Day Trips

GETAWAYS LESS THAN TWO HOURS AWAY

SHIFRA STEIN'S **DAY TRIPS**®

FROM **HOUSTON**

Tenth Edition

Carol Barrington

Revised and updated by

Syd Kearney

The Globe Pequot Press

GUILFORD, CONNECTICUT

The prices and rates listed in this guidebook were confirmed at press time. We recommend, however, that you call establishments before traveling to obtain current information.

Copyright © 1984, 1985, 1988, 1991, 1993, 1995, 1998, 2000, 2002, 2004 by Carol Barrington

Day Trips is a registered trademark.

ISSN 1535-8097
ISBN 0-7627-2750-0

Manufactured in the United States of America
Tenth Edition/First Printing

Contents

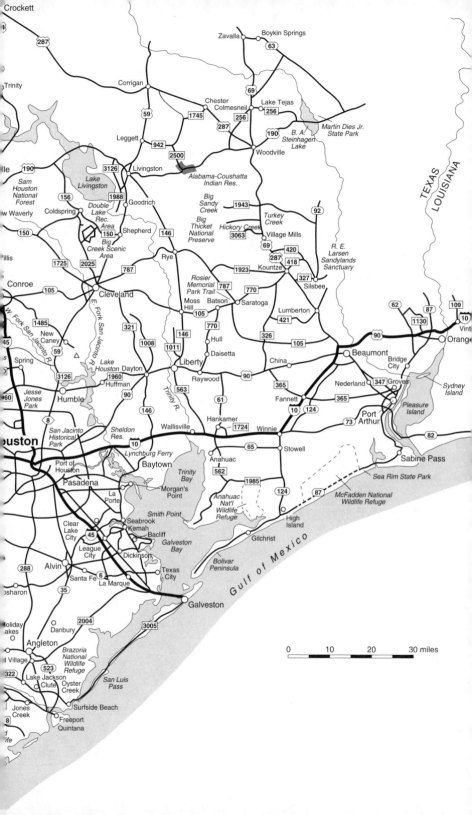

Preface

When money and time are in short supply, nothing is more pleasing than a day trip.

Short and often sweet, day trips provide a change in scenery, a family outing without distractions, the opportunity to share a childhood memory with a new spouse, or the chance to rekindle a romance.

So pack a picnic basket, load up the minivan, and put Houston in your rearview mirror, if only for a few hours.

The possibilities are seemingly limitless: There are seventeen state parks within 100 miles of Houston, scores of historic small towns, enough museums to wear out several pairs of sneakers, and more barbecue stands and taco huts than stars in the sky.

Before you let out the parking brake, make sure you've got a good Texas map. Using it with the "Wandering the Backroads" sections of this book will let you mix and match portions of adjacent trips to suit your personal interests and available time. Do call ahead if you have your heart set on a particular stop. One of the more frustrating things about putting together a guidebook is that facts often change the instant they appear in print. Also, many of the restaurants and special activities listed are individual enterprises and sometimes economically fragile. Before you make the drive, call to make sure hard times haven't claimed yet another victim.

Be aware, too, that in many cases a day trip's total itinerary is too rich to do everything in a single day. The "What to Do" suggestions are designed to cover a variety of interests, so pick and choose the stops that appeal to you before leaving home.

Travel writer extraordinaire Carol Barrington spent eighteen years putting the bulk of this book together and lovingly updating it. I am the caretaker for this tenth edition, with one goal: to tenaciously build on its legacy.

As you travel the backroads of Texas, make some time for opportunities that may not be covered between the pages of this guide. You never know what you'll encounter during a morning hike or on a canoe ride through a marsh. A doe with fawns, a perfect wildflower, a chatty waitress with big hair and a bigger smile, an enormous spiderweb glistening in the sunlight.

And save a little time for getting lost. The best adventures come when you put away the map and let curiosity be your guide. And let us know what you find.

—Syd Kearney

Using This Book

In most cases hours of operation are omitted because they are subject to change frequently. Instead, telephone numbers and Web sites (when available) are listed so that you can call for specifics. Also be aware that many of the restaurants and activity options are closed on major holidays, although that may not be noted in the text.

Restaurant prices are designated as $$$ (expensive, $17.00 or over), $$ (moderate, $7.00–$17.00), or $ (inexpensive, under $7.00) per person.

Listings in the "What to Do" and "Where to Eat" sections generally are in alphabetical order.

The symbol ☐ denotes that at least one credit card is accepted.

Please note: No payment of any kind is either solicited or accepted to gain mention in this book.

Additional Resources

For a Texas map and travel guide, contact the **Texas Department of Transportation,** Travel and Information Division, P.O. Box 5064, Austin, TX 78714-9248; (800) 452-9292. The travel counselors at that number can also advise on events, lodging, attractions, and trip routings throughout the state. You'll find a great deal of this advice on-line at www.traveltex.com, as well as links for requesting more information.

For information on state parks, wildlife, or fisheries, contact the **Texas Parks and Wildlife Department,** 4200 Smith School Road, Austin, TX 78744; (800) 792-1112; www.tpwd.state.tx.us. You can check availability and reserve campsites, group facilities, and cabins in state parks on-line or by calling (512) 389-8900. To cancel a reservation, call (512) 389-8900.

The **Great Texas Coastal Birding Trail** maps are available for either of the two state resources noted above; the Upper Texas Coast version is relevant to the areas covered in this book.

The **East Texas Tourism Association** puts out a free fun map. Contact the association at 421 North Center, Longview, TX 75601; (903) 757-4444; www.easttexasguide.com.

For information on the **Sam Houston National Forest,** contact the Sam Houston Ranger District, 394 FM-1375 West, New Waverly, TX 77358; (936) 344-6205. For information on the **Davy Crockett National Forest,** contact the Davy Crockett Ranger District, Route 1, Box 55FS, Kennard, TX 75847; (936) 655-2299. You'll find on-line information for both parks at www.southernregion.fs.fed.us/texas.

The **Texas Forestry Association** puts out a booklet on woodland hiking trails: P.O. Box 1488, Lufkin, TX 75902; (936) 632-8733; www.texasforestry.org.

For lists of Christmas tree farms, wineries, farmers' markets, and pick-your-own fruit farms statewide, contact the **Texas Department of Agriculture,** P.O. Box 12847, Austin, TX 78711; (512) 463-7624; www.agr.state.tx.us. Information is also available at the Texas Agricultural Extension Service, 2 Abercrombie Drive, Houston, TX 77084; (281) 855-5600; http://harris-tx.tamu.edu/.

The Houston Audubon Society maintains a "Texas Rare Bird Alert" hotline: (281) 992-2757. Find more information on-line at www.houstonaudubon.org.

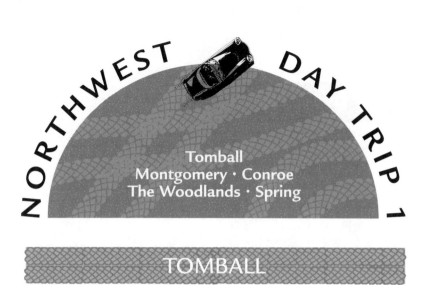

NORTHWEST DAY TRIP 1

Tomball
Montgomery · Conroe
The Woodlands · Spring

TOMBALL

One of the most scenic drives from Houston into the Brazos Valley or to the Lake Conroe area begins by following TX-249 (Tomball Parkway) north through rural woodlands. Although none of the towns included in this day trip is of major interest in and of itself, together they have enough interesting stops to make a great drive.

First up is the farming community of Tomball, named for early-twentieth-century congressman Thomas H. Ball. Turn east on Main Street at the TX-249/FM-2920 intersection to find numerous antiques stores in the heart of town. For advance information and an excellent map of the Tomball/North Harris County region, contact the Tomball Area Chamber of Commerce, P.O. Box 516, Tomball, TX 77377-0516; (281) 351-7222; www.tomballchamber.org. If you're traveling on a weekday, you'll find that office at 14011 Park Drive, Suite 111.

WHAT TO DO

Burroughs Park. 9738 Hufsmith Road, 1.3 miles east of FM-2978. This beautiful, 320-acre park offers a large lake with floating piers for catch-and-release fishing (largemouth bass and catfish), 8 miles of nature trails, a playground accessible to handicapped children, an elevated boardwalk, baseball and soccer fields, and extensive picnic facilities. For pavilion rentals call (281) 353-4196; www.cp4.hctx.net/parks/burroughs/. Developed at a cost of more than

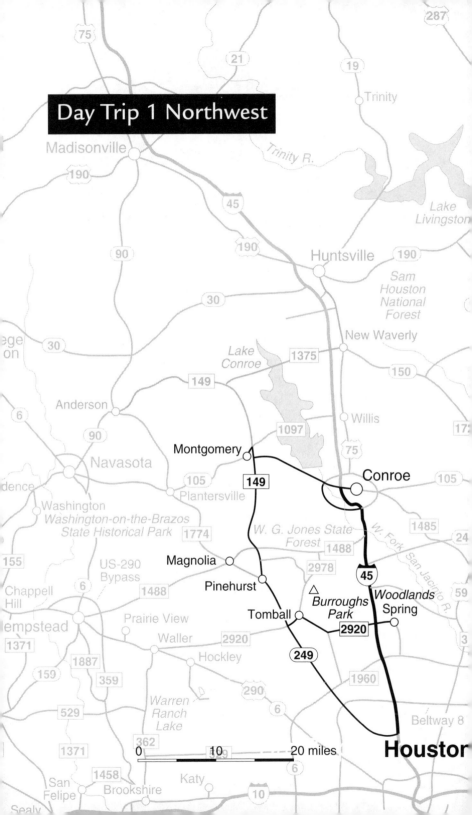

Day Trip 1 Northwest

$3.2 million, this rural park preserves classic Big Thicket growth, including blackjack oak, bogs and water-elm ponds, canebreaks along creeks, short-leaf pines, stands of hickory, and holly and farkleberry bushes. Open daily, dawn to dark.

Camelot Horse Center. 18010 Burkhardt Road (1 block south of FM-2920 and 7 miles north of US-290 via Cypress-Rosehill Road). This full-service horse training facility is devoted to classic English riding, including dressage. The public is welcome to visit, observe, and attend horse shows and demonstrations; no rental horses or trail rides are available. Appointments required; closed Monday; (281) 351-8368.

Christmas tree farms. Although tree cutting officially begins Thanksgiving weekend, many tree farms offer great family activities such as barnyard animals, educational tours, hayrides, hot dog roasts, and so on during other times of the year. Call the following for information and directions: Merry Christmas Tree Farm, (281) 351-0818, merrychristmastree.com; Old Time Christmas Tree Farm, (281) 370-9141; or Spring Creek Growers, (281) 259-8114, www.springcreekgrowers.com.

Flying High at David Wayne Hooks Airport. 20803 Stuebner Airline, Spring (at FM-2920); (281) 376-5436; www.hooksairport.com. The largest privately owned airport in Texas, this sprawling place offers numerous ways to get a bird's-eye view of Houston. Looking for an unusual birthday or anniversary present? Helicopter Services (look for sign on large hangar) offers demonstration rides in a Robinson R-22 (introductory flights $60-$200), or a panoramic exploration of Houston, including the Ship Channel and River Oaks (minimum one hour, $200 per hour). This is a federally licensed facility; all aircraft are maintained to federal standards; (281) 370-4354.

Hooks is home to numerous flight schools that offer sight-seeing tours as well as discovery flights (usually $20-$35 for one person), during which you actually put hands on the controls. Longer pleasure flights and sight-seeing tours generally start at $60 to $75 per hour. For specifics call Mercury Flight Services, (281) 376-9141; National Aviation, (281) 370-5235; United Flight Systems, (281) 376-0357; or Wings of Houston, (281) 376-6644.

For $995 Texas Air Aces will strap you into the front cockpit of a TX-34 Mentor aircraft for air combat, aerobatics, and formation training in the skies over northwest Houston. *Not to worry:* A qualified pilot can override your moves from the second seat. These high-performance airplanes have laser gun systems, gunsights, threat detection/warning systems, and integrated, four-camera video recording equipment. Your five-hour adventure begins with an extensive preflight suit-up and briefing session that instructs you in offensive tactics, defensive maneuvers, use of the weapons system, and safety. After flying you review your air battles via videotape, which you then take home. Reservations are required, at least one month in advance for weekend flights. *FYI:* More than 80 percent of these novice "aces" have never flown before, and anyone over 4 feet 8 inches tall is welcome, regardless of age; clients have ranged from nine to ninety-three. Observers are welcome at no charge. Look for Hangar A-5 at the south end of Hooks; call (281) 379-2237 or (800) 544-2237; www.airaces.com.

The Kleb Farm Museum. 19027 Stuebner-Airline Road (west side of road, north of Louetta), Klein. Descended from early German and French settlers in the Spring/Klein/Rosehill region, Thornwell Kleb (pronounced *Clayb*) has collected farm memorabilia and equipment nearly all his life, a hobby he now enjoys sharing with school groups and the general public. Almost all items came from local sources, including articles used by one of his ancestors at the Confederate powder mill on Spring Creek. Kleb's farm alone qualifies as a museum in this rapidly developing area. Visitors welcome by appointment, at no charge; (281) 376-5960.

Kleb Nature Preserve. 20605 FM-2920 (Waller-Tomball Road), on south side, 7 miles west of Tomball. In addition to picnic tables, a pavilion, and toilet facilities, there's a mile-long trail through dense, second-growth forest, ideal for birding or a walk in the woods. This mini-Big Thicket is what much of north Harris County looked like before the subdivision era. Open daily, dawn to dusk.

The Matt Family Orchard. 21110 Bauer Hockley Road. This 145-acre farm has 22 acres under cultivation. You are welcome to pick mayhaws April-May, thornless blackberries May-June, figs July-September, Asian pears August-September, jujubes August-October, and Asian persimmons September-November. Charges are by the pound. They also host group tours year-round, offer bow hunting by advance arrangement, and put on an extended Harvest Festival in

October and early November. The festival usually includes hayrides and activities for kids, including pumpkins, dressing scarecrows, jumping in a haystack, assorted games, and face painting; picnickers are welcome. Open daily, but call for hours and directions. There are no entrance fees for adults, but they do charge per child; (281) 351–7676 or 467–9758; www. mattfamilyorchard.com.

Rosehill Herb Farm. 14914 Treichel Road, off FM–2920, 1 mile west of Tomball. In addition to special programs on the cultivation and use of herbs, this place sells plants, herbal merchandise, and bundles of fresh-cut herbs by the pound. Call for hours; (281) 351–2641.

Silverado Farms. 30337 Dobbin Huffsmith Road. Hidden deep in the woods northeast of Tomball and best accessed via FM–2920 East, FM–2978 North, and Hardin Store Road, this unusual, twenty-seven-acre facility includes a museum inside the Outback Western World store. Weekend visitors often find rodeo-style competition going on in the farm's arena. Picnickers welcome. Free. Open Monday–Saturday; (281) 259–9378.

Spring Creek Park. On Brown Road, 1 mile north of Tomball via T-249; watch for sign. On weekdays this oak-shaded park is a delightful place for a picnic. There's a large children's play area, and a rough, asphalt-banked ramp for skateboarders. Unfortunately, this park often is spoiled on weekends by rowdy crowds; (281) 353–4196; www.cp4.hctx.net/parks.

Tomball Community Museum Center. 510 North Pine Street. Clustered on this cul-de-sac are some bits of the past collected by the Spring Creek County Historical Association. The Trinity Evangelical Lutheran Church was a volunteer construction project of local German families in 1905, and all furnishings and appointments today are original to this white clapboard structure. Now often used for weddings and christenings, it also glows with public services on Thanksgiving morning.

The Griffin Memorial House is next door. Built in 1860 by one of Houston's earliest pioneers, Eugene Pillot, it stood at the intersection of Willow Creek and an early stage route known as the Atascosita Trail. Sam Houston frequently spent the night in this house, waiting for the morning stage, and it also was a local gathering place. The antique furnishings are of the later Victorian period and in themselves constitute the Magdalene Charlton Memorial Museum. The complex's other transplanted buildings include the pioneer country doctor's office where Dr. William Ehrhardt practiced for more than fifty years; a museum containing early farm machinery, tools, and a hundred-year-old gin moved from nearby Spring; a log house and corncrib built in 1857 in Serbin; the Henry Theis House, built locally prior to 1866; a 1940s four-room oil-camp house with furnishings; and a 1920s one-room schoolhouse with period furnishings, brought in from Bellville. Free, but donations are greatly appreciated. Open Thursday midday and on Sunday afternoon; hours vary. Tours also by appointment; (281) 255-2148.

Wunderlich Farm. 18318 Theiss Mail Road, on the Doerre Intermediate School campus. Now the centerpiece of a historical museum focused on the Klein area, this farmstead includes the furnished home built in 1891 by early settlers Peter and Sophie (Krimmel) Wunderlich, as well as a barn, smokehouse, chicken coop, and other outbuildings. Smaller artifacts are displayed in the school's library. Open, with guided tours, from 11:00 A.M. to 3:00 P.M. on the last Saturday of each month, except for May, November, and December; (281) 320-4170.

WHERE TO EAT

The Bake Shoppe. 22516 TX-249 (Tomball Parkway), Houston, in the Spring Cypress Village Shopping Center. This tidy, family-run place has lunches and pastries like those you wish Mom did make. The sandwiches come on homemade bread, and the cranberry chicken lunch entree is popular. Expect a line if you come between noon and 1:00 P.M.; the good food here draws executives from nearby Compaq. Open Monday–Friday until 4:00 P.M., Saturday until 2:00 P.M. $; ☐; (281) 320-2253.

Goodson's Cafe. 27931 TX-249 (Tomball Parkway). Mrs. Goodson hung up her potholders and closed down her ramshackle but famous cafe on the outskirts of Tomball years ago, and she has gone to her reward. But her recipe for hang-off-the-plate chicken-fried steak lives on at this second-generation eatery. The menu also offers chicken, burgers, salads, and fish for lunch and dinner daily. $-$$; ☐; (281) 351-1749.

Mel's Country Cafe. 24814 Stanolind Road. Alternately described as "chicken-fried heaven" and "home of Houston's best burger" by its legion of fans, this tiny hole-in-the-wall turns out country cooking at its best. You can't go wrong with the chicken-fried steaks, mashed potatoes and gravy, and jumbo onion rings. Have an appetite? Check out the MegaMel Burger loaded with more than two pounds of beef and cheese. Tums are extra. Open weekdays for lunch. $; (281) 255-6357.

Rancho Grande. 30134 TX-249 (Tomball Parkway). This family favorite serves Tex-Mex with creative twists; the "No-Name Enchiladas" are tasty enough to start a trend. Open daily for lunch and dinner. $-$$; ☐; (281) 351-1244. The Carillo brothers also operate a second Rancho Grande at 2207 North Frazier Road in Conroe; (936) 441-0440.

The Rib Tickler. 28930 TX-249 (Tomball Parkway). Half-pounder hamburgers and hickory-smoked barbecue are the house specialties. Open for lunch and dinner, Tuesday–Sunday. $-$$; ☐; (281) 255-9431.

Stillwater Grilling Company. 28900 Tomball Parkway, (FM-249). This lively spot specializes in steaks and seafood and shares both parentage and a parking lot with The Rib Tickler Restaurant. Open for lunch and dinner Tuesday–Friday (closed 2:30–5:00 P.M.), for dinner on Saturday, and for lunch until 4:00 P.M. on Sunday. $-$$$; ☐; (281) 290-9200; www.stillwatergrilling.com.

The Whistle Stop Tea Room. 107 Commerce. Whether you're a devout "foodie" or diligent budget-watcher, this very affordable spot makes Tomball a repeat destination. Top honors go to the chicken salad (no, they won't give you the recipe!), followed by the tortilla soup, daily specials, and homemade desserts. Other good choices include salads, sandwiches, and quiche. Open for lunch Monday–Saturday. $; ☐; (281) 255-2455.

CONTINUING ON

From Tomball this day trip continues north approximately 7 miles on TX-249 to the signal at Pinehurst. There you must make a choice: either to continue this day trip to Montgomery by turning right onto FM-149 or to follow TX-249 (which becomes FM-1774 at Pinehurst) north to Magnolia (Day Trip 4, this sector).

The first option, FM-149 (a historic route known as The Montgomery Trace), roams through rolling woodland toward Montgomery's antiques shops and Lake Conroe. Fond of dewberries? The

brambles that edge the railroad tracks in several places along The Trace usually offer sweet pickings in May. Come prepared with a bucket, gloves, a long-sleeved shirt, stout shoes, and a stick for scaring away snakes before you reach into those bushes.

MONTGOMERY

An Indian trading post later settled in 1837 by Stephen F. Austin's fourth (and last) colony, Montgomery prospered for half a century as a regional center for mercantile activity. It is now a tiny village—population 489—with a 6-block collection of homes immediately north of TX-105. Home tours in April and December give peeks behind some of those doors. In addition to exploring Montgomery's ever-growing number of antiques shops, take time to wander the graveyard at the old Methodist Church. According to the Montgomery Historical Society, more than thirty local sites are on the state historic register. Guided tours can be arranged for groups by calling the society; (936) 597-4899.

A bit of trivia: The town is the birthplace of Texas's Lone Star flag. The flag—along with the state seal—was designed by Dr. Charles B. Stewart, who moved to Montgomery in 1831. The symbols were approved by Republic of Texas President Mirabeau B. Lamar and the legislature in 1839.

WHAT TO DO

Bridgewood Farms. 11680 Rose Road, Conroe. Day programs at this facility benefit more than 160 mentally challenged teens and adults, and the public is welcome to picnic on the grounds, shop in Nichol's Niche gift shop, explore the small greenhouse, and walk the nature trails on this seventeen-acre rural property. Ask about their unique, handmade rugs, so beautiful that one graces the corporate headquarters of Mitchell Energy. There's also a possibility of hayrides if they know you are coming, plus you can cut a live Christmas tree here during the holidays (see following listing). Open weekdays, but call for directions and to make sure the campus will be open when you plan to visit; (936) 856-6460.

Christmas tree farms. There are a couple of these cut-your-own places in the Montgomery-Plantersville area. Call for directions: Bridgewood Farms, (936) 856-6460, and Red Caboose Christmas Tree Farm, (281) 259-9776.

Hoffart's General Store. From Montgomery go west on TX–105; turn south on FM-1486 in Dobbin. The country equivalent of a 7-Eleven, this is the kind of place that has homemade sausage in the meat case and often free puppies and kittens in pens on the front porch. Open Monday–Saturday; (936) 597-5460.

Lolly Farms. 16350 FM-149. Visit with the barnyard set at this petting zoo, about 2 miles north of the city's historical district. The attraction is home to more than ninety farm animals and exotics, including miniature horses, pygmy goats, and pint-size sheep. And please, feed the animals. Admission is $5.00. Pony rides and hayrides available for a fee. Open weekends. Call (936) 449-5551; www.lolly farms.com.

The N. H. Davis Pioneer Complex and Museum. 307 Liberty. Restoration and furnishing of both the Davis Cottage (1851) and the N. H. Davis Law Office (1831 and 1844) are ongoing projects for the Montgomery Historical Society. For now, both of these old log structures are open only by advance arrangements and during special events; (936) 597-4899.

Secret Garden. 23405 Martha Williams Road. Originally a cottage garden surrounding an 1800s dog-trot house, this two-acre plot has been expanded by current owners Bob and Stephanie Wallace to include more than 1,000 rose plants. Some one hundred varieties are for sale in containers year-round. Previous owner Martha Williams planted countless bulbs, wisterias, and flowering trees, so a spring visit is prime. That old home now is a gift shop, there's a small lake, and children get a kick out of the dogs, cats, and chickens. Open Thursday–Sunday; closed during inclement weather; (936) 851-2229.

WHERE TO EAT

The Depot. 402 Liberty (on FM-149, just south of TX–105). Popular with families heading home after a day on Lake Conroe, this place is known for its old-fashioned hamburgers. Lunch and dinner daily. $-$$; ☐; (936) 597-6733.

Heritage House. 1304 Eva (1 mile west of FM–149 on TX–105). A favorite stop on the Houston-to-College-Station run, this spot is known for its country cooking, chicken-fried steak, and homemade pies and rolls. Open for lunch and dinner, Tuesday–Saturday, and until 3:00 P.M. Sunday. $–$$; ☐; (936) 597–6100.

Mexican Chefs True Flavors. 109 Liberty (FM–149 North). The extensive menu is light-years away from standard Tex-Mex. Instead, this is the classic cooking of Mexico City. The semi-open kitchen serves breakfast any time, and the menu explains all, right down to the sauces. The $6.50 lunch specials draw crowds; where else can you get half a roasted chicken for that price? Open daily for breakfast, lunch, and dinner. $–$$; ☐; (936) 597–6633.

Touch of Texas. 605 Eva (TX–105). Housed in a revamped 1954 Texaco station, this small spot serves sandwiches, soups, salads, and desserts. Open for lunch on weekdays, dinner on Friday and Saturday. Closed Sunday. $–$$; ☐; (936) 597–7700.

Other restaurant choices in the TX–105/Lake Conroe area, a short drive east of Montgomery, are listed in the Conroe section.

WANDERING THE BACKROADS

To continue this day trip from Montgomery to Conroe and Spring, travel east on TX–105. A turn west on TX–105 will connect you with Trips 3 through 6 in this sector.

Or you can continue north on FM–149 through Montgomery to Anderson (Trip 5, this sector). From Anderson you can return to Houston via Navasota and Hempstead on TX–90 and TX–6.

How about heading east to New Waverly and Huntsville (Trip 2, this sector)? From FM–149 on the northern outskirts of Montgomery, turn northeast on FM–1097; this enjoyable road arcs east to Willis, crossing Lake Conroe in the process.

CONROE

In 1880 the Central and Montgomery Railroad had a line running from Navasota to Montgomery. With the extension of the track in 1885 to a small sawmill run by Isaac Conroe some 15 miles to the east, the town of Conroe came into being. Within five years Conroe was thriving with 300 citizens and aced Montgomery out of the county seat honor by some sixty-two votes. Always the center of a prosperous lumber industry, it hit the financial big time with George Strake's discovery of oil southeast of town in 1931.

Conroe today needs no introduction to Houstonians, as it is a prosperous business and bedroom satellite 39 miles north on I-45. Although little history has been preserved here, it's fun to visit the Crighton Theater (circa 1930) near the courthouse on North Main. Restored in vaudevillian style, it again hosts the performing arts upon occasion; (936) 441-7469; www.crightonplayers.org. To day-trippers, however, Conroe is attractive primarily as the gateway to an extensive forest and water playground and as a locale for great factory discount shopping, courtesy of the fifty-six-store Conroe Outlet Center (www.conroeoutletcenter.com) north of town on I-45. For those who want to stay over to play another day, Heather's Glen Bed & Breakfast offers Victorian-style lodgings in the former Wahrenberger Mansion in downtown Conroe; (936) 441-6611; www.heathersglen.com.

For more information on the Conroe area, including Montgomery, contact the Greater Conroe/Lake Conroe Chamber of Commerce, P.O. Box 2347, Conroe, TX 77305; (936) 538-7112; www.lakeconroecvb.org. For on-site information weekdays, stop at 505 West Davis.

WHAT TO DO

Heritage Museum of Montgomery County. 1506 North I-45. Take the TX-105 exit from I-45 North and stay on the frontage road to Candy Cane Park. The Grogan and Cochran families jointly owned and operated twenty-five sawmills in Montgomery County, the first of which was on the 55,000 acres later developed as The Woodlands. This makes their 1924 frame home a fitting matrix for local history. One gallery features "Glimpses of Montgomery County," including Dr. Charles Stewart's original drawings of the Lone Star flag and state seal of the Texas Republic (still in use). A second gallery focuses on people and events that influenced the area. Free, but donations gratefully accepted. Open Wednesday–Saturday; (936) 539-6873; www.heritagemuseum.us.

HuckleBerry Hill Family Park and Petting Zoo. 4401 North Frazier, Conroe. This shady and pleasant place is a child's dream—plenty of small animals to experience as well as extensive play zones. Kids love to burn energy at the hippity-hop corral, Big Wheel track, and western town. Open to the public on weekends when weather permits; reservations otherwise required. It's best to always call ahead to make sure they'll be open. Fee; (936) 856-1700; www.huckleberryhill.com.

Lake Conroe. Numerous points of access from I-45, TX-105, and FM-149. The dam, a small county park on the lakefront, several of the larger marinas, and the entrances to three major resorts lie 10 to 12 miles west of I-45 in Conroe via TX-105. The upper west side of the lake can be reached from Montgomery via FM-149 and FM-1097; the east side can be accessed by both FM-1097 and FM-1375 from I-45 north of Conroe.

One of the most beautiful lakes in the state, Lake Conroe is 15 miles long and covers 22,000 acres. A complete list of marinas, campgrounds, and public services is available from the Lake Conroe Chamber of Commerce.

Want an affordable weekend escape? Several resorts on Lake Conroe welcome guests with advance reservations. Inquire about accommodations and available activities at the following: April Sound in Montgomery, (936) 447-3262, www.aprilsoundrentals.com, and Landing at Seven Coves in Willis, (936) 856-5162, www.sevencoves.com.

Del Lago Resort and Conference in Montgomery has numerous package vacations, a golf course, a long sand beach and lagoon, and a full-service marina offering watercraft rentals and guided fishing via pontoon boat; (936) 582-6100 or (800) 335-5246; www.dellago.com.

Located 7 miles west of I-45 via TX-105, Lake Conroe Park & Pavilion offers swimming, two fishing piers, a playground, and picnic facilities, but no boat ramp. Admission ($2.00 for those ages five and older) is charged from March through Labor Day; thereafter the park is free. (936) 788-8302.

The *Southern Empress,* a replica of an old-time paddle wheeler docked at Seven Coves, offers a variety of extended lake cruises. Reservations are required for lunch and dinner cruises. $$-$$$; ☐; (936) 588-3000 or (800) 324-2229; www.southernempress.com.

Moorhead's Blueberry Farm. 19531 Moorhead Road. Who says you can't grow plump, luscious blueberries in Texas? Sid Moorhead has fifteen acres planted with thirty-five different varieties that ripen from early June through late July. Cost is $1.50 per pound, and the best picking times are in the early morning and late afternoon. Mr. Moorhead also grows the nonastringent Fuju persimmons, known as the apple of the Orient, which ripen in November. What do you do with persimmons? He has great recipes—and this fruit is good to eat out of hand or use in pies. Other pickin' crops include figs in late August through mid-September and blackberries in early summer. His farm is deep in the woods between Conroe and Porter. From US-59 North take the Porter exit, go west on FM-1314 for 10 miles, turn left into Bennette Estates, and then follow signs. From I-45 take exit 83, go east on Crighton Road 2.5 miles, turn right on FM-1314 for 7.4 miles, and turn right into Bennette Estates. Open daily, dawn to dusk; (281) 572-1265; www.mooreheadsblueberry farm.com.

WHERE TO EAT

Caddy Shack Bar & Grill. 13101 Walden Road, Montgomery. A million-dollar renovation of the cafe inside the Walden Country Club has resulted in one of the most attractive eateries in the region. Informal and relaxed, this nice spot even looked super when sampled for a Monday lunch on a bleak winter day. Large windows look out on Walden's putting green and a terrace roofed in oaks, and bright flowers fill manicured flower beds. Hungry golfers eat here, so the portions are ample; choices are several cuts above the usual sandwiches and hamburgers. The hot dip appetizers serve three to four and can serve as light suppers in themselves. Alternative choices include Lake Conroe "crab cakes" (made from catfish). Open for lunch daily, dinner Wednesday–Saturday. $-$$; ☐; (936) 582-1111.

    Captain Jack's on the Lake. 15949 Highway 105 West, Montgomery. All the S's—salads, soups, sandwiches, steaks, and seafood—are available here, along with hamburgers, homemade desserts, and the daily specials. Open for lunch and dinner Tuesday–Sunday. $-$$; ☐; (936) 588-3902.

    Dixie's Bayou Victuals. 1202 North Frazier. This family-owned spot is well known locally for its Cajun and Creole offerings, including gumbo, jambalaya, gator strips, red snapper, and BBQ crabs (in season). Open for lunch and dinner Tuesday–Sunday, lunch only on Monday. $-$$; ☐; (936) 441-1177.

Giovanni's Continental Cuisine. 10104 Highway 105 West. Considered by many people to be the best fine dining restaurant on the TX–105 strip, this pleasant place offers exceedingly good (and often unusual) beef, veal, fish, pasta, and chicken entrees at prices substantially under the Houston area's going rates. Chef Giovanni grows fresh herbs out back, and they make all the difference. In addition to the day's special offerings, top choices include chicken artichoke, mussels garlic, and rack of lamb. Service is excellent, and the wines by the glass are affordable. Open for dinner Monday–Saturday. $–$$$; ☐; (936) 588–4666.

Hooks Seafood Restaurant. 820 North Loop 336. If Cajun appeals, this family-run spot serves all those favorites, from fried catfish and shrimp to assorted broiled dinners. The crawfish étouffée comes steaming and well seasoned, and the seafood po'boys arrive on warmed sourdough bread. Open for lunch and dinner daily. $–$$; ☐; (936) 539–4665.

Kiva. 600 Del Lago Boulevard, Montgomery, in the Del Lago Resort and Conference Center, Montgomery. From TX–105 West turn north on Walden Road to the resort entrance. For tasty but unusual dining, this colorful, almost hidden eatery is hard to beat. Menu adventures include crab cakes with roasted tomato corn relish, pit-smoked chicken rubbed with ancho-orange glaze, tortilla-crusted filet mignon, and Southwestern jerked pork. Desserts are divine, particularly the margarita cheesecake. Open daily (staggered hours) for lunch and dinner; reservations suggested. $–$$$; ☐; (936) 582–6100; www.dellago.com.

La Casona Mexican Restaurant. 6035 Highway 105 West. Expect plenty of cars in the parking lot for this family-owned spot. The menu is filled with interesting departures from standard Tex–Mex fare, plus the lunch specials top out at $6.95. Open daily for lunch and dinner. $–$$; ☐; (936) 441–2101.

McKenzie's Barbeque. 1501 North Frazier and 225 Simonton. When you want smoky barbecue or sandwiches, this is a reliable bet. Open for lunch and dinner Monday–Saturday. $–$$; ☐; (936) 539–4300; www.mckenziesbarbeque.com.

Moonstruck Cafe. 330 North Main Street. If deli sandwiches, quiche, salads, soups, cheesecakes, homemade chili, and gumbo sound good, hunt up this small place across from the Montgomery County Courthouse in downtown Conroe. You'll also find smoothies and an incredible variety of coffees and lattes. Open for breakfast and lunch until 4:00 P.M. Monday–Friday and until 8:00 P.M. on Saturday. $; ☐; (936) 756-5282.

Nadine's Creekwood Restaurant and Bar. 12820 Highway 105 West. This upscale setting has had several restaurant "lives," and locals are hoping this one lasts. Nice table linens, professional quality service, live piano music, and a menu that ranges from Mexican to steaks and seafood make this a good choice for a special meal. Open for dinner nightly. $–$$; ☐; (936) 588-2288.

Papa's on the Lake. 14632 Highway 105 West, Montgomery (7 miles west of I-45). One of the hot spots on Lake Conroe, this bar and grill serves pizzas, salads, sandwiches (including muffalettas), and a variety of snacks as well as beer and wine. There's a large deck overlooking the lake and live music on summer weekends. Open daily for lunch and dinner. $–$$; ☐; (936) 447-2500; www.papason thelake.com.

Vernon's Kuntry Barbecue. 5000 West Davis (Highway 105) on the north side of Highway 105, 3.5 miles west of I-45. This beer garden serves delicious brisket, ribs, links, hamburgers, and chicken. Open daily for lunch and dinner. $–$$; ☐; (409) 539-3000.

Vernon's Kuntry Katfish. 5901 West Davis (Highway 105) 6.5 miles west of I-45. Even if you don't like catfish, come here. Tasty choices run from frog legs to chicken-fried steak and burgers, and the homemade desserts and breads are terrific. Even *Gourmet* magazine has taken favorable notice of this eatery; you'll find the framed write-up near the cashier's desk. Open for lunch and dinner daily. $–$$; ☐; (409) 760-3386.

Villa Italia. 213 Simonton. This "Italian Ristorante" serves outstanding rack of lamb, Dover sole, chateaubriand, and assorted veal entrees, along with California and French wines. The menu also offers pastas, seafood, chicken, and steak. Open for lunch and dinner Monday–Saturday (closed 2:30–4:30 P.M.). $–$$$; ☐; (936) 539-5599.

CONTINUING ON

To continue this day trip to The Woodlands, travel south from Conroe on I-45 to exits 78–76.

THE WOODLANDS

North of downtown Houston some 27 miles via I–45, the lakes and neighborhood parks of this extensive master-planned development are for residents only. Several other recreations, however, are open to the general public. More than 50 miles of trails thread beautiful woods, just right for hiking, jogging, in-line skating, or biking. Bring your own wheels and park by the visitor center. Nonmember golfers (for a fee, of course) are welcome on The Woodlands Country Club's Tournament Players Course, former home of the Shell Houston Open; (281) 364–6368, www.thewoodlandscc.com.

WHAT TO DO

Cynthia Woods Mitchell Pavilion. 2005 Lake Robbins Drive. April-to-October playbill offerings at the Woodland's beautiful outdoor performing art center range from bluegrass to ballet and Broadway shows, rock to Rachmaninoff, Gershwin to Willie Nelson; the setting recalls Tanglewood and Interlochen. In all, there are 5,000 seats available by reservation. Get advance tickets from Ticketmaster outlets or by calling (713) 629–3700; www.ticketmaster.com. Tickets are also available at the Pavilion's box office Monday–Saturday and on event days through intermission. Except for specific classical arts "picnics," no food, coolers, or beverages are allowed. There is space for an additional 12,000 people on the grassy hill flanking the seating area; blankets are permitted, but lawn chairs must be rented at the Pavilion ($5.00, but $1.00 is rebated when you return the chair). Recorders, cameras, umbrellas, and pagers are also *verboten*. Parking is free. ☐ For event information, call (281) 363–3300, or access www.woodlandscenter.org.

The Great Western Trading Company. 6445 Old FM-1488, Magnolia. Located midway between The Woodlands and Magnolia, this bit of old Texas welcomes everyone to their Saturday-night horse and tack auctions. The action starts around 7:00 P.M. There's a small concession stand on the premises (hamburgers, hot dogs, and so on) in case you get hungry; (281) 356–2165.

North Houston Horse Park & Carousel Farms Riding Academy.

137 Lexington Drive, 2.5 miles east of I-45 via TX-242 (Needham Road), then right on Lexington. One of the largest hunter/jumper riding schools in South Texas, this spiffy facility welcomes visitors who call ahead. Owner Melany Kirsch also offers a thirty-minute free trial lesson by appointment to introduce both adults and children (age five and up) to this elegant sport, plus she hosts free horse shows twice a year; (936) 273-5600.

Portofino. East side of I-45 in Shenandoah, immediately north of The Woodlands. At this water-themed experience, enjoy a break from shopping at stores such as Old Navy and Oshman's at this Italian-inspired "lifestyle" center by taking a ride on a gondola (fee). You can also stroll among Roman fountains and linger alongside 10-foot waterfalls. For current events and activities information, call (281) 292-5953; www.portofinocenter.com. Also helpful is the Shenandoah Convention & Visitors Bureau, 29811 IH-45 North, Shenandoah, TX 77381; (281) 292-5953; www. shenandoahtxcvb.com.

Rudy's Peach Orchard. 1737 Sawdust Road, 1.7 miles west of I-45. This four-acre farm grows nine varieties of peaches, plus it has "pick your own" patches for strawberries and blackberries. The picking season stretches from May 1 through July 4, nature permitting, but call to check what's available before you go. This farm also sells blackberries at various times of the year, as well as jams, jellies, and picante sauce made from the farm's own produce. Open daily; call for hours. Tours available for groups. Call the fruit hotline, (281) 298-5464, for an update on what's available; (281) 367-4578.

Southwest Paddle Sports. 26322 I-45 North, The Woodlands. This firm operates inexpensive quiet-water kayaking and canoe trips on Lake Woodlands, the San Jacinto River, and numerous other waters in the greater Houston area. They also teach basic canoeing and kayaking skills and organize group trips. Want to go birding by kayak in Christmas Bay (near Freeport) or sea kayaking offshore from Matagorda Island? How about kayaking Spring Creek from Jesse Jones Park to Forest Cove Marina or paddling under a full moon? These are the folks to call. Open daily. ☐; (281) 292-5600 or (800) 937-2335; www.paddlesports.com.

The Woodlands Resort & Conference Center, 2301 North Millbend Drive, The Woodlands. Make a weekend of it. Check out the tennis, golf, and pampering packages. This swank resort boasts five restaurants and a spanking new, family-friendly Forest Oasis Water-scape. The Waterscape features a 30-foot racing slide, underwater murals, children's "sprayground," and, for adults, a relaxation pool and super-size spa. Call (281) 367-1100 or (800) 433-2624; www.woodlandsresort.com.

Woodlands Town Center. Tucked into the community's pride-worthy pines, Town Center is so well designed that most motorists zipping past on I-45 can't really get a feel for the enormity of this mall/leisure complex, which comprises more than 400 shops, restaurants, hotels, and entertainment venues. Town Center, the Woodlands Pavilion, and The Woodlands' downtown are linked by a 1.5-mile "river" complete with water taxis. For information, contact The Woodlands Town Center Improvement District, 1450 Lake Robbins Drive, Suite 410, The Woodlands, TX 77380; (281) 363-2447; www.town-center.com.

W. Goodrich Jones State Forest. Five miles northwest via I-45 and FM-1488 West. Logged in 1892 and burned in 1923, these 1,725 acres again are a verdant wildlife refuge, now under the watchful eye of the Texas Forest Service and part of the Texas A&M system. The Sweet Leaf Nature Trail is self-guided, and a small lake offers picnicking as well as fishing for catfish and bass. A prime birding spot, this park now provides excellent habitat for the red-cockaded woodpecker. Horseback riding is allowed if you bring your own steed. Open all weekends; weekdays by arrangement. Guided tours available for groups; (936) 273-2261.

WHERE TO EAT

Although numerous franchises offer good eats along I-45 in the vicinity of Woodlands Mall, the following are worth searching out.

Alpenhaus Restaurant and Biergarten. 18450 I-45 South, Shenandoah. Take exit 79 going north, exit 78 going south. You'll find authentic and delicious German food here, thanks to the expertise of owner-chefs Dieter and Helga Henze, formerly of the Cologne area of Germany. If the daily specials don't appeal, try the house specialties: goulasch, sauerbraten, schweinebraten, and jaeger-schnitzel. There's also a good assortment of American food for the timid. Open daily for lunch and dinner. $-$$; ☐; (936) 321-4416.

Amerigo's Grille. 25050 Grogans Park Drive. When it's time to eat Italian, come here. The atmosphere equals the high quality of the food; save room for the tiramisu. Open for lunch and dinner weekdays; dinner only on Saturday and Sunday. $-$$$; ☐; (281) 362-0808.

The Glass Menagerie. 2301 North Millbend Drive. A longtime favorite of Woodlands residents, this beautiful and dressy restaurant seems only to improve with age. The dinner menu ranges through some Continental standards—lobster, red snapper, filet mignon, chicken Wellington, grilled Muscovy duck, ribeye of lamb—and the Sunday champagne brunch truly earns the title of "lavish spread." Do what the locals do: Come hungry and make it your meal of the day. Open Tuesday-Saturday for dinner, Sunday for brunch; reservations strongly suggested. $$-$$$+; ☐; (281) 364-6326; www.woodlandsresort.com.

Hyden's Dockside. 25130 I-45 North, Spring. There may be no water in sight at this casual seafood eatery, but take a bite of the perfectly fried shrimp or expertly prepared Pompano and you can almost feel the sea breeze. Owner Elizabeth Kraft developed the bulk of the menu, much of which has a decidedly Cajun flare. Go hungry, as you'll want to try the crawfish pie, the étouffée, *and* the gumbo. Open daily for lunch and dinner. $-$$$; ☐; (281) 367-9735.

Pallotta's Italian Grill. 27606 I-45 North, Spring (in the Woodridge Shopping Center across the interstate from The Woodlands Mall). If the luscious refrigerated desserts displayed in the entry don't spark your appetite, the daily specials will. Menu choices range from pastas to ribeyes, with pizzas and sandwiches alternate choices. Open daily for lunch and dinner. $-$$; ☐; (281) 364-9555.

Paris Cafe & Bakery. 4775 West Panther Creek, Suite 430. Although the lunch menu is limited to a relatively small selection of soups, quiches, sandwiches, and salads, all are tasty. The crisp, narrow baguettes of French bread and the tempting French desserts are habit forming. White linen tablecloths and fresh flowers make this seem like a fancier place than it really is. The dinner entree changes nightly, so call to make sure it fits your desires. Two chefs—owner Patrick Rebiere from France and Guiseppe Greco from Italy—share the cooking duties, so expect authentic fare. They also teach in the cafe's cooking school. Open Monday-Saturday for lunch, Thursday-Saturday for dinner. $-$$; ☐; (281) 363-9890.

Skeeter's Mesquite Grill. 4747 Research Forest Drive (in the

Cochran's Crossing Shopping Center). If you have small bread-snatchers in tow, this sports bar for kiddies is a great place to fill them up. Between electronic games and drawing on the paper table covers, they'll almost be too busy to order from the hamburger/sandwich/burrito type of menu. House specials also range from fish tacos to grilled chicken and Cajun catfish. Open daily for late breakfast, lunch, and dinner. $–$$; ☐; (281) 364–1094; www.skeetersgrill.com.

CONTINUING ON

From The Woodlands, Day Trip 1 swings south on I-45 to the Spring-Cypress Road exit. Turn left (east) under the freeway and follow Spring-Cypress to the railroad tracks.

SPRING

Back in the 1870s, a community called Spring sprang up to serve the International and Great Northern Railroad as a switching station north of Houston. As the railroads prospered through the turn of the twentieth century, so did the town, and in 1902 the Wunche Brothers' Saloon was built within a toot of the roundhouse. It had eight rooms upstairs to house railroad personnel.

But we all know what happened to the railroads of America and to the many small towns that depended on them. By the 1920s the roundhouse had relocated to Houston, and the Texas Rangers had enforced Prohibition laws by shooting every bottle in the saloon. Then came the depression of the 1930s, and when I-45 bypassed Spring in the 1960s, it was the final blow. The old town area lapsed into civic limbo as businesses began to thrive around the new freeway interchange a mile west.

So much for yesterday. Today Old Town Spring is in its second bloom and is a great day-trip destination. More than 150 specialty shops, eateries, antiques stores, and art galleries are right at home in the quaint old houses. In general, the shops are open Tuesday–Saturday and on Sunday afternoon. If you are coming north from Houston, take the 70A exit from I-45 and swing east (right) at the signal on Spring-Cypress Road. When you see the OLD TOWN SPRING sign, you're there; (281) 353-9310; www.oldtownspringtx.com.

B&B also is a possibility here. McLachlan Farm, a 1911 home on thirty-five acres 1 mile south of Old Town Spring, welcomes overnight guests; (281) 350-2400; www.macfarm.com.

WHAT TO DO

Note: The following are not in Old Town Spring unless so noted.

Carter's Country. 6231 Treaschwig Road. From I-45 take the FM-1960 exit east; then turn north onto Aldine-Westfield Road to Treaschwig. Tucked away in the woods, this well-designed place offers pistol, rifle, trap, skeet, and country clay shooting at a variety of distances. Children can shoot BB guns here if they have adult supervision. Open daily. Fee; ☐; (281) 443-8393.

Cypress Trails Stable. 21415 Cypresswood Drive, Humble. Actually located midway between Spring and Humble, this is one of the very few places in the region that offers public horseback riding. You'll be in good hands: Owner Darolyn Butler has won the National Champion Endurance Rider championship three times. Now in addition to riding lessons, horse leasing and sales, training, and horsemanship clinics, she offers a nice string of spirited Arabian horses for adventure trail rides through the woods along Cypress Creek. Small children can be hand-led on ponies. Cost is $30 for the first hour, $15 per hour thereafter. She also organizes parties focused on horseback riding for groups. ☐; (281) 446-7232.

Mercer Arboretum and Botanic Gardens. 22306 Aldine-Westfield Road. This 214-acre county park is a sleeper, often overlooked by day-trippers. What they miss is an outstanding collection of native Texas plants, a series of self-guided nature trails, a bird sanctuary, special gardens (ferns, ginger, water lilies, azaleas), picnic areas, and educational programs, all along a wooded stretch of Cypress Creek. There's also a canoe launch site here. Free and open daily; (281) 443-8731; www.cp4.hctx.net/mercer/.

Splashtown USA. 21300 I-45 North (exit 70A). When summer's heat hits, there's no better cooler than the thrill slides, tube rides, and wave pool at this forty-six-acre water park. You're not allowed to bring your own food and beverages inside the gates, but you are welcome to bring lunches and coolers for a family picnic on the outside grounds. Food also can be purchased inside the park. Open daily from June to mid-August; weekends only in May and from mid-August to October 1. Live entertainment and special events often highlight those off-season weekends. Fee; ☐; (281) 355–3300; www.sixflags.com/parks/splashtown.

Spring Historical Museum. 403 Main Street (at western entrance to Old Town Spring). The human stories of the members of this small community from its German homesteading days in the 1840s to our times are well illustrated here. Open daily Thursday–Saturday and on Sunday afternoon. Donations appreciated; (281) 651–0055.

WHERE TO EAT

Note: All the following eateries are in Old Town Spring.

Bluebonnet Cafe. 123 Midway. This is a good spot to rest while munching on soups, salads, sandwiches, and lunch specials. Open for coffee and lunch Tuesday–Saturday. $; ☐; (281) 288–4882.

British Trading Post. 26303 Hardy Road. Have a hankering for meat pies, mushy peas, or a shandy? This is the place. Owner-chef Maureen Corless-Vlcek also serves delicious fresh scones as well as several memorable signature entrees such as Crab Diane casserole and Shrimp Sarah. Everything comes on bone china, and nothing is fried. Her meat pies also can be ordered in advance for takeout. Open for lunch only Tuesday–Sunday. $–$$; ☐; (281) 350–5854.

Hyde's Cafe. 26608 Keith. Formerly the Spring Cafe, this local institution still brags that it has the best food and slowest service anywhere. The old Spring Cafe was widely known for its marvelous hamburgers, and the tradition continues, including the time-honored thirty- to sixty-minute wait. If that's too long, try the fried veggie tray, buzzards' chili, BBQ, or sausage-on-a-stick. Open for lunch and dinner Tuesday–Sunday. $; ☐; (281) 350–8530.

Javajazz Coffeehouse. 419 Gentry, Suite 103. A strong relief from the lady-lunches and hamburger offerings that dominate in this shopper's paradise, this small place of mixed decor serves up cannoli, pasta, calzones, and sandwiches. And when the shoppers head back to Houston, the coffeehouse transforms into a teen hot spot complete with garage band concerts. Open Tuesday–Sunday; lunch until 5:00 P.M. $; ☐; (281) 528–8129; www.javajazzcoffeehouse.com.

Noble Cottage Cafe & Bakery. 200–2 Noble Street. A bit off the beaten track, this is worth searching for, if only to buy a loaf of Jerry and Mary Beth Fitzgerald's superb beer bread. Want to sample it first? They'll give you a taste, or you can try one of their lunch specials. Italian crème cakes are a house specialty, as are pies, cookies, and kolaches. Open Tuesday–Sunday until 5:00 P.M. $–$$; ☐; (281) 288–3433.

Puffabellys Old Depot Restaurant. 100 Main. Burgers, spuds, salads, and sandwiches served amid peanut-shells-on-the-floor decor in a 1902 train depot. Kids eat free on Thursday night, longnecks are cheap on Friday night, and catfish is all-you-can-eat on Saturday night. Save room for the outstanding desserts, and don't forget to blow the train whistle when you leave. Fun to know: This old depot, a near duplicate of Spring's original depot, which burned some years back, was built in 1902 in Lovelady to serve the International and Great Northern Railroad; it was moved onto this site in 1985 and rebuilt in 2000 after a fire. Open for lunch Tuesday, Wednesday, and Sunday; lunch and dinner Thursday, Friday, and Saturday. $–$$; ☐; (281) 350–3376.

Rose's Patio Cafe. 219 Main (Spring-Cypress Road). A favorite with shopkeepers and locals, this tiny spot offers freshly made salads as well as a variety of sandwiches on home-baked bread. Some outside tables. Open for lunch through 5:00 P.M., Tuesday–Sunday. $; (218) 288–0512.

The Rose Tea Cup Tea Room. 315 Gentry (in Gentry Square). When you want to surround yourself with all things feminine and dine on finger sandwiches, freshly baked scones, clotted cream, and assorted homemade dainties, come here. Lunches run to quiches, lasagna, salads, and luscious desserts. Almost everything is made fresh on-site. Lunch is served until late afternoon, Tuesday through Sunday. $–$$; ☐; (281) 353–5566.

Wunsche Brothers' Cafe and Saloon. 103 Midway. This historic landmark, circa 1902, offers some nifty live music (everything from progressive country to rock and roll) Tuesday–Saturday evenings, along with loads of down-home food. Lunch ranges from burgers to sandwiches and salads, and the sideboard holds free samples of Texas-grown jellies (fig, dewberry, mayhaw, tomato, muscadine, and elderberry). Save room for dessert—the chocolate whiskey cake is a house specialty. Open for lunch on Monday; lunch and dinner Tuesday–Saturday. $–$$; ☐; (281) 350–1902; www.wunschebroscafe.com.

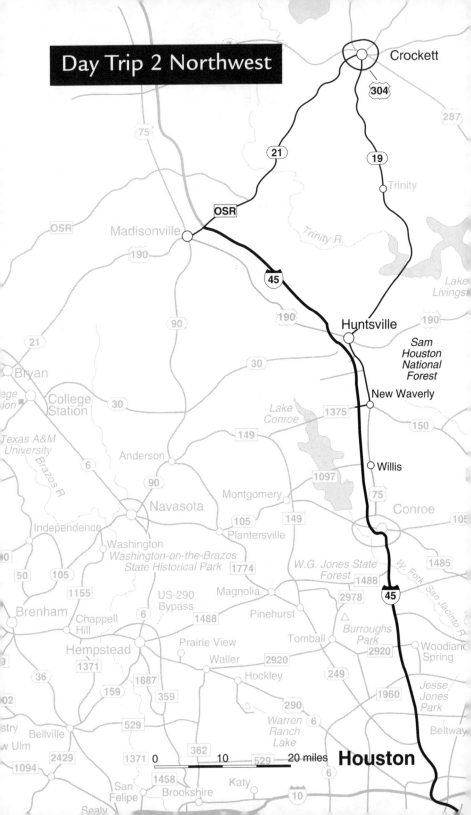

Day Trip 2 Northwest

Crockett

304

287

75

21

19

Trinity

OSR

OSR

Madisonville

45

190

Trinity R.

Lake
Livings

190

90

190

Huntsville

30

Sam
Houston
National
Forest

21

Bryan

30

New Waverly

150

ege
ion

College
Station

30

Lake
Conroe

1375

Texas A&M
University

6

Anderson

149

1097

Willis

Brazos R.

90

Montgomery

75

Conroe

10

Navasota

105

149

W.G. Jones State
Forest

1485

Independence

Plantersville

W. Fork San Jacinto R.

Washington
Washington-on-the-Brazos
State Historical Park

1774

1488

50

105

Magnolia

2978

45

1155

US-290
Bypass

Pinehurst

Burroughs
Park

Woodland
Spring

Brenham

Chappell
Hill

6

1488

Prairie View

Tomball

2920

Jesse
Jones
Park

Hempstead

Waller

2920

249

1371

36

1887

Hockley

1960

Beltwa

159

359

290

6

02

529

Warren
Ranch
Lake

Bellville

362

w Ulm

2429

1371

0   10   529   20 miles

Houston

1094

1458

Katy

San
Felipe

Brookshire

10

Sealy

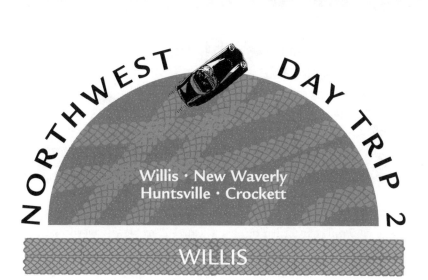

WILLIS

Eight miles north of Conroe, Willis was founded in 1870 as a timber town. Among its historical treasures are two churches, including one that predates the town. The Thomas Chapel Methodist Episcopal Church, South, was organized in 1867. Members worshipped in log buildings and brush arbors until its Gothic Revival–style sanctuary with bell tower was completed in 1899. The other spiritual landmark is Willis Methodist Church, completed about 1878.

Perhaps most interesting is the town's history, albeit short-lived, as a tobacco titan. After the Civil War, farmers began experimenting with tobacco and by the early 1890s enormous fields of extremely high-quality crops were supporting more than a half dozen cigar factories. Unfortunately, the smoke cleared—and the industry evaporated—shortly after the turn of the century, when the United States lifted tariffs off Cuban tobacco.

WHAT TO DO

Jungle Eyes Refuge. 10134 Calvary Road. Where do domesticated lions, tigers, panthers, cougars, and leopards go when their original homes disappear? Thirteen exotic cats now have permanent sanctuary on a shaded, thirteen-acre spread in north Montgomery County. The nonprofit rehabilitation center also cares for wolves, prairie dogs, snakes, and other wildlife that have nowhere else to go. In fact, Jungle Eyes cares for more than 200 creatures, native and exotic. Humans with advance reservations and appointments are welcome to tour the facility April through October. The center also can schedule field trips, birthday parties, and other events. (936) 856-2848; www.jungledomain.org.

NEW WAVERLY

Begin this day trip by driving north on I-45 from Houston approximately 60 miles and turning east at exit 102 to New Waverly. Settled in the 1850s, the community of Waverly thrived for a time on pioneer cotton and cattle businesses. Fearing damage to their cattle and the town's economy, residents turned down the International and Great Northern Railroad Company's request in 1870 for a right-of-way through town, a fatal mistake. The tracks were laid 6 miles west, people began relocating around the station of "New" Waverly, and the original Waverly was doomed. Visitors to the latter now find only an old cemetery with interesting headstones and the visually charming Waverly Presbyterian Church, built around 1904 and still filled every Sunday. "Old" Waverly is 6.8 miles east of I-45 on TX-150.

New Waverly had a heavy Polish immigration from 1870 to 1902. After working in the fields to pay back the area's landowners who had advanced their passage money, the Poles began their own businesses and left a strong ethnic stamp on this community. Stately, Gothic-style St. Joseph's Catholic Church in the heart of town is one of their legacies. Built between 1905 and 1908, it is well worth a visit.

WHAT TO DO

Christmas tree farm. Call Iron Creek Farms for directions; (936) 767-4541; www.ironcreek.com. This is also good birding territory, so bring binoculars.

The Sam Houston National Forest. Although not fully developed, this extensive woodland offers fishing, hunting, camping, hiking, photo opportunities, berry picking, bird-watching, picnicking, and boating access to Lake Conroe. For additional information on locations listed, contact the U.S. Department of Agriculture, Forest Service, Sam Houston Ranger District, 394 FM-1375 West, New Waverly, TX 77358; (936) 344-6205; www.southernregion.fs.fd.us/texas. *Note:* The ranger station, 3 miles west of New Waverly on FM-1375, is open on weekdays.

Unless otherwise noted, all the following are free-use facilities.

Cagle Recreation Area. From I–45 at New Waverly, take FM–1375 west 4.2 miles; then turn southwest on FSR–205 for 3 miles. Facilities restricted to parking lot ($2.00) and boat ramp into Lake Conroe. No rest rooms, electricity, or potable water.

Kelly's Pond Campground. From I–45 at New Waverly, take FM–1375 west 11 miles, turn south 1 mile on FSR–204, and then drive west 1 mile on FSR–271. This scenic spot offers limited primitive tent camping (fire grates and picnic tables but no rest room facilities or water) and fishing in three small ponds. Nice for a picnic, but no boating or swimming.

Little Lake Creek Wilderness Area. From I–45 at New Waverly, take FM–1375 west 14 miles; turn south on FM–149 for 4 miles. Good for hiking.

Off-road vehicle trails. Two ORV loops total 56 miles of trail. No vehicles more than 40 inches in width are allowed, however; check ORV regulations posted at the Sam Houston Ranger Station. East trailhead access: From New Waverly take FM–1375 approximately 4 miles west to FSR–233; turn north and follow signs approximately 3 miles. West trailhead access: From New Waverly take FM–1375 approximately 11 miles west to FSR–215; go north (right) for 1 mile and bear left on FSR–208; trailhead is on immediate left. *Note:* Hikers may be happier on the quieter Lone Star Hiking Trail, accessed from Stubblefield Recreation Area (see below).

Scott's Ridge. From Willis exit of I–45, take FM–1097 West 8 miles, then FSR–212 North for 1 mile. No facilities aside from boat ramp accessing Lake Conroe. Parking fee.

Stubblefield Lake Recreation Area and Campground. From I–45 at New Waverly, take FM–1375 West 11 miles to FSR–215; turn north and follow pavement to signs. That latter road passes a seventy-acre woodpecker cluster with numerous cavity trees, a National Forest Service effort to save the endangered red-cockaded woodpecker. The birds are active primarily at sunrise and sunset. Situated on the wide and shallow west fork of the San Jacinto River, this park offers twenty-eight campsites for either tents or RVs (up to 20 feet in length). Fee. You'll find tables, fire rings, and hot showers. Swimming not recommended (broken glass, possible alligator problem), but shallow-draft boating, canoeing, and bass fishing are pleasures in these beautiful headwaters of Lake Conroe. The park also accesses the Lone Star Hiking Trail. Interested in joining the Lone Star Hiking Trail Club, Inc.? Call the National Forest Service, (936) 344–6205; www.lshtclub.com.

WHERE TO EAT

Old Station Marketplace. 9304 Highway 75 North. This soup-salad-sandwich spot is easily identified by the old-style Texaco gas pumps out front. Open for lunch weekdays. $; ☐; (936) 344–0086.

Waverly House. 9337 Highway 75 South (at the intersection of FM–1375 and TX–75 on the western edge of New Waverly). When a Houston newspaper asked its readers to vote for the Best Country Cafes in Texas in 1989, this friendly place was in the top ten, and nothing's changed. Known for its homemade cream pies, it also dishes out freshly baked cobbler almost year-round. Order the chicken-fried steak only if you're starving or sharing; it laps over both sides of the plate. If you are in New Waverly on a weekday, don't pass up the workingman's steam-table lunch. Open for breakfast and lunch until 2:00 P.M. daily, for dinner on Friday and Saturday; (936) 344–6552.

CONTINUING ON

From New Waverly continue this day trip by driving north on I–45 to Huntsville.

HUNTSVILLE

In the early 1830s an adventurous frontiersman named Pleasant Gray thought this rolling, wooded wilderness looked like his former home in Huntsville, Alabama. Because there were good springs nearby, he settled in and established an Indian trading post. By 1836 the tiny settlement of Huntsville was thriving, and in 1848 Sam Houston built his family home and plantation, Woodland, at the southern edge of town.

Sam's home now is right downtown, across from the Sam Houston State University campus, and those old Indian trails long since have been formalized into highways. Today's visitors can "stand with Sam," however: A somewhat startling 67-foot-high statue of this Texas legend borders I–45, the centerpiece of a visitor center and park. This is the world's tallest statue of an American hero. Open daily, the Sam Houston Statue Visitor Center also distributes Texas state maps and official travel information, the only such resource in the north-from-Houston region. Access is exit 109 from I–45 North, exit 112 from I–45 South; (800) 289-8389; www.samhoustonstatue.com.

To reach downtown Huntsville from either direction on I–45, take the TX–30 exit and head east. You'll soon find a main square retrogressing visually to the 1860s, courtesy of an ongoing trompe l'oeil program designed to bring back the style and architecture of the city's past.

Driving-tour booklets are available weekdays from the Sam Houston Statue Visitor Information Center or the Huntsville Chamber of Commerce, 1327 Eleventh Street, P.O. Box 538, Huntsville, TX 77342-0538; (936) 295-8113 or (800) 289-0389; www.huntsvilletexas.com. Weekend explorers will find area information available outside that office. Expect numerous antiques stores around the square as well as an interesting museum and an old-fashioned soda fountain.

Want to overnight? B&B is provided at several vintage homes. In town The Whistler is an 1859 Victorian that has been in the same family for six generations; (936) 295-2834 or (800) 432-1288; Bluebonnet Bed and Breakfast is a 1912 beauty, recently moved from town to seven acres on FM–1374; (936) 295-3072. Jordan Ranch is a restored 1892 farmhouse 17 miles north of Huntsville on FM–1696; (936) 295-1844. A stay at this working longhorn ranch includes a tour, fishing, and hiking.

WHAT TO DO

The Blue Lagoon. North of Huntsville on Pinedale Road, off FM–247. Also known as Cozumel in the Pines, this old rock quarry offers some exciting scuba territory to certified divers. There are two large lakes, both with 40-foot underwater visibility and sunken shipwrecks to explore. You must have your C-card with you to be admitted, and no children under fourteen, pets, or glass containers are allowed. Open Friday–Sunday in winter, daily in summer. Closed January and February. Call for directions and more information. $$. (936) 291-6111.

Christmas tree farms. This is prime tree-cutting territory. Call either of the following for directions: A-C Christmas Tree Farm, (936) 295-9523; or Mill Hollow Christmas Tree Farm, (409) 377-4044, www.millhollowtexas.com.

Gibb Bros. Building. 1118½ Eleventh Street, on the corner of Eleventh Street and Sam Houston Avenue, across from the court-house. Started in 1841 as a store, this business evolved into the town's first bank because Thomas and Sanford Gibbs owned the only safe. The third structure on this site, the current building dates from 1890 has been restored to its early appearance after being disguised for decades by a modern brick front. The Gibb Brothers banking offices continue on the second floor, making this the oldest business in Texas still on its original site and under the same family ownership.

The Gibbs-Powell Home. 1228 Eleventh Street (Eleventh Street and Avenue M). This excellent example of Greek Revival architecture was built in 1862 and can be toured on weekend afternoons and by appointment. Donation. For group tour information contact the Huntsville Chamber of Commerce; (800) 289-0389 or (936) 295-2914; www.huntsvilletexas.com.

H.E.A.R.T.S. Veterans Memorial Museum. 2 Financial Plaza. Located inside the West Hill Mall (exit 116 from I-45, and turn west). The initials stand for Helping Every American Remember Through Serving, and the exhibits include first-hand accounts of what specific wars and battles were actually like, recorded by soldiers who were there. Open Tuesday–Saturday. Donations appreciated; (936) 295-5959; www.heartsmuseum.com.

Henry Opera House. Twelfth Street and Avenue K. Such elegance as this must have represented in the 1880s is hard to visualize. Only the tall windows on the upper floor give a hint of the building's cultural past. Built as a Masonic investment in 1883, it soon became the property of Major John Henry, who installed Huntsville's first department store on the ground floor and used the second floor as an opera house.

Huntsville State Park. Eight miles south of Huntsville via I-45, then west on Park Road 40. Here 2,000-plus acres center on Lake Raven and offer swimming, canoeing, and limited sailing and motor-boating. Hiking and birding are excellent, and Lake Raven Stables offers trail horseback riding year-round; (936) 295-1985. The forest is dominated by loblolly and shortleaf pine, dogwood, sweet gum, sassafras, and assorted oaks. Good camping and picnicking. Fee. Open daily; (936) 295-5644 or (800) 792-1112; www.tpwd.state.tx.us.

Oakwood Cemetery. Two blocks north of Eleventh Street on Avenue I. (Those 2 blocks of Avenue I are TX-1, the shortest official highway in the state.) Sam Houston sleeps with good company in this historic cemetery. Deeded as a free burial place in 1847 by Huntsville's founder, Pleasant Gray, Oakwood has several tombstones carrying burial dates as early as 1842. Self-guided tour information is available at the Sam Houston Statue Visitor Center.

Sam Houston Memorial Park and Museum. 1836 Sam Houston Avenue (between Seventeenth and Nineteenth Streets). During a turbulent life that saw him the governor of Tennessee, a general in the Texas Army, the victor at the battle of San Jacinto, and the first president of the Republic of Texas, Sam Houston had many homes. None was as lovely or as beloved by him as Woodland Home, built on this site in 1847. Restored in 1981, this square log house with its white clapboard siding is just one of the pleasures in this shady park/museum complex.

Start at the museum, touring the right wing first to keep the chronology straight, and then visit Woodland, its separate kitchen, Houston's law office, and a blacksmith shop. Close by are the War and Peace House and the unusual Steamboat House, where Houston died in 1863. The docents in both homes speak of Sam and his wife, Margaret, as if they might return at any moment. The park's small lake was a fresh, bubbling spring during Houston's residency here; today it is reshaped to resemble the state of Texas and is a pleasant spot for a picnic lunch. Spring visits get a bonus of flowering dogwood and azaleas. Sam Houston's grave also is interesting, across town in Oakwood Cemetery. Part of the Sam Houston State University complex, the park and museum are open Tuesday–Sunday; (936) 294-1832; www.samhouston.org.

Sam Houston State University. Five blocks south of the town square on Sam Houston Avenue (US-75). Founded in 1879 as a normal (teacher-training) institute, SHSU's campus landmark is Austin Hall (1853), the oldest educational facility in the Southwest.

Guided walking tours of this picturesque campus are offered weekdays by appointment; (936) 294-1844. Many cultural, sports, and special events are open to the public. Call the public relations office, (936) 294-1833, to find out what's going on when you're planning to be in town.

The on-campus planetarium hosts public "Star Parties," and the SHSU Observatory north of Huntsville offers sky viewing through a 24-inch telescope; call (936) 294-1601 for schedules. You also can arrange tours of the school's agricultural operations, including the plant science greenhouse, as well as animal facilities focused on beef cattle, horses, and goats; (936) 294-1215.

Texas Prison Museum. 491 TX-75 North, P.O. Box 1271, Huntsville. Want to keep your kids on the straight and narrow? Bring them here for a look at a 9-by-6-foot cell. Guides also explain other exhibits that include Bonnie and Clyde's rifles and some blood-chilling photos from their area escapades; "Old Sparkie," the actual electric chair used through 1964; rare balls and chains; and assorted contraband confiscated with the nearby prison. Moved to new digs in 2002, this interesting museum can special-order any type of prisoner-made leather goods, from "Bubba" belts to snuffcan holders, dolls to artwork. Prices are reasonable and the craftsmanship excellent. Open daily. Admission is $4.00, $2.00 for children; (936) 295-2155; www.txprisonmuseum.org.

The Walls. Three short blocks east of the town square. This is the original main unit of the Huntsville State Prison. *Of interest:* The "prisoner count" whistle that blows daily at 7:00 A.M. and again in the late afternoon assures Huntsville residents that all's well—every felon is accounted for. Self-guided tour information for the prison is available at the Sam Houston Statue Visitor Center.

WHERE TO EAT

The Cafe Texan. 1120 Sam Houston (at the corner of Twelfth Street on courthouse square). Chicken-fried steak and pepper steak are "home-cooked" here. Open for breakfast, lunch, and dinner daily (specials at lunch). $-$$; ☐; (936) 295-2381.

The Catfish Place. 3400 State Highway 19. Between the freshly roasted peanuts on the table and the numerous catfish/shrimp/oyster selections, you won't go hungry here. Open for lunch and dinner Wednesday–Sunday. $-$$; ☐; (936) 295-8685.

The Homestead on 19th. 1215 Nineteenth Street (across from Sam Houston Memorial Park and Museum). No contest, this is the best fine dining in Huntsville, a destination in itself. Owner-chef John Eschenfelder serves innovative American cuisine within an interesting historic matrix: conjoined log cabins circa 1834–1850 that were moved to this shady site in 1980. The courtyard between the cabins now serves as a shady setting for special events. In a hurry? How about a Black Angus tenderloin done in whiskey butter or stuffed with garlic and fresh mozzarella cheese? With a phone call, these and other tasty entrees are available as take-out. Open for dinner Tuesday–Saturday. $$-$$$; ☐; (936) 291–7366.

The Junction Restaurant. 2641 Eleventh Street. Just look for an 1849 plantation house with an old-fashioned buggy on the front porch. Inside, the house specialties are catfish, fresh seafood, steaks, and chicken. Open daily for lunch and dinner. $-$$; ☐; (936) 291–2183.

King's Candies & Ice Cream. 1112 Eleventh Street (on the square). First cousin to King's Confectionery on The Strand in Galveston, this old-fashioned sweet shop makes traditional shakes, malts, and banana splits at its soda fountain, squeezes lemons for the lemonade, makes its own candy, and serves Blue Bell ice cream. It's also a good place for a lunch sandwich or salad. Open Monday–Saturday. $; ☐; (936) 291–6988.

McKenzie's Barbeque. 1700 Eleventh Street. These folks smoke their tasty meats in three pits out back. Open daily for lunch and dinner. $-$$; ☐; (936) 291–7347; www.mckenziesbarbeque.com.

The New Zion Missionary Baptist Church. 2601 Montgomery Road (FM-1374), 2 miles east of I-45. A few years back a Houston housepainter named D. C. Ward volunteered to paint this country church, and when his wife, Annie Mae, began fixing some barbecue ribs for his workday lunch, the wonderful aroma stopped traffic. The congregation took the hint and began selling the Wards' barbecue on weekends from a shady spot near the church.

Next came a "real" kitchen and dining room, serving up some of the best barbecue in East Texas, the profits from which built a new brick church with stained-glass windows. In a hurry? Just ask for the $8.00 family-style special—four meats, beans, potato salad, iced tea, and tax—that arrives as fast as the staff can dish it up. Open 11:00 A.M. to 6:00 P.M. Wednesday–Saturday. $-$$; (936) 295–7394.

WANDERING THE BACKROADS

The OSR turnoff, 40 miles north of Huntsville on I-45, is a meandering country drive with more than a touch of history. The initials stand for Old San Antonio Road, but it also is known as El Camino Real, because it was created by the order of the king of Spain in 1691. The Spaniards, through their control of Mexico, claimed Texas from 1519 to 1821, but the French also coveted this rich, wild land, sending explorers into Texas in the late 1600s. To reinforce its claim, Spain created a series of missions in East Texas and blazed this road to bolster and serve those primitive outposts. Today TX-21 follows, after a fashion, that historic route from San Marcos northeast to the Louisiana border, one portion linking the Madisonville area to Crockett. If you love vistas of rolling fields edged by ancient oaks, don't miss this drive.

Turning west on OSR from I-45 takes you through pretty countryside en route to Bryan–College Station (Trip 3, this sector).

If you're hungry and out roaming, take I-45 23 miles north from Huntsville to Madisonville for a tasty meal at the vintage Woodbine Hotel. Now owned by noted chef Reinhard Warmuth and his wife, Susan, this B&B hotel's dining room serves soups, salads, and sandwiches for lunch Tuesday–Friday, and outstanding dinners Tuesday–Saturday. The evening menus usually include herb-crusted chickens and steaks, grilled salmon topped with one of several flavorful sauces, and prime rib (Thursday–Saturday). $-$$$; ☐; (936) 348-3333; www.woodbinehoteltexas.com.

Fun to know: The Woodbine is a survivor, built in 1904 by joining two kit houses (one in Eastlake style, the other Queen Anne) possibly ordered from Sears Roebuck. Its saloon, now called Brimberry House (circa 1870) and relocated to this site in 1920, is the oldest building in the county. Now on the National Register of Historic Places and a Texas Historic Landmark, the hotel sported Madisonville's only telephone back in 1904; that original phone booth is still there.

CONTINUING ON

From Huntsville, two routes take you to Crockett, the final stop on this day trip. A longer but very scenic alternative travels 30 miles north to Madisonville via either US-75 or I-45, then swings northeast 36 miles to Crockett via TX-21, part of the previously mentioned Old San Antonio Road.

A shorter route to Crockett follows TX-19 northeast from Huntsville for 49 miles, passing through the communities of Trinity and Lovelace en route. If overnighting appeals, you'll find B&B in Trinity at The Parker House, (936) 594-3260 or (800) 593-2373; and at the Sanderson Estate, (936) 594-2007; www.sandersonbb.com.

CROCKETT

Davy Crockett and two companions had to do some fast talking here. Local folks found Crockett's campsite near this area in 1836 (the trio were en route to their destinies at the Alamo) and nearly hanged them as horse thieves. The fifth-oldest town in Texas and loaded with vintage buildings, Crockett has a history that is easy to trace.

Visitors should start at the traditional square in the heart of town—good gift-shopping territory—and then go exploring. For advance information contact the Houston County Chamber of Commerce, 1100 Edmiston Drive, P.O. Box 307, Crockett, TX 75835; (936) 544-2359 or (888) 269-2359; www.crockettareachamber.org. More than 210 historic markers and sites in Houston County reflect its heritage as the first county of the Republic of Texas (1837). For a list contact the Houston County Historical Commission, Second Floor, Houston County Courthouse, Crockett, TX 75835; (936) 544-3255, extension 238.

Consider turning this day trip into an overnight with accommodations at Warfield House, built in the 1890s and now elegantly restored as a B&B lodging in the heart of town; (936) 544-4037.

WHERE TO GO

Davy Crockett Horse & Rider Camp. On TX-21, 10 miles east of Loop 304 in Crockett; watch for signs. Owners Jerry and Cindy Gentry offer hour-long guided trailrides through the Davy Crockett National Forest ($20 per hour, per person), as well as a two-hour "Ribeye Trail Ride" that ends with a candlelight steak dinner served in your own rustic log cabin ($99 per person, including overnight). You also can overnight here without the horseback ride and steak ($50 per person), and you can bring your own horse and ride on your own. The community bathrooms have hot showers. Open daily, year-round. ☐; (936) 546-0690; www.davycrockettduderanch.com.

Davy Crockett Spring. West Goliad at the railroad underpass, west of the town square. Though not much to see, the spring still flows and serves as a public drinking fountain at what is thought to be Crockett's campsite.

Downes-Aldrich Historical Home. 207 North Seventh Street. Listed in the National Register of Historic Places, this Victorian survivor now is the historical and cultural activities center for the town. Open Wednesday, Saturday, and Sunday afternoons. Fee; (936) 544-4804.

Monroe-Crook Home. 709 East Houston Avenue. Built in 1854 and listed in the National Register of Historic Places, this Greek Revival home is open for public tours on Wednesday morning and weekend afternoons, March–December. Fee; (936) 544-5820.

Salmon Lake Park. P.O. Box 483, Grapeland. Twelve miles north of Crockett, this old-fashioned swimming hole and recreational vehicle park is open to day-trippers and overnighters. The privately owned park is the site of several festivals each year, including an August bluegrass festival nearing its thirtieth birthday. Fifteen cabins are available for rental. (936) 687-2594; www.salmonlakepark.com.

WHERE TO EAT

Betty Boop's Sandwich & Soup Shop. 509 East Houston Avenue. If you're looking for a quick bite while strolling Crockett's courthouse square, drop in here. Open weekdays for lunch. $; (936) 544-4297.

Brass Lantern. 1117 East Loop 304. Standard menu here, plus a good buffet and lunch specials. Open for lunch and dinner Tuesday–Saturday. $–$$; ☐; (936) 544-4091.

Camp Street Cafe. 215 South Third Street. Owned by the same family since its stagecoach days, this restored but rustic, western-styled property is back in business as a lively country-style entertainment venue. In addition to assorted bluegrass, blues, and folk music, there's often cowboy-style entertainment on Saturday evening, courtesy of Guy and Pip Gillette. Professional performers who were named the best duo by the 1998 Academy of Western Artists, the Gillettes specialize in cowboy poetry mixed with country music, and they play to standing-room crowds when on tour. Crockett residents, they now have a prime performance setup close to home. Inquire about food service. ☐; (936) 544–8656.

Fowler's Bar-B-Que. TX-7 East and Loop 304. Check out the daily specials at lunch and dinner at this long-established local favorite. Open Tuesday–Sunday. $–$$; ☐; (936) 544–9690.

Stockman's Steakhouse. Highway 21 West, 3 miles west from Loop 304, inside the Houston County Livestock Auction Barn. Nothing like going to the source for great steaks. The seafood entrees are good bets as well. Open Thursday for lunch and dinner, Friday and Saturday for dinner only. $–$$; ☐; (936) 544–3545.

WANDERING THE BACKROADS

There are numerous possibilities if you feel like extending your drive well beyond the two-hour limit of this book. First option is to continue north on OSR (TX-21) from Crockett through the Davy Crockett National Forest to the Mission Tejas State Historical Park, (936) 687–2394; www.tpwd.state.tx.us. The Rice family log home is special here, built between 1828 and 1838 and used as a stage stop. Nearby is a commemorative log structure similar to the old Spanish mission established here in 1690 to serve the Tejas Indians. That mission was the first of its kind in Texas.

Continuing northeast another 7 miles on OSR brings you to Caddoan Mounds State Historic Site, 6 miles southwest of Alto. In addition to two large ceremonial mounds, archaeological digs have led to a full-size replica of a Caddoan house built with Stone Age–type tools. A visitor center explains all. Open Thursday–Monday. Fee; (936) 858–3218.

A second option from Crockett follows TX-7 approximately 18 miles east to the Ratcliff Lake Recreation Area in the Davy Crockett National Forest. A picturesque forty-five-acre swimming and fishing lake surrounded by extensive picnic areas and campgrounds, this facility also sports canoe rentals and countless deer amid a hardwood forest that's particularly beautiful in spring and fall; fee; (936) 655–2299. The 20-mile-long Four C Hiking Trail begins here and continues northeast to the Neches Bluff Overlook on the Neches River, just south of TX-21 northeast of Weches. For more trail information contact the Texas Forestry Association, P.O. Box 1488, Lufkin, TX 75902; (936) 632–8733.

A third long-drive alternative is FM-229 northwest from Crockett to Houston County Lake. Locally, this is considered the best bass fishing in the state.

Following US-287 southeast from Crockett takes you through the Kickapoo Recreation Area near Groveton and hits the northern limit of the Livingston–Woodville day trip (Trip 2, Northeast sector).

And finally, there's Lufkin, which was founded in 1872. About 43 miles east of Crockett, this town was built on the railway and lumber industries. Today it attracts nearly a million visitors annually. Among its attractions are The Texas Forestry Museum, the Museum of East Texas, and the surprisingly good Ellen Trout Zoo. Only the latter charges admission, but its diverse collection is worth the small fee. For zoo information, call (936) 633-0399; www. ellentroutzoo.com.

For general information, including special events and lodging options, contact the Lufkin Convention & Visitors Bureau at (800) 409-5659; www.visitlufkin.com.

BRYAN–COLLEGE STATION

From Houston follow TX-6 and US-290 north to Hempstead and continue north on TX-6 through Navasota into Bryan and College Station.

These joint communities tend to have a single connotation to Houstonians—Texas A&M University. While visitors to that sprawling campus will find much of interest, there are several other things to do near Aggieland.

Bryan and College Station today flow into a combined metropolitan area that ranked first in growth in the state and sixth in the entire country in the 1980 census. Not bad for a slow starter. This rich sliver of agricultural land, bounded by the Brazos River on the west and the Navasota River on the east, was sparsely settled until the advent of the Houston & Texas Central Railroad in 1866. The Reconstruction years after the Civil War were rough on the young town of Bryan, and it wasn't until the formal opening of Texas A&M College in 1876 that the area settled down to some semblance of respectability.

Some footnotes on Bryan's past are interesting. The original street grid inadvertently provided for present-day traffic by making Main Street wide enough to turn a five-yoke oxen team, and the college was deliberately sited on the open prairie 5 miles south of town so as to be well removed from the influence of demon rum, which flowed freely in Bryan's saloons.

39

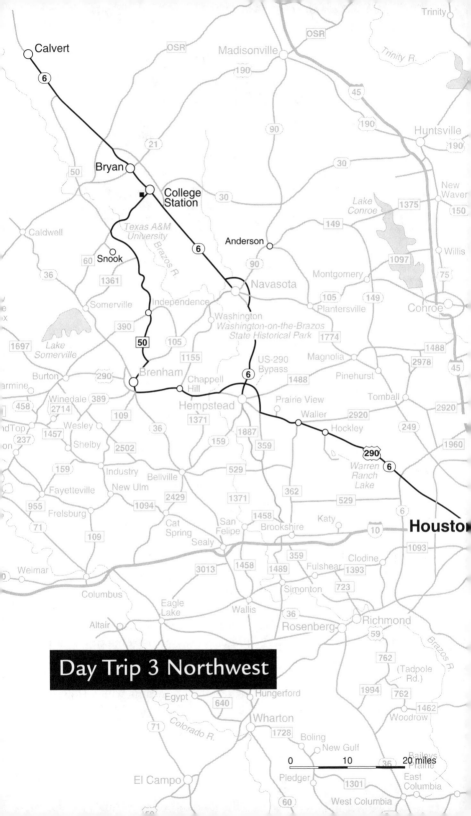

Day Trip 3 Northwest

An information-loaded historic guide and map covers Bryan's old commercial and residential districts, as well as the remains of several small pre–Civil War settlements outside town. This and other area guides are found at the Bryan–College Station Chamber of Commerce Convention & Visitor Bureau, 715 University Drive East, College Station, TX 77840; (979) 260-9898 or (800) 777-8292; www.bryan collegestation.org. Open Monday–Friday only; contact in advance for maps and brochures if you intend to explore on a weekend.

Leaving Texas A&M to its own section following, here are some suggestions of what to see in Bryan and College Station.

WHAT TO DO

Birding. The Brazos Valley hosts an enormous variety of bird life. A self-guided tour covering five areas and a list of birds common to the Brazos County Arboretum are available from the Convention & Visitor Bureau.

Brazos Center. 3232 Briarcrest, Bryan. Take the Briarcrest exit east from the TX-6 bypass. This is the special-events place for the area, hosting giant weekend antiques shows in February, July, and October. Year-round visitors can enjoy the Brazos Valley Museum of Natural Science and a small nature trail on the grounds. Open Tuesday–Saturday, September through May; Monday–Saturday, June through August. Free; (979) 776-8338 (center); (979) 776-2195 (museum).

Canoeing on the Brazos River. First, so you'll sound like a native, it's pronounced *Braa-zas*, not *Bray-zos*, as you might expect from the spelling. Although its water is muddy with sediment, the Brazos generally is quiet and otherwise scenic, a good one- or two-day float if you have your own canoe. As of this writing there are no canoe rentals available in the Bryan–College Station area. You'll find float information in several river books available at major bookstores.

The Children's Museum of the Brazos Valley. 202 South Bryan Street, Bryan. Make-believe and creativity thrive in this hands-on learning environment. Children can pretend to grocery-shop or drive an ambulance, dress up and strut their stuff on a small stage, play a piano, or actually paint a Volkswagen "Bug." Open Tuesday–Saturday. Fee; (979) 779-5437; www.mymuseum.com.

J. P. Seven Christmas Trees. Call for directions; (979) 846–7916.

Lake Bryan. From TX-6 north of Bryan, take the FM–2818 exit south for approximately 5 miles. At Sandy Point Road (blinking yellow light), turn right and go 3.4 miles; lake is on the right. Operated by the City of Bryan Parks and Recreation Department, this 886-acre lake is surrounded by 1,700 acres of oak-shaded land, of which 150 acres are developed for both primitive and RV camping, picnicking, and other recreational uses. There's lots of water access, including a sand beach and a special restricted area for jet-ski operation. Other popular activities here include sailing (no water-skiing), walking and nature trails, and mountain biking along 20 miles of challenging terrain, much of it in view of the lake. Although the park is open year-round, lake hours are seasonal; inquire. Primitive camping is $8.00 per night; RV sites with water and electricity are $15.00. Admission is $5.00 per car. For information or to reserve an RV site, call (979) 361–0861 or 209–5207.

Messina Hof Wine Cellar and Vineyard. 4545 Old Reliance Road, Bryan. Exit TX-6 at Boonville Road; stay on access road going north; turn right on Old Reliance Road; winery is 3 miles east. Follow signs. Paul and Merrill Bonarrigo began planting grapes in 1977; their successful vineyard now covers forty-six acres and produces about 250,000 gallons (780,000 bottles) annually. Using the classic European grape Vinifera grafted onto Texas root stock, they bottle sixteen varieties of wine, including chardonnay, cabernet, port, red and white zinfandels, and champagne. Harvest time is July and August, and you can pick and stomp grapes yourself by signing up in advance for their Pickers' Club (free). The early-twentieth-century Howell manor house has been restored as the winery's retail sales and tasting room; it is open daily, and there are winery tours at specific times. The Bonarrigos also invite the public for Springfest in April and a premiere party for new wines and vintages in November. Other special events occur monthly throughout the year (get on their mailing list). If a luxurious weekend retreat sounds good, inquire about overnighting at The Villa at Messina Hof (ten nonsmoking rooms furnished in European antiques). Visitors also rave about the food at the winery's Vintage House restaurant (see "Where to Eat"); (979) 778–9463 or (800) 736–9463; www.messinahof.com.

The Texas Gallery. 2501 Texas Avenue South, Suite 105-C, College Station. Exhibits, juried shows featuring regional artists, and outstanding handcrafts make this a place to stop and shop. Open Monday–Friday. (979) 696-2787.

EXPLORING TEXAS A&M UNIVERSITY

Even if you haven't a prospective student in tow, this handsome 5,250-acre campus has much to offer. Located in the heart of College Station and hard to miss on the west side of TX-6, Texas A&M was the first public institution of higher education in the state. Originally an all-male military college, it now has a coed enrollment of approximately 44,000 and is in the top ten schools nationally in expenditures for research.

Aggie traditions are stories in themselves. Ask about the Elephant Walk, the Twelfth Man, and Silver Taps at the Visitor Information Center in Rudder Tower for an insight into what makes Aggies so loyal to their alma mater.

Footsteps, a book of suggested walking tours on campus, can be bought in the student bookstore, (979) 845-8681, in the Memorial Student Center, or in advance from the Texas A&M University Press, (979) 845-1436. First-time visitors should begin at the Visitor Center in the lobby of Rudder Tower, (979) 845-5851; see Rudder Tower information below. For visitor information by mail, write Aggieland Visitor Center, Texas A&M University, MS 1372, College Station, TX 77843-1372; www.tamu.edu.

WHAT TO DO

Note: All the following are on or near the Texas A&M Campus.

The Clayton W. Williams Jr. Alumni Center. Corner of George Bush Drive and Houston Street. Displays include an Aggie ring collection. (979) 845-7514.

The George Bush Presidential Library Center. Take the University Drive exit from TX-6 in College Station, turn west, and follow signs. This $42-million project dedicated to the first Bush presidency sits amid ninety acres of oaks and greenbelt on the western edge of the A&M campus. As the nation's tenth (and most computerized) presidential library, it houses all George Bush's vice-presidential and presidential records as well as memorabilia and personal documents from his public service career as congressman, ambassador to the

United Nations, chairman of the Republican National Committee, liaison to China, and director of the Central Intelligence Agency.

Unique museum exhibits include a replica of President Bush's Laurel Library at Camp David, precise down to the books on the shelves and paper clips on the desk; a section of the Berlin Wall; a mock-up of the cabin of Air Force One; and a replica of the cockpit of a Navy Avenger, the plane Bush flew as a fighter pilot in World War II.

Museum archives also hold extensive memorabilia from the Gulf War, including a Humvee, an Iraqi missile launcher, and an old wooden door from Kuwait, listing in gold the names of all the American service personnel who perished during that conflict. Gifts from heads of state dazzle, yet the human side of George Bush's rich personal life comes via exhibits of his favorite fly rods and a baseball glove worn when he played first base on Yale University's College World Series team. There's also a restored 1947 Studebaker, the same make and model Bush drove to Midland after his graduation from Yale. Fee. Open daily; call for hours and information on changing exhibits; (979) 691-4000; http://bushlibrary.tamu.edu.

Horticultural Gardens and Field Laboratory. On Hensel Drive, between Texas Avenue and South College Drive; watch for signs. Several beautiful test gardens are open for walking here seven days a week. Come on a weekday, however, and you can pick up a guide brochure that tells you what you're seeing. All gardens are maintained by students and funded by grants for testing and research; (979) 845-3658. Want to know what's wrong with your flowers or vegetables? Call the Department of Horticultural Sciences; weekdays only; (979) 845-3658.

Horticulture/Forest Sciences Building. On the west campus. Don't miss the Benz Gallery of Floral Art, open during weekday business hours. Exhibits include paintings, sculptures, primitive art, ceramics, and gold orchids. (979) 845-5341.

Kleberg Animal and Food Sciences Center (Kleberg Center). From George Bush Drive, go right on Wellborn, left at the second stoplight (Old Main Drive), and left on Olsen Boulevard; Kleberg Center will be in front of you, on the left. The walls of the northeast stairwell contain 254 panels burned with the major brands of every county in Texas. Open weekdays.

Memorial Student Center (MSC). Part of the University Center complex. Ask at the visitor center in Rudder Tower as to the current locations of the Buck Schiwetz paintings and the Texan Campaign Staffordshire China (circa 1850). Also of interest are the Centennial Wood Carvings in the corridor between the student lounge and the cafeteria (six walnut panels that trace the history of the school from 1876) and assorted art exhibits in the University Center Galleries. For a current schedule of what's showing and where, call (979) 845-8501. Don't miss shopping in the student bookstore.

Memorial Student Center Opera and Performing Arts Society. This campus group presents a full professional program every year, ranging from jazz bands to ballet. For current production information call (979) 845-1234.

Nuclear Science Center. Off campus, near the Easterwood Airport. This multimillion-dollar facility houses the largest nuclear reactor on any campus in the Southwest and produces radioactive isotopes for scientific research. Tours Monday–Friday; (979) 845-7553, 845-7551, or 845-7552.

Rudder Tower. At University Center on Joe Routt Boulevard. The visitor center in the lobby introduces you to the university with maps, an excellent movie and booklet about the school, and campus guides. Visitor parking (fee) is adjacent to the building. Tour reservations must be made at least two weeks in advance. Open Monday–Friday and on football weekends; call for hours, (979) 845-5851.

Sam Houston Sanders Corps of Cadets Center. Built with private funds in 1992 and dedicated to the past, present, and future of the university's famous corps, this outstanding facility exhibits several one-of-a-kind artworks, as well as the Metzger-Sanders Gun Collection (antique and historic firearms). Open Monday–Friday and on football weekends; (979) 862-2862.

Tours also can be arranged through the Cyclotron Institute, (979) 845-1411; the Computing Services Center, (979) 845-4211; and the Veterinary Medicine College, (979) 845-5051.

WHERE TO EAT ON THE A&M CAMPUS

The Creamery. In the Meat Science and Technology Center, adjacent to the Kleberg Building. The best chocolate ice cream in the world is sold here, along with milk, butter, cheese, eggs, and meats produced on the university's farms. Open weekdays. $; (979) 845-5652.

Memorial Student Center. Two choices here: the cafeteria

(979–845–1118) and Hullabaloo, a food court on the lower level (979–847–9464). $.

WHERE TO EAT IN THE AREA

Black Forest Inn. 11319 TX–30, Anderson; on the north side of TX–30, 22 miles east of Bryan–College Station toward Huntsville. Robert and Diane Johnson's skill with the classic Continental food of Europe as well as our own fresh Gulf seafood brings devotees from as far away as Austin and Dallas, just for a meal. Everything is fresh (no additives or preservatives) and made from scratch, including Diane's own mayonnaise and salad dressings. Reservations are a necessity, particularly on weekends or if your party numbers four or more. Open for dinner Wednesday–Saturday. $$–$$$; ☐; (936) 874–2407.

Cafe Eccell. 101 Church Avenue, College Station. Housed in what was the old city hall, this classy bistro features California-style food so fresh even the fish have never been frozen. Barbecued chicken pizza is a best-seller, along with award-winning desserts such as the fresh strawberry tart. In addition to daily specials, the basic menu changes seasonally, and the wine list is considered one of the best in town. Open for lunch and dinner Monday–Saturday, brunch on Sunday. $–$$; ☐; (979) 846–7908.

Chicken Oil Company. 3600 South College, Bryan. This giant wooden building is filled with antiques and memorabilia, and its hamburgers have been voted the best in town in local polls. Open for lunch and dinner daily. $; (979) 846–3306.

Clementine's. 202 South Bryan, Bryan. Located amid the antiques of Old Bryan Marketplace, this delightful spot adds Continental flair to tearoom standbys such as quiche, sandwiches, and salads. Romantics should reserve for a candlelight Saturday night dinner. Open for lunch Monday–Wednesday, lunch and dinner Thursday–Saturday. $–$$$; ☐; (979) 779–2558.

Czech-Tex Barbeque Steakhouse and Bakery. In Snook, 10 miles west of College Station via FM–60. No address is necessary for this popular eatery; just look for the biggest building in Snook. An assortment of Czech food on the menu echos the area's strong ethnic heritage, but the big draws are the generous, handcut steaks. Open Tuesday–Saturday for lunch and dinner. $–$$$; ☐; (979) 272–8501.

Dixie Chicken. 307 University Drive, College Station. Among this venerable watering hole's claims to fame is the title of "best college bar," bestowed by *Playboy* magazine in 2002. Several generations of Aggies have crowded this eatery for brews, burgers, and chicken finger baskets. Wanna fit in? Order a Shiner Bock and Frito Pie. Mmmmmm, good. $; ☐; (979) 846-2322; www.dixiechicken.com.

Epicures Cafe. 2319 Texas Avenue South, College Station. For great food in a very informal atmosphere, try here. Their catering business has expanded into this small eatery featuring custom sandwiches, cold salads by the pound, sandwich wraps, and some unusual hot entrees—many of them heart-healthy. Open for lunch and dinner Tuesday–Saturday, brunch on Sunday. $-$$; ☐; (979) 695-0985.

Fajita Rita's. 4501 Texas Avenue South, Bryan. Great Tex–Mex and margaritas, served in a bright cantina atmosphere. Open for lunch and dinner daily. $-$$; ☐; (979) 846-3696.

Tom's Bar-B-Que & Steak House. 3610 College Avenue South, Bryan, and 2001 Texas Avenue South, College Station. No question what to order in this longtime local favorite, but the fact that your food comes on butcher paper accompanied by a slab of cheese and a butcher knife (no forks or spoons) may come as a surprise. Open daily for lunch and dinner. $-$$; ☐; (979) 846-4275 in Bryan, (979) 696-2076 in College Station.

Vintage House at Messina Hof. 4545 Old Reliance Road, Bryan. If this well-designed restaurant were closer to Houston it would be mobbed every night. As it is, unless you go early, it's best to reserve to ensure a table. Lunches, served until late afternoon, offer unusual quiches, lasagna, salads, and sandwiches, all with appropriate vino tie-ins, of course. Dinners include such classics as Beef Wellington, lamb chops, fish, and chicken, each designed with a fine wine touch. Both the horseradish-crusted salmon and the Gorgonzola Pinwheel breast of chicken are local favorites. Whenever and whatever you eat here, save room for the house special: the memorable Port 'n' Cream Sundae. Open daily for lunch (closes at 3:00 P.M. on Sunday), Thursday–Saturday evenings for dinner. $$-$$$; ☐; (979) 778-9463, extension 31, or (800) 736-9463; www.messinahof.com.

WANDERING THE BACKROADS

From College Station turn west on FM-60 at the University Drive signal and follow the local folks some 15 miles to Snook. The big attractions include fresh sausage from Slovacek's, (979) 272-8625, and a chance to chow down at Czech-Tex Barbecue Steakhouse and Bakery (see "Where to Eat" listings for Bryan–College Station).

As an alternative to returning home from Snook through College Station, backtrack only as far as FM-50 and swing south to Independence and Brenham (Trip 6, this sector). Those fine fields you pass north of Independence are part of the Texas A&M Experimental Farms.

If wanderlust really takes over and you want to stretch the two-hour driving limit of this book, continue north on TX-6 from Bryan some 45 miles to Calvert. Established in 1868, this nice old town is the unofficial antiques center of Texas, and you can tour some outstanding vintage homes during the Robertson County Pilgrimage in spring and the Christmas celebration in early December. Calvert's Main Street is a four-block collection of old brick and iron-front buildings, most of which now house antiques shops that are open Wednesday–Sunday. For information on B&B accommodations in the area, call (800) 290-1213. For information on Calvert call the chamber of commerce, (979) 364-2559, Monday–Wednesday, or (800) 670-8183.

You can return to Houston from Bryan–College Station one of three ways. The first is the simplest—just reverse the route you followed coming up.

The second is more scenic. Follow TX-6 South to Navasota and swing east on TX-105 toward Conroe. Turn south on FM-1774 for a forest drive through Plantersville and Magnolia before connecting with TX-249 South at Pinehurst. *Note:* This route is to be avoided on weekends from October 1 to November 15 because of Renaissance Festival traffic. TX-249 South from Pinehurst ultimately intersects I-45 North inside the Houston city limits.

If you feel like exploring farther, go east on TX-30 to Huntsville (Trip 2, this sector) and then scoot south on I-45 to home.

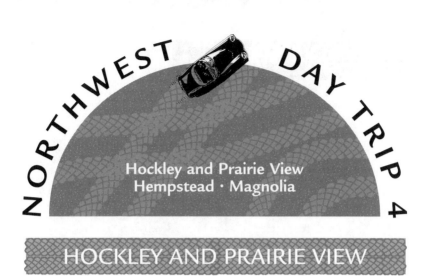

Hockley and Prairie View
Hempstead · Magnolia

HOCKLEY AND PRAIRIE VIEW

The primary path from Houston into this northwest sector is US–290, rambling its way through Cypress and a lot of interesting country en route to Austin and points west. Hockley is pure country—ranches, the remains of an old general store, and a great fishing hole. Prairie View at present is home to Prairie View State University, but just over a century ago it was the site of the Kirby Plantation, known as Alta Vista. Deeded to the state in 1876 for use as a college for black youths, the old mansion was the school's first educational building. It is gone now, along with de facto segregation, but look for St. Francis Episcopal Church, a small frame building (1870) moved to the campus from Hempstead in 1958. The first Episcopal church north of Houston, it still has the original pews, handmade by its first congregation.

WHAT TO DO

Bird-watching at Warren Ranch Lake. In Hockley turn west at the tallest rice dryer and follow Warren Ranch Road 3.4 miles. The lake will be on the left. It is private and a protected refuge, but the viewing (with binoculars) is excellent from the shoulder of the road. The largest winter concentration of ducks and geese in North America is found in the rice fields of this area, and the fifty wild acres of this lake have been known to host as many as 20,000 ducks and geese at one time. With luck you may spot a bald eagle, America's national bird and, happily, now removed from the endangered species list. For

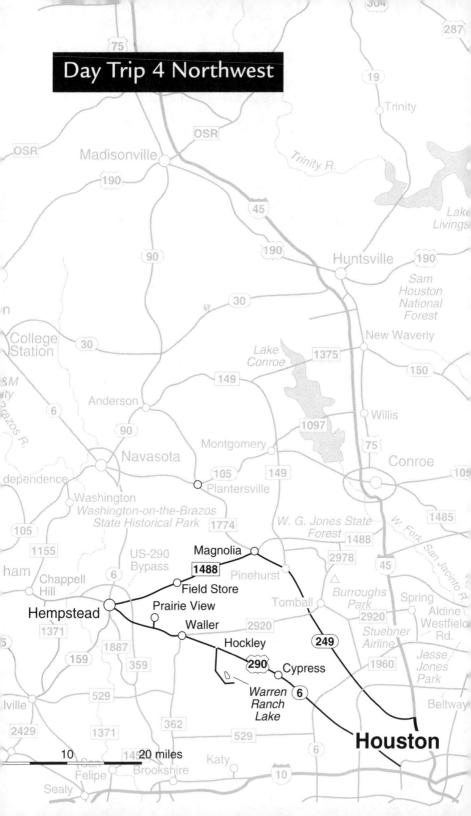

information call the Houston Audubon Society at (713) 932–1639; www.houstonaudubon.org.

Cypress Fairbanks Rodeo. 11206 Telge Road, Cypress (at US–290, Cy-Fair High School area). This popular summer event has kept Friday nights lively in the Cy-Fair High School area for more than thirty years. Standard rodeo events bring out the local buckaroos, plus there's a free calf scramble for ages twelve and under and a free goat scramble for ages six and under. All proceeds benefit the Cy-Fair FFA (Future Farmers of America). Fee. Call for June–July schedule; (281) 955–8558.

The Fishin' Hole. 14120 Cypress-Rosehill Road, Cypress (just north of old US–290). These two fishing lakes are stocked with farm-raised catfish, and the motto is "Catch all you want—Keep all you catch." No license is required, and bait is available. Your catch is weighed and charged at $2.10 per pound live, $2.50 per pound filleted. If it's hot and sunny, bring your own shade. Open Wednesday–Sunday year-round. ❑; (281) 373–0123.

MVP (Most Valuable Pilot) Aero Academy. 21904 US–290, Cypress (Weiser Air Park, between Huffmeister and Telge Roads). Want to see Houston from the air or check out a budding interest in flying lessons? This firm offers "flightseeing" or discovery flights in a Cessna 172 ($35 for thirty minutes, $70 for sixty minutes). ❑; (281) 469–3009.

Oil Ranch. P.O. Box 429, Hockley. Go 20 miles northwest of Houston via US–290, then turn right on Hegar Road and right on Magnolia Road. Families are welcome to play "cowboy for a day" at this pleasant spread. Activities include pony rides in the corral, swinging on ropes in the hay barn, hayrides through the pastures, and exploring a large maze inside Fort George Bush. There are also an Indian village, petting zoo, swimming pools, and miniature golf course, and kids can hand-feed the cattle and learn about the cattle industry. Special events include barn dances and free pumpkins in October. Reservations required; groups welcome. Fee. Open all year. Call for a free brochure and/or reservations. ❑; (281) 859–1616; www.oilranch.com.

Skydive Houston. 15355 Penick Road, Waller. From US–290 turn left on FM–362 (3 miles south of Waller) and follow signs. Care to float above the countryside? When weather permits, this company welcomes both neophyte and experienced skydivers. First-timers can choose between a tandem dive, static line dive (military style), or accelerated free fall; more advanced lessons are available. Cost ranges from $179 to $295, depending on style of jump. Open daily. ☐; (936) 931–1600 or (800) 586–7688; www.skydivehouston.com.

Steam trains at Zube Park. From the intersection of US–290 and the Sam Houston Tollway, go north on US–290 for 17 miles, then north on Roberts Road for 1.2 miles; watch for a large gazebo and park on the right. Thanks to a $1.00 per year annual lease between Harris County and the Houston Area Live Steamers Inc. club, ridable model steam trains now chug along 4,000 feet of 7.5-gauge track at this county park. Want to ride? The public is welcome aboard (free) on the third Saturday of every month, weather permitting. March through November. Each of the coal- or oil-fired steam engines pulls three to five cars capable of holding up to three adults. All are scale models of past or existing trains. Club members also operate model steamboats on the park's pond. For information on the steamers club or to confirm that the trains will be operating, call (713) 758-4949; www.hals.org.

WHERE TO EAT

Stockman's Restaurant. 2014 US–290, Waller. Where else can you get all-you-can-eat charbroiled steak, this place's Tuesday-night special? In addition to a full menu, Thursday's special is charbroiled or deep-fried quail, and Friday's is all the catfish and popcorn shrimp you can handle. There's also a hot-plate lunch daily. Open Monday–Saturday for breakfast, lunch, and dinner; Sunday for breakfast and lunch. $-$$; ☐; (936) 372-2060.

HEMPSTEAD

Resist the opportunity to zip past Hempstead via the US–290 bypass. You'll find a lot of history, some discount shopping, and good eating in this quiet town.

Given its somewhat sleepy air today, it's hard to believe that Hempstead once was known as Six-Shooter Junction, and that for several decades after the Civil War, it was a wild and woolly place. The rolling land south of town was settled as early as 1821, although only scattered historical markers tell the stories now.

The town was platted in 1856–57 as the terminus for the Houston and Texas Central Railroad, an early line that tooted over much of Waller County before expanding north to Bryan–College Station. During the Civil War the railroad made Hempstead a major supply and troop depot for Confederate forces, and when the war ended, the defeated men began their long walks home from here.

Hempstead was the turning point in Texas's battle for independence from Mexico. Sam Houston and his retreating forces camped and regrouped here from March 31 to April 14, 1836, and then began an aggressive march to San Jacinto, site of their ultimate victory over Santa Anna and his Mexican Army. A brief jaunt down FM-1887 now finds a historical marker about the Texian Army camp.

Hempstead slowly is reawakening to its heritage, but at present all vintage structures remain in private hands and are not open to the public. A windshield tour of the quiet residential streets on either side of US-290 offers such rewards as Coburn Cottage, 327 Twelfth Street; the Ahrenbeck-Urban Home, 1203 Bellville Highway; and the Houx House, on the corner of US-290/TX-6 and New Orleans Street.

Another good reason to stop in Hempstead is Dilorio's thriving produce market on US-290 at the southeastern edge of town.

WHAT TO DO

Frazier's Ornamental and Architectural Concrete. 48639 Highway 290. Escape the concrete jungle of Houston's freeway system with a visit to this two-acre retail center. You'll discover a wonderland of concrete products, ranging from garden statuary to tabletop creations, as well as aluminum garden decor and furniture and the fixings for backyard fountains and waterfalls. Open daily except Wednesdays; (979) 826-6760; www.fraziers concrete.com.

Lawrence Marshall Antique Cars. P.O. Box 964, Hempstead (on the north side of US-290 at the FM-1736 intersection, 2 miles west of Hempstead). It's impossible to miss this place. Just watch for a considerable number of folks literally hanging on the high game fence that surrounds this car lot and museum facility. They've temporarily abandoned their own wheels along the shoulder of the road to gaze longingly at more than twenty-six acres of vintage and special-interest cars. The 300-plus stock inventory ranges from a 1914 depot hack to street rods and high-performance muscle cars and includes rare editions of Thunderbirds and Corvettes. An additional one hundred rolling rarities fill an antique car museum (fee) behind the sales lot, and all are for sale; generally speaking, prices range from $5,000 to $50,000. Open Monday–Saturday; (877) 353-2277; www.marshall antiquecars.com.

Lawrence Marshall Family Recreation Center. On US-290 at Urban Road, northwest of town. Formerly the Hempstead Country Club, this multipurpose facility offers a nine-hole, par 36 golf course; swimming pool (season pass required); picnic area; tennis courts; volley and basketball courts; and a ten-acre fishing lake stocked with catfish and bass. There's also a quaint chapel, which can be rented for weddings and receptions, and a replica of a 1930s-era gasoline station. The latter houses game trophies and vintage cars. All are a gift to the city of Hempstead by former auto dealer Lawrence Marshall. Open daily, year-round. Entrance is free, but there are modest charges for individual sports facility use. ☐; (979) 826-4001.

Liendo Plantation. From US-290 in Hempstead turn northeast at the FM-1488 signal and then right on Wyatt Chapel Road; the plantation's gate will be 1 mile down on the right. Originally a Spanish land grant of 67,000 acres, Liendo was one of the earliest cotton plantations in Texas, and its large Greek Revival–style home was built by slave labor in 1853. During the Civil War Liendo served as a Union camp for Confederate prisoners directed by George A. Custer, and from 1873 to 1911 it was the home of sculptress Elisabet Ney and her husband, Dr. Edmond Montgomery. Both are buried on the grounds. Now privately owned, this gracious old home has been restored and furnished much as it would have been during its cotton-growing days. Liendo is a Texas Historic Landmark and is on the National Register of Historic Places. Docents give guided tours at specific times on the first Saturday of almost every month; groups with reservations are welcome at any time. A wonderful public event, the Old South Festival at Liendo, shows off this handsome and historic home every spring. "Civil War Weekend"—reenactments of what older Southerners often term the "Late Unpleasantness"—draws visitors the weekend before Thanksgiving. At other times this is a private residence; please do not wander the grounds without an advance appointment. Fee. Call for details; (979) 826-3126; www.liendo.org.

Liendo's resident owner, Will Detering, also operates Liendo's Restaurant, a charming Texana shop and tearoom in downtown Hempstead, as an extension of the plantation (see below).

Peckerwood Garden. Just south of FM-359 and the Business 290 intersection, near Hempstead. This seven-acre, private experimental garden near Hempstead emphasizes Mexican trees, shrubs, and perennials and their counterparts from Texas, the Southeast United States, and Asia. Dry-land gardens dramatically contrast with lush woodlands and formal topiary. Tours are available by appointment ($60 per hour for one to six persons, $80 per hour for seven to ten persons; two-week advance notice required). The gardens also are open to the public on the third weekend of each month (afternoons only), March–October. For tour information call (979) 826-3232. The Yucca Do Nursery is open Thursday–Saturday, February–October. Plant catalog available; contact them at P.O. Box 907, Hempstead, TX 77445. (979) 826-4580; www.peckerwoodgarden.com.

Poe's Catfish Ranch & Burger Barn. On the south side of FM-359, 7 miles west of US-290. Don't let the faded side dissuade you. Two nice ponds at this mom-and-pop spot offer day fishing; no license required. Open Thursday–Sunday. Call for rules and prices; (979) 826-2136.

WHERE TO EAT

Julio's Mexican Restaurant. 425 FM-1488. You'll find several departures from standard Tex–Mex here, starting with the shrimp enchiladas and special steak plates. Open daily for lunch and dinner. $-$$; ☐; (979) 826-3435.

Liendo's Restaurant. 936 New Orleans Street (at US-290 in downtown Hempstead). The third (and hopefully the final) Hempstead nest for this inventive restaurant, this home (1882) has served many masters. Now revamped into an offshoot of nearby Liendo Plantation, it's known as a spot to indulge in creative soups, salads, sandwiches, and daily specials. Portions are ample, there's usually a fisherman's catch, and you can count on homemade breads and desserts. Open daily for lunch, Friday and Saturday for dinner. $-$$; ☐; (979) 826-4400.

CONTINUING ON

From Hempstead this day trip now swings east on FM–1488 en route to Magnolia, passing through rolling, oak-studded terrain that rates with the prettiest countryside in the state. If you've already explored the FM–1488/Magnolia area, however, Hempstead offers several other travel choices.

The easiest is to continue on US–290 West to Chappell Hill and do all or part of Day Trip 5, this sector. Or you can swing southwest 16 miles on TX–159 to Bellville and pick up Day Trip 5, West sector.

If you elect to continue this day trip to Magnolia via FM–1488, you'll pass through the barely-there community of Fieldstore. This crossroads area got its name back in the late 1800s because there used to be a store here owned by the Fields family. Beginning more than a century ago, neighbors would gather here on the Fourth of July to clean the local cemetery and have a picnic.

WHERE TO EAT

Fieldstore Smoke House. 30291 FM–1488, Field Store. Taking over the space formerly occupied by popular diner Best Friend's Treasures Cafe, this family-run barbecue joint offers an ambitious steam-table based menu that includes brisket, ribs, links, burgers, fried catfish, and fried shrimp. The friendly service suffices for the dining room's lack of charm; better to take your plate of saucy ribs to the pretty courtyard when the weather cooperates. Open for lunch and dinner Tuesday–Sunday. Breakfast buffet on weekends and karaoke on Friday nights. $-$$; (936) 372-3605.

MAGNOLIA

This crossroads market town is of interest to day-trippers primarily for its growing collection of antiques stores, the majority of which are open Tuesday through Saturday.

WHAT TO DO

The King's Orchard. Route 2, Box 653, Plantersville (7 miles north of Magnolia on FM-1774). At various times during summer, you can pick your pleasure of strawberries, blueberries, blackberries, apples, peaches, figs, and Asian pears at this forty-five-acre farm. Open Tuesday–Sunday from the third Saturday in March to early September. Call for fruit availability. There's also a large picnic area as well as a small store selling drinks, jams and jellies, hats, and assorted small sundries; (936) 894-2766; www.kingsorchard.com.

Texas Opry House. 32243 Old Hempstead Road. Country music in a country setting, this tidy, family-run operation has put on a lively two-hour music show featuring local entertainers every Saturday night, year-round, since 1986. Expect singers, dancers, actors, and comedians at this mini–Grand Ole Opry, all backed by the house band. Have you always had a hankering to be in show biz? Give them a call; they hold tryouts on a regular schedule. No alcohol is served or allowed, but the concession stand does a land-office business in homemade cakes and brownies. Bring the kids. Fee; (281) 356-6779.

The Texas Renaissance Festival. Six miles north of Magnolia on FM-1774, 6 miles south of TX-105 in Plantersville. For seven weekends starting around October 1, the sights and sounds of Merrie Olde England brighten up this fifty-acre woodland park. Visitors are encouraged to dress to the sixteenth-century theme and cavort with the jugglers, sword swallowers, harpists, belly dancers, and jesters to their heart's content. Swordsmen fence, Shakespeare enlivens the Globe Theatre stage, and King Henry and his royal court parade around the grounds at high noon. Grand fun for the entire family, with full-contact jousts, assorted craftspeople, stout food, and more. Fee, but ask in advance about sources for discount tickets. Children four and under are free. Also, plan some alternate routes home; the departing traffic south via FM-1774 and TX-249 is always bumper-to-bumper from 3:00 P.M. on; (800) 458-3435, (281) 356-2178, or (936) 894-2516; www.texrenfest.com.

WHERE TO EAT

Hickory Hollow Restaurant. 18537 FM-1488 (in the Renaissance Center). Barbecue in all its forms, plus steaks, chicken, and catfish highlight the extensive menu at this popular family spot. There's often live country music in the back room on Friday night. Open for lunch and dinner daily. $-$$$; ☐; (281) 356-7885.

Las Fuentes Mexican Restaurant and Bar. 18306 FM-1488. Lots of choices here, many beyond the usual tacos, enchiladas, and refritos. Open daily for lunch and dinner. $-$$$; ☐; (281) 356-9923.

Old Magnolia Gardens. 1002 Goodson Road, at FM-1488. Stop here if you're interested in homemade salads, soups, sandwiches, and hot entrees. House specialties range from broccoli-cheese soup to outstanding pies, cobblers, and cakes; the chicken salad club sandwich is a winner. Open for lunch Monday–Saturday, dinner Friday and Saturday. $-$$; ☐; (281) 259-7606.

Rancho Grande Mexican Restaurant. 18914 FM-1488. Spirits perk up as you come through the door of this lively, well-decorated spot, and appetites follow as soon as you've checked the menu. Signature dishes include Atomic Tacos (flour tortillas filled with shrimp jalepenos) and a ribeye steak cooked with fresh jalepenos, tomatoes, and onions. Eight additional shrimp entrees get their own menu selection as do eleven steak/chicken offerings, and all are a far cry from standard Tex-Mex. Combination lunch specials run from $4.25 to $5.75, and happy hour ('Ritas and domestic beers, $2.50) runs from 2:00–6:00 P.M. weekdays. Open daily for lunch and dinner. $-$$; ☐; (281) 356-1700.

Relay Station Restaurant. 15680 TX-105, Plantersville. This combination icehouse and saloon is pure country, from the wood barstools carved like horses' rear ends to the corral out back. Come on a Wednesday or Friday night and you may catch the local cowboys doing some team penning practice. No surprises on the menu, unless you take up their challenge: The eighty-five-ounce steak with trimmings is free if you eat it all in seventy-five minutes. Open 10:00 A.M.–10:00 P.M. on weekdays, until 11:00 P.M. on weekends. $-$$$; ☐; (936) 894-3111.

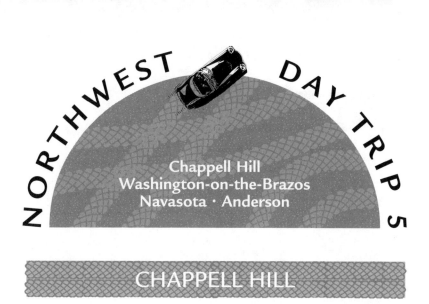

CHAPPELL HILL

From Houston this day trip follows US–290 northwest approximately 60 miles through Hempstead to the intersection of FM–1155. A short jog north then takes you to the first stop, Chappell Hill.

This charming village just north of US–290 may seem like the Brigadoon of Texas, so true is it to its time. Settled in 1847 and named for early Texas hunter Robert W. Chappell, Chappell Hill thrived as a stage stop on the Houston-to-Austin/Waco run and became the cultural center of Washington County, the home of two four-year universities. But the fickle tides of progress soon flowed on, and visitors today often feel they have stumbled on a quiet place left over from the 1880s.

The universities have long closed, their charters transferred to become the seeds of Southwestern University in Georgetown, Southern Methodist University in Dallas, and the University of Texas Medical Branch in Galveston. But the old Stagecoach Inn is still here, a private home restored to its antique glory, and the local bank, circa 1900, has its original brass teller's cage. *Fun to know:* This was the last bank in the region to register its customers by name instead of magnetic codes and computers.

More than twenty-five historical medallions are scattered throughout this four-street settlement. Three treasured homes currently offer B&B accommodations: Browning Plantation (circa

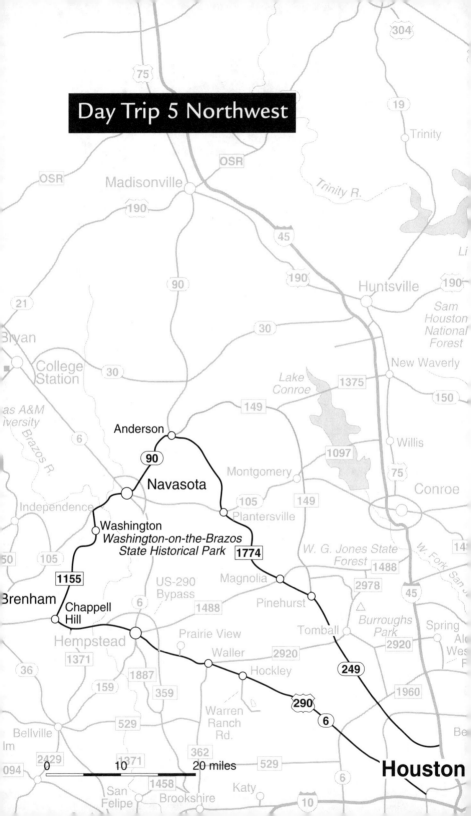

Day Trip 5 Northwest

304

75

19

Trinity

OSR

OSR

Madisonville

190

Trinity R.

45

190

Huntsville

190

Li

21

90

30

Sam
Houston
National
Forest

Bryan

College
Station

30

Lake
Conroe

1375

New Waverly

150

as A&M
iversity

6

Brazos R.

149

Willis

Anderson

90

Montgomery

1097

75

Conroe

Navasota

105

149

Independence

Plantersville

W. G. Jones State
Forest

W. Fork San

14

Washington
*Washington-on-the-Brazos
State Historical Park*

1774

1488

50

105

1155

Magnolia

2978

45

Brenham

Chappell
Hill

6

US-290
Bypass

1488

Pinehurst

Burroughs
Park

2920

Spring

Al
Wes

Hempstead

Tomball

1371

Prairie View

Waller

2920

249

1960

Be

36

1887

Hockley

290

6

159

359

Warren
Ranch
Rd.

Bellville
lm

529

362

529

Houston

2429

1371

0   10   20 miles

094

1458

San
Felipe

Brookshire

Katy

6

10

1850s), (888) 912-6144, www.browningplantation.com/; Lockhart
Plantation, (979) 836-1139; and Southern Rose Ranch, (979)
251-7871, www.southernroseranch.com.

Buy an ice-cream cone at the Bluebonnet House Gift Shop and
then, if it's open, take a nostalgic walk through Lesser's General
Store, stocked with kerosene, seed spuds, local sausage, and jams just
as it was in great-grandfather's day. Other portions of Main Street
and seven additional local sites are on the National Register of Historic Places, and several of them now house antiques shops.

This community hosts a number of family-friendly events
throughout the year, including fall's fabulous Scarecrow Festival.
Contact the chamber of commerce, (979) 277-1122; www.chappel
hilltx.com.

WHERE TO GO

Browning Plantation. 9050 Browning Street (1 mile south of
US-290, off FM-1371). Also listed in the National Register of Historic Places, this three-story wood home was built as the heart of a
2,000-acre plantation in 1856 by Colonel W. W. Browning, a loyal
Confederate supporter and one of Chappell Hill's leading citizens.
By the early 1980s, however, the house was a teetering ruin surrounded by 170 acres of wild country. Completely restored in 1983,
this 6,000-square-foot house is once again an elegant charmer and
filled with antiques. Tours are given by appointment, and four bedrooms are available for classy B&B, as are two bedrooms and two
baths in a replica of a Southern Pacific Railroad depot near the
swimming pool. Don't miss the "before" photos in the downstairs
parlor. Fee. ◻; (888) 912-6144; www.browningplantation.com/.

Chappell Hill Historical Museum and Methodist Church. On
Church Street, 1 long block east of Main. The museum is in the old
school and is staffed Wednesday–Saturday and on Sunday afternoon. The church has stained-glass windows worth seeing and is
open for Sunday services. Donations are appreciated; (979) 836-6033;
www.chappellhillmuseum.org.

Chappell Hill Sausage Co. 4255 Sausage Lane (on westbound
side of US-290, 3.5 miles east of Chappell Hill). Six different kinds
of sausage are made here, primarily for supermarkets around the
state. You can watch the sausage-making process and buy your

favorite to take home. Closed Sunday. $; (979) 836–5830; www.chsausage.com.

The 1873 Providence Baptist Church. Notable for the stone baptistery under its pulpit, this handsome old building on the east side of Chappell Hill's main street sparkles with fresh paint, courtesy of its new owners, the Chappell Hill Historical Society. Church doors are open to the public only during special events or for groups with advance reservations; (979) 836–6033.

Old Masonic Cemetery. Turn west at the four-way stop at Main and Chestnut Streets in Chappell Hill, then right on the first road for 0.5 mile. At least twenty-four Confederate soldiers are buried here, along with assorted Crocketts and the son and daughter of William Barret Travis. The latter were longtime residents of Chappell Hill.

Cemetery lovers also will enjoy the old Atkinson Cemetery, south of town on County Road 87.

Rock Store Museum. 5070 Main Street (east side of Main Street near the bank). The prime display is the town's history, embroidered and appliquéd on two 30-foot cloth panels. Open weekend afternoons in spring or when the locals feel like socializing. Donations are appreciated. Special appointments; (979) 836–6033.

Shiloh Ranch. 12009 FM–1155 East, Brenham. If a horseback trailride through the beautiful Washington County countryside appeals to you, give this place a call; (979) 836–0599; www.shilohranch texas.com.

Texana Cigar and Coffee Company. 5080 Main Street (east side of Main Street, next to the Rock Store). A strong tobacco trade flourished in this Brazos River Bottom area during the plantation era, and this small shop recalls the tradition. Non-smoker? Try their specialty coffees and pecan-smoked jerky, another local specialty. Open daily; (979) 251–7500.

WHERE TO EAT

Bevers Kitchen. 5162 Main Street. This combination house and restaurant serves salads and sandwiches, homemade soup and chili, chicken and dumplings, and chicken-fried steak. Mexican dishes are added on Wednesday. Open for lunch through 3:00 P.M. Monday–Saturday. $–$$; ☐; (979) 836–4178.

WASHINGTON-ON-THE-BRAZOS

From Chappell Hill continue north 18 miles on FM-1155 to Washington-on-the-Brazos. Early settlers used this same route. This portion of Texas was crossed by countless trails that were the interstate highways of the seventeenth and eighteenth centuries, and numerous historical markers presently comment on three major routes. The Old San Antonio Road ran to the Louisiana border and passed to the north of Bryan–College Station. The Coushatta Trail through Grimes County to the north was part of the Contraband Trace, used for smuggling goods from Louisiana into Spanish Texas. A third trail, La Bahia, went from Goliad to the lower Louisiana border, sometimes running in tandem with the Old San Antonio Road.

In 1821 one of Stephen F. Austin's first settlers started a small farm and ferry service where the busy La Bahia Trail forded the Brazos River. In 1835 the settlement was capitalized as the Washington Town Company, lots were auctioned, and the raw beginnings of an organized town began to emerge on the river's west bank. It was to become a pivot point for history.

March of 1836 was a fateful month for Texas. While Santa Anna was devastating the Alamo, fifty-nine men were creating a sovereign nation, the Republic of Texas, at the constitutional convention at Washington-on-the-Brazos. Washington later served twice as the capital of Texas but ultimately lost that honor to Austin. Later bypassed by the railroads, the original settlement faded into obscurity and then literally disappeared after the Civil War. Today, a state park (see below) on the site honors Washington's status as "the birthplace of Texas." A major expansion has added a second visitor center, interactive exhibits, a restaurant/conference center, and a living history farmstead focused on the early Texas frontier.

There's a lot to see and do in the Washington-Brenham area, so consider making advance reservations for lodging. Choices include Barrington, built around the original steps of the Anson Jones home 3 miles west of the park, (936) 878-2844 or (800) 591-9894; and Somerside, a restored one-hundred-year-old German farm home furnished with antiques, (936) 878-2433; www.sommerside.com.

Contact the Washington County Chamber of Commerce for a complete list; (888) 273-6426; www.brenhamtx.org.

WHAT TO DO

The J. M. Brown Plantation. The future of this architectural treasure near Washington-on-the-Brazos State Park is uncertain. At press time, the Greek Revival mansion, built in 1855 and now listed on the National Register of Historic Places, is on the marketplace. Its most recent use was as an elegant antiques shop that specialized in eighteenth- and early-nineteenth-century English and American antiques. Surrounded by centuries-old oak trees, the mansion features 12-foot ceilings and a 40-foot-long center hall.

Live Oak Ranch Family Nudist Resort. Off TX–105 in Washington. This pretty, twenty-five-acre facility is dedicated to "the Joy of Natural Living," which means no one wears clothes. All ages are welcome, and first-timers are permitted to remain clothed for a reasonable time until they feel comfortable being in the nude. Facilities include a swimming pool, a hot tub, a water slide, a clubhouse with a big-screen TV, volleyball courts, pool tables, dart machines, and so on. The resort also offers RV hookups, tent campsites, rental cabins, and a full-service restaurant. No overtly sexual behavior is tolerated, and "undue" demonstrations of affection are considered to be in very poor taste. If you've always wondered what it would be like to go skinny-dipping or live without the constraint of clothing, this is the place. After a few tough minutes of wondering where to put your eyes, the scene becomes very natural, almost asexual. Although there are no age limits (families very welcome), persons under twenty-one must be accompanied by their parents. Fee; ☐; (936) 878-2216; www.liveoakresort.com/.

Washington-on-the-Brazos State Historical Park. On FM–1155 at the Brazos River in Washington; follow signs. Only a handful of relatively new buildings mark where the Republic of Texas began in 1836. However, a $4.3-million legislative grant has expanded this 154-acre park to "living plantation—circa 1830" status. Additional land has been purchased, a restaurant and visitor center have been opened, and both the Star of the Republic Museum and Anson Jones's historic homeplace, Barrington, have changed in many ways.

Start at the visitor center, and do bring a hamper to enjoy the shady picnic grounds along the Brazos River; (936) 878-2214; www.tpwd.state.tx.us.

All the following are within the park's boundaries:

Barrington Living History Farm. This re-creation of plantation life in early Texas (1850s) centers on Barrington (1844-45), the restored antebellum home of the last president of the Republic of Texas, Anson Jones. A costumed staff, working with tools and livestock common to that period, go about their daily lives as though the Civil War had never happened. Even the cookbooks used in the kitchen are from the 1830-50 period. Visitors are welcome to pitch in with the chores, the better to understand what life was like before the advent of the gasoline engine. The site includes a barn, log cabin slave quarters, a functional kitchen separate from the main farmhouse, a smokehouse, and a visitor center. Open Wednesday-Sunday, year-round.

Independence Hall. This simple frame building is a reconstruction of the original structure on this site, in which the signing of the Texas Declaration of Independence took place. Open daily year-round. Fee.

Star of the Republic Museum. Greatly benefiting from the historical park's multimillion-dollar rejuvenation, this outstanding place is full of new exhibits. Children love the interactive experiences provided by the Showers-Brown Discovery Room, while adults become immersed in learning about the various cultures that shaped the Lone Star state. Open daily, except for major holidays. Fee. For more information contact Star of the Republic Museum, P.O. Box 317, Washington, TX 77880; (979) 878-2461; www.starmuseum.org.

WHERE TO EAT

At this writing the restaurant inside the visitor center at Washington-on-the-Brazos State Historical Park was without a concessionaire. Call (979) 878-2214 and hit "0" to check on the availability of food service when you intend to visit.

CONTINUING ON

After exploring Washington, continue north on FM-1155 to the TX-105 intersection, and turn right to Navasota.

NAVASOTA

Settlers responding to Stephen F. Austin's advertisements for colonists founded this town in the 1820s. A generation later cotton was king of the plantation economy, thriving here on the rich bottomland of the Brazos River.

The coming of the railroad in the 1850s brought even larger profits, and the wealthy farmers splurged on lavish town homes in Navasota, many of which remain in fine shape today and are worth a "windshield" tour. Some line Washington Avenue (TX–105) as it flows through town, and others require short detours onto Johnson, Holland, and Brewer Streets.

One of those mansions, LaSalle House at 400 East Washington, is an 1897 Queen Anne Victorian that houses an antiques co-op; house tours (fee) are available on weekends; (936) 825–3865. Shoppers will find numerous other antiques shops and malls scattered around town.

Groups of fifteen or more can tour several other historic structures in and around Navasota by reservation. Information and walking- and driving-tour brochures are available from the Grimes County Chamber of Commerce, 117 South LaSalle (P.O. Box 530), Navasota, TX 77868; (936) 825–6600 or (800) 252–6642; www.navasotatx.com.

Not too surprisingly, Navasota stood heart and soul with the South during the Civil War, but unpaid Confederate soldiers angrily burned much of the town in 1865. A yellow fever epidemic two years later dealt the final economic blow. This quiet community of 7,000 now lies in the heart of horse-farm country, its downtown a National Historic District.

Even fewer traces of the area's Indian and Mexican history survive, and visitors often are startled to find a statue of French explorer La Salle in the center of the main road. It memorializes his death nearby in 1687 at the hands of his own men.

WHAT TO DO

Bank of Navasota. 109 West Washington Avenue. This 1880s building has been restored to its original look and use. Open Monday–Friday and Saturday morning.

Gibbons Creek Reservoir. On FM-244 in Carlos, approximately 20 miles north of Navasota via TX-90. Operated by the Texas Municipal Power Authority, this 2,500-acre lake draws heavy-duty fisher-folk from as far away as Oklahoma and Arkansas. Bass, crappie, catfish, and perch thrive here, stocked by Texas Parks and Wildlife, and while boating and picnicking are allowed, water sports and camping are not. In fact, there's a long list of rules and regulations. Closed Wednesdays and holidays. Fee; (936) 873-2013.

Horlock History Center. 1215 East Washington. Navasota's past is documented in this restored 1892 Victorian house. Open Friday–Sunday. Fee; (936) 825-6744.

Navasota Livestock Auction Co. 7846 Highway 90 South. Three miles east of Navasota on Highway US-90 (also see Cow Talk Steak House in "Where to Eat" listings). Ranchers from Grimes, Washington, and Brazos Counties bring their livestock here for sale, making this auction the state champ in terms of volume and dollars. Visitors are welcome to watch the action, but don't scratch your nose or tug on your ear—you may go home with a live calf as a souvenir. Saturday sales start at 12:30 P.M.; (936) 825-6545.

Navasota Theatre Alliance. 104 West Washington, Navasota. This local theater group uses professional directors and set designers for five or six quality productions by major playwrights each year. Call for schedule; (936) 825-3195.

Rudolph's Treeland Farm. After Thanksgiving call for directions, (936) 825-3052. Amenities include a playground, hayrides, live reindeer, and a lodge with fireplace.

The Wood Factory. 111 Railroad Street, Navasota. *Victoriana lovers' alert:* This antique millwork business welcomes visitors to its showroom in what was Navasota's old P. A. Smith Hotel. Whether you need any gingerbread trim or not, take a peek; many pieces of their early-twentieth-century equipment are as old as the designs they produce. Open business hours on weekdays only; (936) 825-7233.

WHERE TO EAT

Cow Talk Steak House. 7846 Highway 90 South (at the Navasota Livestock Auction Company, 3 miles east of Navasota on US-90). Nothing like going straight to the source for good hamburgers and steaks. Open for breakfast and lunch Tuesday–Saturday. $–$$; (936) 825–6993.

The Golden Palace. 201 North LaSalle. Locals say that this Chinese food is worth the drive from Houston and that the daily lunch buffet is an excellent buy. Open daily for lunch and dinner. $–$$; ☐; (936) 825–8488.

Guadalajara Mexican Restaurant and Cantina. 1000 South Loop 6 (Highway 6 bypass). Don't be fooled by this eatery's location, adjacent to the Cedar Creek Inn Motel. It could well stand on its own, anywhere. The extensive menu covers the expected dinners Mexicana and combination plates, but you also should consider the shrimp fajitas served with all the trimmings. The long house-specialties list also shows flare. Open daily for lunch and dinner, plus there's a noon buffet that's a budget-pleaser at $5.50. $–$$; ☐; (936) 825–2217.

Joe's Place. 206 West Washington. One of the town's newest, this casual place serves up satisfying soul food, including barbecue ribs, smothered pork chops, and crawfish étouffée. Breakfasts are a treat at this very friendly spot. Closed Mondays; $; (936) 825–2686.

La Casita Mexican Restaurant. 9416 Highway 6 Bypass. Super clean and bright, this place always seems packed with Hispanics, a very good sign. If you're traveling early in the day, stop here for breakfast. Open daily for breakfast, lunch, and dinner. $–$$; ☐; (936) 870–3040.

Ruthie's Bar-B-Que Cafe. 905 West Washington. This seemingly undistinguished barbecue place is a Texas classic—six kinds of meat pit-smoked over oak and mesquite. It's so good that it has been mentioned in *Texas Monthly* magazine. Open Wednesday–Saturday for lunch and dinner. $–$$; (936) 825–2700.

Sgt. Pepperoni's. 119 East Washington. One of downtown's historic buildings now houses a good spot for New York–style pizza. Pastas, subs, and salads also are available. Open Monday–Saturday for lunch and dinner; $–$$; (936) 870–4068.

CONTINUING ON

From Navasota this day trip travels to the tiny town of Anderson, 10 miles northeast via TX–90.

ANDERSON

Time stopped here about 1932, and the entire town looks like a stage set for *Bonnie and Clyde*. Fact is, one member of the Barrow gang was tried here in the old courthouse, a tidbit duly noted on the building's historical medallion. But Anderson's history reaches back much farther than the 1930s.

Established in 1834 as a stage stop on the La Bahia Trail, the town became an important assembly point and arms depot during the Civil War. Those days of glory live again during Texian Days in late September, when local folks don period costumes and open their homes to visitors. The entire town—everything you can see from the top of the courthouse—is listed in the National Register of Historic Places. Antiques stores have begun to fill some of the vacant buildings along Main Street. For information on the town, call Historic Anderson, Inc., (936) 873–2662 or 873–2111.

WHAT TO DO

Baptist Church. East side of Main Street, 2 blocks south of FM–1774. Built of native rock by slaves in 1855, this handsome church still has regular Sunday services. LBJ's granddaddy once was Anderson's preacher.

Fanthorp Inn State Historic Park. South end of Main Street on the left. One of the first stage stops in Texas and the seed that started the town, this old inn was built in 1834 and led to Anderson's being, for a time, the fourth largest town in Texas. Owned by the Texas Parks and Wildlife Department since 1977, the inn has been restored and returned to a somewhat rumpled 1850s appearance; visitors have a sense that one stage has just departed and another is on its way. A barn of that period has been reconstructed to house a Concord stagecoach (reproduction) as well as exhibits describing the early stage routes across Texas. Staffed with an interpreter, the inn is open Friday through Sunday for self-guided tours. If you want to tour on Wednesday or Thursday, call ahead; there's usually someone there. Want to ride through the streets of Anderson in a horse-drawn stagecoach? Come for Stagecoach Days on the second Saturday of every month. And for a look at what holiday travel was like in the mid-1800s, don't miss the candlelight festivities on the Saturday of Thanksgiving weekend. *Note:* No overnight or dining facilities are available at the inn. Fee; (936) 873-2633; www.tpwd.state.tx.us.

Grimes County Courthouse. Top of Main Street. Built in 1894 of hand-molded brick with native limestone trim, this oldie has its original vault. Note the handsome pressed-tin ceilings with rounded cove moldings in the main hall. Open weekday business hours; (936) 873-2111.

Historic Anderson Park. South of the intersection of FM-1774 and TX-90. Several architectural relics of Anderson's past are preserved here, including the Steinhagen Log Cabin, built in 1852 by slaves and notable for its walls of unspliced hand-hewn timbers; the Steinhagen Home, with a wing furnished to its 1850s period; and the Boggess Store, filled with early-twentieth-century merchandise. These old buildings can be toured only during special events or by arrangement; (936) 873-2553.

New York Row. Parallels Main Street 1 block east. This is where the town swells lived during Anderson's heyday. That was a long time ago, so you'll need to use your imagination.

WANDERING THE BACKROADS

For anyone who likes country drives, getting to and/or from Anderson via FM-1774 is pure pleasure. While spring is prime because of the wildflowers, an autumn drive recalls the rolling hills of western Massachusetts. The oaks turn color with the first frost, and Anderson's lone church steeple pokes up through the landscape like a sentinel on a hill.

Brenham · Burton
Dime Box · Somerville
Independence

BRENHAM

If it wasn't a 72-mile commute on US–290 each way, Brenham would be overrun with refugees from Houston. This thriving community of slightly more than 12,000 is close to the ideal American small town—old enough to be interesting but enterprising enough to keep up with the times.

Shaded residential streets still sport a number of antebellum and Victorian homes, and many of the early-twentieth-century buildings downtown are spiffed up and in use. Designated a Main Street City by the Texas Historical Commission, Brenham has recently undergone major renovation in the form of new pocket parks, benches, and sidewalks. You'll also find new businesses in some of the remodeled downtown buildings.

Just blocks away it's open country again—thousands of acres of beautiful farmland. In spring the bluebonnets and other wildflowers are magnificent, a carpet of color rolling to all horizons.

Founded in 1844 and settled by German immigrants over the ensuing two decades, Brenham was occupied and partially burned by Union troops during the Civil War. Most of the town's surviving history can be seen on a windshield tour, courtesy of a free map and visitor's guide available from the Washington County Chamber of Commerce, 314 South Austin, Brenham, TX 77833; (979) 836–3695 or (888) 273–6226; www.brenhamtx.org. Call in advance to arrange a guided tour of the downtown historic district. Groups should inquire about tours and use of the Citadel, a former country club (circa 1924) that has been restored to *Great Gatsby* elegance. Highly

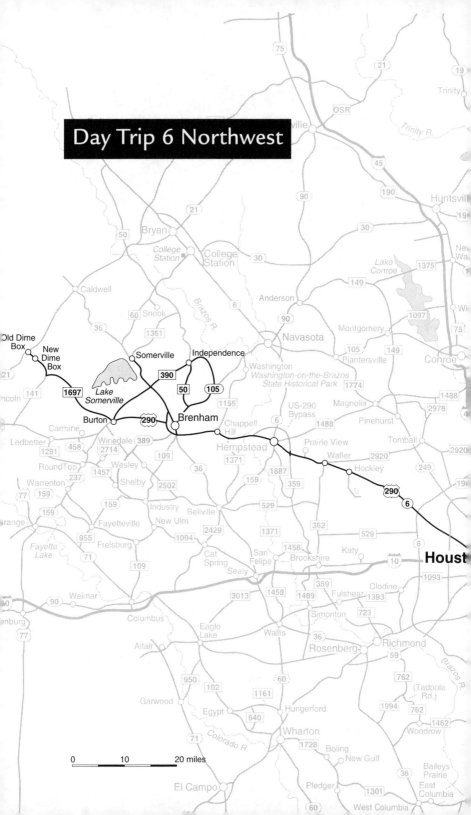

visible on the westbound side of US-290, it looks like a massive plantation house sitting in the middle of a young vineyard 3 miles east of town.

Should you enjoy Brenham too much to leave, there are a number of B&B establishments in town. Among them are the highly regarded Ant Street Inn, (979) 836-7393, www.antstreetinn.com; Far View, (979) 836-1672, www.farviewbedandbreakfast.com/; Mariposa Ranch B&B, (979) 836-4737, www.mariposaranch.com; Secrets, (979) 836-4117; Ingleside B&B, (979) 251-7707; The Brenham House, (979) 830-0477; and the James Walker Homestead, (979) 836-6717.

Nearby Burton (next stop on this day trip) also has B&B accommodations.

WHAT TO DO

Ant Street Historic District. This downtown section of Brenham has been undergoing a colorful renovation for several years and now sports numerous fresh exteriors. The historic district extends to the old Savitall Market at Commerce and Baylor Streets, now handsomely renovated into the Ant Street Inn and Gallery, a fourteen-room B&B hotel similar in quality to the Tremont House in Galveston. If you're planning a big party or wedding, check out the ballroom; that space also is used for frequent antiques auctions. (800) 805-2600.

Bassett & Bassett Banking House. Corner of Market and Main Streets. This vintage bank has been restored as part of a Main Street revival program and is open during normal business hours.

Blue Bell Creameries. Take the FM-577 exit from either US-290 or TX-105 and go north on FM-577. If you want to tour the ice-cream plant, call ahead to confirm space; tours are not offered every day or on weekends, and reservations are required. Fee. The Country Store and Ice Cream Parlour (where you can buy a bowl of your favorite Blue Bell flavor) is open Monday–Saturday from 9:00 A.M. to 3:00 P.M., March–December; (800) 327-8135; www.bluebell.com.

Brenham Brewery. 201 West First Street. Thought to be the only family-owned-and-operated brewery in Texas, this spot invites you in for a free tour and a taste at 1:30 P.M. on Saturday. Sorry, aside from a few promotional gift items, this is not a retail outlet; you won't be able to buy any brew; (979) 830-0854.

Brenham Heritage Museum. 105 South Market. Housed in the refurbished and quite grand Federal Building (1915), this museum offers artifacts and memorabilia dating from 1844, the year Brenham was founded. Displays change monthly, and an 1879 Silsby steam-powered fire engine resides permanently in an exterior showcase; a train exhibit that depicts Brenham in the early 1900s is under way. Open Wednesday–Saturday; call for hours. Fee; (979) 830-8445.

Ellison's Greenhouses. 1808 South Horton (0.75 mile south of Blue Bell Creameries on Loop 577). Whatever the holiday, celebrate it early by touring this colorful wholesale nursery. Seasonally, some five acres of greenhouses are filled with poinsettias, tulips, Easter lilies, hydrangeas, and much more. Retail trade is welcome, and visitors love the unique accessories and gifts. Tours (fee) are given at 11:00 A.M. and 1:00 P.M. on Friday and Saturday; by appointment Monday–Thursday. Closed days prior to major holidays. *Nice to know:* Ellison's is particularly spectacular during their annual poinsettia celebration (fee) on the weekend prior to Thanksgiving. More than 80,000 poinsettias fill several greenhouses with Christmas cheer, and some of those plants go on to grace the State Capitol, the governor's mansion, and the George R. Bush Presidential Library. Fee; ◻; (979) 836-0084; www.ellisonsgreenhouses.com.

Fireman's Park. 900 block of North Park Street. This shady city park has a fully restored C. W. Parker carousel, manufactured for carnival touring prior to 1913 and one of only a few antique merry-go-rounds remaining in Texas. Now visible behind protective glass panels, this wonderful antique operates by appointment and whenever Brenham has a civic celebration in the park; (979) 836-3695.

Gerson Artworks. 307 West Alamo. Only the colorblind will have trouble finding artist Alan Gerson's multi-toned purple house with its front yard filled with crazy sculpture. Look closely, and you'll see that one of the huge pieces on display began its useful life as a Volkswagen trunk lid. Not sure if you've found the right place? Watch for a fried egg on the front walk and slashes of red and blue neon in the windows. Gerson also sculpted the horses that pull the city's old steam fire engine outside the Brenham Heritage Museum, 105 South Market. Gerson's gallery usually is open daily; call to make sure he'll be there; (979) 836-4935.

Giddings-Stone Mansion. 2203 Century Circle (near South

Market and Stone Streets). This twelve-room Greek Revival home, with its imposing galleries, was built in 1869 on a hill in what was then south of town. Now owned by the local Heritage Society, it has been restored to its early-twentieth-century elegance and is considered by historical architects to be one of the ten most significant old homes in Texas. Tours (fee) are offered on weekends, April–June; groups by appointment. It also can be rented for special events such as weddings and meetings; (979) 836-1690; www.brenham-mansion.com.

Giddings-Wilkin House. 805 Crockett. Built in 1843, this is thought to be the oldest house still standing in Brenham. Now the property of the Heritage Society, it sometimes is open as a museum and can be toured by appointment; (979) 836-1690.

Glasco's Gardens. 601 North Horton. This professional landscaping company welcomes visitors to its water and perennial gardens during business hours, Monday–Saturday. Tour groups welcome. ☐; (979) 836-3210; www.glascolandscape.com.

Miniature Horses at the Monastery of St. Clare. 9300 Highway 105 (9 miles northeast of Brenham via TX-105). The breeding, training, and sale of miniature horses are self-support ventures of this cloistered order, the Franciscan Poor Clares, and three of the nuns are permitted to show the public around this ninety-eight-acre facility. The grounds, chapel, and gift shop are open from 2:00 to 4:00 P.M. daily, plus there's a self-guided tour that shows off these pint-size animals. Spring visitors see twenty to thirty foals, each about 18 inches tall, cavorting in fields filled with wildflowers; there is a public show in September. Individuals and families are welcome year-round; bus tours only by advance reservation. You'll also find a picnic area here. Fee for guided tours; self-guided tours are free; (979) 836-9652; www.monasteryminiaturehorses.com.

Nueces Canyon Ranch Resort and Equestrian Center. 9501 US-290 west (8 miles west of Brenham). This well-designed horse show and training complex has something going on—cutting horse competitions, hunter/jumper shows, barrel racing, and so on—nearly every weekend. Passersby are welcome to watch the action and walk through the training barns, and there's a pretty area where you can picnic. Groups with advance arrangements can tour this working ranch (fee), which also offers B&B for both humans and horses; (979) 289-5600 or (800) 925-5058; www.nuecescanyon.com.

Pleasant Hill Winery. 1441 Salem Road, Brenham. From US–290 turn south on TX–36 (the Belleville Road) to Salem. Free tours of this vineyard follow the path of the grape as it makes its transition from vine to fruit to wine. You then get to taste the results. Open weekend afternoons year-round; (979) 830–8463; www.pleasanthillwinery.com.

Unity Theatre. Corner of Church and Commerce Streets, Brenham. This nonprofit playhouse abandoned its spot on the city's popular square in the spring of 2002 for spacious new digs in a nearby historical warehouse. Combining professional and amateur talent, the company produces a variety of musicals and dramas throughout the year, and it generally plays to full houses. Call for a performance schedule, and consider overnighting at one of the area's bed-and-breakfasts. Performance tickets start at $18; reservations are recommended; (979) 830–8358; www.unitybrenham.org.

WHERE TO EAT

A Place in Thyme. 102 South Ross Street. This pleasant tearoom is a good spot for lunches, desserts, or just a snack. Open weekdays for lunch until 2:00 P.M. $; □; (979) 277-9770.

Country Inn II. 1000 East Horton, across from the Washington County Fairgrounds on Loop 577. Beef steaks with all the trimmings are the house specialty, generously cut with good ol' boys' hearty appetites in mind. The menu also offers fish, shrimp, and hamburgers. Open for lunch and dinner Monday–Saturday. $-$$; □; (979) 836-2396.

The Fluff Top Roll Restaurant. 210 East Alamo. The staff at this gingham-decked cafe bakes fresh yeast rolls daily, and the blue-plate specials are substantial and popular with the downtown Brenham business community. Open for breakfast and lunch Tuesday–Sunday. $-$$; (979) 836-9441.

Garden Alley. 202 Commerce (inside The Pomegranate shop). Need a coffee fix or snack? This tiny spot serves cappuccino, espresso, latte, etc., along with biscotti, baklava, and a variety of gourmet foods and candies. Open Monday–Saturday, 8:30 A.M. to 5:30 P.M. $; □; (979) 836-1199.

Glissman's. 106 West Main. In addition to a 1950s-era soda fountain where you can order sweet treats, you'll also enjoy the authentic 1924 fixtures of this vintage pharmacy. Closed on Wednesday and Sunday. $; (979) 830-9100.

Legends Billiards and Grill. 100 West Main. A sports bar with big-screen TV, this spot also serves a variety of freshly grilled hamburgers. Open daily from 11:00 A.M. until midnight. $-$$; ☐; (979) 251-7665.

Main Street Coffee & Trading Co. 201 East Main Street. Freshly rejuvenated, this old-fashioned soda fountain features Blue Bell ice cream, other frozen treats, and a selection of coffees. Open business hours Monday–Saturday. $; ☐; (979) 836-3258.

Manuel's Mexican Restaurant & Taqueria. 409 West Main. While handy with all the standards, this place is well liked locally for its weekday lunch buffet and chicken, pork, and beef fajitas. Open daily for lunch and dinner. $-$$; ☐; (979) 277-9620.

Must Be Heaven Ice Cream and Sweet Shop. 107 West Alamo. These folks have a strong local following for their tasty cookies, pies, and other pastries. There's Blue Bell ice cream, along with homemade soups, salads, sandwiches, and quiche. Open Monday–Saturday for breakfast and lunch (until 5:00 P.M.) and Sunday midday. $-$$; (979) 830-8536.

Purcell's Country Style Buffet. 2800 Highway 36 South. You pay first and then feast on all the food you want, served from the long steam tables in the center of this clean and spacious eatery. Entrees come multiple choice, from herbed chicken to carved beef and ham, plus there's a seafood buffet on Friday night. Open daily for lunch and dinner. $-$$; ☐; (979) 836-9508.

Tex's Barbecue. 4807 Highway 105. When the thought of open-pit barbecue stirs up an appetite, try here. If the weather's nice, try the picnic area or take-out service. Open for lunch Wednesday–Sunday. $; (979) 836-5962.

Volaré. 205 South Baylor Street. Chef Sylvio DiGennaro brings the flavors of his native Sicily to numerous Italian entrees here. The Victorian-styled setting in a historic building is stylish and airy, making it a nice spot for lunch or dinner, Wednesday- Sunday. $$; ☐; reservations recommended; (979) 836-1514.

BURTON

Continue west from Brenham on US-290 to visit the reviving small town of Burton, population 325. One of the few vintage cotton gins in Texas is under restoration here as a National Historic Landmark, and there's an interesting old shoe-repair shop next door. In all, this historic zone covers nine acres and several additional buildings common to small farm town life from 1914–1974. The visitor center, 307 Main Street, is open Monday–Saturday, but guided tours are scheduled only on Friday and Saturday at 11:00 A.M. and 1:30 and 3:00 P.M. Fee. Group tours of ten or more are available on other days by appointment. A brochure detailing an interesting walking tour of town also is available here. Contact the Visitor Center, P.O. Box 98, Burton, TX 77835; (979) 289-3378. You also can tour these pieces of the past during Burton's Cotton Gin Festival, held annually on the third weekend of April.

Burton also has two vintage B&Bs: Long Point Inn, (979) 289-3171; and the Knittel Homestead, (979) 289-5102.

WHERE TO EAT

Brazos Belle Restaurant. 600 North Main. André Delacroix, a French-born chef (formerly at the Four Seasons Hotel in Houston), and his wife, Sandy, serve deliciously untrendy country food with French touches in one of Burton's most venerable buildings. Expect blue-and-white checkered place mats, fresh vegetables, exceptional breads, and a changeable feast of professional-quality art on the walls, most of which is for sale. Delacroix's skill shines in the Belle's signature dish, a grilled fillet of Norwegian salmon that's seasoned in a fresh lemongrass marinade and topped with a fresh tomato-caper sauce. You'll want to come back, as well, to sample other menu items such as large Gulf shrimp seasoned in a lavender marinade, a spicy cassoulet, and medallions of filet mignon. Open for dinner Friday and Saturday, brunch on Sunday. Reservations suggested. $$-$$$; (979) 289-2677; www.brazosbellerestaurant.com.

The Burton Cafe. 12513 Washington Street (on FM-390, behind the post office). Homespun vittles and charm carry the day at this friendly place, considered by many people to be one of the best country cafes in the state. The roast beef platters are great, the home-made bread and veggies are locally produced, the pies are made from scratch, and the breakfasts are humongous. Want to know what's going on in the Brenham-Burton neighborhood? Just sit a spell and listen; you'll soon know as much as the locals. Open Monday, Thursday, Friday, and Saturday for breakfast, lunch, and dinner; Tuesday and Wednesday for breakfast and lunch. $-$$; (979) 289-3849.

CONTINUING ON

From Burton you can complete this day trip by swinging northwest on FM-1697 and FM-141 to Dime Box and some areas of Lake Somerville. Or you can bypass Dime Box and reach Somerville by fol-lowing FM-390 northeast to its intersection with either FM-1948 (turn north) or TX-36 (turn northwest).

An alternative route follows TX-105 northeast from Brenham to Navasota (Trip 5, this sector), or you can jog south from Brenham on FM-389 (Trips 4 and 5, West sector).

DIME BOX—OLD AND NEW

The name alone of these two separate communities brings some explorers. Perhaps this explanation will save some time, gasoline, and tempers.

Old Dime Box is on TX-21, sort of around the corner a few miles from new Dime Box on FM-141. The only things of visitor interest in both places are the historical plaques explaining that the town name comes from the old custom of leaving dimes in the commu-nity mailbox on the Old San Antonio Road (TX-21) in return for items brought by rural delivery from Giddings.

If you do explore in and around Dime Box, you can get back on your original day-trip route by following TX-21 northwest to Cald-well and then TX-36 south to Somerville. Continuing on TX-21 northeast from Caldwell brings you to College Station, Trip 3 in this sector.

SOMERVILLE

Who would think that three little creeks could combine to form a 24,000-acre lake? Dammed in the early 1960s as a flood control and water conservation project, Lake Somerville has become a favorite water playground 88 miles northwest of Houston on TX-36.

The town itself serves only as a gas and grocery supply depot—the lake is the big attraction. Popular with boaters, this lake offers excellent fishing for largemouth and white bass, white crappie, and channel catfish. Deer and other wildlife abound, particularly on the islands within this relatively shallow lake. Birding is varied enough to warrant a special brochure and field checklist, available free from the Texas Parks and Wildlife Department, Resource Management Section, 4200 Smith School Road, Austin, TX 78744; (800) 792-1112; www.tpwd.state.tx.us.

Campers, picnickers, boaters, hikers, and equestrians should investigate the following:

Rocky Creek Park, Yegua Creek Park, and *Overlook Park,* operated by the U.S. Corps of Engineers, (979) 596-1622 or 596-2383; for campsite reservations sixty to ninety days in advance, call (877) 444-6777.

Welch Park, operated by the City of Somerville, (979) 596-1122.

Birch Creek Park, (979) 535-7763, and *Nails Creek Park,* (979) 289-2392, operated by the Texas State Park system, (800) 792-1112.

WHERE TO EAT

Beefmaster Restaurant. On the west side of TX-36, opposite the Exxon station on the northern outskirts of Somerville. It's easy to miss this small white cottage set well back from the road, but if you do, just turn around and try again; it's worth the search. Although the menu offers a large selection of burgers, sandwiches, catfish, and shrimp, the big draws here are the affordable, thick steaks and the daily lunch buffet. Open daily except Tuesday for lunch and dinner. $-$$; ☐; (979) 596-1828.

Country Inn. 900 Avenue B (on west side of TX-36 South on the southern edge of town). This Aggie-land favorite serves many things but is known for its huge, tender steaks. The smallest is a one-and-a-half to two-pound T-bone priced at $12.95, and both the bounty and the doggie-bag hauls increase from there. Come hungry: The medium (two and one-half to three pounds—$16.50) and the large (three and one-half pounds—$19.50) sirloins literally fall off their serving plates. Open for lunch and dinner daily except Monday. Reservations are taken Tuesday–Friday but not on weekends. If the weather's nice, expect a very long wait for space in this sixteen-table spot. $–$$$; ☐; (979) 596–1222.

Mariachi Mexican Restaurant. 100 Avenue B (on east side of TX–36 on the southern edge of town). Is there any town in Texas that doesn't have a Mexican restaurant? When Tex–Mex sounds good, stop here. Luckily, the menu also stretches from crabmeat and shrimp quesadillas to pork chops, catfish, steaks, and chicken. Open for lunch and dinner Monday–Saturday. $–$$; ☐; (979) 596–2313.

CONTINUING ON

Your day trip continues south on TX–36 from Somerville to FM–390. Turn northeast (left) to Independence. This scenic route (FM–390) follows portions of old La Bahia Trail, a prehistoric track that was by the 1830s one of three main highways in Texas. La Salle met his death on this trail (near Navasota) in 1687. Stephen F. Austin and his followers knew it well, and Davy Crockett used it to reach Goliad, en route to the Alamo. Today it's just a glorious country ramble, a two-lane exploration of horse ranch country that follows a high ridge through Washington and Grimes counties. Take time to explore some of the side roads, and to admire the old Seward Plantation, a white ghost from the 1850s that crowns one oak-covered hill. A brochure covering other historic highlights is available from the Washington County Chamber of Commerce (see Day Trip 6, this section).

INDEPENDENCE

As far as Washington County is concerned, Independence is where it all started. Originally called Coles's Settlement for its first pioneer, John P. Coles, the town changed its name in 1836 to celebrate

Texas's independence from Mexico. Coles was a member of Stephen F. Austin's original 300 families, and his cedar log and frame cabin, built in 1824, stands just east of town at the entrance to Old Baylor Park. The town's interesting cemetery, about 2 miles north of the park entrance on County Road 60, is equally old.

When Brenham won election as the county seat by two votes, Independence began a century-long slide into obscurity. Today it is a mecca for Texana lovers because of its old stone church and historic ruins. The second house east of the TX–50/FM–390 intersection was the last home (circa 1863) of Mrs. Sam Houston; unfortunately, it currently is closed to the public. A second Houston homesite across from Old Baylor Park has a granite marker. For B&B contact The Captain Tacitus T. Clay House, (979) 836–1916; or Country Place Cottage, (979) 836–6429.

WHAT TO DO

The Antique Rose Emporium. 9300 Lueckemeyer Road, Brenham (0.5 mile south of the FM–390 intersection on FM–50). More than 200 varieties of old garden roses, documented to have grown in Texas during its years as a republic, thrive here on the site of the Hairston-McKnight Homestead, settled in the 1840s. The remains of an old stone kitchen (circa 1855) have been restored as the center of a typical cottage garden of those times, a converted barn is now the office and bookstore, and an old corncrib has become a gift shop featuring rose-related items. There's also a selection of native Texas trees, shrubs, vines, wildflower seeds, and other plant species appropriate to the climate and locale. Open daily. (979) 836–5548 (retail) or (800) 441–0002; www.weareroses.com.

Independence Baptist Church. 10405 FM–50, Brenham (at the intersection of FM–50 and FM–390). Organized in 1839, the church's present stone building was finished in 1872 and still hosts services every Sunday. Sam Houston saw the light here and was baptized in nearby Rocky Creek; (979) 836–5117.

Old Baylor Park and Ruins of Old Baylor University. One-half mile west of the church on FM–390. This birth site of Baylor University now is marked only by a few ghostly columns and some old oaks and is a good place to enjoy a picnic. It's also prime territory for bluebonnets in March and early April. The Coles

Cabin has been relocated here and can be toured by appointment, as can a one-room schoolhouse. Tours also on weekend afternoons in March and April. Donation, (979) 830-0230.

Seward Plantation. 10005 FM-390, Brenham (0.7 mile west of FM-50 in Independence). The headquarters of a 1,000-acre plantation in the 1850s cotton era and on the Texas Register of Historic Sites, this handsome old place has been owned and occupied by the same family since its foundation was laid. This gracious piece of the past still has many of its original furnishings and is now undergoing a slow but steady restoration. The grounds also include log slave quarters and barns. Visitors are welcome on weekends, March through May. Fee; (979) 830-5388.

Texas Baptist Historical Center and Museum. 10405 FM-50, Brenham. Adjacent to the Independence Baptist Church, this museum houses pre-Civil War artifacts as well as old church and family records. Mrs. Sam Houston (Margaret Moffet Lea) and her mother are buried in a somewhat unlovely site across the street. Open Tuesday-Saturday. Free; (979) 836-5117.

WHERE TO EAT

Independence Kountry Kitchen. 9655 FM-50, Brenham (opposite the Antique Rose Emporium). This place offers a full menu but specializes in ribeyes, sirloins, chicken-fried steak, shrimp, half-pound hamburgers, and catfish. Open Monday-Saturday for lunch and Thursday-Saturday for dinner. Closed 2:00 to 5:00 P.M. $-$$; ☐; (979) 277-0316.

WANDERING THE BACKROADS

Independence is the last stop on this day trip, but you can easily extend your travels. Following FM-390 east brings you to TX-105. Turn northeast (left) and you can tour Washington-on-the-Brazos, Navasota, and Anderson (Trip 5, this sector). An alternative is to continue south from Independence on FM-50 to TX-105 and Brenham, connecting there either with FM-389 and Trips 4 and 5 in the West sector or with TX-36 South to Bellville and home.

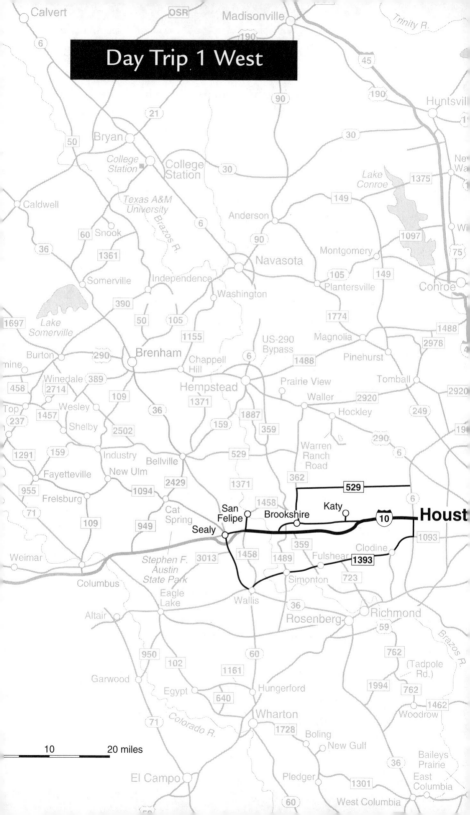

WEST HOUSTON

Because this day trip begins with a drive west on I–10, consider stopping on the western outskirts of town for one of the following activities:

WHAT TO DO

Albert Alkek Velodrome. 19008 Saums Road in Cullen Park. Take the Barker-Cypress exit from I–10 and go north 1 mile to the park. Built for the 1986 U.S. Olympic Festival, this is one of only twenty Olympic-quality velodromes in the country and often the site of national cycling events. The overall program includes general riding sessions, developmental cycling classes for beginners, races for graduates of that program, and a Friday-night racing series open only to USCF-licensed riders. Helmets and track bikes can be rented on site; spectating is free. For a brochure and seasonal schedule, call (281) 578-0693; www.ci.houston.tx.us/alkekvelodrome.com.

Flying at West Houston Airport. 18000 Groeschke Road, Houston. Take Barker-Cypress exit from I–10 and follow the airport signs north to a left turn on Groeschke Road. You too can discover the wonder of flying in a four-seat Cessna; discovery flights (thirty minutes) are $49 in this high-winged plane. Sight-seeing and photography flights also can be reserved, starting at $110 per hour in the four-seater. Reservations required; (281) 492-2130; www.westhoustonairport.com.

Hot-air ballooning. Several companies will take you silently floating over Houston for sixty to ninety minutes in a three-person basket suspended below a giant hot-air balloon. Most liftoffs are at sunrise to take advantage of the still air, and costs are in the range of $300 and up per couple, including champagne at the end of the trip. Pricey but worth it for a once-in-a-lifetime experience. Get the particulars from Adventure Ballooning, (713) 774-2359; Bear Creek Balloons, (281) 463-0080, www.bearcreekballoons.com; or Soaring Adventures, (800) 762-7464, www.800soaring.com.

CONTINUING ON

To continue this day trip, take I-10 West to the Katy exit.

KATY

Founded as a rice and railroad town, Katy now is of interest to day-trippers primarily as a great spot to eat, play, shop, and experience China. You'll find a smattering of gift and antiques shops in "Old Towne" and several places to picnic. It's also a good food stop Tuesday–Saturday if you're returning to Houston on I-10 from points west.

WHAT TO DO

Forbidden Gardens. 23500 Franz Road. From Houston take the Grand Parkway exit from I-10, turn north, then west on Franz road; watch for orange pagoda roofs. Block some time for this handsome, forty-acre, open-air museum which authentically replicates major scenes from China's history, starting in the third century B.C. Hand-made in China by gifted artisans who then installed their work on the Katy prairie, the exhibits include a huge and intricate scale model of Beijing's Forbidden City; detailed models of Chinese palaces; a one-third-scale reproduction of the entire 6,000-piece terra-cotta army (no two soldiers are alike) found in burial pits of China's first emperor; and replicas of the weapons used by that first emperor to conquer and meld several warring states into one empire. Future exhibits will include a scale model of the Great Wall of China and a reproduction of the beautiful mountains of Guilin, complete with canals and riverboats for visitor enjoyment. Also here is a 100-foot-long model of Su Zhou, a city known as the Venice of China, detailed with various types of houses, shops, and temples as well as miniature figures of people going about their daily routines. Hourly guided tours are included in admission fee ($10.00 per adult, $5.00 for students and seniors, five and under free with a paid admission). Parking is free; ◻. Open Wednesday–Sunday, 10:00 A.M.–5:00 P.M., weather permitting (call ahead to confirm times); (281) 347-8000; www.forbidden-gardens.com.

Katy Heritage Museum. 6202 George Bush Drive. Opened in the spring of 2002, this museum pays tribute to Katy's farming roots. Among the exhibits here are a 1914 Model T roadster, a 1925 truck once used to haul rice to market, and artifacts from the old Robertson Store, including a coffee grinder, scale, and rice shovel. Next door to the Heritage Museum is the Veteran's Memorial Museum, known locally as the "G.I. Joe Museum." (281) 391-4800.

Katy VFW Veterans Memorial Museum and Community Park. George Bush Drive and Avenue D. This oak-shaded retreat offers picnic tables, a small playground, and indoor exhibits focused on America's participation in foreign wars. Park is open daily; museum is open Saturday and Sunday, noon to 5:00 P.M.; (281) 391-8387. Open 10:00 A.M. to 2:00 P.M. Tuesday and Thursday; ci.katy.tx. us/museums.html.

Mary Jo Peckham Park and Katy City Park. Franz Road and Avenue D. These blended play spaces offer miniature golf, playgrounds, picnic areas, a fishing lake, a caboose, and the old Katy Railroad depot. Open daily; (281) 391-4840.

Waterfowl hunting trips. For guided hunts on the Katy and Eagle Lake prairies, call (281) 392-8999 or 391-6100.

WHERE TO EAT

John & Ann's Pie Shoppe. 5608 Fifth Street. Need a box lunch to eat here or to go? For $6.50 you get a great sandwich, chips, drink, and a slice of their super homemade pie. This tiny spot also makes a special quiche daily as well as fruit, cream, and specialty pies to order. Prefer sugar-free? Just let them know. Open Tuesday–Saturday for lunch. $-$$; (281) 391-8088.

BROOKSHIRE

Brookshire's history is brief. This small community was established in the early 1880s by the MKT Railroad to serve a rich agricultural area. Its ethnic past ranges from Polish to German, Greek to Czech, Swiss to Armenian. The Waller County Festival is an energetic melding of these cultures every October.

WHAT TO DO

Blue Barn Fun Farm. On FM-1458, approximately 0.5 mile west of FM-359. This ten-acre country learning experience is run with loving care by longtime farmers Dan and Paula Brubaker to educate children about country life. Following a basic program set up with the assistance of Texas A&M, pint-size visitors learn how to milk a cow and get to try the hands-on method themselves. They also pet calves, baby chicks, and a soft-shell turtle; jig for crawfish; and get up close to doves, bullfrogs, pigs, deer, geese, ducks, quail, golden pheasants, bobwhite quail, guinea hens, ring-necked pheasants, rabbits, goats, chickens, and turkeys. A small plastic horse is used to teach children how to mount and rope. A tractor-drawn hay wagon then hauls everyone to a picnic area shaded by huge oaks, so pack a hamper when you come; cold drinks are sold on premises. July visitors are given free watermelon, August visitors get stone-ground cornmeal and a recipe for corn bread, October and November visitors receive free pumpkins, and December visitors go home with candy canes. Cost is $6.00 per person in groups of twenty or more; $7.00 per person (including children) for individuals. Open daily. Absolutely no admittance without advance reservations; (281) 375-6669; www.bluebarnfunfarm.com.

  The Brookwood Community. 1752 FM-1489, 1 mile south of I-10 (signs). This handsome, 475-acre country facility is a privately funded community for functionally disabled adults (mentally and/or physically handicapped), aided in part by volunteers. Institutional gloom is not found here, however. Brookwood looks like the home most people only dream about and functions like a successful company. Last year the 120 persons in the program produced $2 million worth of horticultural and/or crafts products. Their bedding and potted plants and art are sold not only on the premises but also through Brookwood's four retail outlets in the Houston area. Tours are given the first Wednesday of every month by appointment; (281) 375-2100. In addition to lunch in the Brookwood Cafe (see "Where to Eat"), visitors can purchase Brookwood's original ceramics, garden sculptures, silk-screened notes and cards, and plants at the Garden Center, open Monday–Saturday 9:00 A.M. to 4:30 P.M.; Sunday noon to 4:30 P.M. ☐; (281) 375-2100; www.brookwoodcommunity.org.

Nelson Water Gardens. Just south of I-10 on FM-1489. Where else in Houston can you find acres of exotic goldfish amid blooming lotus and water lilies? The shop sells everything needed to rejuvenate or create your own water garden, but visitors are welcome to just browse among the thirty production ponds out back. These folks also publish a large color catalog and even mail goldfish. Open daily in summer, Monday–Saturday in winter. ☐; (281) 391-4769; www.nelsonwatergardens.com.

The Waller County Historical Museum. 4026 Fifth Street (at Cooper). Built in 1910, this nice old home houses period furnishings, historical artifacts and documents, and some interesting vintage photos. Free, but donations are welcome. Open Wednesday, Friday, and Saturday midday. Call for hours; (281) 934-2826; www.wlrctyhistsoc.org.

WHERE TO EAT

Brookwood Cafe. 1752 FM-1489. When you want a midweek lunch under the care and feeding of a chef trained at the Culinary Art Institute and formerly with Maxim's, call in advance for reservations here. The menu offers hot entrees, salads, and desserts. Open for lunch only, Tuesday–Saturday. $$; (281) 375-2400.

WANDERING THE BACKROADS

If you are coming from the FM-1960/TX-6 area of Houston and prefer backroads, swing west on FM-529 and then south on FM-362 to Brookshire. Going home, just reverse those directions to miss the traffic crunch on TX-6 near Bear Creek.

If you love country drives, save some time for wandering south of I-10 on FM-1489. This is horse and cotton-growing country, and the ranches and farms are beautiful. The road passes through the small communities of Simonton, Wallis, and East Bernard, an excellent route into the southwest sectors described in this book.

CONTINUING ON

To find San Felipe either drive west from Brookshire on I-10 for 8 miles and watch for the exit signs to Stephen F. Austin State Park, or follow the country route via FM-359 northwest to Pattison and then west on FM-1458. The latter is a great country ramble along the route of the pioneers.

SAN FELIPE

Alas, how fleeting is fame. From 1823 to 1836 San Felipe collected enough "firsts" to secure its niche in Texas history. Then known as San Felipe de Austin, it was the original settlement and capital of Stephen F. Austin's first colony. It also was the site of the first Anglo newspaper and postal system in the territory and the founding spot of the Texas Rangers. The town was burned in 1836 to prevent its use by the advancing Mexican Army. Although rebuilt later in that decade, San Felipe never regained its earlier momentum.

In addition to visiting the oldest post office in Texas, visitors today find some pieces of San Felipe's past in and around the state park. Stop first at the small historical park where FM-1458 crosses the Brazos and search for the still visible traces of wagon ruts that lead to the old ferry crossing. A dog-trot log cabin replicates Austin's headquarters, and the J. J. Josey Store, built in 1847, has been restored as a museum; unfortunately, neither is open very often. Bring a lunch; there's a shady picnic ground along the river on the other side of the road.

Stephen F. Austin State Park is nearby and open daily, year-round; watch for Park Road 38 turnoff from FM-1458. This park offers an outstanding eighteen-hole golf course, as well as picnicking, camping, fishing, and numerous other family activities. As an oak-shaded retreat, it's wonderful on warm weather weekends. Fee; (979) 885-3613 or (800) 792-1112; www.tpwd.state.tx.us.

WHAT TO DO

Willow River Farms. Take exit 723 from I-10, go north 2.7 miles on FM-1458; after crossing the Brazos River, turn left on FM-3318 and go 2 miles to the farm. This 310-acre farm is home to sixty mentally challenged adults who contribute to their keep by producing herbs, ceramics, handmade papers, woven goods, produce in season, potted plants, and hanging baskets. Their products are for sale at the community hall near the front gates. Visitors are welcome weekdays from 9:00 A.M. to 4:30 P.M.; on weekends by appointment; (281) 375-5594; www.cri-usa.org.

CONTINUING ON

After enjoying San Felipe and the park, resist the temptation to take backroads to Sealy; the route that forks to the right immediately outside the park gate is frustrating and nonscenic. Instead, return to I-10 and continue west to the Sealy exit.

SEALY

San Felipe sold a portion of its original 22,000-acre township to the Gulf, Colorado, and Santa Fe Railroad in the 1870s to create the town of Sealy in 1879. That town now bills itself as the "Best Little Hometown in Texas" and collects a few more refugee Houstonians every month.

Is there any connection with the Sealy mattress? Yes, indeed. A Sealy businessman named Haynes made the first tufted mattress early in the twentieth century, and folks referred to it as "that mattress from Sealy." Haynes later sold the patent and the name, but his factory with its original equipment is still intact, awaiting an "angel" to finance its refurbishment as a museum sometime in the future.

Visitors enjoy a drive down Sealy's oak-shaded Fifth Street, with its early-twentieth-century homes, and a walk around the downtown area, which is being restored to its original appearance. There are numerous antiques shops, most of which have free walking maps of the town.

For information on Sealy, San Felipe, or Frydek, contact the Sealy

Chamber of Commerce, 309 Main Street, Sealy, TX 77474; (979) 885-3222; www.sealy-tx.com.

WHAT TO DO

Lone Star Raceway Park. 120 Old Columbus Road. Coming from Houston, take exit 713 from I-10, go over the Interstate, and turn right on the feeder road; the race track will be on your left. Motorcycles, modified cars, and dragsters (some with drivers in the eight-to-sixteen age category) test their stuff on this ⅛-mile dragstrip; spectators are welcome. Open weekends year-round, weather permitting. Call for race information. Fee; (979) 885-0731; www.lonestar racewaypark.com.

Port City Stockyards. North of Sealy on TX-36. This is one of the largest cattle auction operations in America, and visitors are welcome. Cattle are auctioned on Wednesday afternoon year-round; (979) 885-3526.

Santa Fe Park Museum. On Main Street. Includes artifacts from the early days of Sealy and Austin County. Just look for the small tin building with bright flowers, a flagpole, and a grader in the front yard. Open by appointment; (979) 885-3222.

Sealy Outlet Center. On I-10. Westbound, take exit 721; eastbound, take exit 723. Some twenty stores offer direct-from-manufacturer savings at this mall, a sister to the outlet mall in Conroe. Most are names you know: Spiegel, Mikasa, Van Heusen, and Florsheim. Discount coupons are available for groups; contact the mall office, 1402 Outlet Center Drive, Suite 250, Sealy, TX 77474. Open daily; call for seasonal hours; (979) 885-3200.

WHERE TO EAT

Hinze's Bar-B-Que. 2101 Highway 36 South. Well known for outstanding meats and sauce, this spot has been featured several times in the *Houston Chronicle* and was voted one of the ten best BBQ restaurants in the state by the readers of an Austin newspaper. Open daily for lunch and dinner. $-$$; ☐; (979) 885-7808.

Tony's Restaurant. 1629 Meyer (TX-36). Breakfast anytime and a full menu and noon buffet make this a popular eatery. Open daily for breakfast, lunch, and dinner. $-$$; ☐; (979) 885-4140.

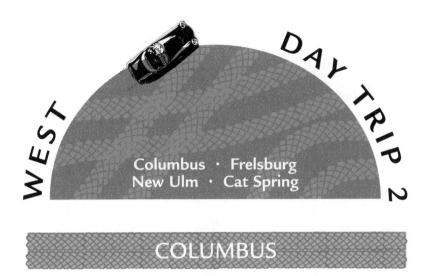

**Columbus · Frelsburg
New Ulm · Cat Spring**

COLUMBUS

Some 56 miles west of Houston's city limits via I-10, Columbus is in one of the oldest inhabited areas of the state. The early Spanish maps of Texas marked this as a sizable Indian village known as Montezuma, and Stephen F. Austin's first colonists called it Beason's Ferry. Now, as Columbus (population 4,800), it is one of the prettiest and most historic towns in Texas. As you stroll through the shady town square, it's hard to believe that the busy interstate zips by less than 1 mile to the south.

Back in 1823 Stephen F. Austin brought a survey party to this fertile land looped by the Colorado River, thinking it would make a fine headquarters and capital for his first settlement. The river was deep enough for commerce, and the busy Atascosito Trail crossed the river nearby. But this was Karankawa country—the Karankawas were a fierce Indian tribe labeled by history as cannibals—and the threat made San Felipe a better choice.

Some of Austin's colony did settle here, however, and a tiny village named Columbus was laid out in 1835. Its life was brief. In March 1836 General Sam Houston and his Texian forces retreated from Gonzales and camped in Columbus on the east bank of the Colorado River. The pursuing Mexican Army settled in on the west bank, where it soon was reinforced by additional troops.

Knowing his position was weak and that an attack on the Mexicans would be suicide for both his men and the cause of Texas independence, Houston elected to retreat farther. Moving to Hempstead

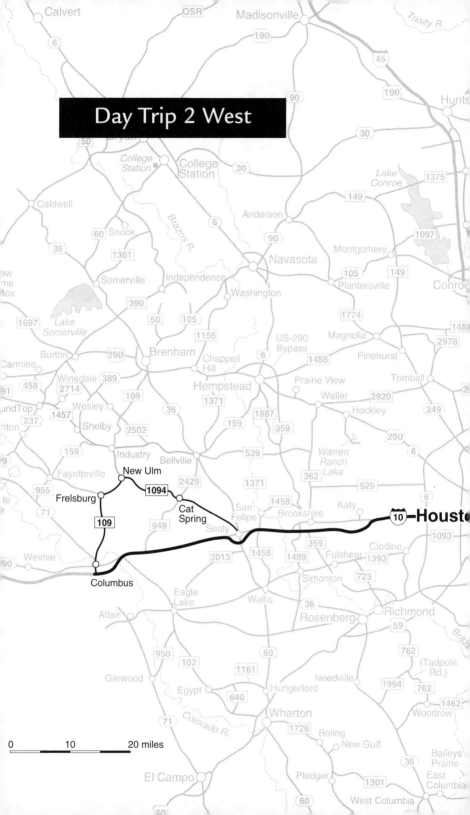

(Trip 4, Northwest sector), he ordered all the buildings in and around Columbus burned so that they would be of no use to the Mexicans. Caught in the middle, the local residents fled east to safety, a migration termed by history as the "Runaway Scrape."

Houston's strategy was vindicated by his victory over Santa Anna and the Mexican Army at San Jacinto the following month, and slowly Columbus began to build again. Today it is a delightful small town full of live oak and magnolia trees; if you're into superlatives, drive by the massive oak at 1218 Walnut, the second largest in the state. Thanks to large natural deposits of sand and gravel, Columbus literally is where Houston comes from—approximately 90 percent of the aggregate used to construct Houston's skyscrapers was excavated nearby.

The town's mainstay always has been the river on its doorstep. Early settlers floated their construction lumber downstream from pine forests near Bastrop, and by the mid-nineteenth century paddle wheelers were making regular runs between Columbus, Austin, and Matagorda. Dressed up with names like *Moccasin Belle, Flying Jenny,* and *Kate Ward,* these flat-bottom boats also carried cotton from large plantations south of town to the shipping docks at Matagorda Bay (Trip 1, Southwest sector).

The river still figures in the town's life but with a lighter touch. Columbus children grow up "floating around the bend," and local high school seniors traditionally celebrate graduation with all-night float trips. The most popular stretch for recreation starts at the North River Bridge (TX–71 North) to the East River Bridge (US–90), a distance of about 0.5 mile by land and 7 miles (about four hours) by water. Canoe rentals and livery service come and go in Columbus; check with the chamber of commerce for current status. You may need your own canoe and two cars, one of which should be parked at the East River Bridge takeout.

Wide and smooth (and usually opaque with sediment), with only a few small rapids, the Colorado River at Columbus is relatively safe for novice canoeists. The numerous long sandbars make night floats a timeless experience. Moonlight glows from these freshwater beaches, and the wildlife show is fascinating as the river comes alive with beaver, deer, and raccoons.

Exploring Columbus and its numerous heritage medallion homes is easy with the *Historical Talking Houses Audio Tour,* prepared by the

Columbus Convention and Visitors Bureau and available weekdays at 435 Spring Street, across from Courthouse Square. It's also available by mail: P.O. Box 98, Columbus, TX 78934; (979) 732-5135 or (877) 444-7339. The CCVB also can advise you in regard to the historical homes offering B&B and on the best wildflower routes in spring. Check those out at www.columbustexas.org.

WHAT TO DO

Alley Log Cabin. 1230 Bowie. Built in 1836 by Abraham Alley, one of Stephen F. Austin's original "Old Three Hundred" colonists, this square-notch oak cabin was moved into town in 1976 from its original site at the Atascosito crossing of the Colorado River. Open daily.

Canoeing. Howell Tire Center, 1223 Walnut Street (US-90), operates the Float the Colorado Tube and Canoe Rental. Trips of three hours to three weeks on the Colorado River can be arranged covering the stretch from Austin to the Gulf. Open Monday–Friday. Call to arrange tubes and canoes for weekend trips; (979) 732-3816.

Colorado County Courthouse. Bounded by Spring, Milam, Walnut, and Travis Streets on Courthouse Square. Built in 1890–91, this is the third courthouse on the same site and still the county seat. The four-faced clock is original, but its steeple fell in a 1909 hurricane and was replaced by a neoclassic dome. A full restoration completed in 1980 uncovered a handsome stained-glass dome above the district courtroom, hidden for generations behind a false ceiling. The courthouse is open Monday–Friday.

Take special note of the stump of the famous Courthouse Oak, 2,000 years old and the site of the first district court held in 1837. At that time the first courthouse on this site had been burned by Houston's forces, and a second one had yet to be built. Judge R. M. Williamson, known as "Three-Legged Willie" because of his false leg, elected to hear cases under this tree.

Columbus Opry. 715 Walnut Street (The Oaks Theatre). Named the best of its kind in the nation in 1996, 1997, and 1998 by the Country Music Association, this bit of Nashville in the heart of Texas showcases outstanding local and regional C&W talent and regularly draws professional scouts on Saturday nights. There's lots of audience-performer interaction and a wholesome "no alcohol, no smoking" environment suitable for families. $; free for children under six; (979) 732–9210 or 732–6510; www.columbusopry.com.

Confederate Memorial Museum and Veterans Hall. On the southwest corner of Courthouse Square. This old water tower was built 400,000 bricks strong in 1883. Dynamite didn't dent it in a later demolition attempt, so the United Daughters of the Confederacy decided it was a safe repository for their treasures. The exhibits feature clothing, small possessions, articles, documents, and pictures of early Columbus, including artifacts from the "Old Three Hundred," as Stephen F. Austin's first colony was known. Donation. Open during the May homes tour and for groups by prior arrangement; (979) 732–8385.

Dilue Rose Harris House. 602 Washington. Built of tabby in 1858, this house museum is filled with Texas primitives and early Victorian furniture. Open during May homes tour and by private arrangement; (979) 732–8385.

Fishing. Bass and catfish await in the Colorado River. You'll find a public boat ramp at the North River Bridge.

Grave of the Infidel. Odd Fellows Cemetery on Montezuma Street. Like all frontiers, the Columbus area attracted characters. Back in the 1890s Ike Towell made a name for himself as an outspoken atheist. The town marshal, he also was instrumental in the establishment of Jim Crowism in the area. He wrote his own funeral service, and his tombstone reads "Here lies Ike Towell, an infidel, who had no hope of heaven or fear of hell."

"Gunsmoke" at the Brune Land and Cattle Company. Take the TX–71 (Austin) exit from I–10 for 7 miles, turn left on FM–1890, and watch for signs. A nonprofit organization that promotes the sport of cowboy action shooting and safe gun handling, the Texas Historical Shootist Society holds cowboy shoot-outs here every third Sunday of the month. The society also hosts "Trailhead," a yearly shoot-out and gathering for society members on the fourth weekend of March that includes a trail ride through bluebonnet country, shooting competitions, a vendors' row, games, crafts, a campfire sing-along, liar's contest, and so on. Visitors are welcome to come and watch, but no children under eight, please. For information contact the Texas Historical Shootist Society, P.O. Box 216, Barker, TX 77413; www.thss.org.

Hunting. Colorado County is happy hunting grounds for deer, quail, dove, and geese. Every winter it becomes the goose capital of the world because of its location on the central flyway. Arrangements to hunt can be made through the Blue Goose Hunting Club, (979) 234-3597; and Clifton Tyler (goose and wild duck guide, day and season hunting), 1139 Fannin, Columbus, TX 78934; (979) 732-6502, www.texasgoosehunt.com.

Live Oak Arts Center. 1014 Milam. Housed in a historic building, this gallery's exhibits change monthly and feature both local and internationally known artists. Open Thursday–Saturday; (409) 732-8398.

Mary Elizabeth Hopkins Santa Claus Museum. 604 Washington. Push Santa's nose on the doorbell of this nice old home and you're greeted with "Santa Claus is coming to town!" Actually, he's already here, more than 2,000 strong and in every form imaginable. This lady's lifelong collection fills several rooms and includes jewelry, paperweights, cookie jars, music boxes, samplers, and more, in addition to the expected ornaments and mantel decorations. Open Monday and Thursday. Fee.

Nesbitt Memorial Library. 529 Washington. Root-tracers prize this library's new archives room for its regional genealogical information; children and collectors love it for its antique doll and toy collection. Open weekdays, Saturdays until 4:00 P.M.; (979) 732-3392.

Preston Kyle Shatto Wildlife Museum. 1002 Milam. Animal trophies from around the world are shown here in simple dioramas. Donation. Open 10:00 A.M. to 2:00 P.M. on the first and third Thursdays, September–June. Call ahead to confirm operating hours; (979) 732-8385.

Restored 1886 Stafford Bank and Opera House. 425 Spring Street (across from Courthouse Square). Built by millionaire cattleman R. E. Stafford in 1886 for a reputed $50,000, this elegant old building originally housed Stafford's bank on the first floor and a 1,000-seat theater upstairs, where such headliners as Lillian Russell and Al Jolson performed. Today the show-biz names may not be so grand, but the theater is, thanks to an eighteen-year, $1.5-million restoration financed entirely by local residents. The original 15-foot chandelier and the first elaborate stage curtain have been reproduced, and a variety of entertainments once again bring up the foot-

lights. There are monthly dinner theater performances September–
July. Don't miss either the museum on the first floor or the unusual
marble cornerstone. The opera house also is open to visitors
Monday–Friday and during the homes tour in May. Fee for tours;
(979) 732-8385.

WHERE TO EAT

Hackemack's Hofbrau Haus. On FM-109, 10 miles north of Columbus and 1 mile south of Frelsburg. You can't miss this place—it's a
Bavarian chalet in the middle of a small pasture, surrounded by
flying flags. And you shouldn't miss it, because the German food is
great (as are the steaks, seafood, and hamburgers), and there's lots of
live oom-pah-pah when the yodeling house accordionist is joined by
other local talent on the guitar, a "squeeze box," or the rhythm rake
'n bench. Their Friday and Saturday night repertoire ranges from
Bavarian tunes through C&W to rhythm and blues; call ahead to see
what's going on fun-wise if you are coming this way on a weekend.
Open for lunch and dinner Friday–Sunday year-round. $–$$; ☐;
(979) 732-6321.

　　Mikeska's Barbeque. Located at exit 698 in Columbus and known
as the BBQ king of the Southwest to local folks, Jerry Mikeska not
only sells his tasty ribs, sausage, and brisket in Columbus but also
caters for events as far away as Washington, D.C. Open for lunch and
dinner daily, with a buffet on Sunday morning. $; (979) 732-3101.

　　. . . of the day/A Cafe. 1114 Milam (on Courthouse Square).
There's a New Orleans feeling to this small place, thanks to imaginative restoration of a vintage building. Chef-owner Penny Miekow
explains her cafe's unusual name by saying that she not only uses
what's freshest that day but also changes the menu to fit trendy
things going on in the cooking world. That means you may find the
latest fad food or some old-fashioned favorites on the lunch blackboard specials. One of her standards is Columbus sausage (from the
butcher next door) braised in Shiner Bock beer. For the timid she
excels at sandwiches, homemade breads, and soup of the day. Open
Tuesday–Friday for lunch. $–$$; (979) 732-6430.

　　Poody's. 2002 Highway 71 South. A Quonset hut is a humble setting for chef Wade Schindler's creative cuisine, which includes spicy
shrimp and scallops linguini in a chipotle sauce and crème brûlée

with raspberry coulis. The salads are memorable. Open for lunch Tuesday-Saturday, dinner Thursday–Saturday, and brunch on Sunday. $-$$; ☐; (979) 733-9370.

Schobel's Restaurant. 2020 Milam. Convenient from I-10, this family restaurant cuts its own steaks, grinds its own hamburger meat, and makes its own pies. The menu also includes seafood and Mexican dishes, and there are large buffets at the daily lunch and on Friday night. Open daily for lunch and dinner. $-$$; ☐; (979) 732-2385.

CONTINUING ON

Columbus is the gateway to all of Austin and Fayette counties, rolling farmland that still looks much as it did when it was settled by Polish, German, and Czech immigrants in the 1800s. FM–109 North continues this day trip through that territory to the small German communities of Frelsburg and New Ulm.

FRELSBURG

When you stop to chat in this region, don't be surprised to hear strong German accents. The ethnic heritage of this community, 12 miles north of Columbus via FM–109, runs deep. The town is named for John and William Frels, who settled here in the 1830s.

You'll see Saints Peter and Paul Catholic Church on a hill as you approach on FM–109. Although this particular Catholic sanctuary was built in 1927, the parish it serves was organized in 1847 and is the oldest in Texas. Visitors are welcome either to celebrate Mass or to view the three carved wood altars. Nearby and a bit more humble in its architecture, St. John's Lutheran Church (1855–56) and its churchyard look like New England transplants.

Heinsohen's General Store has served this area for generations. If you stop in to buy a cool drink, you'll find it stocks everything from the latest in electronic games to pegged pants. Don't leave without buying some of the home-done pickles.

The big doin's in Frelsburg is the annual Fireman's Picnic on the second weekend in June. A fund-raiser, it also is an enjoyable look at a small, still very German community in the heart of Texas.

WHAT TO DO

Texas Falls Golf and Country Club. Three miles east of FM-109 via Dr. Neal Road, between Frelsburg and New Ulm; watch for signs. The golf course of this large real estate development is ranked fifth in Texas among golf pros, a demanding eighteen holes designed by Jay Riviere and Dave Marr. Expect bent-grass greens, a series of clear-water lakes, and numerous waterfalls. Golf fees vary; call for tee times three days in advance if possible. The resort's restaurant is open on weekends. $-$$; ❑. Two-bedroom villas with kitchens and swimming pool privileges also are available for overnight guests. Closed on Tuesday; (979) 992-3123; www.thefallsresort.com.

CONTINUING ON

From Frelsburg continue north on FM-109 to the more sizable community of New Ulm, population 650.

NEW ULM

Also founded by Germans and Czechs in the early 1800s, New Ulm soon may be in for its second golden age. Back in the 1940s the entrepreneurial Glenn McCarthy made some Texas-size bucks in the nearby Frelsburg oil field and brought lots of his Hollywood friends to the quiet streets of New Ulm. New wells are hinting at another wave of prosperity sometime in the future. In the meantime enjoy the simplicity and old-time rural architecture of this crossroads settlement as part of a country drive. This also is spectacular wildflower territory in the spring.

WHAT TO DO

Green Gate Ranch. Owned by Roberta Ellis, this 500-acre spread breeds, trains, and sells Peruvian horses, a relatively rare breed that's noted for its even temperament and smooth gait. Please, do not enter the grounds of this ranch without advance arrangements. Visitors who call ahead, however, are welcome (during spring foaling is a great time to come); (979) 992-3441; www.greengateranch.com.

WANDERING THE BACKROADS

This day trip continues on to Cat Spring via FM–1094 East. Other options from New Ulm include taking FM–109 North to Industry and then jogging either northwest on FM–1457 to Winedale and Round Top or turning east on TX–159 to Bellville. All are part of Trip 4, this sector.

CAT SPRING

When the wildflowers bloom in late March and early April, this tidy crossroads community looks like a calendar picture. As you come into town on FM–1094 from Frelsberg, watch for an unusual twelve-sided building on a rise to the left. This is the Cat Spring Agricultural Society Hall, built in 1902 and still the heart of community activities.

The Cat Spring Agricultural Society was founded in 1856 and is considered the forerunner of today's Texas Agricultural Extension Service. Early German and Czech farmers pooled their knowledge through this society, keeping explicit planting and production records of their small cotton and grain farms in a central book. All entries were written in German until America entered World War I; the practice was then deemed unwise, and all records thereafter were written in English. They are still used as a reference by local farmers.

If you want to use Cat Spring as a touring base, consider overnighting at Southwind Bed and Breakfast, (979) 992–3270, a working spread for registered Texas Longhorns. If you have a horse and would love some country riding, bring it with you; Southwind has an old restored barn with twelve stalls. Other pets are also welcome, as are day visitors who call ahead for an appointment.

WHAT TO DO

Rancho Texcelente. This 250-acre working ranch holds open house on Saturday for visitors interested in Paso Fino horses (appointments preferred). They love to show off their beautiful stock and even offer riding lessons ($30 per hour) to visitors who would like to saddle up for a guided trail ride. Also here: stock-tank fishing and

bed-and-breakfast accommodations for those who want to experience ranch life. Call for directions; (979) 865-3636; www.paso.net.

WHERE TO EAT

Cross Road Tavern. At the corner of FM-949 and FM-1094. This
gasoline station also sells hamburgers at lunch daily and puts on all-
you-can-eat catfish fries on Friday nights. $-$$; ◻; (979) 357-4808.

WANDERING THE BACKROADS

From Cat Spring you have several choices. A turn southeast on
FM-1094 takes you to Sealy and access to I-10 east for a swift return
to Houston. If, however, you want to journey on, swing northeast on
FM-2429 to connect with TX-36 north to Bellville (Trip 4, this
sector).

Yet another alternative is to head home the slow way, taking in
some sights as you go. To do the latter from Sealy, take FM-3013
southwest 11 miles to the Attwater Prairie Chicken National Wildlife
Refuge. This 8,000-acre preserve is the happy "booming" grounds
(mid-February through April) for the nearly extinct Attwater's
prairie chicken. Each male prairie chicken has his own domain and
protects it with a war dance, a real sight to see. Rangers may restrict
public access, however, to protect the birds, so inquire before you
make this jaunt. Day visitors usually can drive 5 miles of road
through this preserve, plus there are two walking trails; binoculars
are highly desirable. This refuge also has a high resident bird population and harbors migratory flocks in winter as well. More than 250
species of flowering plants have been recorded here, which makes a
spring visit exceptional. This refuge is open year-round, with some
picnic facilities, but call in advance for advice; (979) 234-3278.

A second option from Sealy follows TX-36 south to Wallis and a
visit to Guardian Angel Catholic Church, one of the most beautiful
painted churches in the state. Watch for signs to the church. Organized in 1892 by several Czech families, this church's interior and
stained-glass windows rival those found near Schulenburg (Trip 3,
this sector). The church doors normally are open during the day.

From Wallis, FM-1093 East more or less parallels I-10, ultimately
becoming Westheimer Road in far west Houston.

The area around Cat Spring is threaded with small country roads, and rambling is a joy. Be sure, however, that you have a good state highway map in hand if you care where you end up.

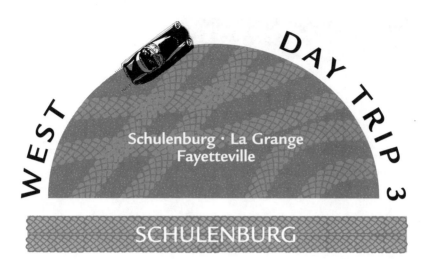

SCHULENBURG

Begin this trip by driving due west from Houston on I-10 to the Schulenburg exit and turning south on TX-77.

Like Sealy, this is a railroad town, created in 1873 when the fledgling Galveston, Harrisburg, and San Antonio Railroad purchased a right-of-way across Louis Schulenburg's farm and built a station. Folks living in nearby High Hill used log rollers pulled by oxen to move their homes and business buildings 3 miles south to the new townsite, and Schulenburg began to thrive.

Local residents still tell time by train whistles, and day-trippers find an architecturally interesting Main Street (particularly the 400–600 blocks), numerous historic sites, and a string of "painted churches" beautifully representative of the area's strong Czech, Austrian, and German heritage. Another local oldie, the 1930s Schaefer Observatory, has been featured on the television show *The Eyes of Texas*. Open only to serious amateur astronomers, this working observatory has a 14-inch telescope; (979) 743-3448 (weekdays only).

Strong ethnic traditions make the Schulenburg Festival a big event the first full weekend in August. For additional information and a driving-tour map, contact the Schulenburg Chamber of Commerce, 101-B Kessler Avenue (P.O. Box 65), Schulenburg, TX 78956; (979) 743-4514 or (800) 504-5294; www.schulenburgchamber.org.

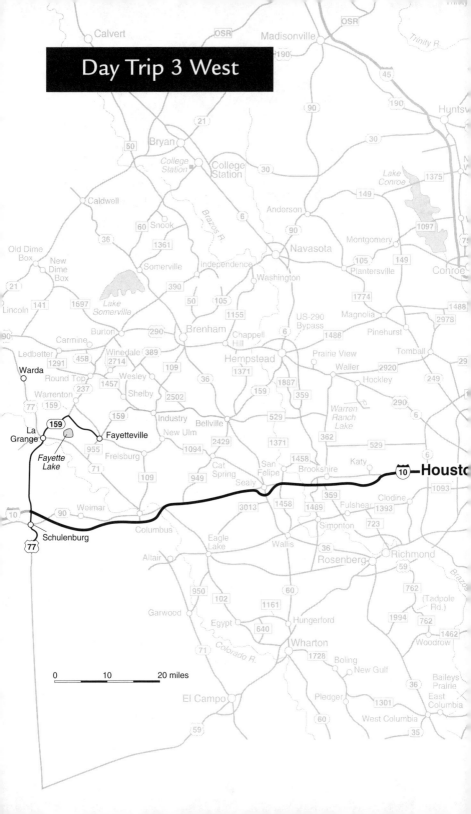

Day Trip 3 West

0   10   20 miles

WHAT TO DO

Itsy Bitsy Burro Company of Cedar Grove Farm. North of Schulenburg; call for an appointment and directions. Basically a breeding farm for miniature donkeys, this place also has a potbellied pig and a llama, and cattle fields line the long drive up to the 1860s ranchhouse. This is an ideal place to show off the best of country life to children, but appointments are required; (979) 247–4965; www.lildonk.com.

The Old Anderson Place. 510 South Main Street. Built before 1857 and later the home of Louis Schulenburg, this is thought to be the oldest occupied house in the area. Privately owned, it is not open for tours. Do not disturb the occupants.

Painted Church Driving Tour. An interesting map to the rural countryside around Schulenburg is available from the chamber of commerce. It will lead you to the tiny Czech settlement of Dubina and its beautifully frescoed Saints Cyril & Methodius Catholic Church; to Ammannsville and the unusual stenciled Gothic interior of St. John the Baptist Catholic Church; to Praha and the painted murals of the Blessed Virgin Mary Catholic Church; and to High Hill and the painted murals of St. Mary's Catholic Church. En route and worth seeing are a Russian-styled house and (near Dubina) a century-old iron bridge over the Navidad River. Most of the churches are still in use and may or may not be open; best consult in advance with the Schulenburg Chamber of Commerce, which also provides guided tours by advance appointment; (979) 743–4514.

Schulenburg Historical Museum. 631 North Main. Visiting this old store-turned-museum is wonderful on Sunday afternoon. There are few cars around, and the atmosphere is that of a quieter time. Lots of old stuff here, and it's fun to poke around. Donations welcome. Also open by appointment; (979) 743–4887.

Stanzel Model Aircraft Museum. 311 Baumgarten. This petite but first-rate museum focuses on the mechanical and marketing genius of native sons Victor and Joe Stanzel, whose toy factory operated in the area for more than fifty years. The brothers held over twenty-five patents, including one for a rocket-inspired carnival ride. A must-stop for flight and toy enthusiasts. Closed Tuesday and Thursday; fee; (979) 743–6559.

WHERE TO EAT

Frank's Restaurant. At the intersection of I-10 and TX-77. A favorite stop for travelers roaming between Houston and San Antonio, this spot has been serving up the Texas standards since 1929. Open daily for breakfast, lunch, and dinner. $-$$; ☐; (979) 743-3555.

Kountry Bakery. 110 Kessler (US-77 North). While a great spot for homemade breads, cookies, pies, sweet rolls, and the like, this fragrant place also serves salads, breakfast tacos, stew, chili, soups, burgers, sandwiches, and daily specials. Check the blackboard for the cook's selections. Closed on Wednesday. Open other weekdays from 5:30 A.M. to 5:00 P.M., Saturday until 2:00 P.M. $; (979) 743-4342.

Oakridge Restaurant & BBQ Smokehouse. At the intersection of TX-77 and I-10; exit 674. This long-established family restaurant smokes its own meats and makes its own sausage, but you'll find chicken, burgers, fish, and buffet offerings here as well. In addition to patio dining on nice days, there's a small playground for children and a gift shop. Open daily for breakfast, lunch, and dinner. $-$$; ☐; (979) 743-3372 or (800) 320-5766.

WANDERING THE BACKROADS

If you want to explore farther, consider deviating briefly from this day trip itinerary to visit Flatonia, 12 miles farther west and well beyond the 110-mile limit of this book. While I-10 and US-90 are hardly backroads, they are time-savers and the most direct routes. Another railroad town, Flatonia was established in 1875 and is where many of the eggs sold in Houston are laid. Prime sights include a historical museum in the old Flatonia Bank Building, an 1886 mercantile (open daily except Sunday), and the oldest operating newspaper (1875) in the county. For information call the Flatonia Chamber of Commerce at (361) 865-3920 weekdays.

While you're in the territory, visit Praha on FM-1295, off US-90, 3 miles east of Flatonia. The first Czech settlement in Texas, this tiny community and its large church host Czechs from all over America for homecoming in mid-August, a festival that began in 1856.

LA GRANGE

There are two ways to get to La Grange from Houston, but they both follow I-10 West some 56 miles to Columbus. There you can either take TX-71 northwest 26 miles to La Grange or continue on the interstate another 21 miles to the US-77 exit, then go north 16 miles to your destination.

Long before TV personality Marvin Zindler focused the bright lights of TV publicity and traditional morality on Miss Mona and her Chicken Ranch on the outskirts of town *(Best Little Whorehouse in Texas)* some years ago, La Grange had a colorful personality. A bear of a man known as Strap Buckner was running an Indian trading post here by 1819, and local legend says he cleared the site of La Grange in a wild wrestling match with Satan.

Whatever the truth, a small community began about 1831 where the La Bahia Trail crossed the Colorado River, and some of Stephen F. Austin's first colony helped tame the land. By 1837 the town known as La Grange was the seat of government for Fayette County. The courthouse, built in the 1890s, stands in the town square, and its original clock still chimes the hour.

Pause for a moment under the once glorious Muster Oak on the square's northeast corner. Through six conflicts starting with the Mexican attack of 1842, La Grange's able-bodied men have gathered here with their families before leaving for battle. The tradition took a 1990s twist during Iraq's occupation of Kuwait. When area army reserve units came through La Grange, they found Muster Oak wrapped with a giant yellow bow.

La Grange is a nerve center for wildflower tours in the spring, and the local chamber of commerce will help you plan a driving route. Whenever you come, spend some time exploring the city's historical square, slowly being restored to old-time character via the Main Street Program. Walking-tour brochures as well as guides to area antiques shops and cemeteries are available at the chamber of commerce, 171 South Main, La Grange; www.lagrangetx.org. Those offices are housed in what was the old Fayette County Jail, built in 1883 and used until 1985. Now renovated, the old jail serves also as a tourist information center and as a museum displaying relics and memorabilia of former law enforcement officers; (979) 968–5756 or (800) 524–7264.

Should you decide to linger, you'll find bed-and-breakfast at the Guest House at Dos Lagos, (979) 247–4465; La Grange Bed and Breakfast, (979) 249–3646; the Tree House at Colorado Landing, (979) 968–9465, www.coloradolanding.com; and Waldhutte, (979) 247–4802.

WHAT TO DO

Fayette County Heritage Museum and Library. 855 South Jefferson Street (across from the Faison home). A local bicentennial project, the museum has changing exhibits and special humidified archives to preserve historic documents. Open Tuesday–Sunday, but hours vary; (979) 968–6418.

Hermes Drug Store. 148 Washington (across from the courthouse). Established in 1856, this is the oldest drugstore in continuous operation in Texas. Visitors expecting a vintage site will be disappointed, however; although many of the original fixtures and beveled mirrors remain, the interior otherwise is very much of our times. Open Monday–Friday, Saturday until noon; (979) 968–5835.

Holy Rosary Catholic Church in Hostyn. From La Grange take US–77 South approximately 5 miles; then turn west on FM–2436 for 1 mile. Even non-Catholics enjoy strolling on this hilltop, noted for its large stations of the cross, grottoes, shrines, Civil War cannon, and replica of the first log church on this site.

The Jersey Barnyard. 3117 State Highway 159. More than 300 cows are milked at this dairy twice a day, and you're welcome to see how it's done. This guided educational tour includes a tractor-pulled hayride to the milking barns, a milking demonstration, plus the chance to pet or feed goats, chickens, fish, calves, cows, pigs, ducks, bunnies, and a donkey. *Fun to know:* This is home to "Belle, the Singing Cow" of Blue Bell ice cream commercial fame. Open daily except Wednesday by advance appointment only. Fee; (979) 249–3406; www.texasjersey.com.

KatySweet Confectioners. 4321 West Highway 71. If you call in advance for reservations, these folks will show you how they make bonbons, pralines, fudge, and other indulgences; tastes are part of the tour. Open weekday business hours. ◻; (979) 242–5172.

Monument Hill and Kreische Brewery State Historical Park. 414 State Loop 92 (2 miles south of town off US–77). Even after the Texans' historic victory at San Jacinto, the Mexican Army continued to raid this portion of Texas through the following decade. The tragic 1842 Dawson Massacre near San Antonio and the ill-fated Mier Expedition are the focus of this memorial. Both are lesser-known but interesting chapters of Lone Star history. This popular picnic site, high on a bluff overlooking the Colorado River, features a nature walk through the woods and one trail designed for the handicapped. The view north from the overlook includes the old La Bahia Trail crossing on the river.

In 1978 the adjacent Kreische Brewery and homesite were added to the facility and subsequently restored. Kreische was a skilled stonemason and brewer from Europe who established this first brewery in Texas between 1860 and 1870 below his home on what is now Monument Hill. Ultimately it became the third-largest brewery in the state, and his product, a dark beer called Frisch Auf, was sold at his beer garden. The restoration has cleaned out the springs that provided water for the brewery and stabilized the old buildings. Guided tours down to the brewery are given on weekends. Open daily. Fee; (979) 968–5658; www.tpwd.state.tx.us.

Mountain Biking at Bluff Creek Ranch. 537 Owl Creek Road, Warda. From the Columbus exit on I–10 West, take TX–71 North to La Grange, turning north on US–77 10 miles to Warda. Turn right on Owl Creek Road (Fayette County Road 152) and go 0.5 mile to a red and white sign. This private, 200-acre longhorn cattle and Arabian horse ranch offers 10 miles of challenging mountain bike trails through meadows and creeks as well as forested and hilly terrain. Rated intermediate to expert, some of the hard dirt trails are easy enough for new riders. Bluff Creek hosts several major races annually. Bikers also can camp here—there are rest rooms with showers— and there are rental bikes and a shop on-site. Fees. The property recently was put on the market, so do not come without calling first to make sure the ranch and trails are open; (979) 242–5894; www. bcrwarda.com.

N. W. Faison Home and Museum. 822 South Jefferson Street. The nucleus of this gracious frontier home is a two-room cabin built of pine around 1845. Bought in 1866 by N. W. Faison, a Fayette County clerk and land surveyor who survived the Dawson Massacre, the home remained in the Faison family until 1960. Open only for group tours by prior arrangement. Fee; (800) 524-7264.

St. James Episcopal Church. 156 North Monroe. Built in 1885 and still painted its original rust and cream, this small church has retained its original furnishings, handmade by the first rector and his congregation. Visitors are welcome at the 10:00 A.M. Sunday service and by appointment; (979) 968-3910.

WHERE TO EAT

Boss' House of Steaks. 710 West Travis. This Victorian home with its three-story fireplace has more to offer than just outstanding steaks, seafood, and Mexican entrees. Well done on a western theme, it also sports a massive antique bar and collections of guns, barbed wire, and Indian arrowheads. Open for dinner Tuesday–Saturday. $-$$$; ☐; (979) 968-8886.

Emilio's Southern Grill. 658 South Jefferson. In addition to Southern dishes, the daily buffet also includes Mexican entrees and fresh vegetables. Open for lunch and dinner daily, breakfast also on weekends. $-$$; ☐; (979) 968-6612.

Frank's Place. 235 West Travis. A varied selection of steaks and seafood here, with a salad bar. Although no mixed drinks are sold, take note of the 200-year-old bar. Open for breakfast and lunch Tuesday–Friday and breakfast on Saturday. $$; ☐; (979) 968-3759.

Holman Valley Steakhouse. 10204 FM-155 (9 miles south of La Grange in the crossroads community of Holman). Judy and David Hajovsky have turned this old country store and meetinghouse into an excellent and much needed eatery for the region. In addition to steak the menu includes seafood and chicken. Open for dinner Wednesday–Saturday. Reservations advised. $-$$; (979) 263-4188.

Main Street Bistro & Wine Bar. 155 North Main. Located across the street from the County Court House, locals consider this airy eatery among the area's best. Lunch features ample salads and hefty sandwiches, but the dinner menu is much more ambitious. Sample the grilled duck or indulge in the Shiner Bock Marinated Ribeye Steak. Open for lunch Monday–Saturday, for dinner Thursday–Saturday, and for brunch on Sunday; $-$$; ▯; (979) 968-9665, www.mainstbistro.com.

Prause's Market. 253 West Travis (on the town square). Fresh and smoked meats here, as well as barbecue to eat on-site or take out. Open Monday–Friday and on Saturday morning. $; (979) 968-3259.

Reba's. 108 South Main. This spot is known locally for its sandwiches, salads, homemade soups, freshly baked breads, fresh lemonade, and brick-oven pizzas. Open Saturday–Thursday for breakfast, lunch, and dinner. $-$$; (979) 968-4932.

WANDERING THE BACKROADS

Before continuing on from La Grange to Fayetteville and the conclusion of this day trip, consider a detour north/northwest to the tiny community of Serbin. Settled from 1854 through 1900 by Wends (Sorbs) from Lusatia in East Germany, this is the only Wendish village in Texas where you can still hear the Wendish language occasionally. Sights include St. Paul's Lutheran Church, completed in 1871 and still in use, (979) 366-9650; and the Texas Wendish Heritage Museum, open Tuesday–Sunday. Fee; (979) 366-2441. The latter exhibits Old Country folk dress, manuscripts, personal papers, photographs, and painted Easter eggs in addition to two log buildings built in the 1850s. Group tours that include a Wendish meal can be arranged by calling the museum. To reach Serbin take US-77 North from La Grange for approximately 7 miles and turn west (left) on FM-153 for 8 miles. Turn north (right) on FM-448 and go 9 miles to FM-2239; Serbin then is 2 miles west (left). You'll be driving through lovely countryside all the way.

If hunger strikes, you're out of luck in Serbin. The closest food source is a true taste of rural Texas: the Warda Store (and post office, gas station, restaurant, and bar). Located in Warda on US-77 about halfway between La Grange and Giddings, this spot is locally famous for its "Warda-burgers." Open daily (call for hours) but only after 4:00 P.M. on Sunday; (979) 242-3366.

Delaying an exploration of Fayetteville for another day, you'll also find road food as well as a picturesque 1899 octagonal courthouse in Giddings, about 5 miles northeast of Serbin via FM–448. From Giddings it's a straight shot home to Houston via US–290 East, unless you detour just east of Carmine onto TX–237 South, which connects you with Day Trip 4, this sector.

CONTINUING ON

If you do not jaunt off to Serbin, your next stop on this day trip is Fayetteville. From La Grange follow TX–159 northeast 15 miles on its zigzag course through the countryside.

FAYETTEVILLE

If you like the big time and bright lights, move on. This small town keeps a low profile, tucked away in the rolling farmland east of La Grange. If too many folks fall in love with it, it's bound to change, and that would be a pity.

Some of Austin's first colonists were sharp enough to settle here in the early 1820s, and by 1833 the tiny community was a stage station on the old San Felipe Trail, with service to Austin via Round Top and Bastrop. The town officially was mapped in 1847, and the next decade saw extensive German and Czech immigration, an ethnic blend that continues.

In the town's settlement days, free food was served to all comers, but occasionally the vittles ran out before the customers did. Late arrivals were told to "lick the skillet," and Fayetteville was nicknamed Lickskillet as a result. The town celebrates the Lickskillet Festival the third weekend of October with parades, fun, and a big meal (not free!) in the town square.

Fayetteville looks much as it did at the end of the last century: a series of 2- and 3-block streets in a grid with a central square. The town's pride and heart is the rare Victorian precinct courthouse in the center of that square, a small wooden structure built in 1880 for the heady sum of $800. The four-faced clock in the steeple resulted from a ten-year fund-raising effort by the Do Your Duty Club and was installed with much civic horn-tooting in 1934.

City folks cherish this small town as a wind-down place. The best way to get on Fayetteville time is to pick up a walking map from one of the stores and take a slow stroll around town. While Fayetteville retains its sleepy charm, its days of relative obscurity are numbered. Houstonians are buying Fayetteville's old homes as country get-aways, and many of the vintage buildings around the square are metamorphosing into Victorian-style shops, galleries, or lodgings.

Fayetteville's shops usually are open Tuesday–Sunday, but the first and third Friday and Saturday are the best times to come to town and stay late. That's when Baca's Historic Saloon and Confec-tionery on the square usually swings with live music, ranging from Czech and German polka tunes to contemporary country. This is a good-old-boy country band, the likes of which are rare in rural Texas today. Call for schedule; (979) 378-4911. Bring your dancing shoes and plan to stay over via an advance reservation at one of Fayette-ville's ten bed-and-breakfast establishments. For reservations and maps call (888) 575-4553. For additional overnight options in the region, consult the Round Top (page 119), Brenham (page 71), and La Grange (page 109) sections of this book.

WHAT TO DO

Citywide Garage Sale. Dozens of families participate in Fayette-ville's Citywide Garage Sale each July. A free map pinpoints their locations. (979) 378-4021.

Fayette Area Heritage Museum. 117 Washington Street (on the square). Lots of local lore here, with docents to add the human com-mentary. Open Monday–Saturday, or by appointment; (979) 378-2210.

Fayette Lake. From TX-159 bass fishermen may want to detour east on County Road 196 to this 2,400-acre lake, the cooling pond for the Fayette Power Project. Open year-round, it offers fishing, camping, swimming, and powerboating from both Park Prairie and Oak Thicket Parks, with a multimillion-dollar upgrading under way at this writing. Bait and tackle shops dispense necessi-ties and advice at the entrances to both. Fee; (979) 249-3344 for Park Prairie Park; (979) 249-3504 for Oak Thicket Park.

WHERE TO EAT

Hackemack's Hofbrau Haus. Between La Grange and Frelsburg on FM-109. (See Trip 2, this sector.)

Keilers Restaurant. On the square in Fayetteville. Take your pick: In addition to daily lunch specials, the menu offers fried catfish, steaks, hamburgers, and seafood platters. Save room for the homemade pies. Open for lunch and dinner Wednesday–Saturday. Lodging rooms upstairs. $-$$; (979) 378-2578.

Orsak's Cafe. On the square in Fayetteville. There's nothing fancy about this clean and basic cafe, but the food is acceptable and affordable. In addition to daily lunch specials and a regular menu, Wednesday night brings fried chicken; Thursday night, pork chops; Friday night, seafood; and Sunday, barbecue. You'll want to linger long enough to visit with local residents; nearly everyone who comes to town drops in for at least a cup of coffee, to pick up messages, and otherwise to stay in touch. Open Tuesday–Sunday for breakfast, lunch, and dinner; until 2:00 P.M. on Monday. $-$$; (979) 378-2719.

WANDERING THE BACKROADS

After touring Fayetteville you can continue east on TX-159 to Bellville and then home (Trip 4, this sector). Or you can reverse the order of this day trip, touring Fayetteville first and then continuing to La Grange. See the map with this section for your route options. It's also easy to connect with tours of Round Top and Winedale (Trip 4, this sector) or Brenham (Trip 6, Northwest sector), if you prefer.

If you are traveling in any part of this territory from late March through May, contact the La Grange Chamber of Commerce in advance. It scouts the best routes for color during the wildflower season. For information call (800) 524-7264.

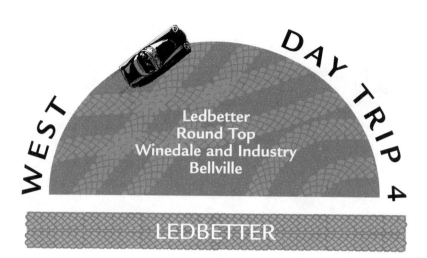

WEST

DAY TRIP 4

Ledbetter
Round Top
Winedale and Industry
Bellville

LEDBETTER

Begin this day trip by driving northwest from Houston on US–290 to Ledbetter, 25 miles west of Brenham. If it's Saturday, antiques shoppers will want to spend some time in the whistle-stop town of Carmine, a few miles east of Ledbetter.

Both Carmine and Ledbetter are railroad towns, the latter platted in 1870 by the Texas and New Orleans Railroad. Folks anticipated big things—those old plats show a big depot from which wide streets with pretty names stretched in all directions. The depot did become a reality, the first and largest in Fayette County. The town, however, maxed out at about 1,000 residents in 1900 and began a steady decline after World War II. The last passenger train whistled through in 1952, the last freight in 1979. Now even the tracks are gone, and Ledbetter has a permanent population of approximately one hundred souls. Perhaps the town is best defined by what it doesn't have: gas stations, fast-food franchises, supermarkets, traffic lights, noise, and crowds—in short, Ledbetter is a perfect pause in another era.

Looking for a place to lay your head for the night? Check out Czech Inn. Comprised of two turn-of-the-century farmhouses, this beautiful bed-and-breakfast in the woods is 1 mile north of Ledbetter on US–290; (979) 278–3626; www.czechinn.com.

WHAT TO DO

Alice Darnell Studio. Between Ledbetter's buggy shop and general store. This artist specializes in spinning local wool into thread on

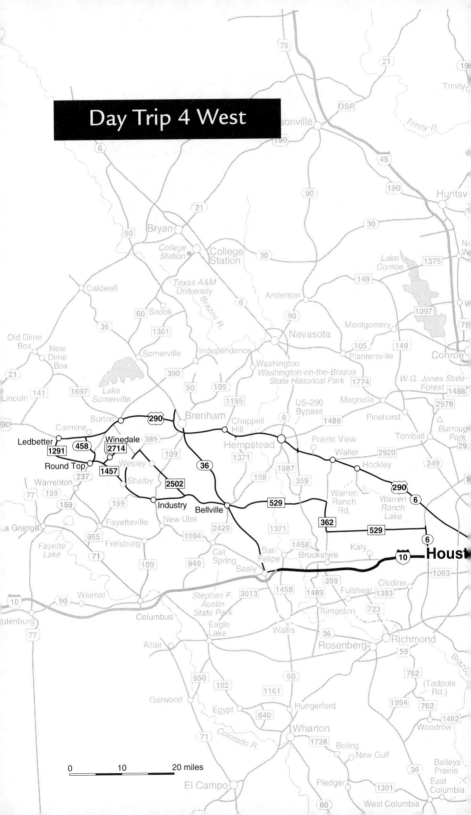

antique equipment and then hand-looming that thread into handsome cloth. She also restores and sells antiques and artwork. Open by appointment; (979) 249-5234.

Stuermer's General Store and Working Museum. 100 FM-1291, Ledbetter (at the intersection of US-290 and FM-1291). No one knows exactly when this old place was built, but the two antique bars (one dated 1836 on the back) were part of a saloon established here by the owner's great-grandfather in 1890. Today Chris Jervis and her mother, Lillian Stuermer Dyer, sell sandwiches and Blue Bell ice cream from those bars, and the rest of the two-story store is filled with memorabilia and antiques (not for sale), along with those sundry items no one can do without. Kids love this place; the jukebox and pool table are free. This is the oldest flag stop on the Kerrville bus route, and when the shutters are closed, the store is closed (usually Sunday except during wildflower season); when the shutters are open, come on in.

Jay and Chris Jervis also have fifteen B&B lodgings, one in a charming 1880s country cottage known as Granny's House. All the units have private baths and include full country breakfasts in their basic $60–$105 nightly rate. Guests also have access to a party house, complete with indoor swimming pool; (979) 249-5642 or 249-3066.

CONTINUING ON

To reach Round Top take either FM-1291 South from Ledbetter or TX-237 South from Carmine.

ROUND TOP

When it comes to vintage Texas villages that have retained the essence of their past, Round Top is the champ. Officially founded in 1835 by settlers from Stephen F. Austin's second colony, it was first called Jones Post Office and then Townsend, after the five Townsend families who established plantations in the area. The name of Round Top originally applied to a stage stop 2 miles north, a landmark by 1847 because it had a house with a round top. When the stage line between Houston and Austin moved its route slightly south, the town and the name followed.

Driving into Round Top is like passing through a time warp. A small, white meetinghouse in the middle of the village green is part of the town's charm. In fact, Round Top is so small, so compact and neat, that visitors often feel like giants abroad in Lilliput.

Those first Anglo settlers were followed by Germans, many of whom were intellectuals oppressed in their native country. Others were skilled carpenters and stonemasons whose craftsmanship marks numerous area buildings that survive today. A drive on the lanes around Round Top is a lesson in enduring architecture.

Nice to know if you hate to leave: The numerous bed-and-breakfast lodgings in the Round Top area include Briarfield at Round Top, (979) 249-3973, www.briarfieldatroundtop.com; Cole Cottage, (888) 922-3691; Gaste Haus, (979) 249-3308, www.texaspioneerarts.org; Heart of My Heart Ranch, (800) 327-1242; A Light unto My Path, (979) 249-5620, www.alightuntomypath.com; Oak Grove House, (800) 716-3931, http://oakgrovehousebandb.com; Outpost at Cedar Creek, (979) 836-4975, www.outpostatcedarcreek.com; Round Top Cottages, (877) 756-2681, www.roundtopcottages.com; Anderson's Round Top Inn, (979) 249-5294, www.andersonsroundtopinn.com; and The Settlement at Round Top, (979) 249-5015, www.thesettle ment.com.

With its current population of eighty-one, Round Top holds two distinctions. Not only is it the smallest incorporated town in the state, it has what many think is the oldest Fourth of July celebration west of the Mississippi. Local folks have been kicking up their heels on Independence Day since 1826, and the annual tradition now runs to orations, barbecues, a trailride, and the firing of the cannon in the town square.

Whenever you visit, just park your car near the square and walk around. Round Top folks welcome visitors and have lots of tales to tell, so stop and chat as you explore. Unless you are passionate about country antiques and/or folk art and don't mind major crowds, avoid coming to Round Top on the first full weekend of both April and October when literally thousands of people attend the Round Top Antiques Fair, one of the finest events of its kind in the world. More than 270 dealers from all parts of the country participate in this blue-chip show, but that's not all. Riding the fair's coattails is a seemingly endless antiques and flea market scene along many of the region's roads. Farmers rent field space to all comers, and hunting for bargains and treasures is the rule of the day. Nerve center for the latter scene is Warrenton, 3 miles south of Round Top on TX–237 (toward La Grange), and the action begins the weekend prior to the Round Top show.

For information on the area, contact the Round Top Chamber of Commerce, P.O. Box 216, Round Top, TX 78954; (979) 249-4042; www.roundtop.org. If you're already in town and need information, stop at the Round Top Visitors Center, 203 Washington, just off the square. A display of local heritage and attractions, it's open mornings only, Monday–Saturday.

WHAT TO DO

Bethlehem Lutheran Church. Up the hill from Moore's Fort and 1 block southwest. This sturdy stone church was dedicated in 1866 and is in use still. The front door usually is unlocked, so enter and climb the narrow wood stairs to the loft. Not only will you get a strong feeling for the simplicity of the old days, but you'll see an unusual cedar pipe organ, one of several built by local craftsman Johann Traugott Wantke in the 1860s for area churches. The old churchyard cemetery is charming and ageless, enclosed by a hand-laid stone wall reminiscent of New England.

Henkel Square. On the square in Round Top. Back in 1852 a German immigrant named Edward A. Henkel bought twenty-five acres in Round Top to establish a mercantile store. The following year he built a two-story home that now is the keystone of Henkel Square, a historical open-air museum operated by the Texas Pioneer Arts Foundation.

Dedicated to preserving the history of this region, Henkel Square is a collection of sixteen historically important structures scattered across eight acres of pasture in the heart of town. The docents are local women who explain each home or building, its furnishings, and how it fit into early Texas life. Don't miss the old Lutheran church, which doubled as a school. Its painted motto translates from German to "I call the living to my church and the dead to their graves," a reference to its two-clapper bell. One rings; the other tolls.

Five of the buildings were moved to Henkel Square from sites in surrounding communities, and the lumber needed for restorations was cut in the local woods, just as it was in pioneer times. Using old

tools and techniques, present-day craftsmen have kept each structure faithful to its period, an attention to authenticity that has won
Henkel Square awards for restoration excellence.

The entrance is through the Victorian building that once housed
Round Top's apothecary, and several of the homes have outstanding
wall stenciling and period furniture. Open Thursday–Sunday afternoons year-round, except for major holidays. Fee; (979) 249-3308.

International Festival-Institute at Round Top (Festival Hill).
P.O. Box 89, Round Top, TX 78954-0089 (on Jaster Road, off
TX-237, 0.5 mile north of the town square); www.festivalhill.org.
What once was rolling open pasture graced only by birdsong is now
a mecca for music lovers throughout the world. Back in 1968 noted
pianist James Dick performed near Round Top and fell victim to its
bucolic charm. Returning in 1971, he held the first of his musical
festival-institutes in Round Top's tiny town hall, a venture that has
grown into permanent quarters on Festival Hill. Every summer sixty
young professional musicians from various parts of the world attend
master classes taught by a professional guest faculty and perform
with internationally known musicians in a series of public concerts.

Two handsome old homes have been moved onto the Festival Hill
grounds. The William Lockhart Clayton House, built in 1870 in La
Grange, is now staff living quarters, and the C. A. Menke House, originally an old ranch house in Hempstead, is used as a conference center.

An Early Music Festival on or near Memorial Day weekend kicks
off a series of summer concerts (through mid-July) in the new and
air-conditioned Festival Hall, and monthly afternoon performances
are offered from August to April. Tickets can be ordered in advance
or purchased at the box office prior to curtain. There usually is a free
concert for children in mid-June, as well as assorted educational
museum forums at various times of the year.

Picnic facilities are free for the summer concerts, and you can even
leave the food packing to someone else. Both Royers' Round Top
Cafe, (979) 249-3611, and Klump's Country Cooking Restaurant,
(979) 249-5696, prepare box picnics to go if you call in advance.
During the August-to-April series you can reserve a Saturday night
pre-concert dinner at Festival Hill ($$$). Limited overnight accom-
modations also are available by advance reservation during those
months. P.O. Box 89, Round Top, TX 78954; (979) 249-3129. Exten-
sive herb gardens amid rock and cloisters adjacent to Menke House

are open daily under the supervision of herb gurus Madalene Hill and Gwen Barclay. For a guided tour (fee), call (979) 249–5283. Those ladies also offer monthly "Herb Days at Festival Hill," which include a guided tour of the gardens, a three-course luncheon, and a short lecture on the use and enjoyment of herbs. Cost is $30 including tax and gratuity. They also teach educational workshops on various "herb" topics and organize the Round Top Herb Festival annually in the spring. For information and/or program reservations, write Gwen Barclay, Director of Food Service, P.O. Drawer 89, Round Top, TX 78954; (979) 249–5283.

Also available to groups for seminars and conferences, Festival Hill houses extensive art, notably the David W. Guion Americana Collection and the Anders and Josephine Oxehufwud Swedish and European Collection. Guided tours ($5.00 per person) can be arranged by calling (979) 249–3129.

Moore's Fort. On TX-237, 2½ blocks south of Round Top's square. Now integrated into the Landhaus-Ramsey restaurant's site (see "Where to Eat"), this double log cabin with an open dog-trot center was the frontier home of John Henry Moore. Built about 1828 near the Colorado River in La Grange, it was used primarily as a defense against Indians.

Round Top Area Historical Center. 304 North Washington (TX-237 North). Housed in the town's former blacksmith shop, this young but growing museum displays regional memorabilia from 1820 through the 1850s. This also is a good source for local genealogical information. Currently open from noon to 3:00 P.M. on weekend afternoons, or by appointment; (979) 249–3042; www.texas pioneerarts.org.

Round Top General Store. On the TX-237 side of the town square. Stop at this circa 1847 store for antiques, gifts, and fudge. Open Friday–Sunday afternoons; (979) 249–3600.

Sterling McCall Old Car Museum. Located in Warrenton, about 5 miles southwest of Round Top, this nonprofit museum displays more than eighty-eight cars built between 1909 and 1959. Among its treasures: a hand-built 1956 Lincoln Mark II, Arthur Godfrey's 1956 Studebaker, and the re-creation of a 1950s-era service station. Open Thursday–Sunday and by special appointment. Admission is $5.00; (979) 249–5089; www.oldcarcountry.com.

WHERE TO EAT

Klump's Country Cooking Restaurant. On the west side of the square in Round Top. House specials run to Mexican food on Wednesday night, fresh catfish fillets on Friday night, and fried chicken at Sunday noon. Owner Liz Klump also offers memorable apple pie, barbecue, steaks, and hamburgers for lunch and dinner Wednesday–Saturday; breakfast and lunch (until 2:00 P.M.) on Tuesday and Sunday. $–$$; ☐; (979) 249–5696.

   Landhaus-Ramsey German-American Kitchen. 109 Bauer Rummel Road (2½ blocks south of the square on TX–237). A perfect complement to the deep German roots of the area, this handsome spot currently has a born-in-Germany chef, Tony Schmidt, in residence. In addition to turning out superb classics such as sauerbraten with dumplings, authentic Hungarian goulash, rouladen, and assorted schnitzels, Schmidt is also training one of the owners, Rick Ramsey, which bodes well for continued high food quality. This kitchen also does equally well by chicken, beef, and hamburgers, and Friday brings a super fish special. The apple strudel and Black Forest cake are baked especially for this eatery by the retired owner of Roland's Swiss Bakery in Houston. There's outdoor seating on a large deck built around a huge, 200-year-old oak in the front yard.

   Cuisine notwithstanding, that oak and the site's buildings alone draw many folks who just want to take a look around. The main dining room is housed in what was originally a Texas dog-trot–style house built in Frelsburg around 1870 and moved to Round Top years ago by the creative force behind Henkel Square, the late Faith Bybee. Moved again to its present site, Frelsburg House has been restored with a strict eye for historical integrity and expanded to include a first-rate kitchen. An even earlier structure, Moore's Fort (circa 1828; see "What to Do" listings) is adjacent and has been restored for private party use. Landhaus-Ramsey is open for lunch and dinner Thursday–Saturday and on Sunday from 11:00 A.M. to 3:00 P.M. Reservations are welcome and strongly suggested for weekends and event days. $–$$$; ☐; (979) 249–2080.

   The Oaks Restaurant. In Warrenton, 3 miles south of Round Top. A local favorite, it serves most of the Texas standards as well as steaks,

Italian, and daily specials. *Tip:* Sunday often brings all-you-can-eat cold shrimp (you peel). Open for lunch and dinner Thursday–Sunday. $–$$; (979) 249–5909.

Royer's Round Top Cafe. On the square in Round Top. Owned by Bud and Karen Royer and operated by their adult children, this small spot has been justly praised by numerous food writers and publications and is now a destination in itself—a very good reason to make a day trip to Round Top. Originally the menu was "the kind of food you come to the country for," and that still predominates. However, the taste bar has been raised to include more sophisticated offerings. Winners range from a luscious fresh salmon to the pricey but perfect Angus tenderloin; Royer's also serves a unique BLT layered with one-quarter pound of grilled shrimp. One off-menu item, Bud's fork-tender chicken-fried steak, is pure country and worth what is often a two-hour wait for seating; folks usually just settle down on the hay bales out front.

Good to know: There are two exceptions to Royer's "no reservations/no credit cards" rule. On nonevent weekends you can phone ahead and Bud will put your name on the seating list (a move that usually results in a shorter wait), and on event weekends you can guarantee your arrival at a certain time via a credit-card deposit. You will still have to pony up the price of your meal via cash or check, however.

Sweet frills run to Blue Bell ice-cream cones (vanilla only) and homemade desserts. Real apples and pumpkins go into the pies—no canned or processed fillings are used—and if you are lucky it will be dewberry cobbler day. The pies are available to go—they sell several hundred every weekend—so call ahead to reserve your favorite. Royer's normally is open Thursday–Saturday for lunch and dinner; Sunday noon to 7:00 P.M. The days and hours of operation change seasonally, however, so call. For example, this cafe is open on Wednesday in March and April, but closed on Sunday during Antique Week and on Easter, Mother's Day, and Memorial Day. $–$$$; (979) 877–7437.

CONTINUING ON

To visit Winedale take FM–1457 North for 4 miles to FM–2714 and turn northeast.

WANDERING THE BACKROADS

If you have lingered too long in Round Top and now must head home, why not take the scenic route? TX–237 South (connecting to TX–159 South) to La Grange (Trip 3, this sector) is one of the nicest country rambles in the state. Take a few minutes to travel east or west of the highway on the many graded county roads. You'll pass gracious old homes, log cabins, churches flanked by tiny cemeteries, and numerous historical landmarks. As you enter Warrenton on TX–237 South, watch for a large two-story rock house on the west side of the road. This is the Neece House, built in 1869 and now available for special events. You'll also pass St. Martin's, locally called the smallest Catholic church in the world; it holds only twelve people. Concurrent with the Round Top Antique Fair on the first full weekends in April and October, Warrenton blossoms into a giant antiques, crafts, and collectibles market, with plenty of hearty country food on the side. Warrenton's old grocery store has been renovated into a B&B, Warrenton Inn, (979) 249-3074. If you're wandering here on a weekend, have a look at the Sterling McCall Old Car Museum on TX–237 (fee), (979) 249-5089. (See a description on page 123.)

From La Grange follow TX–71 southeast to Columbus (Trip 2, this sector) and I–10 east to Houston.

WINEDALE AND INDUSTRY

Winedale provides another look at yesterday's Texas. The settlement is blink-small: a gas station and a few homes tucked into a valley threaded by Jack's Creek. That old-style split-rail fence on the right, however, encircles one of the most ambitious restoration projects in the state, the Winedale Historical Center.

Administered by the University of Texas Center for American History, this 225-acre outdoor museum illustrates many pages of the past. The basic farmstead was part of a Mexican land grant to William S. Townsend, one of Austin's second colony of settlers. He built a small house on the land about 1834 and in 1848 sold the farm to Samuel Lewis. He in turn expanded the home and the plantation, and by the mid-1850s this old farmhouse was a stage stop on the main road between Brenham and La Grange.

Although Winedale's grounds are open daily for wandering, guided tours (fee; weekends or by appointment only) are the only way to access the buildings. Starting at the visitor center, the first stop is a simple 1855 farm building known as Hazel's Lone Oak Cottage, often used as a gallery for an exhibit on Winedale's history. From there the tour moves to the focal point of the entire museum complex, the Lewis-Wagner House. This two-story farmhouse is notable for its authentic Texas primitive furnishings and beautiful wall and ceiling frescoes painted by a local German artist of the time, Rudolph Melchior. Other rare examples of Melchior's art can be seen in several of the Henkel Square houses in Round Top.

The Winedale complex also has assorted dependencies, such as a smokehouse and pioneer kitchen. The old barn, built in 1894 with cedar beams salvaged from an early cotton gin, now rings with the ageless words of Shakespeare in July and August, courtesy of University of Texas English students. The performances are Thursday- Sunday evenings, seats must be reserved in advance ($), and an inexpensive hunter's stew dinner is served before the Saturday-evening show. You also are welcome to bring a picnic basket and blanket and feast in the field. For picnics to go, contact either Klump's or Royer's eateries, listed in the Round Top section of this trip (pages 124–25).

A ten-minute trek through the back pastures of Winedale leads to the McGregor-Grimm House, a two-story Greek Revival farmhouse built in 1861 and moved to Winedale from Wesley in 1967. As the Lewis-Wagner House represents the earlier, rather simple plantation home of the area, the McGregor-Grimm House is more gracious and elaborate, typical of pre–Civil War cotton-boom wealth.

Winedale hosts numerous special fests, symposia, and exhibitions throughout the year, many of which focus on early Texas antiques and crafts. The complex also includes a nature trail and herb garden. Picnickers are welcome. For more information call (979) 278-3530, or write the Winedale Historical Center, P.O. Box 11, Round Top, TX 78954.

CONTINUING ON

From Winedale turn southeast (left) on FM-1457 and go approximately 9 miles to the intersection with TX-159. Turn east (left), and it's then 19 miles to Bellville—beautiful country all the way.

En route take a few minutes to explore Industry, settled in 1831-33 and the oldest German community in Texas. An 1838 Republic of Texas post office still stands, now surrounded by Friedrich Ernst Memorial Park just north of the FM-159/FM-109 intersection. Stop also at Lindemann's General Store, in business since 1884 and a great place to buy local sausage, custom-cut meat, and cold drinks (open daily). The current building, however, is a relative newcomer—it's only twenty years old. The original Lindemann's Store on Industry's old Main Street (2 blocks west of the intersection of FM-109 and TX-159) has a historical marker, and the building itself now houses the Lindemann Store Museum, open on the fourth Friday of every month. Two other vintage buildings in Industry—an early-twentieth-century house and an 1860s church that's still used for services once a month and at Christmas—also will be open to the public soon, on a limited basis. For information call (979) 357-2722 or 357-2237.

Two other bits of the past are open by appointment: a 1920s doctor's office, (979) 357-2772; and Welcome Hall (1899), (979) 357-2729. Originally called Halle Das Welcome Maennerchor (Hall of the Welcome Men's Choir), the latter was the community's social center for years.

The old Welcome Store, a landmark in the area since 1890, is 4 miles north of Industry on FM-109. You'll find cut tree trunks neatly holding up the porch's shed roof, enough groceries on the shelves to keep locals from having to drive into Brenham, and some friendly old farmers probably playing dominoes. Alas, age claimed the traditional potbellied stove some time back. Open Monday-Saturday and 4:00-9:00 P.M. on Sunday; (979) 836-7378.

WANDERING THE BACKROADS

An alternative route from Winedale to Bellville follows FM-1457 only as far as the tiny town of Shelby and then angles north (left) on FM-389. At the intersection with FM-2502, turn right and go 3 miles to Wesley, an early Czech-Moravian settlement. Watch on the east side of the road for the turnoff to the community's historic church, the first church of the Czech Brethren faith built in North America (1866). This simple structure's rock foundation is original, and a huge oak log (visible from the rear) supports the center of the building. Unfortunately, this small sanctuary usually is locked, preventing visitors from viewing its hand-painted interior decorations.

From Wesley you can either connect with Brenham (Trip 6, Northwest sector) by returning north on FM-2502 to FM-389 and then turning northeast (right), or you can continue on this day trip to Bellville. To do the latter, go south on FM-2502 to TX-159 and turn east (left). On your immediate left will be the Four County Auction Barn, home to the Cattleman's Country Restaurant; it serves breakfast, lunch, and dinner Monday-Saturday; $-$$; (979) 357-2848.

BELLVILLE

Settled in 1848 and the Austin County seat, Bellville was named for Thomas Bell, one of Stephen F. Austin's "Old Three Hundred," as his first colony has been labeled by history. The best time to visit is during the spring Country Livin' Festival, when nature lines the routes into the town with bluebonnets and Indian paintbrush. During that festival the chamber of commerce sets up roadside booths where you can get maps and directions to the best flower displays. They also sell packets of bluebonnet seeds in the hope that you will sow some of next year's color yourself. For information on Bellville, including antiques shops, galleries, and such, contact the chamber of commerce, 4 West Main (P.O. Box 670), Bellville, TX 77418; (979) 865-3407.

Restoration is bringing back the architectural integrity of the old town square. Numerous building fronts have been returned to their original design, and more than a dozen housed antiques stores at last count. There also are new boutiques and art galleries, most of which open on Sunday afternoon. Plan your trip to take in Market Day on the Square on the first Saturday of every month (March-December).

Although there are many historical markers in town, no vintage homes currently are open for scheduled tours. For a modest donation, however, members of the Bellville Historical Society (979-865-9116) can open some of those doors for you on a private guided tour. One of the special sites they access is Sam Houston's Texian Army encampment at Raccoon Bend on the west bank of the Brazos, currently undergoing an archaeological dig.

The following offer in-town bed-and-breakfast: Lewis House, (979) 865-1208; and the Bluebonnet Inn, (979) 865-0027, www. bluebonnet-inn.com. Three others are more rural: Somewhere in Time, on five acres west of town, (979) 865-9547, http://somewhere intimebb.com; Outpost at Cedar Creek, a restored German farmstead on thirty acres, (979) 836-4975, www.outpostatcedarcreek. com; and Lonesome Pine Ranch, (979) 865-3647, www.texasranch life.com. The latter is a 1,100-acre cattle ranch between Chappell Hill and Bellville with six historical cabins, all comfortably furnished with antiques or period reproductions. The B&B fee includes catch-and-release bass fishing on thirty-five lakes, excellent birding opportunities, and all of the ranch atmosphere you care to absorb. Wagon rides and trailrides carry additional fees, as do the March and September cattle roundups, which are offered on a day-visit basis.

WHAT TO DO

Bluebonnet Farms. This hundred-acre farm near Bellville breeds, raises, and trains American saddlebred horses and has several national champions in its paddocks. Visitors are welcome only if they have a sincere interest in the riding and training of horses; no sight seers or casual drop-ins, please. Appointments required; (979) 865-5051.

The 1896 Jailhouse Museum. 36 South Bell Street. The sheriff's office and county jail (with original gallows) have been furnished to their early-twentieth-century look, and monthly exhibits include artifacts from the Texian Army encampment at Raccoon Bend as well as assorted weapons, many of which were confiscated from prisoners during the jail's serious years. Open Saturday 11:00 A.M. to 3:00 P.M. Call to confirm hours as the building currently is being renovated. Fee; (979) 865-9116.

The Turnverein (dance hall). On FM-529 in the city park, immediately east of Bellville. Now celebrating its centennial, Bellville's dance hall was the first (1897) of five wooden pavilions in Austin County attributed to Joachim Hintz, a German immigrant carpenter. Still in continuous use, this quaint, twelve-sided hall has hosted many an oom-pah band and schottische as well as countless county fairs, antiques shows, and so on. Other examples of Hintz's dance halls include the Sealy Liedertafel Hall on Main Street in Sealy (circa 1914 and under restoration); Peter's Hacienda Schuetzen Verein (circa 1900), 5 miles north of Bellville on TX–36, then 1 mile west on Trenckman Road; the Coshatte Turnverein (circa 1928; call the Bellville Historical Society at 979-865-9116 for directions); and the Cat Spring Landwirth Schaftlide Verein (circa 1902), on FM–1094 in Cat Spring.

WHERE TO EAT

Granny's Bar-B-Q. 515 East Hellmuth Street (½ block off TX–36). Real pit barbecue here, with all the fixings. Open for lunch and early dinner Monday–Saturday. $-$$; (979) 865-5752.

    The Hill. 758 West Main, Bellville. Clean and crisp to look at with its red-black-white color scheme, this hamburger spot seems one of the best of its genre. No surprises here—but do try the shakes, malts, and floats. Open for lunch and dinner Monday–Saturday. $; (979) 865-3607.

    The Lemon Tree/Amber's Garden. 412 East Main. Take one historic building in need of an angel, add a relocated caterer from Houston, and mix in buckets of renovation money. The result is an exciting new destination eatery like this one. Rejuvenated, owned, and operated by Wanda Buntzel and her daughter, Shawn Rosa, what was the venerable but unlovely Dr Pepper Building now sports a front porch and landscaping on the outside, and a big fireplace, antiques, and great food on the inside. Lunches feature three specials daily along with a number of salads, sandwiches, and homemade breads and desserts. Dinners range from a memorable beef tenderloin and steaks to seafood, chicken, and pasta. The veggies are fresh, the coffee choices multiple, and you can buy some fresh flowers from the on-site garden shop to take home. Open for lunch Wednesday–Sunday; dinner Friday and Saturday. $-$$; ☐; (979) 865-1552.

    Manuel's Mexican Restaurant. 1416 South Front (TX–36 South). Fajitas and shrimp enchiladas are two of the house specialties. Open daily for lunch and dinner. $-$$; ☐; (979) 865-8408.

    Newman's Bakery. 504 East Main. This coffee shop is a local favorite for breakfast as well as soup and sandwiches for lunch. Open daily, 6:00 A.M. to 5:00 P.M. $; (979) 865-9804.

WANDERING THE BACKROADS

To return to Houston from Bellville, you again have a choice. FM-529 East is a rural route that intersects TX-6 north of the Bear Creek business area in northwest Harris County. If you live in south Houston, your best bet from Bellville is TX-36 South 15 miles to Sealy (Trip 1, this sector), then east on I-10 toward home.

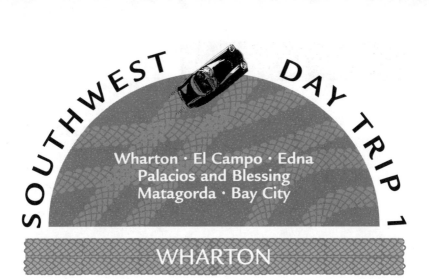

Wharton · El Campo · Edna
Palacios and Blessing
Matagorda · Bay City

WHARTON

The trip through Wharton, El Campo, Edna, Palacios and Blessing, Matagorda, and Bay City covers a lot of territory, so you may want to make a weekend out of it with an overnight in Palacios. Take your fishing and crabbing gear and have fun.

Start your trip via US–59 South to Wharton. While not a gee-whiz destination in itself, Wharton offers several pleasures. This rich agricultural land drew Stephen F. Austin's early settlers, and the town of Wharton began about 1846. *Fun to know:* Playwright Horton Foote, winner of the 1995 Pulitzer Prize for *The Young Man from Atlanta* as well as two Academy Awards at various times in his career, is a Wharton native and still maintains a home here. Many of his plays take place in "Harrison," a thinly disguised stand-in for his hometown.

Although no homes are open to the public on a regular basis, it's pleasant to drive down Wharton's oak-shaded streets. For information on local events as well as a list of antiques shops and an interesting driving map of "the Caney Run" through Wharton, Colorado, and Matagorda counties, contact the Wharton Chamber of Commerce, 225 North Richmond Road, Wharton, TX 77488; (979) 532–1862; www. whartontexas.com.

WHAT TO DO

Cotton ginning. There are not many places left in Texas to watch a cotton gin do its thing. If you are interested and plan to visit Wharton during the August–October ginning season, you can visit

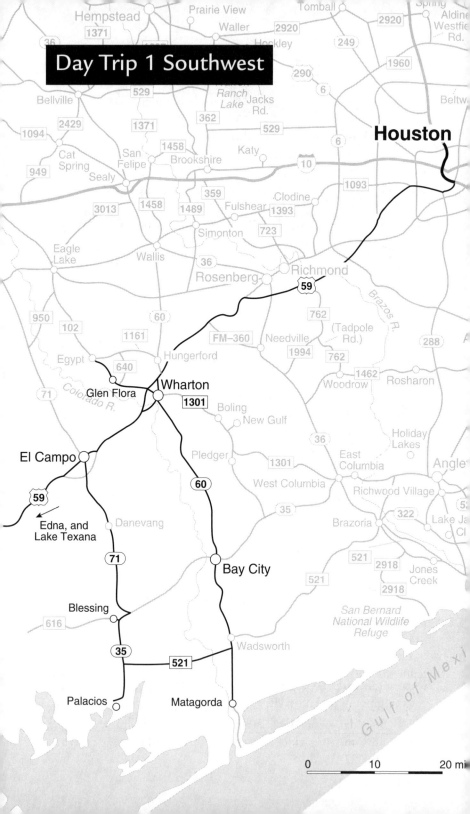

Day Trip 1 Southwest

Hempstead
Prairie View
Waller
Tomball
Spring
Aldine
Westfie
Rd.
2920
2920
Hockley
249
36
1371
1960
290
6
529
Ranch
Lake
Jacks
Rd.
Houston
Bellville
Beltw
2429
1371
362
529
1094
6
San
Felipe
Katy
1458
Cat
Spring
Brookshire
1093
949
Sealy
10
359
Clodine
3013
1458
1489
Fulshear
1393
Simonton
723
Wallis
36
Rosenberg
Richmond
Eagle
Lake
59
Brazos R.
950
60
762
102
1161
FM-360
Needville
(Tadpole
Rd.)
288
Egypt
640
Hungerford
1994
762
1462
Woodrow
Rosharon
Glen Flora
Wharton
71
Colorado R.
1301
Boling
New Gulf
Holiday
Lakes
El Campo
Pledger
36
East
Columbia
Angle
59
1301
5
West Columbia
Richwood Village
Edna, and
Lake Texana
Danevang
60
35
Brazoria
322
Lake Ja
Cl
71
521
2918
Jones
Creek
Bay City
521
2918
Blessing
616
35
Wadsworth
San Bernard
National Wildlife
Refuge
521
Palacios
Matagorda
Gulf of Mexi

0   10   20 mi

the Moses Gin through advance arrangement with the Caney Valley Cotton Co., Box 470, Wharton, TX 77488; (979) 532-5210 or 532-3522.

Egypt Plantation. On FM-102 at its intersection with FM-1161, 10 miles north of Wharton. This crossroads was settled by Austin's second colony in 1827 and was, for several generations, a bustling center of commerce. Today's visitors find a single row of wooden buildings that originally housed a store and a feed warehouse, several slave cabins, the historic Heard-Northington family cemetery, and that family's old homeplace, Egypt Plantation. Still occupied by the Northington family, this durable pink-brick home (circa 1849) welcomes visitors with advance reservations (adults only). Fee; (979) 677-3562. The house tour includes the Northington-Heard Museum, a remarkable collection of country Texana housed in what was the old Egypt-Santa Fe Railroad depot. The grounds also sport antiques/crafts/collectibles shows on the first weekend of some months; the Egypt Plantation Antique Barn usually is open Thursday-Sunday. Call for specifics; (936) 677-3232.

The town's old saloon and country store house more artifacts. Vintage cars and farm equipment often are on display outside on weekends (weather permitting), and tour groups can reserve barbecues at any time inside these interesting old buildings. To arrange that food service, call Carolyn Northington at (281) 242-7658 or (832) 541-6321.

Geese and duck hunting. Numerous outfitters guide visitors to excellent shooting on this region's vast prairies. For a list contact the Wharton Chamber of Commerce at the address previously given.

James G. Martin Nuts. 117 South Sunset. This local pecan broker has six mechanical pecan crackers that rarely stop during the harvest months of October through January. You are welcome to stop in and watch. He sells both wholesale and retail, so you can pack some home. Open Monday-Friday; Saturday until noon; (979) 532-2345.

Peachland (Gundermann's) Orchard. Take the Eagle Lake exit from US-59 South and follow FM-102 North into Glen Flora. Watch for signs. If tornadoes, freezes, and droughts have left the crops intact, visitors will find organic veggies here, fresh from the field. Open daily May-July, weather permitting. Country arts and crafts and sometimes cider also are sold here. Call for crop information; (979) 677-3319.

Riverfront Park at the Port of Wharton. This seventeen-acre civic project has a playground, picnic tables, walking trails, rest rooms, and a deck overlooking the river. Concessionaires are often here during summer, offering rental canoes, paddleboats, and bicycles; check the current situation with the Wharton Chamber of Commerce. Stop here with your picnic, and then tour the nearby Monterey Square in front of the 1888 courthouse. The square is one of the Main Street projects fostered by the National Trust for Historic Preservation.

Skydive USA. At Wharton Regional Airport, 1 mile south of Wharton on US–59 (past FM–961 on southeast side). In addition to supplying airlift services to certified skydivers, this firm offers two types of jumps to "never-evers," folks who just want a taste of this exhilarating sport. The first, a tandem jump, requires no classroom time or solo parachute—you just ride along with a certified tandem jumpmaster in a double-parachute harness ($169). The second type of one-day jump includes five to seven hours of ground-school orientation, followed by a sixty-second freefall skydive wearing a supplied parachute system and assisted by two certified jumpmasters using harness grips on each side of the novice ($279). The latter jump can be a one-time ride or the first in a series of approximately twelve skydives that result in complete certification. The entire course costs $1,200. Skydive USA is fully certified and licensed by the U.S. Parachute Association. Open Tuesday–Sunday, weather permitting. Advance reservations required, but spectators are welcome. ☐; (979) 282-8002 or (281) 561-5867.

Wharton County Historical Museum. 3615 Richmond Road. Some interesting bits and pieces of Wharton's past are gathered here. Farm and ranch exhibits focus on early settlement days, and the childhood home of a local boy who made the big time, CBS news anchor Dan Rather, was moved onto the museum grounds in 1992; call for times of guided tour. The museum also sponsors living-history events and historical reenactments several times a year; call for dates. Open daily Monday–Friday and on Saturday and Sunday afternoons. Fee; (979) 532-2600; www.whartoncounty museum.com.

WHERE TO EAT

Fibber's Cafe. 315 East Milam. You'll find freshly ground hamburgers here, along with steaks, seafood, and a buffet lunch with daily specials and fresh veggies. Open daily for breakfast and lunch. $-$$; ☐; (979) 532-8761.

Glen Flora Grocery. 114 Bridge Street, Glen Flora (6 miles north of Wharton on FM-102). Don't come here expecting luxe. This is primarily a locals' spot, and you'll be sitting at card tables and folding chairs in the middle of a small country grocery store while chomping into very good hamburgers. As for the daily specials, proprietor Patsy Rawlinson consults the local bush telegraph before deciding what to make and how much. After more than twenty-five years behind the store's old worn counter, she knows who is out of town or deer hunting, who likes what and is likely to come in for lunch, and so on. This is about as small-town "country" friendly as it gets. A smattering of antiques stores, mostly carrying general "junque" and open Wednesday–Sunday, are across the street. Lunch is served from 10:30 A.M. to 2:00 P.M. Monday–Saturday. $; (979) 677-3206.

Hinze's Bar-B-Que. 3940 Highway 59 Loop. Local folks think this family-run place has the best pecan-smoked, succulent barbecue in the region, not to mention the homemade chocolate, coconut, and pecan pies. Try Hinze's for takeout. Open for lunch and dinner daily. $-$$; ☐; (979) 532-2710.

Must Be Heaven. 100 South Houston. This is a good spot for light lunches, soups, sandwiches, pies, and a snack of Blue Bell ice cream. Open Monday–Saturday, 8:00 A.M. to 5:00 P.M. $; (979) 532-4504.

WANDERING THE BACKROADS

Wharton is surrounded by vast cotton, corn, and rice fields, and the early spring months along any rural road in the area produce a vision of fresh green punctuated by bright wildflowers. Local folks think there is no prettier drive in Texas than FM-102 from Wharton north to Eagle Lake. Another nice rural drive is along the Spanish Camp Road, FM-640.

To continue this day trip, follow US-59 South to El Campo and Edna.

EL CAMPO

This spreading town, 68 miles south of Houston on US-59, sits in the middle of a vast coastal grass plain used for open cattle range from the early 1800s. By the 1850s this area was the starting point for cattle drives across East Texas on the Opelousas and Atascosito Trails, heading for the railroad terminals at New Orleans and Mobile.

The railroad eventually made it to this part of Texas, and by the early 1880s the area had an official railroad name, Prairie Switch. Mexican cowboys handling the large herds would camp nearby—thus the name El Campo, which was officially adopted in 1902 when the town was incorporated. Early settlers came from Germany, Sweden, Czechoslovakia, and Ireland, an ethnic mix still found in the area. As you drive around checking out the antiques and crafts stores, watch for the twenty murals on assorted downtown buildings. Taken from old photographs, each depicts some phase of El Campo's early days and has an explanatory plaque. For information contact the El Campo Chamber of Commerce, Box 1400, El Campo, TX 77437; (979) 543-2713; www.elcampochamber.com.

WHAT TO DO

El Campo Museum of Natural History. 2350 North Mechanic (inside the Civic Center on TX-71 North at FM-2765). The main attraction at this extensive, well-done museum is the big-game trophy exhibit, a donation in 1972 from a local family. Over the years numerous other exhibits have been added, including displays on Africa, waterfowl, the Arctic, the jungle, the Alaskan brown bear, and animals native to South Texas. There's also a clown collection and displays of shells and rocks. Interactive computers and information boxes make this an in-depth educational experience. Open Monday–Saturday; call for hours. Donation appreciated; (979) 541-5092; www.elcampomuseum.com.

WHERE TO EAT

Churchill Downs. 105 South Mechanic. This antiques store serves homemade soups and sandwiches. Open Tuesday– Saturday. $; (979) 543–5611.

Greek Bros. Oyster Bar and Saloon. 133 South Mechanic. One of the most popular eateries in the region, this large and lively place puts some tasty twists on seafood, chicken, and other Texas standards. Oysters are always on the menu and are prepared several different ways. Although there's a full bar as well as dancing (live band on Thursday, Friday, and Saturday nights), this is a family kind of place. Open for dinner Monday–Saturday. $–$$$; ☐; (979) 543–1757; www.greekbros.com.

Los Cucos Mexican Cafe. 805 East Jackson. One of several Los Cucos restaurants in the greater Houston area, this spot has more than one hundred items on its menu. Specialty dishes include beef or chicken served with seafood toppings of shrimp, crawfish, and crabmeat. Open daily for lunch and dinner. $–$$; ☐; (979) 578–0612.

Mikeska's Bar-B-Q. 218 Merchant (downtown, across from the police department), and a second location on US–59/Blue Creek Road on the northern outskirts of El Campo. These spots are two of the reasons why Wharton County is considered by many to be the International Capital of Barbecue. Both are good sources for picnic sandwiches, and both are open daily (until 2:00 P.M. on Sunday). $–$$. Only the US–59 location accepts credit cards. (979) 543–5471 (downtown); (979) 543–8252 (US–59).

Pincher's Cajun and Seafood Restaurant. 104 East First Street. This family-style place occupies nicely revamped quarters in the back of a historic brick building that housed a hardware store from 1905–83. In addition to the expected étouffées and gumbos, the menu usually includes sourdough hamburgers, steaks, king and snow crab, fresh fried shrimp, oysters, scallops, freshwater catfish, and numerous selections featuring crawfish. Open for lunch Monday–Friday, dinner Monday–Saturday. Closed midafternoon. $–$$; ☐; (979) 541–5211.

Prasek's Smokehouse. Route 3, Box 18, El Campo (on US–59, 4 miles west of El Campo). Using an old family recipe, Mike and Betty Jo Prasek turn out memorable smoked sausage and both beef and turkey jerky, as well as baked goods. If you call ahead, they'll have a gift box or sandwiches ready to go when you arrive. Open daily from 7:00 A.M. until early evening. $–$$; ☐; (979) 543–8312.

EDNA

Once known as "Macaroni Station," because that's all the New York, Texas and Mexican Railroad commissary on this site stocked, Edna is home to some 7,000 persons and is a commercial center for livestock, oil, and agriculture. It's important to day-trippers primarily as the gateway to beautiful Lake Texana (see below).

Interesting to know: That lake now covers the old townsite of Texana, which was a well-established Indian village at the time of La Salle's expedition in the area in 1685. In 1832 it became the first town founded in Jackson County, and a few years later the Allen brothers decided Texana would be the ideal location for their dream city because of its location on the Navidad River, which provided deepwater access to the Gulf of Mexico. Anticipating that it would be a great port, they offered $100 in gold for the land. When the owner demanded $200, the Allen brothers moved northeast and ultimately bought a tract of land in Harris County upon which they founded their dream city—Houston.

Artifacts from Texana's early days were uncovered by archaeologists before the site was inundated with water; they now are on display at the Lavaca-Navidad River Authority headquarters, north of Palmetto Bend Dam on FM–3131. Free and open weekdays. Another bit of interesting salvage, the Texana Presbyterian Church, which predates the Civil War, now sits on Apollo Drive, next to the Edna Presbyterian Church.

The Jackson County Chamber of Commerce has area bird lists as well as information on Lake Texana, the town of Edna, and assorted historical sites, more than thirty of which have historical markers; P.O. Box 788 (317 West Main), Edna, TX 77957; (361) 782-7146; www.ykc.com/ccc.

WHAT TO DO

Lake Texana. Twenty-one miles southwest of El Campo via US–59; 6.5 miles east of Edna via TX–111 South. Formed by the Palmetto Bend Dam, which backs up the Navidad River for 18 miles, this 11,000-acre lake is noted for its catfish and bass, plus there are good camping, fishing, and picnicking under shady oaks. Much of this mixed oak-and-pecan woodland is usually kept neatly trimmed by resident deer. All water sports are here, either at Lake Texana State Park, (361) 782-5718 or (800) 792-1112, or at Lake Texana Marina and Brackenridge Plantation Campground, (361) 782-7145; you can rent paddleboats and canoes. Birding is excellent in the state park, so much so that it's a stop on the recently developed Great Coastal Birding Trail. For information on the latter, contact the Houston Audubon Society, (713) 932-1392; www.houstonaudubon.org.

Texana Museum. 403 North Wells (TX-111 North). Exhibits here include old volumes of medicine formulas, a rosewood Chickering piano more than 130 years old, a much older violin, artifacts pertaining to the settlement of Jackson County, and a jail out back, built in 1922, complete with hangman facilities. The museum is open Tuesday–Friday afternoons; (361) 782-5431. The old jail now houses the Otto Lawrence Children's Museum. This hands-on experience opens the doors of a vintage country schoolroom, store, and post office. Dress-up clothes and accessories plus old-time games are part of the fun. Open by appointment. Free; (361) 782-3266.

WHERE TO EAT

Dos Hermanos Mexican Restaurant. 106 East Houston Highway (US-59 frontage road; exit 111). If you hanker for Tex-Mex while roaming this way, try here. Open for lunch and dinner daily. $-$$: ☐; (361) 782-3372.

Frontier Barbecue. 608 North East Street. This local favorite does the standards well. Open for lunch daily, dinner Thursday–Saturday. $-$$; (361) 782-5270.

Palmetto Restaurant. 906 West Main. American and Mexican standards here, along with a good noon buffet and salad bar. Don't pass up the homemade rolls. Open for breakfast, lunch, and dinner Monday–Saturday; breakfast and lunch on Sunday. $-$$; ☐; (361) 782-2471.

CONTINUING ON

To reach Blessing and Palacios from Edna, take TX-111 East from Edna for 29 miles (you'll cross Lake Texana) to TX-71; turn south (right) 4 miles, then west (right) on TX-35 for 2 miles to Blessing, 13 miles to Palacios.

PALACIOS AND BLESSING

When you want to get away from it all, take TX-71 South from El Campo to the sleepy fishing community of Palacios. Whatever you want to escape, it isn't here. The big activity for visitors is walking from the Luther Hotel to downtown's eateries, with a short stroll along the refurbished bayfront thrown in for excitement.

The area was named Tres Palacios several centuries ago by ship-wrecked Spanish sailors who claimed they saw a vision of three palaces on this bay. Although the tiny town that began here around the turn of the twentieth century doesn't quite live up to the vision, for day-trippers Palacios is the perfect low-key escape.

There are two lighted fishing piers (bring your own bait and gear), numerous other jetties out into the bay, a nice shell beach, plus several public playgrounds, marinas, piers, and boat ramps. A 1.5-mile lighted walkway curves along the seawall, and a new, rather grand public beach area starts just south of the Luther Hotel.

The old town of Blessing, 13 miles north of Palacios via TX-35, is a real piece of the past. When the tracks of the New York Central (Missouri Pacific) Railroad and the Southern Pacific Railroad finally crossed on the Texas prairie in 1902, legend says that developer J. E. "Shanghai" Pierce said, "Thank God," and set aside 640 acres for a town of that name. The post office demurred, and "Blessing" was chosen as a compromise. Pierce's burial site is here in Hawley Cemetery, along with his likeness atop a 10-foot column so that he could continue to oversee his lands even after death.

For information on the Palacios/Blessing area, contact the Palacios Chamber of Commerce, 312 Main, Palacios, TX 77465; (361) 972-2615 or (800) 611-4567; www.palacioschamber.com.

WHAT TO DO

Birding. More than 450 bird species, including brown pelicans and black skimmers, have been spotted along this portion of the Texas coast, making Palacios an important stop on the Great Texas Coastal Birding Trail; there are five birding sites in the city and six others nearby. For a map to major birding sites, contact the Palacios

Chamber of Commerce, 312 Main, Palacios, TX 77465; (361) 972-2615 or (800) 611-4567. *Encouragement:* Palacios recently won the coveted number-one ranking for number of species sighted (236) during the annual Audubon Christmas Bird Count.

Charter boat excursions. You'll want to overnight to take advantage of the following. For scuba diving contact Don's Diving Service, (361) 972-2177. For fishing charters call Big PaPaw's Bay Fishing, (361) 972-1664; Captain Jay's, (361) 245-1190; Lost Anchor, (361) 972-6325; and Palacios Guide Service (Captain Jim Havens), (361) 972-3897.

Palacios Area Historical Museum. 401 Commerce, Palacios (at Fourth Street). Housed in a 1902 building, this collection of artifacts and antiques covers the period from 1902 through World War II. Open afternoons, Thursday–Sunday. Call for specific hours. Free; (361) 972-1148.

Texas State Marine Education Center. 102 Marine Center Drive, Palacios. Basically an educational facility designed to handle large groups of students, this operation is of interest to individuals and family visitors only for its 700-foot-long pier (strolling is fine, but no fishing) and its self-guided, 1.2-mile nature trail through a coastal marsh. Pick up a trail guide at Hulin House to fully appreciate the trail's abundant freshwater and saltwater wildlife. Birding platforms overlooking the marsh also are accessible, so bring binoculars. Guided group tours that include parts of the educational facility area are available only by advance appointment. Open weekdays only; (361) 972-3774.

WHERE TO EAT

Blessing Hotel Coffee Shop. Avenue B and Tenth Street, Blessing. Built in 1906, the hotel now is owned by the Blessing Historical Foundation and is under slow restoration. What was the hotel's ballroom is now a coffee shop with a well-earned reputation of its own. You pay your money and fill your plate from pots of delicious country-style food lined up on top of old stoves. The breakfasts are incredible, and the lunches are large enough to satisfy a hardworking field hand. No cutesy quiches here; the noon meal on Sunday is like Thanksgiving all year long. Open daily until 2:00 P.M. $; (361) 588-6623; www.hotelblessing.com.

Outrigger Restaurant. 515 Commerce, Palacios. Easy to find—it's opposite the park gazebo—this place offers the Texas standards: seafood, burgers, and chicken-fried steak. Open for lunch and dinner Thursday–Monday. $–$$; ❑; (361) 972–1479.

Palacios Mexican Restaurant. 511 Main Street, Palacios. Seafood gets an olé touch at this eatery. Locals also recommend the chile rellenos as well as the fajitas. Open daily for lunch and dinner. $–$$; ❑; (512) 972–2766.

WHERE TO STAY

Bed-and-breakfast seems a growth industry in the Palacios area. If that's your choice for an overnight, contact the following: Le Jardin de la Mer (Garden by the Sea), (361) 972–5983 or (800) 895–8934, www.bbhost.com/lejardindelamer/; The Getaway (a three-bedroom cottage), (361) 972–2177; The Main Bed & Breakfast, (361) 972–3408; and Moonlight Bay, (361) 972–2232, www.moonlightbaybb.com. The chamber of commerce can provide an extensive list of vacation rental properties.

The Luther Hotel. 408 South Bay Boulevard, Palacios (on the bay between Fourth and Fifth Streets). Quality lasts, and this rambling white frame hostelry has survived many a storm since its construction in 1903. Sited with dignity on a large lawn, this is the kind of place where you contentedly watch twilight creep across Palacios Bay while lounging in a chaise on the front porch. Resort it isn't; relaxing it is. Members of the Luther family still run this historic hotel and suggest you have reservations, as they hang out the NO VACANCY sign with regularity. The rooms are plain but comfortable, with air-conditioning and private baths. Be warned, however; there are no in-room telephones, and two rooms have no television sets. Several of the rooms have kitchens, plus there's a third-floor "penthouse" if you feel like splurging. Except for a complimentary continental breakfast, no food is served at the hotel. ❑; (361) 972–2312.

WANDERING THE BACKROADS

The main route into Palacios is TX–71 and TX–35 South from El Campo. En route a short turn east on County Road 46 (11 miles south of El Campo) brings you to Danevang Lutheran Church and a memorial to the Danish pioneers who settled here in 1894.

TX-60 is an alternate route to Palacios through neat and orderly Bay City. Take a break here at the Matagorda County Museum, 2100 Avenue F, and examine its collection of early Texas maps, carpenter's tools, and other Matagorda-related archival material. Open Tuesday–Friday and on weekend afternoons. Fee. There's also an outstanding historical children's museum in the basement. "Our Town" focuses on the turn of the twentieth century from a child's point of view. Kids play "dress-up" in vintage-style clothing, write on slates in a one-room school, shop in a general store, and so on. Open afternoons Tuesday–Sunday; (979) 245-7502.

CONTINUING ON

To reach Matagorda from Palacios, take TX–35 North approximately 6 miles. Then turn east (right) on FM–521 for 17 miles to the TX–60 intersection at Wadsworth. Turn south (right) on TX–60 for approximately 11 miles to Matagorda. Plan a stop en route at the Houston Light & Power Company's South Texas Nuclear Plant on FM–521. The free visitor center (open Monday–Saturday) explains all, but tours of the project (weekdays only) must be reserved in advance; (361) 972-5023. While driving FM–521 near the power project, watch on the north side for tiny St. Francis Catholic Church and cemetery. Part of an early Polish settlement, only the church was rebuilt after the 1895 hurricane swept all else away.

MATAGORDA

Founded in 1829 with Stephen F. Austin as one of its original proprietors, Matagorda thrived as the Colorado River's port on the Gulf of Mexico and was the third-largest town in Texas by 1834. One of the early freight routes that supplied central Texas with the basics of life ran between Matagorda and Austin; wagons left both cities on the first and fifteenth of every month.

The railroad steamed across Texas by 1853 and bypassed Matagorda in favor of Bay City. A hurricane in 1854 dealt another blow, and Matagorda never regained its early prominence.

Visitors now find two historic churches (1838 and 1839; both thought to be the first of their denominations in Texas), an 1830 cemetery, several homes with historic markers, and a double lock system operated by the U.S. Army Corps of Engineers on the Intracoastal Canal.

If it's crabbing, seining, picnicking, or beaching you want, turn south on FM-2031 (locally called River Road) in the center of town and follow it to the Gulf. There are many fine crabbing and fishing holes along the way, and the road ends at a county park (picnic and rest room facilities) and 20 miles of beach stretching as far as you can see. Pink granite jetties poke out into the Gulf, ideal for fishing. There are several charter fishing operations on River Road, among them Allen's Landing, (979) 863-7729 (summer only), and Raymond Cox, (979) 863-7434. Catches change with the season but generally include trout, flounder, and redfish.

WHERE TO EAT

Moore's Seabreeze Restaurant. Corner of Market and Matagorda Streets. It's a good thing this is a good place to eat, because it's nearly the only game in town. The shrimp salad holds its own against the best of the coast, and the seasonal oysters come from nearby shoals. Contrary to the general rule of "Don't order beef in a seafood restaurant," the burgers and steaks win local raves. Open Tuesday–Sunday for lunch and dinner. $-$$; ☐; (979) 863-7905.

BAY CITY

The county seat of Matagorda County, Bay City is one of Texas's oldest communities. Founded in 1894 just 25 miles from the Gulf of Mexico, it was known then as Bay Prairie. Today it is a center for farming and ranching, as well as nuclear energy.

As birding tourism has taken flight, so has Bay City. In the fall of 2002, the city opened the Matagorda County Birding and Nature Center. This inviting thirty-five-acre preserve on the banks of the Colorado River spotlights three ecological zones with nature trails, six specialty gardens, and a variety of educational programs. Make time for chatting with the helpful volunteers at the park's office;

they can provide details on the most recent bird sightings, as well as offer tips on birding destinations outside the city. The park is located about 1.7 miles west of the city on TX–35; (979) 245–3336.

You may also want to contact the Bay City Chamber of Commerce & Agriculture, P.O. Box 768, Bay City, TX 77404-0768; (979) 245-8333; www.baycity.org.

WHAT TO DO

Matagorda County Museum. 2100 Avenue F. Housed in a 1917 postal building on the town's historical square, this museum showcases a variety of fun exhibits, ranging from a look at Karankawa Indian lore and cowboy life to the story of the *LaBelle*, French explorer LaSalle's ship that sank in Matagorda Bay in 1686. The shipwreck was discovered in 1995, and many of the relics recovered have found their way here. The museum also offers interactive exhibits for children that look at frontier life on the Texas coast. Open afternoons Wednesday-Saturday. Admission is $2.50; (979) 245-7502.

Riverside Park. Located on FM–2668, just south of Bay City, this park is a one-stop destination for family fun. The woodsy park nestled along the Colorado River offers fishing and boating opportunities, jogging and nature trails, picnic areas, a Xeriscape garden, a shuffleboard court, a driving range, and a playground. If you want to overnight, there are forty campsites with full-service RV hookups; (979) 245-0340.

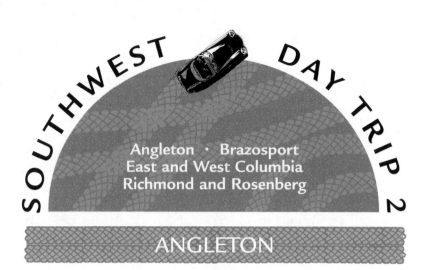

ANGLETON

Two routes—TX-288 and TX-35—come south from Houston and meet in Angleton before continuing to the Brazosport area as TX-288. You'll pass the old Brazoria County Courthouse in Angleton, built in 1896 and expanded in 1916 and again in 1927. It now houses the Brazoria County Historical Museum.

If you enjoy canoeing, explore Bastrop Bayou, about 5 miles south of Angleton via either FM-523 or TX-288. The best put-in for this 5-mile float is at the FM-2004 bridge, south of the intersection with FM-523. The best takeout is 2 miles (by road) farther at the old TX-288 bridge (watch for a railroad track). Even better, float as far as you want and then turn around and paddle back to your car. The current generally is not a problem.

WHAT TO DO

Brazoria County Historical Museum. 100 East Cedar (at intersection with Velasco Street). A general store and a doctor's office from Brazoria County's past are re-created here, along with a plantation bedroom, dioramas, and economic exhibits. A sixty-eight-panel exhibit on the Austin Colony illustrates "Where Texas Began" and includes artifacts from early settlement days, books, documents, and furnished replicas of a log cabin and an antebellum room. Other areas show items salvaged from the blockade runner *Acadia*, a Civil War ship that lies in a watery grave in San Luis Pass. If you're tracing your Texas roots, check out the "Old Three Hundred" genealogical database here. This spot is also worth a stop to shop in the museum's interesting store. Free. Open Monday–Saturday. Call for hours; (979) 864-1208; www.bchm.org.

Brazos River County Park. From TX–288 north of Angleton, turn west on County Road 44, south on FM-521, then west on County Road 30. This seventy-five-acre park on the banks of the Brazos River has picnic sites with grills, pavilions for groups, 0.5 mile of surfaced trail, a man-made lake with a duck island, a two-story observation tower, and a large, well-equipped playground. Lots of small wildlife here, including rabbits, squirrels, and deer. For information or group reservations, call (979) 849-5711, extension 1541.

WHERE TO EAT

Bo's Barbeque. 2024 East Highway 35. If you need a steak or barbecue fix, try here. Open for lunch and dinner daily. $-$$; ☐; (979) 849-0781.

Smithhart's. 2440 North Velasco. Serving numerous Texas standards, this bar and grill enjoys a strong local clientele. Open for lunch and dinner daily. $-$$; ☐; (979) 848-1320.

CONTINUING ON

From Angleton TX–288 South takes you into the heart of Brazosport.

BRAZOSPORT

It's rare to find the name Brazosport on current maps, but that's because it really is nine communities in Southern Brazoria County: Brazoria, Freeport, Lake Jackson, Quintana, Richwood, Surfside, Oyster Creek, Jones Creek, and Clute. Their common bond is the mighty (and usually muddy) Brazos River as it empties into the Gulf of Mexico.

Local folks say that the name has its origins on seventeenth-century nautical charts to mark where the Brazos meets the sea, and Brazosport today is the only mainland community actually on the Gulf-front coast of Texas.

This is historic country—many people from Stephen F. Austin's first colony settled here—but there is little physical evidence left to provide tourist interest. The area's biggest draws are the free and unrestricted beaches. Any sunny weekend finds thousands of cars lined up on the sand, boom boxes and barbecues going full blast. Most of the beach-related businesses shut down after Labor Day, and Brazosport quickly reverts to the industrial and refining community it basically is.

There's something going on in at least one of the nine towns nearly every month of the year. For a schedule of special events as well as information on marinas, vacation rentals, deep-sea charter and party-boat fishing, and so on, contact the Southern Brazoria County Visitors and Convention Bureau, 1239 West Highway 332, Clute, TX 77531; (979) 265-2508 or (800) 938-4853; www.brazosport.org. For local weather information call (979) 798-1212; for surf and tide conditions, call (979) 233-5301; for a fishing report call (979) 233-7351.

WHAT TO DO

Annual Christmas Bird Count. Because of its diversity of habitats, Freeport often leads the nation in number of species spotted during this annual volunteer activity (216 in the 2002 count). Call the visitors and convention bureau above for information.

Beaches. The old mouth of the Brazos River becomes, through engineering, the Brazos Harbor Channel and is framed by two jetties ideal for free fishing and crabbing. This channel also divides the beaches. Northeast to San Luis Pass via FM-3005 and the Bluewater Highway (County Road 257) are Surfside and Follet's Island beaches (14 miles of sand). Southwest of the channel are Quintana Beach and Bryan Beach State Park; both are accessed via TX-288 South (Brazosport Boulevard) and FM-1495.

The latter's 878 acres are undeveloped but good for fishing, beachcombing, and bird-watching; use four-wheel drive and keep a wary eye on the tide or you may be stranded by rising water. Quintana Beach has an excellent county park that includes two restored historic houses, a shore ecology lab, picnic pavilions, rest rooms with showers, a fishing pier, a playground and sports courts, World War II gun mounts, and both primitive camping and RV sites. The latter require reservations. Fee; (979) 233-1461 or (800) 872-7578. Take notice, however, of the park's warning signs regarding snakes, and be aware that the beach often wears storm debris.

With the exception of Quintana and a small section of Surfside, automobile traffic is allowed on all beaches. Camping generally is where you wish. There are no hookups, and public rest room facilities are extremely limited. Surfside has the most commercial development. If it's solitude you seek, Bryan Beach is your best bet. For additional beach information, call (979) 265-2508.

Anglers and RV devotees, note: Two county parks have been designed with you in mind. San Luis Pass County Park and RV Campground is one of the hottest fishing spots on the gulf coast. Day-use facilities include fishing piers, a boat ramp, a playground, and a visitor center with a deck overlooking the water. The RV area has full hookups as well as a bathhouse with showers and laundry facilities (fee); for reservations call (800) 3-PARK-RV. Fisherfolk, birders, and picnickers also find good facilities at Surfside Jetty County Park on the Brazos River Harbor Channel. This Gulf-front park features a deck and patio with picnic tables, rest rooms, showers, lighted volleyball courts and parking, a paved walking trail along a bird-rich lagoon, and an observation tower. Handrails and a concrete walkway allow easy fishing from the jetty.

Big Boggy National Wildlife Refuge. On the northern shore of East Matagorda Bay. Difficult to get to, this wild area is open for seasonal wildfowl hunting only. For information contact the refuge office at 1212 North Velasco, Suite 200, Angleton; (979) 849-6062; http://southeast.fws.gov.

The Brazoria Community Historical Museum. 620 South Brooks Street, Brazoria. Brazoria was an important settlement during the early days of Anglo Texas, and this small museum has artifacts dating from 1827 as well as an interesting re-creation of Dr. Sofie Herzog's medical office. She was the county's first woman doctor and the first female railroad surgeon in the world. Open on Saturday afternoon and by appointment. A program about Dr. Herzog can be part of your tour if you make advance arrangements; (979) 798-2076.

Brazoria National Wildlife Refuge. On the north shore of West Galveston Bay. From TX-288 South in Lake Jackson, turn east on FM-2004 for 5 miles, right on FM-523 for 8 miles, and follow signs.

This 42,338-acre reserve is the winter home to some 40,000 snow geese and small populations of Canada and white-fronted geese. It's open the first full weekend of every month for birding and nature photography, and there's also seasonal access by water only for wild-fowl hunting. Visitors find hiking trails and a 6-mile auto tour through numerous habitats. For information contact the refuge office at 1212 North Velasco, Suite 200, Angleton; (979) 849-6062; http://southwest.fws.gov/refuges.texasmidcoast.index.htm.

Brazosport Center for the Arts and Sciences. 400 College Drive, Clute (on the Brazosport College campus off Texas 288). This 40,000-square-foot cultural complex is of interest to day visitors primarily for the gem of a natural science museum it contains. Exhibits at the Brazosport Museum of Natural Science interpret this coastal region through shells, plants, animals, fossils, minerals, and Indian artifacts. The shell exhibit, the most extensive in the southern United States, is particularly well done and will turn your beach trips into expeditions. The Brazosport Nature Center and Planetarium has star shows for the public on Tuesday evenings. A self-guided nature trail along Oyster Creek reveals more than 200 species of river-bottom vegetation. Closed Monday; (979) 265-7661; www.bcfas.org.

Fishing Charters and Party-Boat Rentals. Captain Elliott's Party Boats offers daily deep-sea fishing trips to the snapper banks 30–60 miles offshore year-round, nine-hour trips on Friday and Saturday nights from May through September, and a twenty-four-hour safari May through October. The company also has (by private charter only) two-hour sight-seeing trips on the Old Brazos River. Fee; □. Reservations advised; (979) 233-1811; www.deep-sea-fishing.com.

Two Surfside firms also offer deep-sea charters. Action Charters operates four boats for parties of four to sixteen people. Call for brochure and rates, (979) 265-0999; www.actioncharterfishing.com. Johnston's Sportfishing has three "six-pack" vessels (for up to six people), (979) 233-8513 or (800) 460-1312. In both cases all you bring is food and drinks. The charter firms provide equipment, bait, and expertise. The visitors and convention bureau maintains a list of fishing charter operations. For additional options contact the bureau at the address and telephone previously given.

Girouard's General Store. 626 West Second Street, Freeport. When *Texas Monthly* magazine labels something the best in the state, it's worth a good look. You'll find the wrenches over the bread, plumber's helpers near the piñatas, and nearly everything else tucked somewhere. This is an outstanding example of a nearly extinct type of store. If you forgot your crabbing or seining gear, just stop here. Open daily except Sunday; (979) 233-4211.

Gulf Coast Bird Observatory. 103 West Highway 332, Lake Jackson. Dedicated to the conservation of birds and their habitat in and around the Gulf of Mexico, this young facility welcomes visitors interested in learning more about birding. Trails wind through much of this forested thirty-six-acre site, plus this is a good source for the upper Texas coast version of the The Great Texas Coastal Birding Trail map. Funds currently are being raised to build a major interpretive center here. Open weekdays during business hours, but ask about special weekend events; (979) 480-0999; www.gcbo.org.

Lake Jackson Historical Museum. 249 Circle Way, Lake Jackson. Debuted in late 1998, this well-done look at the past focuses on the four heritages of the local area. Starting with the Karankawa Indians, the exhibits continue through the mid-nineteenth-century plantation era, the beginnings of the petrochemical industry in 1940, and the subsequent creation of Lake Jackson as a Dow Chemical company town. One of the big attractions here is the Windecker Eagle, a revolutionary airplane invented by a Lake Jackson dentist in the early 1950s. Built of glass and epoxy resins and therefore invisible to radar, it served as the forerunner for today's Stealth aircraft. Suspended here as if ready for takeoff, this is one of nine remaining originals. Fee. Open Tuesday–Saturday and on Sunday afternoon; (979) 297-1570; www.lakejacksonmuseum.org.

Longhorn cattle. Dow Chemical has developed a 600-acre greenbelt and stocked it with Texas longhorn cattle. Best viewing is in the 1200 block of State Highway 332 West.

San Bernard National Wildlife Refuge. Ten miles west of Freeport. From TX-36 South turn southwest on FM-2611, left on FM-2918, then right on County Road 306. This 24,455-acre prairie and marsh preserve can be reached by boat from the Intracoastal Waterway and by car via FM-2004 West from TX-288 in Lake Jackson. Established as a quality habitat for wintering migratory waterfowl and other birds, the refuge has recorded more than 400 species of wildlife and is the winter home to more than 90,000 snow geese. Birding, wildlife observation, hiking, photography, fishing, and waterfowl hunting are the major activities. One loop road encircles Moccasin Pond, and a new walking trail leads to a woodland

area usually rich with birds. For on-site assistance try the mainte-
nance facilities on County Road 306, inside the refuge boundaries.
The gates are always open; no fee. Information: 1212 North Velasko
(P.O. Drawer 1088), Angleton, TX 77516; (979) 849–6062; http://
southwest.fws.gov/refuges.

Scuba diving. For two- and three-day diving trips in the Gulf
from Freeport aboard the MV *Fling* or the MV *Spree*, see any local dive
shop. The visitors and convention bureau maintains a list of scuba
operators in the Brazosport area. Contact the bureau at the address
and telephone previously given.

Sea Center Texas. 300 Medical Drive, Lake Jackson. Technically
the largest red drum (redfish) hatchery in the world, this free-admis-
sion, $13-million facility is reason enough to journey to Southern
Brazoria County. The 15,000-square-foot visitor center has a large
touch pool where folks can handle marine animals such as clams,
snails, anemones, crabs, starfish, and urchins; an impressive coastal
bay aquarium where Gulf species such as red drum, speckled trout,
and snook cruise through 2,200 gallons of water; a 5,000-gallon jetty
exhibit with a variety of fin fish zipping in and out of wooden pilings
and rocks; a 5,000-gallon artificial reef that replicates those found in
the open Gulf; a 1,000-gallon salt marsh where crabs, shrimp, peri-
winkles, and other aquatic denizens scurry around a simulated natural habitat; and a 50,000-gallon Gulf of Mexico aquarium where
500-pound Gordon the Grouper swims amid tarpon, redfish, and
circling sharks.

Visitors also can tour the broodfish tanks in an adjacent hatchery
building and explore several outside culture ponds and a five-acre
marsh area. The latter has elevated walkways, interpretive signing,
and viewing platforms. Open Tuesday–Friday from 9:00 A.M. to 4:00
P.M.; Saturday from 10:00 A.M. to 5:00 P.M.; and Sunday from 1:00 to
4:00 P.M.; (979) 292–0100; www.tpwd.state.tx.us.

Surfside Museum. 1304 Monument Drive, Surfside. Housed in a
1915 Coast Guard station, this small but interesting collection is
worth a look. Open business hours on weekdays; (979) 233–1531.

The Train Museum. 418 Plantation Drive, Lake Jackson. Operated by the Brazos Valley Railroad Society, this exhibit focuses on
Brazoria County in the year 1955 via a 12-by-32-foot layout in HO
scale. Displayed at a child's eye level, the display literally covers the
territory—from rivers and bridges to farms, animals, and homes.
Open weekends. Call for hours; (979) 388–9848.

WHERE TO EAT

Cafe Annice Kitchen & Art Space. 24 Circle Way, Lake Jackson. If beautifully prepared and presented food is high on your list of personal pleasures, make a special trip to this eatery. Owners Leonard and Janel Botello have created a visual cross between a California-style cafe and contemporary Italian trattoria, complete with coffee bar, a challenging menu, and vivid abstract art on the walls. Top honors go to the Texas blue crab cakes, the pasta caliente with jumbo shrimp, and the grilled-chicken caesar salad. Open Monday–Saturday for lunch and dinner (closed midafternoon). $-$$; ☐; (979) 292–0060.

Craft Attic and Picket Fence. 644 Dixie Drive, Clute. If you're hunting for a tasty, home-style lunch, give this popular place a try. Choices include freshly made soups, casseroles, salads, sandwiches, and desserts. Open Monday–Saturday for lunch. $; ☐; (979) 297–7234.

Dido's. County Road 519, Brazoria. From FM–521 in Brazoria turn left on TX–36, right on FM–311, and right on FM–519 to the river. Dido runs his own shrimp boats, which makes for good eating, either in the air-conditioned dining room or on the outside deck. For groups of ten or more, Dido's also operates the *Velasco Princess,* a 72-foot paddle wheeler, on the San Bernard River in southern Brazoria County. Open Thursday–Sunday for dinner, lunch also on Saturday and Sunday; $-$$$. ☐; (979) 964–3167.

D.J.'s Bar-B-Que. 906 West Plantation, Clute. This longtime local favorite is open Monday for lunch only; Tuesday–Saturday for lunch and dinner. $; (979) 265–6331.

On the River. 919 West Second Street, Freeport. The fried, boiled, blackened, or baked fish is great here (particularly the stuffed shrimp and catfish), plus there are plenty of steaks and chicken selections as well. The location is a 1910 building, cozied up with antiques. Open for lunch and dinner Monday–Saturday, dinner only on Sunday (5:00 to 9:00 P.M.). $-$$; ☐; (979) 233–0503.

Red Snapper Inn. 402 Bluewater Highway, Surfside. Locals love this place for its inventive way with fresh fish. Try snapper a la grecque, the shrimp baked with feta cheese and fresh tomatoes, or the sautéed fillet of fresh flounder topped with fresh mushrooms and artichoke hearts, and you'll probably agree. Save room for a slice of house-made cheesecake or apple pie. Open daily for lunch and dinner. $-$$; (979) 239–3226.

Windswept Restaurant. 105 Burch Circle, Oyster Creek. One of the favorite seafood restaurants in the Brazosport area, this place specializes in fresh shrimp dinners and whole flounder. To get here drive east on TX-332 in Surfside, left on FM-523, right on Linda Lane, right on Duncan Drive, and right again on Burch Circle. The restaurant is behind the Oyster Creek water tower. Open for lunch and dinner Sunday-Friday; dinner only on Saturday. $-$$$; ☐; (979) 233-1951.

CONTINUING ON

From Brazosport and environs this day trip continues north to East and West Columbia. Although TX-36 is the swiftest route, you might prefer to mosey awhile along the old river road that runs beside the Brazos from Jones Creek to Brazoria. To do the latter start north on TX-36 at Freeport, turn east (right) on County Road 400, and continue northwest along the river. At the intersection with FM-521, turn west (left) for about 0.75 mile to intersect TX-36 and the original routing for this trip.

WANDERING THE BACKROADS

As you pass through Brazoria, take time to explore. Most of the original town has been flooded by the river, but there are a growing number of antiques stores as well as several historical markers worth a read. As an alternative to continuing on TX-36 to the Columbias, you can follow FM-521 West and TX-60 South to Matagorda (Trip 1, this sector).

EAST AND WEST COLUMBIA

As you drive into these two small towns on TX-36 and TX-35, it's hard to believe they were among the most thriving communities in the state in 1836. East Columbia originally was Bell's Landing, a small port on the Brazos River established in 1824 by one of Austin's first colonists, Josiah H. Bell. Today East Columbia is almost a ghost town, with only a few fine old homes to hint at its early importance.

West Columbia was another enterprise of Josiah Bell. In 1826 he cut a road across the prairie on the west side of the Brazos and created a new town called Columbia. Within three years it was one of the major trading areas in Texas, and by 1836 some 3,000 people lived here, the rich river bottomland nurturing a thriving plantation economy.

After Sam Houston's victory over Santa Anna at San Jacinto, West Columbia really came into its own. The most powerful men in Texas came here, designated it the first state capital, created a constitution, and elected Sam Houston the first president of the new republic.

Such glory was short-lived. The town wasn't big enough to house everyone who came to the governmental proceedings, and in 1837 the legislature moved to Houston. But West Columbia had snagged its place in history, and visitors find several interesting sites as well as antiques shops along Brazos Street. For maps and advance information, contact the West Columbia Chamber of Commerce, 247 East Brazos, West Columbia, TX 77486; (979) 345-3921; www.westcolumbia.org.

WHAT TO DO

Ammon Underwood House. On the river side of Main Street in East Columbia. Built about 1835 as a pole cabin and enlarged twice, this stately old home has been surprisingly mobile. It has been moved three times to save it from tumbling into the Brazos. Currently owned and restored by the First Capitol Historical Foundation of West Columbia, this is the oldest house in the East Columbia community. Many of the furnishings and some of the wallpaper are original, and one room has been left unfinished to show early construction techniques. A log cabin built prior to 1850 has been moved onto the land beside the Underwood home. Open during the San Jacinto Festival and by appointment through the West Columbia Chamber of Commerce; (979) 345-3921.

Columbia Historical Museum. 247 East Brazos, West Columbia. Local antiques, plus exhibits on area ranching, the oil boom days of the 1920s, and present times are the focus here. Children enjoy the display of Indian arrow and spear points and the metal bell once used on a Brazos River steamboat. Open 9:00 A.M. to 2:00 P.M., Wednesday–Saturday, or by appointment; (979) 345-6125.

Hanson's Riverside Park. On the San Bernard River, 2.5 miles west of West Columbia on TX-35. This picnic spot has grills, a playground, a fishing pier, and an old-fashioned swimming hole.

Replica of the First Capitol. On Fourteenth Street, behind the First Prosperity Bank. This successful bicentennial project re-creates the small clapboard building that served as the first capitol of Texas. The original building was a store, which subsequently had a variety of tenants before it was destroyed in the 1900 storm that devastated much of the Texas coast. The shed room to the right as you enter is thought to replicate Stephen F. Austin's office when he served as the first secretary of state for the republic, and the furnishings of the building, while not original, are antiques from that period. Open Monday–Friday by appointment; (979) 345-3921.

The Varner-Hogg State Historic Park. P.O. Box 696, West Columbia (1 mile north of TX-35 on FM-2852). This land was one of the original land grants from Mexico, part of approximately 4,500 acres given to Martin Varner in 1824. Varner built a small cabin, began running stock, and in 1826 built a rum distillery on his holdings. Stephen F. Austin termed the results of this last enterprise the first "ardent spirits" made in the Texas colonies.

Varner sold his holdings in 1834, and the next year the new owner built a two-story brick house that survives today. Varner's original cabin is believed to be incorporated into the house. The bricks of the existing house were made by slaves from clay found in the nearby Brazos riverbed. By the late 1800s this plantation was prospering with sugar cane, cotton, corn, and livestock. In 1901 the first native-born governor of Texas, James Hogg, bought the plantation and regarded the house as the first permanent home his family had. In 1920 the four Hogg children began remodeling the old house. Donated to the state in 1958, it was further restored in 1981. There is a shady picnic area, and house tours are given whenever a small group forms. The park is open daily; the plantation house is open 9:00 to 11:00 A.M. and 1:00 to 4:00 P.M. Wednesday–Saturday and 1:00 to 4:00 P.M. Sunday. Fee; (979) 345-4656; www.tpwd.state.tx.us.

WHERE TO EAT

Brazos Street Grill. 333 West Brazos, West Columbia. This may well be the best tearoom in the greater Texas area, a bright and clean place where the emphasis is on fresh, well-prepared food. Ladies love the surroundings—a shop stuffed with fine women's and children's clothes, accessories, dolls, and so on—and men get a kick out of learning that this building really was a feed store from 1938-98. All patrons are greeted with a demitasse cup of tomato consommé to whet their appetites, and then the choices begin. The sandwiches come on freshly baked croissants or bread, the entrees and soups change daily, the salads come with freshly cut vegetables, and the desserts are worth a drive from Dallas. Think ahead to the three-layer Feed Store Cake, the Acapulco pie, or the toffee mousse when you're selecting your basic lunch; you'll be glad you did. Open Tuesday–Saturday for lunch. $; ☐; (979) 345-6997.

Elmo's Grill. 454 South Seventeenth Street (TX-35), West Columbia. If you're looking for fast, low-cost, no-surprises food, consider this local favorite. No menus here—just bulletin boards listing the normal burgers and Mexican offerings as well as at least one daily special. Open daily for lunch and dinner. $; (979) 345-5127.

Lucy's Mexican Food. 1017 South Columbia Drive, West Columbia. The Tex–Mex here is so popular with local residents that you may have to wait for a table. Both the fajitas and the chicken-fried steak come highly recommended. Open for lunch and dinner Monday–Saturday. $-$$; ☐; (979) 345-5300.

RICHMOND AND ROSENBERG

Enjoy Richmond while you can. Within a decade it may be swallowed by Houston's urban creep, a historic oasis amid acres of subdivisions. For now, just getting to Richmond and its sidekick city of Rosenberg is a pleasure, whether you come north via TX-36 from the Columbias or west on US-90A from Houston. The countryside primarily is farms and ranches, shaded by mature pecan trees and pleasant to pass by any time of the year.

Richmond flows into Rosenberg, the larger of the two towns. An early shipping site on the Brazos, Rosenberg really boomed in 1883, when the railroad came to town. While it remains the commercial center, the two towns have shared a common history for the past century; for day-trippers Richmond is the more historically interesting destination.

In Texas time Richmond is very old, one of the first permanent settlements of Stephen F. Austin's original 300 colonists. For centuries the Brazos River had made a big bend here, each flood leaving more rich soil in its wake. Shortly after Christmas Day 1821, five men staked their fortunes on this fertile land, building a two-room fort just below the bend, thus the name Fort Bend County. Today a marker stands on this site, almost lost between the eastbound and westbound bridges of US-90A as they span the Brazos.

The settlement thrived with the addition of Thompson's Ferry, northwest in the bend of the river, and in 1837 the town of Richmond was formally laid out on the site of the old fort. By 1843 a sugar mill was in operation at nearby Sugar Land, the forerunner of the Imperial Sugar plant, and sugar cane plantations were thriving throughout the area by the 1860s.

Richmond had a number of now-famous residents, among them Mirabeau Lamar, Deaf Smith, and Jane Long. Carrie Nation ran a hotel on the corner of Fourth and Morton Streets before she took up her hatchet-wielding crusade against demon rum.

Visitors find several reminders of Richmond's colonial past, but the overriding feeling is that of exploring small-town America, circa 1940. Somehow it is reassuring to discover a corner drugstore and other small businesses within the shadow of an old-fashioned courthouse. A walk along Richmond's main drag, Morton Street, is a visual antidote to Houston's skyscrapers.

A detailed map guides you along the oak-shaded streets to all the historic sites, courtesy of the Fort Bend County Museum. The maps are available at the museum (see "What to Do" section) or from Rosenberg Tourism Development, P.O. Box 32, Rosenberg, TX 77471; (832) 595-3520; www.rosenbergtourism.com.

WHAT TO DO

Brazos Bend State Park. 21901 FM-762 (Tadpole Road), Needville (20 miles south of Richmond). Turn south on the Crabb River Road exit from US-59 South and follow signs. One of the newest parks in the system, this is 5,000 acres of wild beauty along Big Creek, a tributary of the Brazos. Overnight facilities include screened shelters, trailer sites with hookups, tent sites with water, and primitive sites with no water that require a hike in; almost all are shaded by massive oaks. In addition to two large fishing piers where you can angle for bass, catfish, or crappie, there are hiking/biking and nature trails, several large playing fields, seven photography platforms for "focusing on" the park's exceptional wildlife, and an interpretive center. Rangers lead daily programs, so the center should be your first stop to see what's going on. *Of interest:* Children under seventeen do not need a license to fish in this park. *Caution:* This is alligator country; no one can enter any of the park waters for any reason. All visitors are given a list of alligator etiquette rules when they arrive. A nature trail designed for all, including those with vision, hearing, or mobility challenges, now circles the park's Creekfield Lake. Flat and paved, the trail is 0.5 mile long and has tactile interpretive panels that explain the wetlands ecology. A taped audio tour can be checked out at the park's visitor center. Fee. Park information; (979) 553-5101; www.tpwd.state.tx.us.

Also in the park is the George Observatory, a satellite facility of the Houston Museum of Natural Science that opens at 3:00 P.M. on Saturday. General public viewing through the large telescope is possible from dusk to 11:00 P.M. on summer Saturdays, dusk to 10:00 P.M. in winter. Passes are given out on a first-come, first-served basis beginning at 5:00 P.M. (arrive no later than 4:00 P.M. or you won't get a pass). Several smaller telescopes on the top deck of the planetarium are available for persons without passes. Fee. Adjacent to the observatory, the Challenger Learning Center offers space lore, including a simulated mission to the moon. For information call (979) 553-3400.

Decker Park. North of the railroad tracks at Sixth and Preston Streets, Richmond. Two buildings moved here mark the very slow beginning of a living-history museum: a 1902 railroad depot and the 1850s McNabb House, once owned by Carrie Nation's daughter. The Victorian brick relic across Preston Street was the county jail from 1896 to 1948. It now has been restored to its former architectural splendor and functions as a museum and offices for the Richmond Police. Call for hours and jail tour information, (281) 342-2849.

The Fort Bend County Courthouse. Fourth and Jackson Streets, Richmond. This fifth courthouse was built with an air of majesty in 1908 and was so well refurbished in 1981 that it was cited by the Houston chapter of the American Institute of Architects. It also is the only public building in Fort Bend County listed in the National Register of Historic Places. Notable features are the three-story rotunda, the mosaic tile floors, and the rich woodwork on the stairs and in the main courtroom. Free. Open Monday–Friday.

Fort Bend County Museum. 500 Houston Street, Richmond (at Fifth Street). Just about every aspect of "Life along the Brazos" between 1820 and 1930 is covered here, with displays including items and manuscripts of Mirabeau Lamar, Jane Long, and Austin's first colony. One diorama tells the harrowing tale of early railroad crossings on the Brazos, and special exhibits include the hatchet Carrie Nation used on a Houston saloon in 1905. A clapboard house (known as the Long-Street Cottage) that stood on property owned by Jane Long from 1837 to 1859 is next to the museum; furnished, it gives an excellent picture of 1840s life.

The museum staff also gives demonstrations of frontier skills and guides historical tours of Richmond for groups by advance notice. Closed Monday; (281) 342–6478.

The George Ranch Historical Park. 10215 FM–762 (P.O. Box 1242, Richmond, TX 77406) 8 miles southeast of Richmond. What was life like in rural Texas between 1890 and 1930? This 470-acre living-history project (part of a 23,000-acre working ranch) turns back the years and lets you participate as well. Costumed actors re-create Victorian life at the J. H. P. Davis Home (1896) and more modern times at the George ranch house (1930s); cowboys rope and ride; ranch hands demonstrate cattle-dipping, blacksmithing, woodworking, and so forth; and tractor-drawn carryalls haul you around the grounds. The 1820s Jones Farmstead, an authentically re-created working farm, includes a furnished dog-trot cabin, a barn, a corncrib, croplands, an orchard, and a garden.

Nearly every weekend between Memorial Day and Labor Day has a special theme. Don't miss Texian Market Days the fourth weekend of October. Special events such as rodeos and trailrides can be arranged year-round for corporate meetings, conventions, and private groups. Although there's a small eatery on site, picnickers are welcome. Open daily. Fee; (281) 545–9212 or 343–0218.

Glider rides. This glorious, silent sport now is available in the Rosenberg area. For information call Thrilling Adventures at (800) 762–7464.

John M. Moore House. Fifth and Liberty Streets, Richmond. Built in 1883 on the present Fort Bend County Museum grounds, this gracious old home looks as though it will stand for several more centuries. Now used as a gallery by the museum. Call for exhibit schedule; (281) 342-6478.

Morton Cemetery. On Second Street, north of Jackson Street, Richmond. Used during the 1838–41 period, this is the last resting place of Mirabeau Lamar and the "Mother of Texas," Jane Long.

Museum of Southern History. 14070 Southwest Freeway, Sugar Land. The South *may* rise again. This collection includes muskets, rifles, guns, uniforms, furniture, pictures, money, letters, and other memorabilia relating to both Jane Long and the Civil War. Other exhibits show ship models, maps, and prints. Open Tuesday–Friday and on weekend afternoons. Fee; (281) 269-7171.

Railroad Museum. Corner of Third and Avenue F, Rosenberg. Housed in a replica of an 1883 depot, this family-friendly museum traces the history of Fort Bend County, once home to eight rail lines and a major player in the cattle and cotton industries. Open Tuesday–Sunday. Fee; (281) 633-2846.

Seabourne Creek Park. Highway 36 South, ¼-mile south of US-59. Whenever there's a big celebration in Rosenberg, this 164-acre park plays host. Opened in spring 2001, the park features a four-and-a-half-acre stocked lake with fishing platforms, a 700-foot boardwalk accessing a wetlands basin, and hiking and biking trails; (832) 595-3520.

WHERE TO EAT

Camino Real Mexican Cafe. 4511 Avenue H, Rosenberg. This large spot usually is packed because many locals think it has the best Tex–Mex in town. Open daily for lunch and dinner. $-$$; ☐; (281) 341-1900.

Italian Maid Cafe. 300 Morton Street, Richmond. Delicious pastas, done with an Old-Country touch and served with either salad or soup, are the big draws here. Alternates include daily specials, several unusual soups and salads, and a long list of sandwiches that makes you hungry just to read it. Running short on time? Just pick a menu item noted with an asterisk (*) —you'll be back out day-tripping very swiftly. Open for breakfast Monday–Friday, for lunch Monday–Saturday, for dinner Tuesday–Saturday, and for a brunch buffet on Sunday. $-$$; ☐; (281) 232-6129.

Sandy McGee's. Two locations: 314 Morton, Richmond; and 1207 Sixth Street, Rosenberg. If inventive salads, sandwiches, and daily specials sound appealing, don't miss these charming cafes. Save room for dessert. Open for lunch on weekdays. $-$$; (281) 344-9393 in Richmond, (281) 341-9151 in Rosenberg.

WANDERING THE BACKROADS

An alternate route from Houston to Richmond forsakes US-59 and US-90A and instead rambles west out Westheimer (FM-1093) past its intersection with TX-6 and then turns south (left) on FM-1464. Watch for the Clodine Country Store, opened in 1896 and rebuilt after a 1978 fire. Nearly the last of its kind in the greater Houston area, the store's corrugated tin facade and well-worn front porch draw artists and photographers, as well as folks just wanting drinks, snacks, and chat.

From there continue south on FM-1464 for approximately 8 miles to its intersection with US-90A. A turn west (right) then takes you directly into Richmond's historic district.

To roam among pastures and pecan orchards, go north from Richmond on FM-359 (Skinner Road) and when it curves to the left, stay straight. That puts you on Skinner Lane, one of the prettiest drives around.

Another country ramble takes the long way home. From Richmond turn south on FM-762 (Eleventh Street/Thompson Road) and follow its zigzag southeasterly course through the countryside. Just beyond Crabb, FM-762 turns farther south as the A. P. George Road. Stay on FM-762 as it jogs onto Tadpole Road. At the intersection with FM-1462 at Woodrow, turn east (left) to intersect TX-288 and then north (left) toward Houston and home.

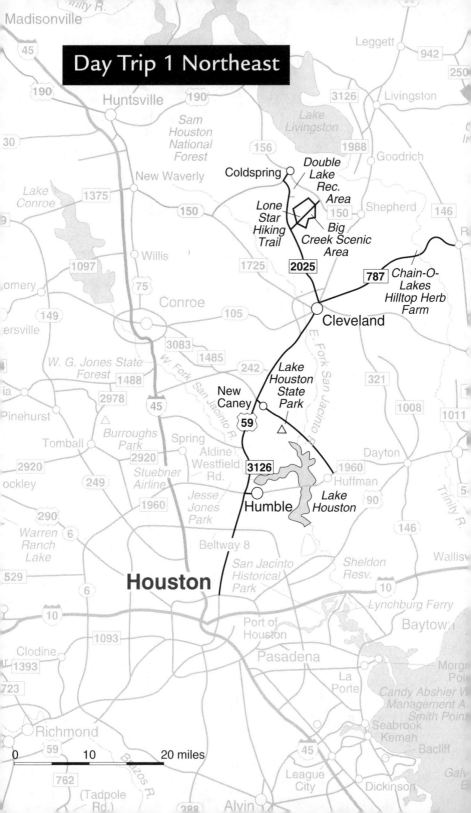

NORTHEAST DAY TRIP 1

Humble · Cleveland
Coldspring

HUMBLE

As with the small town of Spring in north Harris County, there are two Humbles—old and new. The new is easy to find, a plastic forest of franchise signs and shopping centers around the US-59/FM-1960 interchange. Old Humble lies quietly behind, east of the railroad tracks and south of FM-1960.

Back in 1865 a fisherman named Pleasant Smith Humble established a small ferry across the San Jacinto River near where US-59 crosses it today. Things remained quiet until the railroad arrived in 1878, and Humble became a flag stop on the narrow-gauge HE&WT line, running between Houston and Shepherd. Settlers came, and by 1886 Humble was officially a town.

Rich with timber, Humble fed a growing logging industry. Back in 1887 a local lumberman, Jim H. Slaughter, rafted logs down the San Jacinto for milling. Pulling into a small backwater to make an overnight camp, he noticed bubbles seeping along the riverbank. When his match brought a flame, he recognized the presence of natural gas and subsequently bought sixty acres of land in the area. Although he personally didn't profit greatly, this was the beginning of the oil fields in Humble and Harris County.

The first wells came into production in 1904, and by mid-1905 the field was producing more barrels per day than any other in the state. The Moonshine Hill area east of town soon had a population of 25,000, and Humble got busy earning a reputation as one of the toughest towns in Texas. The Texas Rangers often had to be called on to keep some semblance of law and order.

167

In 1909 the Humble Oil and Refining Company was formed in a small, tin-roofed building on Humble's Main Street, one of its organizers being the local feed store owner, Ross Sterling. The company was successful and ultimately became part of the Exxon we now know. Sterling didn't do badly either. He soon bought the Humble State Bank and carved a niche in the state's history as a newspaper publisher, oilman, and governor of Texas from 1931 to 1933.

As quickly as it had come, the oil boom disappeared—no new wells were coming in—and by 1915 Humble once again was a small, quiet community strongly dependent on lumber and agriculture for its financial base. A second oil strike at greater depth in 1929 brought new life, and Humble was chartered as a city in 1933.

Humble's Main Street is now a stroll through struggling small-town Americana, but things are looking up. Fresh interest in restoring Main Street to its original appearance has resulted in several antiques shops, excellent eateries, and a pocket park in the 300 block. The small cottages that line nearby First Street also offer unusual shopping. Stop too at the corner of First Street and North Houston Avenue to see the oldest artesian well in the area, drilled as a wildcat oil venture in 1912. For additional information on the area, contact the Humble Area Chamber of Commerce, 110 West Main (P.O. Box 3337), Humble, TX 77347; (281) 446–2128; www.humbleareachamber.org.

WHAT TO DO

Humble Historical Museum. 219 Main Street. A grassroots result of America's bicentennial, this small museum is bursting with a collection of interesting old things donated by local residents. Open Tuesday–Saturday. Free; donations appreciated; (281) 446–2130.

Jesse H. Jones Park. 20634 Kenswick Drive. From US–59 North go west 1.7 miles on FM–1960 and turn right on Kenswick Drive; the park is at the end of the road. This large wilderness preserve on Cypress Creek has ten hiking trails, a frontier fort–styled playground and picnic area, a pioneer homestead, and a three-acre beach on the creek for fishing (no swimming); with a Texas fishing license, you can angle for white bass, crappie, catfish, and alligator gar. Nature photography is popular here, as are birding and canoeing. About 85 percent of the trails are black-topped for use by the handicapped. Birders can pick up a list at the Nature Center Building, which also has wildlife exhibits, including common poisonous snakes and a cut-away look at a working beehive. On one weekend a month, September to May, the park offers free guided canoe tours on Spring Creek. The four-hour Saturday tour goes from Mercer Arboretum to Jones Park; the one-hour Sunday tour goes two miles from the park to the US-59 bridge. On that same Saturday the park also offers free one-hour pontoon-boat tours for those interested in natural history and bird-watching. Call for full information. Open daily; (281) 446-8588; www.cp4.hctx.net/jones.

Lake Houston. The best play places (picnicking, swimming, boating) are Dwight D. Eisenhower Park and Alexander Duessen Park, both near the dam. Take the Duessen Drive exit from the Sam Houston tollway, and follow signs.

Lake Houston State Park. Take New Caney exit from US-59, go east approximately 2 miles on FM-1485, then turn right on Baptist Encampment Road; the park entrance will be 1.5 miles down on the left. Don't rev your boat motors or load your fishing gear; in spite of its name, this 4,913-acre park has no lake frontage. It's an outstanding spot, however, for birding, hiking and biking (12 miles of trails), and—thanks to hot showers—tent camping. A small, white-sand beach on Peach Creek offers shallow-water play for children. There also are 8 miles of separate equestrian trails, but so far it's BYO horse. Open daily. Fee; (281) 354-6881; www.tpwd.state.tx.us.

Old McDonald's Farm. 3203 FM-1960 East (2.5 miles east of Deerbrook Mall). When the pint-size natives get restless, spend the day in this kiddie paradise. Admission ($6.00 for adults, $5.00 for children) includes pony and train rides, petting and feeding animals in twelve barns, playing in a mountain of sand, jigging for crawfish in a pond, swimming, milking the cow, and gathering eggs. In addition to food concessions, there's also a shady picnic area to use if you bring food from home. Open weekends November–February, daily March–October; (281) 446-4001.

Tour 18. 3102 FM-1960 East (2 miles east of US-59). There are hundreds of golf courses in the greater Houston area, but none other like this $5-million layout. In toto it re-creates eighteen of the greatest holes in the nation, a par-72, 6,807-yard challenge engineered across 200 acres. Want to test your skills against the pros on the 17th at Sawgrass? No. 14 at Pebble Beach? Nos. 11 and 12 at

Augusta? Come try what may be the most difficult course in the
country. Tee times can be arranged up to thirty days in advance.
Open daily. Call for fees. ☐; (281) 540-1818; www.tour18golf.com.

WHERE TO EAT

Brown Bag Lunch. 106 South Avenue B. If you haven't time to pack
a weekday picnic, call these folks instead; they'll have it ready when
you come by. Their sandwiches come on a variety of breads, plus they
offer design-your-own croissants and tortilla wraps, soups, salads,
and some very tasty desserts. Open weekdays until 3:00 P.M. $; ☐;
(281) 540-2233.

Chez Nous. 217 South Avenue G. In addition to a menu that features many French classics, chef-owner Gerard Brach and his wife,
Sandra, offer outstanding daily specials such as fresh Dover sole or
swordfish in an avocado-lime butter or pineapple salsa. French-born
and -trained, Gerard also has taught a wine course at the Four Seasons in New York City, expertise that shows on the wine list. This
jewel of a restaurant is in an unlikely setting, a century-old church.
You'll want to dress up for this dining experience. This restaurant is
worth a trip to Humble if you enjoy fine food prepared with skill and
care. Open Monday–Saturday for dinner; reservations strongly
advised. Ask for specific directions when you call; it's hard to find.
$$-$$$; ☐; (281) 446-6717.

Fuel Cyber Cafe. 120 Main Street. This place dispels the theory
that all the cool spots are located within the I-610 Loop. Patrons
come here to play video games and down massive quantities of caf-
feine. You'll find frappes and lattes of every flavor imaginable,
shakes, and other specialty drinks. Feeling youthful? Try the teen-
centric Peanut Butter & Jelly smoothie, a concoction of strawberries,
peanut butter, strawberry yogurt, vanilla protein, and honey. Open
evenings Thursday–Saturday, with concerts featuring local garage
bands many nights. Cover charges some nights; $; ☐; (281) 540-
3170; www.fuelcybercafe.com.

Hasta la Pasta Italian Grill. 202 FM-1960 East bypass, in the
Corum Humble Shopping Center. Marvelous aromas from the kitchen
start those juices flowing the instant you enter this nicely styled
eatery. In addition to the classic pasta dishes, the emphasis is on
marinated chicken, beef, pork, and fish that are then grilled over a

combination of oak and pecan. Very popular with Humble's business community. Open daily for lunch and dinner. $–$$; ☐; (281) 446-6414.

Humble City Cafe & Bakery. 200 Main Street, at Avenue A. What was the town's old drugstore (built in 1914) has been restored to its original porch-and-balcony appearance to house this popular cafe. Food is Texas home-style stuff, and the portions exceed generous; come hungry. Open Monday–Saturday for breakfast, lunch, and dinner; Sunday until 3:30 P.M. $–$$; ☐; (281) 319-0200.

Menciu's Gourmet Hunan. 1379 Kingwood Drive, Kingwood (in the Kingwood development north of Humble via US-59). Popular with local residents, this family-run place uses only fresh foods to prepare its tasty dishes. The menu is long, so move first to the suggestions in the New Creations section, all of which are cooked with fresh ingredients and original to this restaurant. Second tip: One of the most popular dishes on the regular menu is the Triple Delight. Budget-watchers: The Early Bird Special menu (3:00–7:00 P.M., Sunday–Thursday) offers twenty-two combination plates in the $6.95–$8.25 range, and the lunch specials are excellent values. Open Tuesday–Sunday for lunch and dinner. $–$$; ☐; (281) 359-8489.

The Railroad (Italian) Cafe. 105 Railroad Avenue. This tiny, somewhat shy-looking little building is thought to be the oldest structure still standing in Humble, a concrete symbol of the town's name. You'll be tempted to pass on by, and that would be a huge mistake, because inside is one of the best Italian restaurants in the Houston area. The creative stamp of chef-owner Wayne Falgiano is everywhere—in the quiet chic of the carpeted room, the fresh flowers on the ten tables, the interesting art on the walls, and in the ravishingly fragrant scents coming from the kitchen. Between chats with customers, Falgiano turns out flawless, highly personal versions of Italian specialties such as gnocchi verdi, carciofo, and osso buco, and some surprises as well. Maiale alla Modenese, for example, is a pork loin wrapped in sage and braised in a Chianti wine sauce and cream. Then there's Anitra Frangelico—broiled duck breasts served with a Frangelico cream sauce—and a memorable fresh salmon baked with a sauce of fresh basil, pine nuts, olive oil, garlic, and Parmesan. His pastas and classic Italian desserts also are outstanding. The menu begins, as all good meals should, with an extensive list of Italian wines, including six affordable ones by the glass. Open for lunch Tuesday–Friday; dinner Tuesday–Sunday. $$–$$$; ☐; (281) 319–6244.

Trigg's Cafe. 1712 First Street (at Wilson Road). A bright spot in an otherwise undistinguished shopping center east of the business district, this family-run place offers an all-you-can-eat buffet on Sunday (11:00 A.M. to 3:00 P.M.; $7.95) that draws diners from miles away. The menu also offers steaks, barbecue plates, salads, sandwiches, and assorted fried fish, all in abundant portions for the price. Open for breakfast, lunch, and dinner daily. $–$$; ☐; (281) 540–4801.

Trigg's Humble Inn. 1410 First Street. Hearty breakfasts all day at prices that won't hurt your wallet are the rule here, followed by equally inexpensive sandwiches, burgers, soups, salads, stews, steaks, seafood, and pizzas. Open for breakfast, lunch, and dinner Monday–Saturday. $–$$; ☐; (281) 446–9484.

The Veranda. 2820 Chestnut Ridge, Kingwood. From Kingwood Drive turn left at the first light and go 3 blocks. When cost is no object and exceptional food is your desire, try this small treasure of a restaurant. Selecting from the extensive menu is challenging, but consider two of the house specialties: Veal Veranda (stuffed with prosciutto and topped with lump crabmeat, provolone, and herbed hollandaise) or the grilled Australian lamb chops, frenched and served on a mix of caramelized tomatoes, onions, and mushrooms with mint jus. The crusty-topped crème brûlée is made daily with fresh vanilla beans. Open nightly at 6:00 P.M.; reservations strongly recommended. $$$; ☐; (281) 358–2820.

CONTINUING ON

From Humble it's approximately 28 miles north via US–59 to Cleveland.

CLEVELAND

Back in the 1880s this railroad town on US–59 north of Houston thrived with lumber shipping. Now it is better known as the main gateway to the forest and water wonderland that covers most of San Jacinto County. Entrances to the Lone Star Hiking Trail are marked on FM–1725 and FM–945 near Cleveland, and the Greater Cleveland Chamber of Commerce, 222 South Bonham Avenue, has a brochure listing activities in the area: Box 1733, Cleveland, TX 77328-1733; (281) 592–8786.

Art lovers will enjoy viewing the mural on the face of St. Mary's Church on Highway 105/321, immediately south of the business district. Painted by Arturo Moyers in honor of the millennium, it is entitled *Back to Our Roots; Toward the Future* and appears to be three dimensional.

WHAT TO DO

Berry picking. If you come in early summer, consider picking a year's supply of blueberries at Chain-O-Lakes Blueberry Farm, (281) 592–2150. You also can pick your own blueberries, peaches, plums, apples, and watermelons at Lidiak Farm; (713) 453–6121.

Chain-O-Lakes Resort & Conference Center. One Country Lane. Although no longer open to day visitors, this woodsy retreat welcomes overnight visitors for bed-and-breakfast or camping on weekends (two-night minimum). Lodgings are in authentic log cabins with fireplaces, central air and heat, lofts, and decks with porch swings. Breakfasts are at the adjacent Hilltop Herb Farm (see "Where to Eat"), and horse-drawn carriage rides link the two seasonally. Activities include fishing (no license required), swimming in a two-and-a-half-acre spring-fed lake, hiking, and nonmotorized boating. More than 300 campsites are scattered over nearly as many acres of pine and hardwood forest, with centrally located hot-shower bathhouses, a laundromat, and a general store. Call for rates and directions; (832) 397–4000; www.colresort.com.

Christmas tree farms. Call for directions to the following: A & W Trees, (281) 592–5307; D Bar D Christmas Tree Farm, (936) 628–3114; Keith's Christmas Tree Farm, (281) 592–5032; and the Prairie Merry Tree Farm, (281) 592–1935.

WHERE TO EAT

Hilltop Herb Farm at Chain-O-Lakes Resort. One Victorian Place. From Cleveland go 18 miles east on FM–787; after passing the Trinity River Bridge, turn right on CR–2132 (Daniel Ranch Road) and follow signs to Chain-O-Lakes Resort and Conference Center. Delicious food based on the creative use of herbs is the rule here, along with tours of the herb garden and cooking classes. Call to get on the special-events mailing list. The gift shop sells homemade jams, jellies, chutneys, and herbal teas—you'll want to buy some mint-touched Tranquilitea mix for home. Open by reservation only for breakfast, lunch, and dinner, Monday–Saturday; ask for directions and the day's menu when you reserve. *Note:* Drop-ins generally cannot be served. $-$$$; ❑; (281) 592-5859 or (832) 397-4020; www.colresort.com.

CONTINUING ON

The drive to Coldspring is a day-tripper's delight. From Cleveland take FM-2025 north for 17 miles; then turn east on TX-150 and go another 2 miles. This takes you through a major portion of the Sam Houston National Forest. An alternate route leaves US-59 North at Shepherd and follows TX-150 West 11 miles to Coldspring.

COLDSPRING

This old community (population 569) was called Coonskin when it was founded in 1847. Now the San Jacinto County seat, it is showing signs of life as a budding tourist center. Most of the structures on Main Street were built between 1916 and 1923, the courthouse in 1918. Many of those vintage structures now house antiques and gift shops. There are numerous historical markers in Coldspring, including one on the United Methodist Church (1848), one of the oldest Methodist churches in Texas. Good times to come: Thursday through Saturday, when most of the shops are open, and on Trades Day (arts, crafts, antiques), the fourth Saturday of every month, March- November; (936) 653-2184. For information, contact the Coldspring Chamber of Commerce, P.O. Box 980, Coldspring, TX 77331; (936) 653-2184; www.coldspringtexas.org.

WHAT TO DO

Big Creek Scenic Area. From Cleveland continue on US-59 North 12 miles to Shepherd, then west on TX-150 for 6 miles to Forest Service Road 217. Part of the 350,000-acre Big Thicket that spatters across vast sections of Southeast Texas, this 1,130-acre preserve has numerous hiking trails, wild and varied topography, spring-fed creeks, and abundant wildlife. One segment of the 140-mile Lone Star Hiking Trail (foot traffic only) begins near Montague Church on FM-1725 and loops through the scenic area on a 25-mile jaunt to a trailhead on FM-945. Information: Sam Houston Ranger District, 394 FM-1375 West, New Waverly 77358; (936) 344-6205; www.fs.fed.us.

Christmas tree farms. This is good tree-cutting country in November and December; call the following for directions: Iron Creek Christmas Tree Farm, (936) 767-4541, www.ironcreek.com; or Skyvara Family Christmas Trees, (936) 767-4961.

Double Lake Recreation Area. On FM-2025, 15 miles north of Cleveland. This twenty-five-acre lake is edged by picnic and camping areas and has boat rentals, a beach, and a bathhouse with showers. No large motorboats are allowed, but canoeing is popular. Boat rentals are available seasonally; call. Stocked with bass, bream, and catfish, this also is a great place to take kids fishing. One 5-mile path through the woods links Double Lake with the Big Creek Scenic Area and the Lone Star Hiking Trail; (936) 344-6205; www.fs.fed.us.

Old Town Heritage Center. Coldspring's original Courthouse Square is now home to a small but interesting museum in the old 1880s jail (usually open Thursday–Saturday or by appointment, 409-653-2009) and the transplanted Waverly schoolhouse, circa 1926; the latter now houses an antiques co-op. Other memorabilia are scattered around the grounds, including an old Ford fire engine and the replica of a blacksmith shop; (936) 653-2009; www.oldtowncoldspring.tripod.com.

WHERE TO EAT

Elaine's Restaurant. P.O. Box 289, Point Blank (on TX-150 West in downtown Coldspring). One of the main nerve centers for this small town, this family-run place cuts its own steaks and also puts on a good lunch buffet and salad bar. Open daily for breakfast, lunch, and dinner. $-$$; ☐; (936) 653-4929.

The Hop. P.O. Box 1193, Coldspring (on TX-150 West). Good spot for hamburgers, shakes, and pizza. Open for lunch and dinner daily. $; (936) 653-4889.

M'Honeys. On the square in Coldspring. The offerings here include soups, sandwiches, salads, and desserts. Open for breakfast and lunch on weekdays. $; (936) 653-4845.

Sharon's Cafe. Three-quarters mile west of the courthouse. Expect the East Texas cafe basics here: oilcloth on the tables, plastic-coated menus, large servings, and a friendly staff. In addition to the expected lunch offerings, the house excels at hand-breaded shrimp and onion rings, fried catfish, and chicken-fried steak. Open for lunch and dinner Tuesday–Saturday. $-$$; (936) 653-3777.

WANDERING THE BACKROADS

From Coldspring you can continue west on TX-150 and connect with I-45 at New Waverly (Trip 2, Northwest sector). From there continue your travels by turning north (right) on I-45 to Huntsville (Trip 2, Northwest sector). If it's time to go home, head south on I-45; from New Waverly it's 55 miles to the Houston city limits.

An alternative: If you want to visit the Lake Livingston area (Trip 2, this sector) from Coldspring, take TX-156 North to its intersection with US-190 and turn east. From Livingston take US-59 South to home.

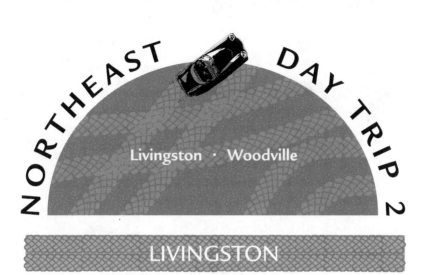

Livingston · Woodville

LIVINGSTON

A fire wiped out three downtown blocks around the turn of the twentieth century, so little is left of Livingston's beginnings back in 1846. Today this timber town is 76 miles north of the heart of Houston via US–59. The seat of Polk County, it is important to day-trippers in several ways. Shoppers come to town for Livingston's Trade Days, held monthly on the weekend preceeding the third Monday of each month. For information call (936) 327–3656.

Every fall the forest around Livingston resembles the rolling hills of western Massachusetts when the frosts bring up the color in the maple, sassafras, oak, sweet gum, sumac, and hickory trees. One of the town's biggest attractions is 90,000-acre Lake Livingston, 15 miles west of downtown. The lake primarily is an impoundment of the Trinity River, and there are three short but beautiful river-float trips possible below the dam. Put-ins for canoes are at the dam, at the US–59 crossing south of Livingston, and at FM–105 near Romayor. The final takeout is at the FM–162 crossing east of Cleveland.

All of Polk County is crossed with old Indian traces, the remains of which are indicated by highway signs. For information on Lake Livingston or the general area, contact the Polk County Chamber of Commerce, 505 North Drew, Livingston, TX 77351; (936) 327–4929. You also will find useful information on-line at www.livingston.net/chamber and www.cityoflivingston-tx.com.

Should you linger too long in the area, you may be interested in the Milam Home Bed and Breakfast in Livingston. The B&B features

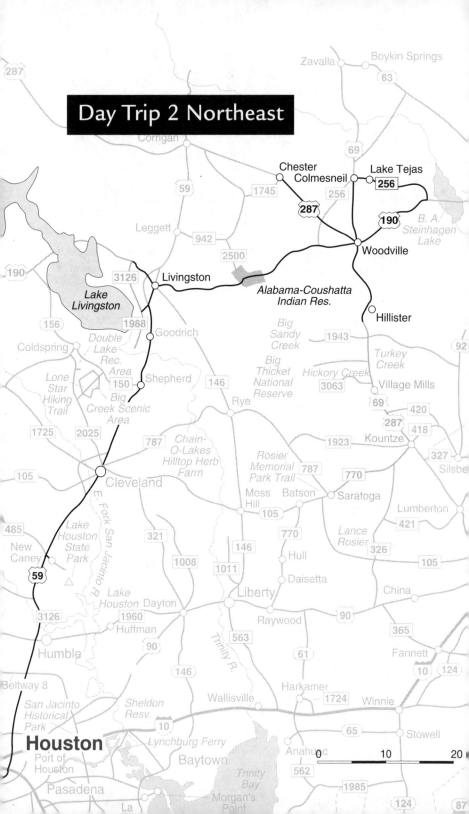

an inviting wraparound porch and four antiques-filled, well-appointed rooms; (936) 327–1173; www.milamhome.com.

WHAT TO DO

Alabama-Coushatta Indian Reservation. Route 3 (on US–190, 17 miles east of Livingston). Established by Sam Houston in 1854, this 4,600-acre reservation in the Big Thicket offers a camping/recreation/tourist complex that has been challenged in recent years.

The tribe, along with the Tiguas in El Paso and the Kickapoo in Eagle Pass, has spent the past several years trying to gain legislative approval for a casino, which proponents say would produce millions in revenue annually. (The Alabama-Coushatta opened a small casino in late 2001 that remained open for eight months before a federal judge's order shut down its 349 slot machines. Before it closed, according to reports, the casino was averaging 4,000 visitors a day and generating more than $1 million monthly for the cash-poor tribe.)

If and when the Alabama-Coushatta get approval for the casino, the tribe plans on building a major gaming center with 3,000 slot machines, 120 gaming tables, and a hotel.

As it stands now, the reservation offers only limited appeal for day-trippers. There's twenty-six-acre Lake Tombigbee, a nice place for quiet camping, picnicking, and swimming. Canoeing and fishing for bass, perch, and catfish are also popular.

More than one hundred species of trees are native to this reservation, including eight varieties of oak, the state champion water hickory and laurel oak, and a huge 200-year-old magnolia.

Tours of the reservation and the Big Thicket in open-air buses are available during a handful of weekends during the summer. Some days visitors can take in tribal dances.

If you're interested in learning about Native American culture, plan your visit for June when the Alabama-Coushatta hosts an annual powwow featuring dance and drum competitions, an Indian arts and crafts market, and other festivities. Fee.

The tribe mans two gift shops, one located on Park Road 56 in the village. The other is in the Shell Station on US–190, just a few miles west of the village. (The Shell Station also boasts a snack bar serving Indian fry-bread.) At the gift shops, you will find for sale some of the

Alabama-Coushatta's beautiful baskets, woven from needles of the rare longleaf pine. Many have lids and are shaped like animals, and all are considered collector's items. Some rare, old baskets also are displayed in the Polk County Museum in Livingston.

The reservation is open daily in the summer, more sporadically in the winter. Call ahead; (936) 563-1329; www.alabama-coushatta. com.

Blueberry farms. You can pick a year's supply at reasonable cost at Sandy Foot Farm, (936) 327-2744. Hamilton's Berry Farm has blackberries as well, (936) 563-4910. *Note:* Blueberry season is late May through July 4.

Johnson's Rock Shop. 5810 Indian Springs (10 miles east of Livingston off US-190 in the Indian Springs Lakes Estates; call for directions). You'll see more than 1.5 million pounds of rock, and just about that many varieties, as well as the equipment used to cut, polish, and finish same. Visitors are welcome, and there's no fee for a personal tour. Open daily; (936) 563-4438.

Lake Livingston. From Livingston take US-59 South 2.5 miles and turn west on FM-1988, then north on FM-3126 to Park Road 65. There is good public access through 640-acre Lake Livingston State Park, open daily (fee). Facilities include a swimming pool, paddle and boat rental, an activity center, hiking and biking trails, horseback riding, picnic areas, campsites, and screened shelters. Private resorts, marinas, and campgrounds along this route offer fishing guides or rent boats. Information: Route 9, Box 1300, Livingston, TX 77351; (936) 365-2201, or call the Lake Livingston Area Tourism Council, (800) 766-5253.

You'll also find major fishing action on the Trinity River immediately below the Lake Livingston Dam. The lake itself has a large shad population, and those passing through the dam locks into the turbulent pool below the dam become feeder fish for incredible numbers of striped and white bass, crappie, and catfish. Fish numbers in this pool are so high that the Texas Parks and Wildlife uses the pool as a source for their restocking program on other state-owned waters. In addition to bank and wade fishing, there's a cable stretched across the river for boats to use as a tie-down. *Caution:* The water force is very strong with dangerous currents. Western access is via FM-3278 East from TX-150, south of Coldspring; eastern access from US-59 is via FM-1988.

Polk County Memorial Museum. 514 West Mill Street, Livingston. Exhibits focus on the early days of Polk County, and there are some interesting Indian artifacts. You may want to hunt up the tiny Jonas Davis log cabin across the street. Donation. Open Monday–Friday; (936) 327-8192.

WHERE TO EAT

Florida's Kitchen. From US-59 in Livingston go west 1 mile on US-90, then turn left on FM-350 South for 0.7 mile; cafe will be on the right. Hard to find but worth the hunt, this simple place serves plentiful and delicious ribs, barbecue, catfish, hamburgers, chicken-fried steak, and other standards. Thursday night is all-you-can-eat ribs; Friday night is all-you-can-eat catfish. Open for lunch and dinner Wednesday–Saturday. $–$$; ☐; (936) 967-4216.

Lone Star Charlie's Family Restaurant. 101 Queens Row Street (1 mile south of Livingston on the east side of US-59). A favorite with truckers, this clean and homey spot serves the usual road-food standards, along with homemade cobblers. Good place if you're on a budget and traveling with children. Open for breakfast, lunch, and dinner daily. $–$$; ☐; (936) 365-3017.

Out to Lunch Cafe. 413 North Washington. This spot is known for its made-from-scratch sandwiches, soups, daily specials, and desserts. Open for lunch Monday–Friday. $; (936) 328-8100.

Shrimp Boat Manny's. 1324 West Church (1 block east of the US-59 bypass). This eatery specializes in seafood prepared Cajun-style. Manny and Nancy Rachal are from Lafayette in "Luziana" and serve a mean étouffée, boiled and fried shrimp, raw and fried oysters, and seafood gumbo. Open daily for lunch and dinner. $–$$$; ☐; (936) 327-0100.

The Texas Pepper. 930 US-59 North Loop. One of the most popular and pleasant eateries in the region, this spacious place serves choice steaks cut on the premises—they hand-bread the country-fried steak as it is ordered and then cook it in peanut oil. They also smoke their own barbecue meats and prepare their Mexican dishes from scratch. Open Monday–Saturday for lunch and dinner, Sunday from 11:00 A.M. to 2:00 P.M. $–$$; ☐; (936) 327-2794.

CONTINUING ON

This day trip now follows US-190 due east for 33 miles through the forest to Woodville.

WOODVILLE

Although history has been relatively quiet here, the town has some surprises in store for visitors who take the time to poke around. Not only are there twenty-one historical markers in the area, but the entire town also is a bird sanctuary. So rich is the birding here that the Woodville-Angelina National Forest-Steinhagen Lake areas provide seven stops on the Big Thicket Loop of the Great Texas Coastal Birding Trail map (upper coast). Woodville also is the northern gateway to the Big Thicket National Preserve.

Founded in 1846–47 as the county seat for the newly created Tyler County, Woodville is aptly named because it is surrounded by miles of rolling forest. The prettiest times to visit here are in late March, when the Tyler County Dogwood Festival stirs things up a bit, and again in fall, after the first cold snap coats the woods with color. Brochures, maps, and updates on the current status of spring or fall scenery are available weekdays or by mail from the Tyler County Chamber of Commerce, 717 West Bluff (US-190), Woodville, TX 75979; (409) 283-2632; www.woodvilletx.com. The courthouse in the heart of town is interesting, as are the antiques shops around the square.

WHAT TO DO

Allan Shivers Library and Museum. 302 North Charlton (2 blocks north of the courthouse). The late Governor Allan Shivers had his roots in Woodville, and this restored Victorian showplace houses his papers as well as memorabilia of the Shivers family and the town. Fee. Open Monday–Saturday, Sunday by appointment; (409) 283-3709.

Big Thicket information. The north district office of the Big Thicket National Preserve is at 507 Pine. Open Monday–Friday, when staff is available; (409) 246-2337; www.nps.gov/bith/.

Blueberry farms. June and July are prime picking months at Mott's Blueberry Farm; (409) 429-3196.

Boykin Springs Recreation Area. From Zavalla go southeast 11 miles on TX–63, then south (right) 2.5 miles on FSR–313. Some 30 miles northeast of Woodville and pushing the limits of Day Trips territory, this nine-acre lake offers swimming, canoeing, and camping (no hookups; fee). Its primary value, however, is as a richly diverse habitat for woodland birds, particularly in the spring and summer. Watch for at least three types of sparrows, painted buntings, and red-cockaded woodpecker groups. Lovely in itself, this longleaf pine forest also is extremely rich in wildlife. Hikers should investigate the 5.5-mile-long Sawmill Trail that links Boykin Springs Recreation Area with Bouton Lake Recreation Area. Adventures along the way include an old sawmill site, explorations of the Neches River bottomlands, and crossing a long swinging bridge over Big Creek. For trail information contact the Texas Forestry Association, (409) 632–8733; www.texasforestry.org. Open daily. Parking fee; (409) 639–8620.

Dogwood Trail. This 1.5-mile walking trail along Theuvenins Creek is maintained by Louisiana-Pacific. Watch for its sign 3 miles east of Woodville on US–190.

Exotic Cat Refuge and Wildlife Orphanage. Kirbyville (Trip 3, this sector).

Heritage Village Museum. US–190 West (P.O. Box 888, Woodville, TX 75979) 1 mile west of Woodville on US–190. Never underestimate the power of people with a mission. When it looked like Woodville's best-known tourist attraction might either close or move in 1987, the Tyler County Heritage Society turned local pockets inside out to buy the property and its restaurant.

Now what was a weathering conglomeration of early Americana is an interesting outdoor museum devoted to Texas history in general, Tyler County and Big Thicket territory in particular. Visitors wander through a replica of a small town, composed of a number of homely historic structures and some artifacts of early pioneer life (barbershop, blacksmith shop, syrup mill, whiskey still, pawnshop, apothecary, newspaper, etc.). Walking-tour maps are available at the office.

A well-done historical musical, *Whispers in the Wind,* turns the village green and surrounding buildings into an open-air stage the last two weekends in June. Costumed to the changing periods, this locally written and produced play follows three generations of a family from the time they settle in East Texas in the 1830s to the coming of the railroad in the early 1900s. Music is live, the horses and old covered wagons are real, and the audience almost becomes part of the show. Tickets ($) can be charged. For all information call (409) 283–2272 or (800) 323–0389.

Another "don't miss" event, the Harvest Festival and East Texas Folklife Festival on the third weekend of October, fills the village with costumed craftspeople demonstrating all the old-time skills. Although smaller in scale, the quality equals that of the Texas Folklife Festival in San Antonio.

Whenever you plan a jaunt this way, call the general information number above in advance to see if a special event is on; Heritage Village hosts several types of music festivals several times a year.

Walkers note: Eleven and a half acres of neighboring woodlands are threaded with trails. The Heritage Society also owns and operates the Pickett House restaurant (see "Where to Eat"), and the gift shop specializes in East Texas handcrafts and art. Want a quilt or pine-needle basket? How about an inlaid domino set? This may be the place. Open daily except major holidays; call to confirm. Fee; (409) 283–2272 or (800) 323–0389; www.heritage-village.org.

James Edward Wheat House. At the corner of Charlton and Wheat Streets. One portion of this house was built in 1848. It is a private residence, but you are welcome to enjoy it from the street.

Lake Tejas. Eleven miles north of Woodville via US–69, then east 1 mile on FM–256 in Colmesneil. When summer's heat hits our neck of the woods, this super swimming hole is the place to be. The sand-bottom lake has a two-level dive platform, sundecks over the water, lifeguards, bathhouse, concession stand, tubes, and paddleboats. Operated by the local school district, the lake is open on May weekends and daily from June to Labor Day. *Note:* Picnicking and camping are available year-round. Fee; (409) 837–2763 weekdays.

Martin Dies Jr. State Park. On the eastern shore of the B. A. Steinhagen Lake, 14 miles east of Woodville on US–190. This 705-acre retreat offers camping (with and without hookups); screened shelters; hiking trails; swimming in two designated areas; fishing for crappie, bass, and catfish; two lighted fishing piers; five boat ramps; and numerous opportunities for wildlife observation, birding, and photography. Visitors also find an interpretive nature center and amphitheater, plus canoe/boat rentals at nearby marinas. Conservation specialists often guide canoe field trips along the Angelina-Neches River. Fee. For information contact Route 4, Box 274, Jasper, TX 75951; (409) 384–5231 or (800) 792–1112; www.tpwd.state.tx.us.

River floating. B. A. Steinhagen Lake, east of Woodville on US-190, also is known as Dam B, an impounding of the Neches River. If you are interested in floating on the Neches below the dam, call the U.S. Army Corps of Engineers at Steinhagen Lake, (409) 429–3491, for a report on conditions.

WHERE TO EAT

The Highlander. 708 South Magnolia (US-69). Ever had Snicker pie? Marinated chicken-fried steak you can cut with a fork? A hot smoked-turkey sandwich with cheese and guacamole? Those are just a few of the well-prepared offerings created by chef-owner Martha Stark. She also makes a memorable New Orleans–style bread pudding with whiskey sauce that will bring you back to Woodville again and again. Open for lunch daily; dinner Thursday–Saturday. $-$$; (409) 283–7572.

The Homestead Restaurant. On US-69, Hillister. Two refugees from Houston, Emily and Otho Sumner, offer country dining with a gourmet touch in a spacious old home they have restored. Built around 1912 in nearby Hillister, the house was moved by the Sumners to its present thirteen-acre shady site and fixed up with charm, including rockers and a swing on the porch. In addition to some nice touches on the standard fish/steak/chicken offerings (the broiled catfish is outstanding), the Sumners make their own salad dressings. Every entree is prepared to order, and it's all-you-can-eat homemade chicken and dumplings on the first Sunday of the month; ditto boneless skinless chicken breasts (batter dipped and fried) on the second Sunday. Because Emily Sumner is a pie lover, she produces an ever-changing selection of unusual pies, such as Toll House, coconut cream, buttermilk pecan, chocolate gold brick, double fudge, and lemon icebox.

While reservations are not essential, they are strongly advised, particularly if you want to sit in a room cleverly adorned with vintage clothing. No liquor is served, but glasses and ice buckets are provided for diners who wish to bring their own wine. Open for dinner Friday and Saturday; lunch only on Sunday. $-$$; ◻; (409) 283-7324. The Sumners also operate The Getaway, a fully equipped guest retreat on the banks of Theuvinens Creek, 6 miles from their restaurant. Available to nonsmoking adults only, this two-bedroom house has a fireplace, a screened porch, and a great fishing hole in bass territory. Don't count on just dropping in; these digs often are booked months in advance; (409) 283-7324 (restaurant); 283-7244 (cottage).

Pickett House. Two miles west on US-190, behind Heritage Village. This old schoolhouse has been converted into an all-you-can-stuff-in kind of place, with bright circus posters on the walls and family-style service. Authentically replicating an East Texas boardinghouse experience during the 1840–1900 period, this eatery serves huge bowls of food family-style (fried chicken, chicken and dumplings, and three veggies) and your choice of fresh buttermilk or made-from-scratch iced tea, watermelon-rind preserves, corn bread, hot biscuits, fruit cobbler, and bread pudding. It's fetch your own drinks and then take your dirty dishes to the kitchen, just like home. Open daily for lunch March–November; dinner on Saturday and Sunday. Closed Monday and Tuesday December through February. Hours fluctuate seasonally; call (409) 283-3371. $-$$; ◻; www.heritage-village.org.

Texas Best. On the south side of US-190, 0.5 mile west of Woodville. Loaded with country atmosphere, this small spot offers barbecue, steaks, sandwiches, salad bar, as well as all-you-can-eat spreads of fish and shrimp on Friday and Saturday. Open for lunch and dinner Monday–Saturday. $-$$; ◻; (409) 283-5249.

Texas Star. 205 North Wheeler, Colmesneil. Stop at this big red barn for country cafe-type food: char-grilled hamburgers, chicken-fried steak, and even surf and turf. Open for lunch and dinner daily. $-$$$; ◻; (409) 837-4444.

The Tree Restaurant. On Highway 69, 8 miles south of Woodville in Hillister. Sharing quarters with a Diamond Shamrock station is an unlikely venue for a good spot to eat, but that's just the case here. Owners Martin and Cindi Riley specialize in open-flame grilling over mesquite and hickory, and the resulting steaks are well worth stopping for. Their menu also runs to breaded shrimp, sandwiches, and plate lunches; the pies and cobblers are made on-site. They prepare tasty takeout, or you can be served outside under the giant oak that gives this eatery its name. Open daily for lunch and dinner. $-$$$; ☐; (409) 283-8040.

WANDERING THE BACKROADS

If you need a swift return home from Woodville, retrace your route back to Livingston via US-190 and turn south on US-59.

From Woodville, however, you can drive northwest on US-287 to the small community of Chester and make a 1.6-mile jog north on FM-2097 East to see Peach Tree Village, composed of lumber tycoon John Henry Kirby's mansion (now a museum) and the community meetinghouse/chapel, built in 1912. Although drop-in visitors are welcome, advance notice helps ensure that both buildings will be open when you visit. The site is an old Alabama Indian headquarters camp called Ta Ku La, and two trails blazed by pioneers crossed here. Recently refurbished as a retreat and summer youth camp, Ta Ku La makes a pleasant picnic destination. For information or to arrange a tour or group retreat, call (936) 969-2455.

Another scenic drive takes you from Woodville to Saratoga and Big Thicket National Preserve (Trip 3, this sector). Take US-69/287 South from Woodville to Kountze, swing southwest on TX-326, and turn right on FM-770 to Saratoga, in the heart of the Big Thicket. To continue home to Houston, follow FM-770 South to US-90 and turn west.

Although the wild azalea canyons near Newton are beyond the geographic scope of this book, they are well worth viewing during their pink and white blooming season, which usually comes in late March. Tip your hat to the Temple Inland for preserving these beauties, and tread carefully; bird's-foot violets, cinnamon fern, and jack-in-the-pulpit wildflowers may be underfoot. Newton is 48 miles east-northeast from Woodville via US-190. For information contact the Newton Chamber of Commerce, Drawer 66, Newton, TX 75966; (409) 379-5527; www.newton-texas.com.

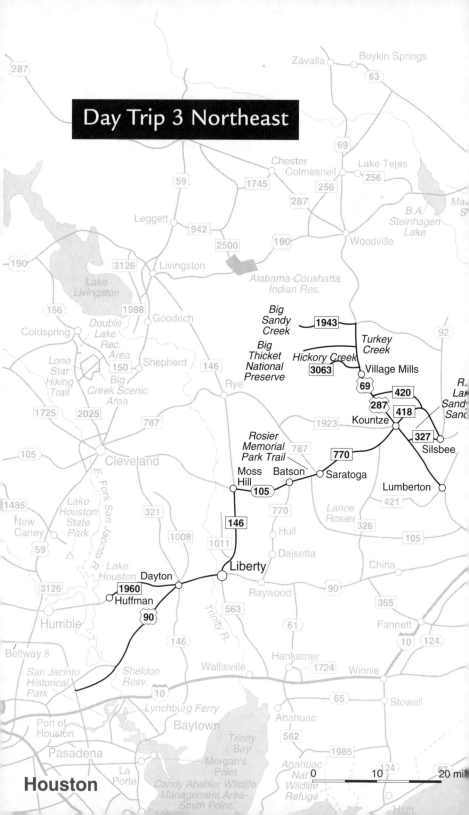

LIBERTY AND DAYTON

Although this area, east of Houston on US-90, is rich with history, much of what survives remains privately owned, and the towns have little to illustrate their heritages to the general public. Take away the historical markers, and the casual tourist might conclude that nothing much has happened here—which is far from the truth.

Originally this entire corner of southeast Texas was called the Atascosito District, a municipality first of Spain and then of Mexico. Now broken into ten counties, the district was built around the outpost of Atascosito, shown as a freshwater spring on maps as early as 1757. To reach the original site of Atascosito today, take TX-146 northeast from Liberty approximately 4 miles and turn west (left) on FM-1011. A marker is just beyond the intersection, and the spring still flows nearby.

After 1821 this wilderness was controlled by Mexico, and Anglo settlers were welcome. For the most part early settlers were independent individuals who came here because they could not gain grants through Austin's colonization farther to the west. They formed settlements like Liberty and Dayton as well as many other places whose names have faded from map and memory.

The Atascosito Road crossed the district, running from Goliad and Refugio to Opelousas, Louisiana. Now its route is roughly paralleled by US-90, and the town of Dayton straddles the historic path.

In 1831 the Villa de la Santissima Trinidad de la Libertad was established slightly south of the spring and officially laid out with six public squares. Now called Liberty, it traditionally is considered to be the third oldest town in Texas.

A map available from the chamber of commerce will direct you to most of the sites of interest, including the Cleveland-Partlow House (1860), 2131 Grand (private); and the T. J. Chambers Home (1861), 624 Milam (private). Graveyard historians love Liberty—there are at least four historic cemeteries in the area. For information contact the Liberty-Dayton Chamber of Commerce, Box 1270, Liberty, TX 77575; (936) 336-5736; www.libertydaytonchamber.com.

Six miles west on US-90 and across the Trinity River is Dayton. It was first called West Liberty and then Day's Town in honor of an early settler, I. C. Day. Originally a lumber and agricultural community, Dayton got financial boosts with the coming of the railroad in the 1870s and oil strikes in the early 1920s. Visitors now find some vintage buildings slowly being filled with interesting shops. As you pass through, take time to read the historical marker concerning the Runaway Scrape (Trip 3, West sector). This marker is on the eastern outskirts of Dayton on US-90 East.

Day-trippers living north or east of Houston can now access this area by taking the Sam Houston Parkway (Beltway 8) to US-90 East.

WHAT TO DO

Christmas tree farms. If you are en route to Dayton or Liberty in late fall, you can pick out your Christmas tree at Hatcher's Christmas Tree Farm (near Liberty), (936) 389-2387; and Keith's Christmas Trees (Dayton), (281) 592-5032.

Cleveland-Partlow House. 2131 Grand, Liberty. Built around 1860 and curated by the Sam Houston Regional Library and Research Center, this vintage home is open to visitors on Tuesday from 9:00 to 10:00 A.M. or by appointment. Fee; (936) 336-5488.

Geraldine Humphreys Cultural Center. 1710 Sam Houston Street, Liberty. An active little theater, the Valley Players, puts on plays and musicals here. For the current playbill call (936) 336-5887. A contemporary bell tower houses an exact replica of the famous Liberty Bell, cast in 1960 by a London foundry from the original pattern and mold. The bell rings twice a year—on New Year's Day and again on the Fourth of July during an old-fashioned Independence Day celebration on the center grounds.

Free. Open Monday–Thursday and on Saturday; (936) 336–8901 (Liberty Library).

Huffman Horse Auction. 7903 FM-1960 East, Dayton (on FM-1960 East, 7 miles east of Lake Houston, 4 miles east of Huffman, and 7 miles west of Dayton; mail goes to P.O. Box 30164, Houston, TX 77249). When you see a big red barn fronted by a large parking lot, you've found a piece of pure redneck Texana. It's open all day on Saturday, but the real action starts at 7:00 P.M. with the auction of tack, then used saddles, then trailers, mules, horses, and ponies. Just watching and walking through the livestock barns is worth the trip, and nonbidding visitors are very welcome. Consider having a pre-auction dinner next door at the Horseshoe Cafe (see "Where to Eat"); (936) 258–9333.

Liberty Opry on the Square. 1816 Sam Houston Avenue, Liberty. If you enjoy live country-and-western music laced with liberal servings of gospel, don't miss this family-oriented, three-hour show featuring musicians from throughout the state. The venue is Liberty's former movie theater (circa 1935), complete with plush red velvet seats, and the curtain goes up on Friday and Saturday evenings year-round. Call for reservations. Fee; (936) 336–1079; www.libertyopry.com.

Old French Cemetery. Approximately 3 miles east of Dayton on FM-1008. Established in 1830, this is the burial place of some of the early settlers of the Atascosito District. One grave notes an 1821 death; others are enclosed inside antique iron fences.

Sam Houston Regional Library and Research Center. P.O. Box 310, Liberty, TX 77575. Go 4 miles north of Liberty via TX-146 and turn northwest (left) on FM-1011. Appropriately sited near the original settlement of Atascosito on a high knoll shaded by mature pecan trees, this massive repository is owned by the state and operated free of charge to the public by the Texas State Library. Within its fireproof vaults are valuable historical records, documents, portraits, and other artifacts of the original Atascosito District, most of which can be accessed by special request.

This also is one of the state's least-known and most interesting museums. There are three public display rooms full of goodies like Jean Lafitte's personal diary and other remnants of the days when Liberty was a major steamboat port on the Trinity River. *Genealogists note:* This library has reprints of the Atascosito census of 1826, valuable because it lists the maiden names of wives.

Several interesting structures dot the museum's grounds: the historic Gillard-Duncan Home (1848), restored and furnished to its period; the Norman House (circa 1883), with changing exhibits drawn from the library's vaults; St. Stephen's Episcopal Church (1898), used for meetings; and the Price Daniel family home, filled with antiques and mementos of former Texas Governor Price Daniel's political years. Admission to the first three structures mentioned is free and available by request when the library is open. Tours of the Price Daniel family home require two weeks' advance notice, but they're worth planning for. Patterned after the original 1856 governor's mansion in Austin, this 6,300-square-foot home is furnished with American Empire antiques. Displays also include the Sam Houston family china, furniture from one of Sam Houston's homes (no longer extant) in Liberty County, and the four-poster bed upon which Sam snoozed the night before the Battle of San Jacinto. Free. Open Monday–Saturday; (936) 336-8821.

Sheldon Lake State Park and Education Center. 14320 Garrett Road, Houston (via Sam Houston Parkway/Beltway 8). Only 13 miles from downtown Houston's skyscrapers and currently improving as a state park, this public preserve covers 1,200 acres of water, 400 acres of marsh and swampland, and slightly more than 600 acres of rice/milo/soybean farmland. The latter is food for an estimated 10,000 ducks and geese that winter at this refuge; huge flocks often are easily viewed from Garrett Road. In addition several heron/egret rookeries exist on barrier islands along the lake's western edge.

Although you can fish from the banks and five fishing piers daily year-round, the lake is open for boat and wade fishing only from March 1 through October (no motors over 10 hp), so as not to disturb the migrating birds. Catches include bass, crappie, sunfish, and three species of catfish. *Note:* This is alligator territory—no swimming. Park rangers are available weekdays at the above address; (281) 456-2800; www.tpwd.state.tx.us.

A free, 600-acre Environmental Education Center opened in late 1998 at 15315 Business US-90 at the southern edge of the park. It offers small displays focusing on park wildlife; a gift shop filled with nature-related items; two fishing ponds for children (open Saturday and Sunday; catch-and-release); and extensive hiking and birding. The staff also conducts fishing clinics, nature hikes, and other outdoor activities for groups (fee). Open Tuesday through Sunday; (281) 456-2800; www.tpwd.state.tx.us.

WHERE TO EAT

Cedar Landing. 10614 FM-1960 East, Huffman. Overlooking Lake Houston at the east end of the FM-1960 bridge, this pleasant place has ribeye steak on the menu, but its real specialty is regional seafood fixed just about every way that's been thought up. If you love fried shrimp, come Tuesday through Thursday for all-you-can-eat ($13.95). Open for dinner Tuesday-Thursday; lunch and dinner Friday-Sunday. $-$$$; ☐; (281) 324-1113.

Jose's Mexican Restaurant. 901 West Clayton Street (FM-1960 East), Dayton. A convenient stop if you're headed home from exploring Beaumont or the Liberty area, this clean and colorful place puts a few flourishes on the standard Tex-Mex menu, plus it also serves "gringo" dinners, salads, and both a half-pound hamburger and breast of chicken sandwich. Open for lunch and dinner daily. $-$$; ☐; (936) 258-5887.

Nina's Diner. 710 US-90 West, Dayton. Breakfast all day is the specialty at this simple place, and lunch specials run to homemade chicken and dumplings, meat loaf, hamburgers, and other Texas standards. Open for breakfast, lunch, and dinner on weekdays; breakfast and lunch on Saturday. $-$$; (936) 258-2998.

CONTINUING ON

This day trip moseys on to the Big Thicket via Moss Hill, Batson, Saratoga, Kountze, and Silsbee. From Liberty take TX-146 north 15 miles to Moss Hill, turn east (right) on TX-105 to Batson, and then northeast (left) on FM-770 to Saratoga and Kountze.

Moss Hill is a farming and ranch area, named for the Spanish moss draped in the surrounding woods. Batson was a small village called Otto prior to the discovery of the Batson Oil Field in 1903 and was the scene of the Batson Round-Up, in which all the unmarried women were gathered up and auctioned to prospective husbands. It's a bit of a racy story—ask locally or check out the faded pictures of the event at Heritage Village in Woodville (Trip 2, this sector).

SARATOGA, KOUNTZE, AND SILSBEE

Saratoga was named for the famous New York spa because it had several medicinal hot springs. A hotel catering to the health seekers burned decades ago, but some of the old foundation still can be found. No word on the fate of the hot springs. Saratoga today is one of the gateways to the Big Thicket.

Kountze got its start with the railroad's arrival in 1881 and owes its continued existence to the lumber industry. The county seat, Kountze soon will be home to the headquarters of the Big Thicket National Preserve.

Silsbee sprang to life when lumber baron John Henry Kirby established a sawmill here in 1894. For comprehensive information on the entire Big Thicket area, contact the Hardin County Tourist Bureau, P.O. Box 400, Kountze, TX 77625; (409) 246–8000 or (800) 244–8442; www.indianspringscamp.net/HCTB.

If you decide you'd like to overnight in the Big Thicket area, consider a stay in an 1840 dog-trot cabin at the Pelt Farm Bed and Breakfast; (409) 287–3300; www.peltfarm.com.

WHAT TO DO

Big Thicket Visitor Information Center. From US-69/287 turn east on FM-420, 7 miles north of Kountze. This new facility will be on your left. If you don't know the Big Thicket, start with this center's slide show, and then study the exhibits detailing the plant and animal life that makes this 86,000-plus-acre national preserve so special. Ask specifically about ranger-led activities, hikes, walks, floats, and canoe routes. Open daily; (409) 246–2337.

Exotic Cat Refuge and Wildlife Orphanage. HC 3, Box 96A, Kirbyville (located 16 miles north of Buna off US-96; call twenty-four hours in advance for an appointment and specific directions). A rural spot in the East Texas woods is a good place to house jaguars, bears, lions, wolves, cougars, several species of tigers, and assorted birds. This nonprofit, federally sanctioned refuge is a permanent home and rehabilitation facility for wild animals that have been confiscated by law enforcement officers as abused or via drug raids. Visitors receive guided, up-close tours among the habitats. *Of interest:* These animals devour $7,000–$10,000 worth of food every month, and the annual medical bills often exceed $25,000. Donations are this facility's lifeblood; it receives no federal funds. Although there is no admission or tour fee, a donation is greatly appreciated. Open Tuesday–Saturday; (409) 423-4847; www.exoticrefuge.org.

Fruit farms. You can pick a variety of things at these various Hardin County patches: B & M Farms (near Silsbee; blueberries in June; jelly kitchen open daily in summer, Monday/Wednesday/Friday the rest of the year), (409) 385-1200; Clegg Blueberry Farm (near Buna), (409) 994-2549 or 994-3425; Ethridge Farms (near Kountze; mayhaws in April, blueberries in June and early July; satsuma oranges, kumquats, and lemons in November), (409) 246-3978; and Lack's Blueberry Farm (Kountze), (409) 246-2193 or 246-3770.

Indian Springs Camp. 6106 Holland Cemetery Road (P.O. Box 32), Kountze. From US-69 between Kountze and Woodville, turn west on Post Oak Road for 1 mile, north (right) on Holland Road for 0.8 mile, and right on Holland Cemetery Road to the first drive on the left; watch for signs. This 200-acre bit of nature offers more than 3 miles of nature trails, a long stretch of frontage on Village Creek, and plenty of Big Thicket wilderness for city folks to experience. Day visitors are welcome ($3.00 per person), and activity options include fishing, picnicking, canoeing, swimming, and walks. Additional fees apply for use of a campground with tent sites and RV hookups; cabins with bunk beds, ceiling fans, and electricity; a bathhouse with hot showers; and a lodge with kitchen that's great for reunions or group retreats. Owners Ronnie and Brenda Stockholm also offer a summer camp for children; (409) 246-2508 or (800) 942-7472; www.indianspringscamp.net.

Kirby-Hill Home. 210 West Main Street, Kountze. This 1902 Victorian mansion is under restoration and open Tuesday–Sunday for tours (call for hours). Fee; (409) 246-8000 or (866) 244-8442.

Silsbee Ice House Museum. 818 Ernest Avenue (at Fourth Street), Silsbee. Housed in the community's old icehouse, this cultural center displays the work of local artists (new shows monthly) and includes a small museum focused on Hardin County history. Open weekdays; (409) 385-2444.

Village Creek State Park. On Alma Drive, off US-96 in Lumberton. This 942-acre facility has more than 1 mile of frontage on Village Creek and is densely forested, an excellent example of Big Thicket terrain. Facilities and activities include camping (some hookups for RVs), picnic areas, hiking, canoeing, birding, fishing, and swimming; several sandbars along the creek make ideal beaches. Floods are common here, which means there are baygalls (small swamps) within the park boundaries. Wildlife is abundant—expect a multilevel frog chorus at night—and more than sixty species of birds have been seen in a single day. This park is a good put-in or take-out spot on a Village Creek float; if you don't have your own canoe, contact one of the outfitters listed in the Big Thicket "What to Do" section. P.O. Box 8575, Lumberton; (409) 755-7322; www.tpwd.state.tx.us.

WHERE TO EAT

Restaurant listings follow in the next section, The Big Thicket.

THE BIG THICKET

The Big Thicket National Preserve is often described as the biological crossroads of North America. It is a unique place, comprised of four major ecosystems where the flora and fauna mix from all points of the compass. Ferns, orchids, dwarf palmettos, mushrooms, several types of pine, four types of insect-eating plants—the abundance and variety of this particular mix is unequaled anywhere else on our globe.

Unfortunately, many folks visit what they think is the Big Thicket and go home wondering what all the shouting is about. The problem is that there are twelve Big Thicket areas in all, and you have to know where to look to find them. The preserve is composed of eight land sections and four river/stream corridors and spreads out over 86,000 acres and seven counties. The beautiful, biologically unique portions lie well away from the highways. Just driving through won't do.

The above statistics refer to acreage already within the national preserve. In general terms the Big Thicket covers 3.5 million acres of Southeast Texas, including portions of Harris County.

All Texans love a tall tale, and the Big Thicket has its share. One concerns the Kaiser Burnout near Honey Island near Kountze. Local residents called Jayhawkers who had no sympathy for the Confederate side of the Civil War hid out in the woods to escape conscription. Charged with capturing them, Confederate captain James Kaiser set a fire to flush them out. Two were killed in a later skirmish, and the rest vanished once again. Some claim the descendants of those Jayhawkers still live in the depths of the Big Thicket. As more people explore this wilderness, there may be an update on the story.

Then there's the mysterious light that spooks travelers on the Bragg Road, a pencil-straight graded lane that follows the old railroad right-of-way between Saratoga and Bragg. Sometimes called a ghost or the "Saratoga light," it appears as a pulsating phenomenon and has been seen by enough people to warrant serious investigation. Some say it is the ghost lantern of a railway worker killed on the old line; other, less imaginative types claim it's swamp gas or the reflected lights of cars on a nearby highway. Whatever, it adds to the Big Thicket mystique. Now protected as the Ghost Road Scenic Drive County Park, this spooky drive begins at a bend in FM-787 that is 1 mile north of the FM-787/FM-770 intersection in Saratoga and runs almost due north for approximately 10 miles to FM-1293.

In addition to the backroads route to the Saratoga area listed in the preceding day trip, Houstonians have several other ways of getting to the Big Thicket. The most direct route follows US-90 East to a left turn onto FM-770 North at Raywood, continuing to Saratoga. An alternative is to take I-10 East to Hankamer, then go north on TX-61 to US-90; turn west and go 4 miles to FM-770, then north to Raywood.

Depending on what unit of the Big Thicket you want to visit, there also is access from Woodville, Kountze, Cleveland, and Beaumont. A good state map is indispensable, as are maps and guides of the area itself. Pick up the latter at the Big Thicket Information Center (previously mentioned) north of Kountze or request in advance by contacting Big Thicket National Preserve, 3785 Milam Street, Beaumont, TX 77701; (409) 839-2689; www.nps.gov/bith/. Do remember that this is a young park, developing slowly on limited funds, and that many of the areas are recovering still from people's earlier abuse. *Note:* There are no accommodations within the preserve.

WHERE TO GO

The National Park Service operates twelve units within the national preserve's sprawling boundaries: Turkey Creek, Beech Creek, Hickory Creek Savannah, Big Sandy Creek, Lance Rosier, Neches (River) Bottom/Jack Gore Baygall, Beaumont, Upper and Lower Neches Rivers, Pine Island/Little Pine Island Bayou, Loblolly, and Menard Creek. For information, maps, and trails listing, stop at the Big Thicket National Preserve Visitor Information Center on FM–420, immediately east of US–69/287 between Warren and Kountze (open daily, except Christmas and New Year's Day); (409) 246–2337.

The Nature Conservancy operates the Roy E. Larsen Sandylands Sanctuary near Kountze. Guided hikes for groups can be arranged by contacting P.O. Box 909, Silsbee, TX 77656; (409) 385–0445; www.nature.org.

The following units are the most easily accessed:

Beech Creek, off FM–2992 southeast of Woodville, is a 4,856-acre plant community composed of beeches, magnolias, and loblolly pines. Unfortunately, a 1975 beetle epidemic killed almost all the loblolly pines, so the forest is not as pretty as it once was. The Beech Woods Trail, a 1-mile loop, passes through a mature stand of hardwoods.

The **Big Sandy Creek** unit includes a rich diversity of plant and animal life. The 5.4-mile Woodland Trail, at the northwestern edge of the unit (near the Alabama-Coushatta Indian reservation), covers a floodplain, dense mature mixed forest, and upland pine stands. The trail entrance is not well marked, 3.3 miles south of US–190 on FM–1276. The trail also offers two shorter loops and is one of the closest to Houston. *Equestrians and all-terrain bikers, take note:* This unit also offers an 18-mile trail designed specifically for horseback riding, hiking, and mountain biking. This trail often is closed during the November–January hunting season, however; call (409) 246–2337 to check.

The **Hickory Creek Savannah** unit, 0.5 mile west of US–69/287 via FM–2827 and a dirt road, combines the longleaf pine forest and wetlands with the dry, sandy soil found in the uplands. This is great wildflower territory in spring. The Sundew Trail (1 mile) is open to the public, and there also is a 0.25-mile loop designed for the handicapped, the elderly, and those pushing strollers.

Roy E. Larsen Sandylands Sanctuary is on TX-327, 3 miles east of Kountze. Although it is considered an excellent example of the arid sandylands, it has 9 miles of frontage along Village Creek. The canoe float from FM-418 to TX-327 has some good swimming holes and white sandbars; about three hours long in paddling time, it is one of the most popular outings in the park (see Boating section under "What to Do" for canoe livery services). If you prefer to walk, a 6-mile trail is open daily, and interpretive brochures are available at the trailhead. Guided tours for groups can be arranged by writing to P.O. Box 909, Silsbee, TX 77656, or calling (409) 385-0445; www.nature.org.

Turkey Creek is noted for changing habitats and carnivorous plants and is best accessed from the visitor information center on FM-420, mentioned above. The Kirby Nature Trail loops out nearby, primarily a 1.7- or 2.4-mile walk to Village Creek. Persons interested in insect-devouring carnivorous plants should ask directions to the Pitcher Plant Trail, and those seeking a longer hike should ask how to connect with the 15-mile Turkey Creek Trail, which rambles the length of the unit.

WHAT TO DO

Biking. Mountain bikes are permitted only on the 18-mile-long Big Sandy Trail.

Birding. Excellent, particularly from late March through early May, when hundreds of species pass on their way north up the Mississippi flyway. The Big Thicket is one of the first stops on the upper Texas coast section of the Great Texas Coastal Birding Trail.

Boating. Guided fishing and sight-seeing trips on the Neches River can be arranged through Timber Ridge Tours, (409) 385-4700. Small watercraft can be launched at several places on the Trinity River, Neches River, Pine Island Bayou, and both Village and Turkey Creeks; road crossings generally provide access. Water levels fluctuate; check before you make firm plans. The national preserve often organizes free trips with a naturalist guide; you must bring your own canoe, life jacket, paddles, and the like. The preserve provides shuttle service at the end of the trip back to the starting point. Reservations required; (409) 246-2337 or 839-2689.

Exploring Big Thicket waterways on your own can be difficult. There are few takeouts, and much of the land bordering the creeks is privately owned, which makes visitors subject to trespass charges. Seek advice and equipment from one of the following canoe livery services: Sharp's Canoe and Kayak rentals in Silsbee, (409) 385-6241; Eastex Canoe Trails and Timber Ridge Tours in Silsbee, (409) 385-4700, www.eastexcanoes.com; Piney Woods Canoe Co. in Kountze, (409) 246-2602, www.canoetexas.com; Village Creek Canoe Rentals in Kountze, (409) 246-4481; or Whitewater Experience in Houston, (713) 774-1028, www.whitewaterexperience.com.

Camping. Primitive backpacking is allowed by free permit from the National Park Service in the Turkey Creek, Beaumont, Jack Gore Baygall/Neches Bottom, Beech Creek, Big Sandy, and Lance Rosier units, as well as the Upper and Lower Neches River corridors; (409) 246-2337. *Note:* All primitive camps must be at least 200 feet from trails. There are no developed campgrounds within preserve boundaries.

Fishing. Allowed in all waters. A license is required, and state regulations apply.

Hiking. Wear sturdy, water-repellent boots. This is rain country at certain times of the year, and the shady trails often have standing water. Mosquito repellent is an absolute necessity. Unleashed pets and motorized vehicles are not permitted on any of the trails, and please register your hike at the trailhead. Be aware that cougars and wild boars may be in the park. Request in advance a list of hiking trails from the visitor center listed previously.

Hunting and trapping. Allowed in specific areas. Permit required. For information and season details, write to the National Park Service, 3785 Milam, Beaumont, TX 77701, or call (409) 839-2689.

Naturalist activities. National Park rangers offer an extensive program that includes talks, guided hikes, and canoe trips. Reservations are required; (409) 246-2337.

Picnicking. Many sites throughout the park, some with fire grates; all are shown on the park map available at the visitor center. Open fires, tree or brush cutting, and wood collecting are prohibited, and bringing your own water is strongly advised.

Photography. There is a great range of natural subjects, particularly if you use macro or long lenses. Most of the beautiful things are found in deep shade, so bring a tripod and high ISO film. Several outstanding photographic books on the Big Thicket are available at Houston libraries and bookstores to start your creative juices flowing.

Swimming. Although there are no designated swimming areas within the Big Thicket, many people enjoy a dip from the Lakeview sandbar area of the Neches River in the Beaumont unit and from numerous sandbars along the Neches River and Village Creek.

WHERE TO EAT

The Cottage. 5125 Old Evadale Highway (1 block north of US-96), Silsbee. This small, ten-table eatery has been serving more than 1,000 folks every week for as long as anyone can remember. Serving "most everything folks are hungry for," they peel more than fifty pounds of potatoes every morning just for the french fries. Menu choices include catfish, steaks, shrimp, burgers, sandwiches, and salads. Open Monday–Saturday 8:30 A.M. to 9:00 P.M. $–$$; (409) 385-9057.

The Highlander. Woodville (Trip 2, this sector).

Homestead Restaurant. Hillister (Trip 2, this sector).

Jack and Sue's Catfish. 205 West Avenue N, Silsbee. Locals recommend this place for its daily lunch buffet and the catfish, but the menu stretches to Belgian waffles as well as filet mignon. Open daily until 2:00 P.M. for breakfast and lunch. $–$$; ☐; (409) 385-3685.

Mama Jack's Restaurant. 215 Pine Street (US-69), Kountze. Owned and watched over by Barbara and Jerry Jackson, this popular eatery specializes in full buffets of home-cooked–style foods, as well as hamburgers and sandwiches. Open daily for breakfast and lunch until 3:00 P.M. $; ☐; (409) 246-3450.

Munchie's Olé. 1198 North Fifth Street, Silsbee. Mexican food lovers will find lots of house specials here, including shrimp fajitas and owner Chris Urbena's Christo Dinner. Open daily for lunch and dinner. $–$$; ☐; (409) 385-5003.

Pickett House. Woodville (Trip 2, this sector).

Red Onion Restaurant. 120 Candlestick, Lumberton. Tucked away behind Wal-Mart, this popular eatery dishes up home-cooked specialties such as chicken and dumplings, grilled pork chops, pot roast, veggie soup, and so on. There's a huge daily all-you-can-eat buffet, with many fish entrees featured on Friday. On a low-fat diet? Look for the green spoons on the buffet. Tiny appetite? Check out the chef specials (smaller portions) for $4.99. No surprise that local folks voted this the best restaurant in the area in 1992. Open daily for lunch and dinner. $-$$; ◻; (409) 755-7422.

Texas Best. Woodville (Trip 2, this sector).

The Tree. Hillister (Trip 2, this sector).

West Texas Bar-B-Que. 3078 US-96 North, Silsbee. (Send mail to 8603 Bussey Road, Silsbee, TX 77656.) It takes four cords of mesquite every month to fuel the smoke pits at this family-run spot. A favorite with the Big Thicket's NPS rangers, the flavorful meat's so tender it often falls off the fork. Locals also love the homemade pies—they buy more than 150 every Thanksgiving. Open for lunch and dinner Monday–Saturday. $; (409) 385-0957.

Wildwood Cafe. Inside the Wildwood Resort development. Entrance is on the west side of US-69/287, midway between Warren and Kountze; ask for specific directions at the entrance gate. This clean, tiny place on the edge of Wildwood Lake makes a great hamburger stop when you're roaming around the Big Thicket. Open for lunch and dinner Tuesday–Saturday. $-$$; (409) 834-6251.

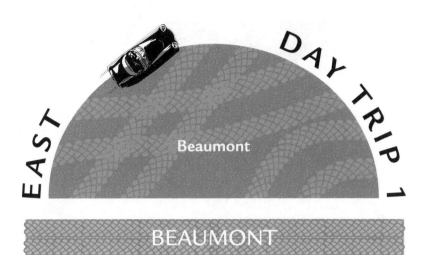

BEAUMONT

The prospect of a day trip to Beaumont may evoke all the wild enthusiasm usually reserved for kissing your sister. But a little exploration in and around this river city may change your mind. There are a surprising number of things to do, not only in Beaumont proper but in the surrounding Golden Triangle area (Beaumont/Orange/Port Arthur). From Houston there's only one way to get there—due east on I-10.

Although history hasn't painted the town with the color found in Austin's cradle country west of Houston, Beaumont is equally old. The first land grant by Mexico to an Anglo in Texas was issued to Noah Tevis and covered 2,214 acres of richly forested area along the Neches River. Today that is downtown Beaumont. By 1825 there was an active trading post here, and Jefferson County, of which Beaumont is the county seat, is one of the original counties formed by the Texas Republic in 1836. Since that time Beaumont has made its own brand of history in several ways.

Most vivid and important to modern America was the Lucas gusher at the Spindletop oil field in January 1901, the greatest oil well in history. Almost overnight Beaumont grew from 8,500 souls to 30,000 folks with advanced cases of oil fever, and a wooden shantytown called Gladys City was hammered into instant life on Spindletop Hill. By the end of that decade, the oil was gone, and Gladys City was a ghost town of wooden shacks. Those glory days live again in the re-creation of Gladys City, 0.5 mile north of its actual site, at Beaumont's successful bicentennial project.

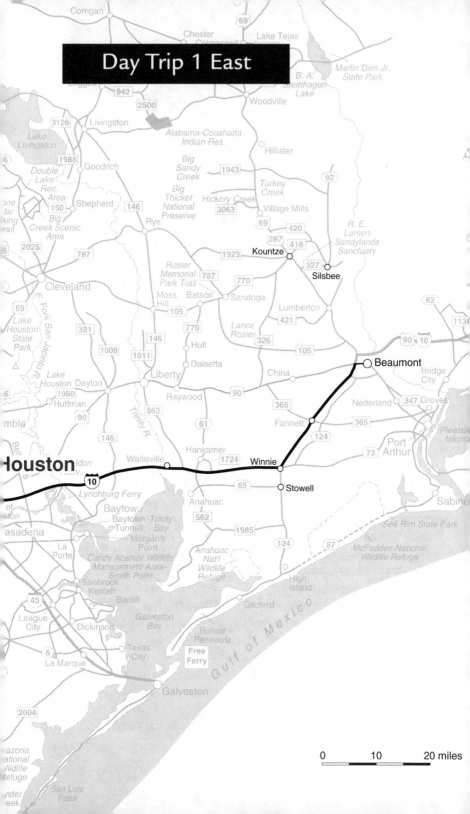

Day Trip 1 East

Economically linked with the volatile oil and petrochemical industry, Beaumont has had its ups and downs in recent years. By the late 1960s shifting financial fortunes had created another ghost town of sorts in the downtown area. But that scene slowly is changing, thanks to major commitments from public and private sectors. During the past decade more than $120 million worth of capital improvements have been made downtown, including new municipal and county government complexes. Work remains under way on multimillion-dollar hotel and office projects, and the $5-million Art Museum of Southeast Texas regularly draws raves. Other commercial projects involve the restoration of classic buildings listed in the National Register of Historic Places.

For free maps, brochures, and advice, stop at the Visitor Information Center in the Babe Didrikson Zaharias Memorial (MLK exit 854 from I-10). Open daily; (409) 833-4622. The Beaumont Convention and Visitors Bureau is another good source, 801 Main Street, City Hall, Suite 100, Beaumont, TX 77701; (409) 880-3749 or (800) 392-4401; www.beaumontcvb.com.

WHAT TO DO

Art Museum of Southeast Texas. 500 Main Street. This handsome, $5-million museum showcases a wide variety of nineteenth- and twentieth-century American art. Exhibits change every six weeks. Open daily. Free. Also here: Cafe Arts (see "Where to Eat" listings); (409) 832-3432; www.amset.org.

Babe Didrikson Zaharias Museum and Visitor Center. P.O. Box 1310, Beaumont, TX 77704 (MLK exit 854 from I-10). In her time this outstanding woman athlete put Beaumont on the map, and the town repaid her with a love and admiration that live on beyond her death from cancer in 1956. This memorial museum chronicles a life and career that saw her six times named Woman Athlete of the Year by the Associated Press. Free. Open daily; (409) 833-4622; www.babedidriksonzaharias.org.

Beaumont Botanical Gardens and The Warren Loose Conservatory. 6088 Babe Zaharias Drive (in Tyrrell Park off Fannett Road [TX-124] on western outskirts of Beaumont). Whether you love flowers or just want to stretch your legs, this ten-acre demonstration garden (free) and its adjacent conservatory (fee) are worth a stop, particularly in spring. Opened in late 1997 and specializing in tender tropicals, the conservatory is the second-largest such facility in Texas. The gardens are open daily from dawn to dusk, but the conservatory is open only on weekends and by advance arrangement. Tyrrell Park also includes a 900-acre constructed wetlands known as Cattail Marsh. Although not always accessible or attractive, it generally provides extensive refuge for numerous aquatic animals and reptiles as well as more than 350 varieties of birds. This park also provides camping, playgrounds, picnic areas, an eighteen-hole golf course, and riding stables. Call the latter for hours and fees; (409) 842–3135; www.beaumontbotanicalgardens.com.

Beaumont Police Department Museum. 255 College Street, downtown. This unique collection of weaponry and other law enforcement paraphernalia dates from the turn of the twentieth century. Open weekdays. Free; (409) 880–3825.

Blueberry farms. Call the following for directions to pick-your-own berry patches: Dishman Brothers Berry Farm, (409) 752–2161; Griffin's Farm, (409) 753–2247; and Lazy D Berry Farm, (409) 296–2882.

Canoeing. Why not take a paddle on the Neches or Sabine Rivers? These rental and livery services provide paddles, life jackets, maps, and basic instruction: Eastex Canoes in Silsbee, (409) 385–4700, and Timber Ridge Tours in Kountze, (409) 385–4700.

Christmas tree farms. Places to cut your own tree in Chambers, Jasper, and Jefferson counties include: B's Christmas Tree Plantation, (409) 794–1593; Beavers Christmas Tree Farm, (409) 253–2372; Dugat Tree Farm, (409) 296–2255; Five "O" Evergreens, (409) 994–3686; K & K Evergreen Farms, (409) 746–2412; Reaves Christmas Tree Farm, (409) 746–2522; and Spell's Golden Triangle Trees, (409) 746-3615.

Clifton Steamboat Museum. P.O. Box 20115, Beaumont, TX 77720 (south of Beaumont on TX–124; call for directions). Opened in 1995, this attraction honors military and civilian heroes with exhibits relating to the Republic of Texas, the Civil War in Southeast Texas and Southwest Louisiana, the steamboat era, and World War II. Visitors also tour a 1938 tugboat, the *Hercules,* and a replica of the Sabine Pass lighthouse and keeper's dwelling. The latter includes a restaurant. Call for information and hours of operation. Fee; (409) 842-3162.

Crockett Street Entertainment and Dining District. Beaumont's beleaguered downtown got a much-needed boost in 2002 with the opening of this $13-million-plus complex spread across five historical buildings. The complex with its brick-paved streets and ornate details includes a huge dance hall, a steak house, a Mexican restaurant, a pub, and a handful of other eat-ertainment venues.

The Edison Plaza Museum. 350 Pine. What was once the old Travis Street substation of Gulf State Utilities now houses various adventures in electricity, including inventions of Thomas A. Edison. Open Tuesday–Friday from 1:00 to 3:30 P.M. and by appointment; (409) 981–3089.

Exotic Cat Refuge and Wildlife Orphanage. Kirbyville (Trip 3, Northeast sector).

The Fire Museum of Texas. 400 Walnut (at Mulberry). This 1927 fire hall now contains a good collection of old fire equipment and memorabilia, including seven major fire-fighting units used from 1779 to the present. A Learn-by-Doing exhibit teaches thirty fire and home safety facts to children ages six to twelve; there's also a child-size safety house, a fire safety theater, displays of toy fire trucks, and a life-size Smokey Bear. The world's largest fire hydrant also is here—a 24-foot black-and-white-spotted fiberglass replica that spouts water. Created by Walt Disney Studios as part of the *101 Dalmatians* craze, it anchors a memorial plaza that honors firefighters from 1881 to our time. Open weekdays; (409) 880–3927.

John Jay French Museum. 2985 French Road (Delaware exit from US-69/96/287 North; turn west and watch for signs). This substantial museum was John J. French's trading post and home back in 1845, now restored and operated by the Beaumont Heritage Society in a beautiful wooded setting north of town. Open Tuesday–Saturday. Fee; (409) 898–0348.

Jefferson Theater. 345 George Jones Place. Listed on the National Registry of Historic Places, this property reopened in the spring of 2003 after extensive renovations. It was built in 1927 and features one of seven existing Robert Morton Wonder organs—and this one is still in working condition; (409) 832–6649.

McFaddin-Ward House. 1906 McFaddin Avenue. Don't leave Beaumont without touring this impressive home; it is one of the few restored Beaux Arts–Colonial houses in the United States. Built in 1906 on land granted by the Mexican government to earlier generations of the McFaddin family, it was occupied by that oil-wealthy and socially prominent family until 1982. Tours begin every thirty minutes with an excellent slide show and continue through numerous rooms, a kaleidoscope of family life and American decor styles from the 1907 period on. Most of the furniture is American, most of the accessories are European, and the 1908 Pink Parlor is particularly grand. Open Tuesday–Saturday and on Sunday afternoon; no children under eight are allowed. The last tours begin at 3:00 P.M. Fee; (409) 832–2134; www.mcfaddin-ward.org.

Old Time Trade Days. 14902 FM–1663, Winnie. From I–10 take exit 829 and follow signs. This buy-and-sell trade market has more than 700 exhibitors on the weekend that follows the first Monday of each month. Parking fee; (409) 296–3300 or 892–4000.

Old Town. East of Calder and Eleventh Streets. When the first Gladys City was in its heyday, this portion of Beaumont was a highly desirable, tree-lined residential neighborhood. It still is. Some of the homes remain impressive, and many now house galleries, restaurants, and specialty shops. A free map helps you find out what's what in this 30-block area. Pick one up at the Tourist Information Center or order it in advance from the Beaumont Convention & Visitors Bureau, Box 3827, Beaumont, TX 77704; (800) 392–4401 or (409) 880–3749.

Port of Beaumont. 1255 Main Street. You'll have a bird's-eye view of the busy port from an observation deck atop the Harbor Island Transit Warehouse; ask the security guard at the Main Street entrance for directions. This modern port handles more than thirty million tons of cargo annually and is one of the four largest ports in the United States in terms of tonnage. The far banks of the Neches River, on the other hand, remain richly forested and undeveloped, just as they were when clipper ships stopped here a century ago. Open daily; guided tours by appointment; (409) 832–1546.

Southeast Texas Entertainment Complex. This spanking new 221-acre complex features an 18,000-seat amphitheater; a 9,500-seat hockey arena, home to the Wildcatters; a 48,000-square-foot exhibition area, and a dozen championship ball fields. For a schedule of events, go on-line at www.setxevents.com.

Spindletop/Gladys City Boomtown Museum. P.O. Box 10070, Lamar University, Beaumont (at the intersection of University Drive and US-69/96/287). Although it lacks the grime of the original, this reconstruction is a good look at 1910 America as well as life in an oil field boomtown. A rickety boardwalk connects most of the structures, just as it did nine decades ago.

The furnished replicas include a surveying and engineering office, the pharmacy and doctor's office, a photographer's studio, a general store, and more. Vintage oil field equipment is scattered around, and the Lucas Gusher Monument is out back on its own site. From I-10 take the US-69/96/287 turnoff to Port Arthur and then the Highland Avenue/Sulphur Drive exit. Signs guide you from there. Open Tuesday–Sunday afternoons. Fee; (409) 835-0823.

Texas Energy Museum. 600 Main at Forsyth (across from the civic center complex). Exhibits about Beaumont before and after Spindletop are featured in this $5-million showcase, along with the entire collection of oil patch artifacts of the Western Company Museum of Fort Worth. Exhibits animated with cine-robots show how oil is created, found, pumped, and refined. Open Tuesday–Sunday. Fee. (409) 833-5100; www.texasenergymuseum.org.

Tyrrell Historical Library. 695 Pearl. People come from all parts of the world to research their roots at this genealogical library; the building was constructed in 1906 as a Baptist church. Open Tuesday–Saturday; (409) 833-2759.

WHERE TO EAT

Al-T's Seafood & Steakhouse. 244 Spur 5 (TX-124), Winnie. Take exit 829 from I-10 and go 1 block south; the restaurant will be on the left. A welcome stopping spot between Houston and Beaumont, this is where the locals go when they want great regional and Cajun food. House specialties include chicken and sausage gumbo, fried gator balls, alligator appetizers, and a ribeye steak topped with a spicy crawfish étouffée. The breakfasts also win raves. Open daily for breakfast, lunch, and dinner. $-$$; ☐; (409) 296-9818.

Brad's Place. 2306 Hazel. From I-10 east, take Seventh Street exit. At Seventh Street turn right to Hazel. Give a creative chef such as Bradley Nelson an old grocery store as a restaurant site, and stand back. The result is a trendy spot with an expo kitchen that serves everything from memorable hamburgers and designer sandwiches you've never thought of to elegant entrees such as salmon strudel. There's no printed menu—what's available changes from meal to meal, day to day—so check the chalkboard when you walk in. You order and pay, and a waiter takes over from there. A number of vegetarian meals are available at lunch. Everything—sauces, breads, gravies, and so on—is made from scratch; they even slice and hand-fry their own potato chips. No alcoholic beverages are sold here, but you're welcome to bring your own wine or beer. Open Tuesday–Saturday for lunch and dinner; closed midafternoon; open Sunday 11:00 A.M. to 9:00 P.M. There's often a Sunday brunch with live jazz—call for an update if that appeals. $–$$$+; ☐; (409) 839-8100.

Broussard's Links Plus Ribs. 2930 South Eleventh (at Washington). All-beef, homemade links bring locals here, along with ribs so tender the meat nearly falls off the bone. All is pit cooked over oak out back. Open for lunch and dinner Monday– Saturday. $–$$; (409) 842-1221.

Bryan's 797. 797 North Fifth Street (at Hazel). Housed in a 1905 home in Beaumont's historic district, this chef-owned restaurant consistently offers some of the finest Continental food in town. *Oenophiles, note:* Their list of California and French wines has won a *Wine Spectator* award of excellence. Chef Bryan Lee trained at Four Seasons Hotel in Taiwan, and it shows. Your best bet is to just ask what's great today, and go with your server's suggestions. Do ask the price of the specials, however; they are not offered voluntarily by the waiter and could lead to sticker shock when you get your bill. Menu choices include a marvelous stacked crab appetizer, numerous entrees featuring Angus beef, and assorted variations on quail and lamb. Open for lunch Monday–Friday, dinner Monday–Saturday; with only fourteen tables, reservations are strongly advised. $$–$$$+; ☐; (409) 832-3900.

Cafe Arts. 500 Main, in the Art Museum of Southeast Texas. Another venture by Debbie Bando. This pleasant spot not only serves in the museum's foyer but also outside when weather permits. Offerings include creative salads, soups, and sandwiches, as well as a quiche of the day. If you're feeling sinful, you can feast just on the desserts. Open for lunch Monday–Friday. $–$$; ☐; (409) 838-2530.

Cajun Kitchen. 105 I-10 North. Lots of good Cajun stuff here at reasonable prices. The menu covers seafood, chicken, barbecued crab, alligator, frog legs, and a great seafood gumbo. If you're in town on a Thursday night, try their all-you-can-eat buffet ($13.95). Open daily for lunch and dinner. $-$$; ☐; (409) 835-7668.

Carlito's. 2610 College Street. If Mexican food appeals to you, give this place a try. Open for lunch and dinner Monday–Saturday, breakfast and lunch on Sunday. $; ☐; (409) 839-8011.

Carlo's. 2570 Calder. If you want Italian and your spouse wants Greek, this is the place; it specializes in both. Paintings by local artists and live entertainment provide a pleasant ambience. Open for lunch and dinner Tuesday–Friday; dinner only on Saturday. $$-$$$; ☐; (409) 833-0108.

Cody's. 6680 Calder. For burgers, fries, and other finger food, this casual restaurant is a good bet. When the weather is nice, request a seat on the patio and kick back. Open daily for lunch and dinner. $-$$; ☐; (409) 866-8511.

Elena's. 1801 College, downtown. In addition to the Mexican standards, this place also serves menudo and chorizo. Open daily for lunch and dinner. $-$$; ☐; (409) 832-1203.

The Green Beanery Cafe. 2121 McFaddin (at Sixth Street in Old Town). This chef-owned restaurant offers tasty, unusual twists on sandwiches, soups, salads, and quiche. Expect a more Continental flair at dinner. Open Tuesday–Saturday for lunch and dinner; closed midafternoon. $-$$.; ☐; (409) 833-5913.

Hoffbrau Steaks. 2310 North Eleventh. This veteran watering hole and steak house is a local favorite. Known for its well-priced, well-done steaks, unchallenging salads, and convivial wait staff, it also offers terrific alfresco dining in the beer garden, which features local bands on weekends. Open daily for lunch and dinner. $-$$; ☐; (409) 892-6911; www.hoffbrausteaks.com.

J&J Steakhouse. 6685 Eastex Freeway. Although many locals come to this family-owned place for affordable steaks and seafood, the big draw for visitors is the unique "Eye of the World" museum in the back room. Hand-carved by the late John Gavrelos, this large display of folk art covers many biblical and patriotic themes. Open for lunch and dinner Monday–Saturday; breakfast also on Saturday. $-$$; ☐; (409) 898-0801.

Log-on Cafe. 3805 Calder. Need to check your e-mail? This clever cafe at the rear of the Gyedco Technology store is set up with numerous individual computer terminals, each with direct Internet service ($7.00 per hour). While you work or play on-line, you can be served unusual snacks, sandwiches, and soups, plus there's espresso and cappuccino. No alcohol. Open Monday–Saturday almost around the clock, but call for update on the hous. $–$$; ◻; (409) 832–1529; www.logoncafe.net.

Novrozsky's. 4320 Calder, 4438 Dowlen, and five other locations. The owners of this small Beaumont chain took their inspiration from a Houston institution and then ran with it. The burgers are hand-shaped, grilled to order, and served "all the way." An extensive appetizer menu features nachos, stuffed jalapeños, and tasty boudin balls. Really hungry? Try the chicken-fried steak and a basket of sweet potato fries. Open daily for lunch and dinner. $; ◻; (409) 898–8688; http://novrozskys.com.

Pig Stand. Two locations: 1595 Calder, (409) 813–1444; and 3695 College, (409) 832–8495. A local favorite since 1921, Pig Stand serves "pig" sandwiches and old-fashioned malts. It's said they served the first onion rings in the United States. The College Street location is open around the clock. $; ◻.

Pine Tree Lodge. 3296 Pine Tree Road (on the east side of LaBelle Road, 2.5 miles north of TX–73; watch for a drive opposite the volunteer fire station). Opened in the 1940s, this low-key family restaurant and bar is a good stop if you're roaming the country roads northwest of Port Arthur en route to or from Beaumont, I–10, or Winnie. While there are plenty of burgers and sandwiches on the menu, locals come here for the seafood platter, chicken-fried steak, pork chops, or ribeyes. If the kids get antsy, there's fishing for white perch, brim, and catfish in the picnic area. Open for lunch and dinner Thursday–Tuesday. $–$$; ◻; (409) 796–1600.

Quality Cafe. 730 Liberty. These folks must be doing something right; they've been in the same location since 1930, and the menu has hardly changed. From buttermilk biscuits and gumbo (Friday only) to plate lunch specials, it's just good Southern home-style cooking. Their Italian salad dressing is so tasty it has become a satellite business; buy a bottle to take home. Watching your weight or cholesterol? Their shrimp pasta salad, fresh fruit bowl, and Dagwood veggie sandwich highlight a heart-healthy menu. Open Monday-Friday for breakfast and lunch. $; (409) 835-9652.

Rao's Bakery. 2596 Calder (also at 4440 Dowlen Road). Grab a seat on the outdoor patio and enjoy the best baked goods in Beaumont. The chocolate éclairs are inspiring (and not a little messy), and no one south of the Mason-Dixon Line does cannoli better. That should be no surprise, because Rao's has been baking since 1941. Reliable soups, salads, and sandwiches for lunch. Open Monday-Saturday for breakfast and lunch. $; ☐; (409) 832-4342; www.raos bakery.com.

Sartin's Seafood. 6725 Eastex Freeway (I-10). This latest venture of the Sartin family brings back the all-you-can-eat barbecued crab and shrimp that made the first Sartin's in Sabine Pass *the* seafood dining destination in Southeast Texas for years. Open daily for lunch and dinner. $$; ☐; (409) 892-6771.

Skip's Outrageous Bar & Grill. 2626 Highway 124, Stowell. From I-10 take the TX-124 exit at Winnie and go approximately 1 mile south. This new eatery is a great stop while day-tripping to Trade Days in Winnie or driving from the Golden Triangle area to the Bolivar Peninsula. Clever in design, the building is certainly an architectural plus for the area, and the kitchen does good things with steak, seafood, and chicken. There's also a wide variety of burgers, sandwiches, and salads. Out of towners: Ask for the Chambers County map and tourism packet they keep on hand and spend some time checking out all the regional memorabilia on the walls. This really is a home-town place, done with vitality. Open daily for lunch and dinner. $-$$; ☐; (409) 296-8860.

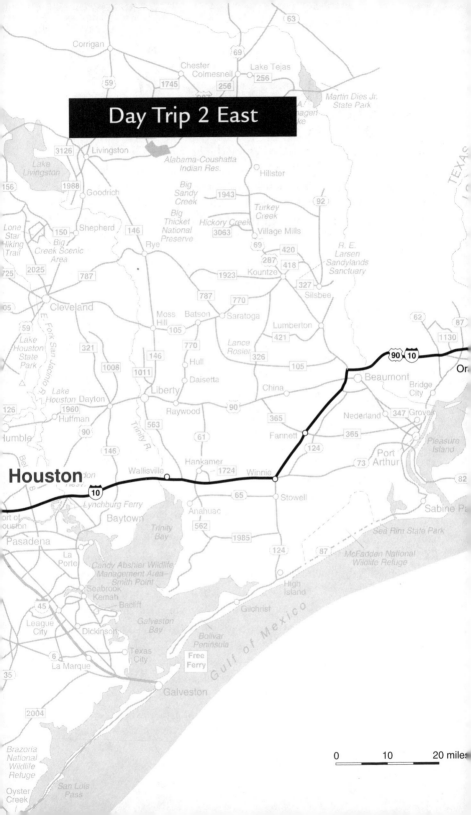

Day Trip 2 East

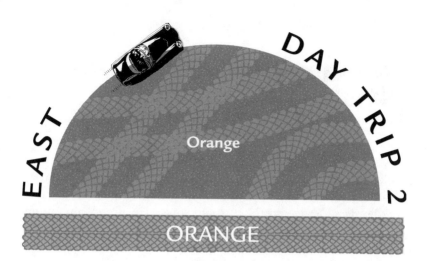

EAST DAY TRIP 2

Orange

ORANGE

Some 32 miles east of Beaumont and the last gasp of Texas on I-10 before you find yourself in Louisiana, Orange has some interesting places to visit.

Officially founded in 1836, Orange has a traceable history that begins about 1600, when the Attacapas Indians settled here. French fur traders came a century later, followed by the Spanish, and the city's name comes from this latter period—early French and Spanish boatmen looked for the wild oranges that grew along the banks of the Sabine River. Anglo settlers ventured west across the Sabine in the early 1800s, but little is left in Orange to mark those times. Most of the city's tourist attractions date from the prosperous lumber and ranching days of 1880 to 1920.

Local information, including a list of antiques stores, can be had from the Orange Chamber of Commerce, 1012 Green Avenue, Orange, TX 77630; (409) 883–1011 or (800) 528–4906; www.orangetexas.org. Do cross the Sabine when you come on this day trip; the Louisiana State Information Center combined with the Sabine National Wildlife Refuge is on the right immediately beyond the bridge. It has an outstanding picnic area and boardwalk through the marshes where you may see numerous water birds, nutria, and so on; bring your camera, preferably one with a long lens. You also may want to play the ponies at Delta Downs racetrack, just over the bridge in Vinton, Louisiana.

Anyone who thinks chili is the definitive Texas dish hasn't been in Orange for the International Gumbo Cook-off on the first weekend

215

in May. More than 20,000 folks mob this annual event, proving that the Cajun heritage thrives in this part of the state.

WHAT TO DO

Adventures 2000+. 333 East Lutcher Drive, No. 12. Trained as a biologist and oceanographer, local resident Eli Tate offers ninety-minute narrated boat tours throughout the Sabine River estuary that borders Orange on the east and south. His deep-V aluminum outboard boats (22- and 26-feet long, respectively) have half-convertible tops, so you will be exposed to weather; dress appropriately. In addition to nature and birding trips through a variety of coastal habitats and ecosystems—sightings of eagles and roseate spoonbills are possible—he also ferries folks to Toscana's Italian Ristorante (see "Where to Eat") for lunch or dinner and to the USS *Orleck* (see below). Cost is $20 for adults, $15 for students and seniors, and $10 for children under twelve, with a $50-per-trip minimum. He also offers sportfishing trips at additional cost. Departures are from the Blue Bird Bait Camp, 1 mile south of I-10 via exit 878; (409) 988-9342 or 883-0856; www.adventures2000plus.com.

Christmas tree farms. Orange County may be the Virginia pine capital of Texas. Call any of the following for directions: K&K Evergreen Christmas Tree Farm, (409) 746-2412 or 746-3268; Reaves Christmas Tree Farm, (409) 746-2522; or Spell's Golden Triangle Trees, (409) 746-3615.

Delta Downs. Twelve miles east via I-10, then north on LA-109. Slightly beyond the two-hour/110-mile limit of this book, this horse racing track is still a good reason to visit the Beaumont/Orange/Port Arthur area, especially since the opening of its all-slot casino. September–March is the racing season for thoroughbreds, and April–Labor Day is reserved for quarter horses. Meanwhile, the casino, with its 1,500 state-of-the-art slot machines, is open twenty-four/seven. For information, contact P.O. Box 175, Vinton, LA 70668; (800) 589-7441; www.deltadowns.com.

Farmer's Mercantile. 702 Division (at the corner of Sixth and Division Streets, just where it has been since 1928). Saddles rest next to bins of nuts and bolts, onion sets are offered just below packets of bluebonnet seeds, and horse collars line the high walls. Whatever you might need, it's here—somewhere. People have been known to dawdle here for hours, remarking on the old wood stoves, bottle cappers, and such. You can't miss the place—just look for hay bales on the sidewalk. Open business hours on weekdays; until 2:00 P.M. on Saturday; (409) 883-2941.

First Presbyterian Church. 902 Green Avenue. One wonders what there would be to see or do in Orange without the Lutcher and Stark families (see entries on W. H. Stark House and Stark Museum that follow). This impressive domed building is a Lutcher/Stark contribution to the city and is thought to be the first public building to be air-conditioned east of the Mississippi. The power plant with the air-conditioning unit was installed during the church's construction in 1908. The handmade stained-glass windows are impressive, as is the entire interior of the church. Tours are available for six or more by advance reservation. If you can't fit those tour requirements, stop in for Sunday services; (409) 883-2097 or 883-4116.

Fishing. Fed by a huge coastal marsh ecosystem, Lake Sabine and its twisting bayous offer excellent seasonal fishing for redfish, speckled trout, and flounder. Additionally, fly fishermen cast for bass and bream in the cypress-tupelo zone of Blue Elbow Swamp, and both the Neches and Sabine Rivers function almost as fish sanctuaries. Brochures available from The Orange Convention & Visitors Bureau detail numerous marinas, fishing camps, guide services, and boat launches. As an alternative, call one of the following: Fishing, the Sabine Connection, (409) 883-0723; Fish-on Guide Service, (409) 735-8761; Skip's Guide Service, (409) 886-5341; or Chuck's Guide Service, (409) 886-5222. For additional information contact the local Texas Parks and Wildlife office, 5550-L Eastex Freeway, Beaumont 77708; (409) 892-8666 or (800) 792-1112. *Tip:* September through December are prime fishing months.

Heritage House. 905 West Division Street. While not as elegant as the Stark House (below), this early-twentieth-century home is worth a stop. Not only is it furnished as an upper-middle-class home would have been in those times, there are several "see-and-touch" exhibits for children, as well as historical items of interest. Fee. Open Tuesday–Friday; (409) 886-5385.

Lutcher Theater for the Performing Arts. 707 West Main (in the Orange Civic Plaza). If you are coming over for the weekend anytime during the September–May season, call to see who and what is playing. Recent offerings have included a touring production of *The Music Man* and *Rent,* and performances by the Nashville Mandolin Ensemble, Monica Gomez, and the Kingston Trio. Tours available weekdays; advance reservations required; (409) 886-5535 or (800) 828-5535; www.lutcher.org.

Piney Woods Country Wines. 3408 Willow Drive. This small vineyard produces some tasty fruit wines—drop in for a sample of Texas-grown sunset muscadine or peach. The tasting room is open daily, except for some weekends and vacation periods. Call ahead; (409) 883-5408.

Stark Museum of Art. 712 Green Avenue (across from the Stark House). William H. Stark was a prominent financial and industrial leader in Orange, who married Miriam Lutcher in 1881. She began collecting European art in the 1890s, and her son Lutcher and daughter-in-law Nelda continued the family tradition with further emphasis on art of the American West and the Taos school of New Mexico. The Audubon print and Steuben glass collections also are particularly worth seeing. This contemporary museum was completed by the Starks in 1976 and houses the varied and impressive collections. Free. Open Wednesday–Saturday and on Sunday afternoon; (409) 883-6661; www.starkmuseum.org.

Super Gator Tours. 108 East Lutcher Drive (on the westbound side of I-10, exit 878). Few thrills compare to skimming over water aboard an airboat. This firm welcomes families for hour-long explorations of the bayous and cypress swamplands that make up the Sabine River. Most trips cover approximately 5 miles of Little Cypress Bayou, with emphasis on Blue Elbow Swamp. Bring binoculars; primeval with huge cypress trees, this area hosts so many birds that it has been named the first stop on the upper Texas Coast section of the Great Texas Coastal Birding Trail. You'll also get close enough to alligators to toss them a marshmallow snack. Tours operate every two hours daily, beginning at 10:00 A.M., weather permitting. May through the first frost of fall is the best time to go. Reservations are requested, but drop-ins may find room in one of the ten-seat airboats. Sunscreen and drinks are advised (coolers are welcome), as are hats that tie on—these airboats reach speeds in excess of 35 mph. Two-hour night tours spotlight alligators, foxes, raccoons, and other animal nightlife. Fee; (409) 883-7725.

Texas Travel Information Center. Exit 880 (Sabine River Turn-around) on I-10. Built with ecological sensitivity on the southern edge of the Blue Elbow Swamp, this travel facility includes a picnic area and the Tony Houseman State Park and Wildlife Management Area. The latter is the first stop on the Great Texas Coastal Birding Trail and includes a boardwalk with informational exhibits regarding the swamp and the flood plain forest. Ask for an upper coast birding map, a state map, and the latest *Texas State Travel Guide;* all three are basic field equipment for exploring the greater Houston region and beyond. Open daily, year-round.

USS *Orleck*. Currently in Ochiltree Inman Park on Front Street, between Sixth and Seventh Streets. This Gearing class destroyer, one of many warships built in Orange in 1945, saw action in the Korean and Vietnam wars. Winner of four battle stars, it was given by the U.S. Navy to the Turkish Navy in the 1960s and finally decommissioned in 1997. Wanting to create a memorial not only to the veterans of the Southeast Texas/Southwest Louisiana area but also to the 1940s shipyard workers, a group of local veterans banded together to form the Southeast Texas War Memorial and Heritage Foundation to raise funds and acquire the ship. Since being towed from Turkey, it has been moored at this small but his-toric park, awaiting a permanent home elsewhere on Orange's waterfront. In the meantime, it is being restored to its appearance in the early 1970s and is open for tours on Tuesday, Friday, Sat-urday, and Sunday. Donations are much appreciated by this non-profit group. For information call (409) 883-8346 or 883-4477; www.ussorleck.org.

W. H. Stark House. P.O. Box 909, Orange, TX 77630 (in the Stark Civic Center complex at Green Avenue and Sixth Street). Built in 1894, this massive Victorian home with its gables and turrets is a visual delight, inside and out. A ten-year restoration project and now on the National Register of Historic Places, this fifteen-room struc-ture can be toured only by advance reservation. No children under fourteen are allowed. Tours start in the carriage house, where an excellent glass collection is on display. Open Tuesday–Saturday. Fee; (409) 883-0871; www.whstarkhouse.org.

WHERE TO EAT

Cajun Cookery. 2308 I-10. Although the regular menu is good, nearly everyone comes here for the Cajun seafood buffet. Open daily for lunch and dinner. $-$$; ☐; (409) 886-0990.

Cody's. 3130 North Sixteenth Street (at I-10). Stop for charcoal-broiled hamburgers, steaks, seafood, and salads. The burgers were rated best in Southeast Texas some years back by *Texas Monthly*. Open for lunch and dinner Sunday–Friday; dinner only on Saturday. $-$$; ☐; (409) 883-2267.

Old Orange Cafe. 914 West Division. In addition to savory lunch plates daily, these inventive folks serve some super salads, sandwiches, spuds, soups, and desserts. They also have special pre-theater dinners prior to certain performances at the Lutcher Theater for the Performing Arts; call for schedule and reservations. Open from 8:00 A.M. to 2:00 P.M. weekdays. $-$$; ☐; (409) 883-2233.

Polo's Restaurant in the Ramada Inn. 2610 I-10 West. If you are eastbound, exit at Sixteenth Street; if westbound, exit at Adams Bayou. Folks come from as far away as Beaumont for the Friday and Saturday night seafood buffets—mountains of fresh shrimp or crawfish, depending on the season. Open daily for standard meals also. $$; ☐; (409) 886-0570.

Tuffy's Eatery. TX-12 at TX-62, Mauriceville (8 miles north of I-10 via TX-62). Expect Southern and Cajun-style cooking here, along with excellent pastries and biscuits. A full menu, plus all-you-can-eat specials (Monday and Friday, catfish; Tuesday, shrimp; Wednesday, chicken and dumplings; Thursday, prime rib), pack in the local folks. Open for lunch and dinner daily. $-$$; ☐; (409) 745-3170; www.tuffyseatery.com.

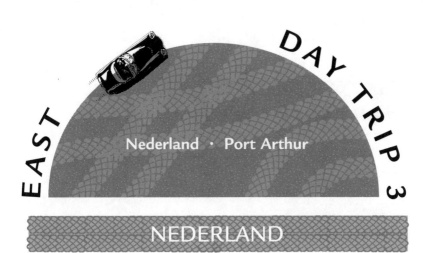

NEDERLAND

When you want to fish or hunt in Southeast Texas, you well could be headed for the Port Arthur area. From Houston the most direct route is I–10 East to Beaumont, followed by a swing southeast on US-69/96/287. For the day-tripper there are several activity options in the area, but first let's take a look at one of the smaller towns you will pass on the way—Nederland.

You'll think you are in Cajun country when you first drive up the main street of this small community—the local market usually is advertising fresh boudin (sausage). Confusion may set in when you see Dutch names on some stores and a windmill at the end of the street. Established as a railroad town in 1897, Nederland first was settled by Dutch immigrants, who were soon followed by French settlers from the Acadiana area of southwestern Louisiana, and both ethnic groups make Nederland what it is today. For information contact the Nederland Chamber of Commerce, 1515 Boston Avenue, Nederland, TX 77627; (409) 722-0279; www.nederlandtx.com.

WHAT TO DO

La Maison Beausoleil. 701 Rue Beausoleil Avenue, Port Neches (off Grigsby Avenue, in Port Neches Park). This fully furnished 1810 Acadian home was barged in from Vermilion Parish, Louisiana. Notable for its mud-and-moss walls that are mortised and pegged with square nails, this "House of Beautiful Sunshine" is fully furnished

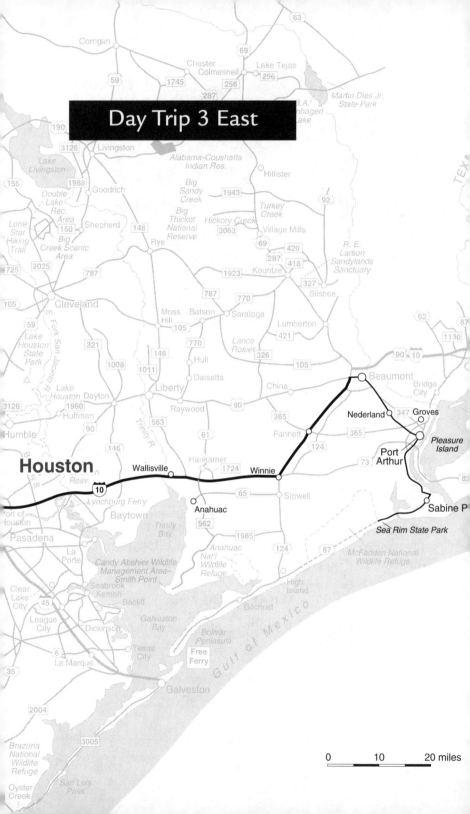

Day Trip 3 East

and open weekend afternoons; weekdays by appointment; (409) 722–1688 or 832–6733.

Windmill Museum and La Maison des Acadiens Museum. 1528 Boston Avenue in Tex Ritter Park. These adjacent museums keep the dual heritage of Nederland alive. The first floor of the authentic Dutch windmill is devoted to mementos of a local boy who made the big time in country-and-western music—Tex Ritter. The remaining two floors have a sparse but interesting collection of assorted cultural treasures. Best is the old pirogue, hollowed out of a cypress log prior to 1845 and in use until bought and donated to the museum in 1969.

La Maison des Acadiens Museum honors the French Cajun culture. A bicentennial project by local volunteers, this authentic replica of a French Acadian cottage has furniture to match. Both museums are open Tuesday–Sunday afternoon March through Labor Day, and Thursday–Sunday afternoon thereafter through February; (409) 722–0279.

WHERE TO EAT

Dorothy's Front Porch. 1000 Smith Road. This family-owned lakefront restaurant is known for steaks and seafood. Open for lunch and dinner daily. $$; ☐; (409) 722–1472.

Sartin's Seafood. 3520 Nederland Avenue. A bit more cozy than its sister establishment in Beaumont, this all-you-can-eat place will stuff you with platters of barbecued crab, shrimp, oysters, crab balls, and other forms of fried fish. You'll find a roll of paper towels on every table, so roll up your sleeves and dig in. Open daily for lunch and dinner. $$–$$$; ☐; (409) 721–9420.

The Schooner. US-69/96/287 at FM–365. Famous for stuffed flounder and stuffed red snapper steak, this restaurant goes all the way with a few stuffed fish and game trophies for decor as well. Open daily for lunch and dinner. $$; ☐; (409) 722–2323.

PORT ARTHUR

From Nederland continue southeast on US-69/96/287 to Port Arthur. The Sabine and Neches Rivers form Sabine Lake, which empties into the Gulf of Mexico 8 miles south of Port Arthur; the town sits on the lake's northwest edge.

Settled as Aurora about 1840, the town became Port Arthur in 1898 as the terminus of the Kansas City-Pittsburgh and Gulf Railroad, and the ensuing oil strike in nearby Beaumont ushered in Port Arthur's golden age of growth. At present the city is primarily a large industrial and refining center with a growing number of things of interest to visitors. Guided tours to the port of Port Arthur can be arranged; (409) 983-2029. The Port Arthur Convention and Visitors Bureau is a good source of specific information, maps, discount coupons, and so on: 3401 Cultural Center Drive, Port Arthur, TX 77642; (409) 985-7822 or (800) 235-7822; www.portarthurtexas.com.

Planning to drive to Port Arthur from Galveston via TX-87? Be aware that, at this writing, that road remains washed out immediately south of Sea Rim State Park. From High Island (on Bolivar Peninsula), go north 29 miles on TX-124 to Winnie, then east 30 miles on TX-73 to Port Arthur.

WHAT TO DO

Airboat rides. This activity comes and goes in Port Arthur. Sea Rim State Park operates airboat and outboard marsh tours (see park entry below), but check either with the park (409-971-2559) or with the visitors bureau (800-235-7822) for an update before you come.

Birding. This is a growing sport here, particularly at Sabine Woods, an Audubon Society-owned preserve on TX-87 south of Port Arthur and 5 miles west of Sabine Pass. Like High Island on the Bolivar Peninsula (Trip 4, this sector), this is a major "fallout" zone for migratory birds in spring and fall. A complete list of birding sites and maps are available from the Port Arthur Convention and Visitors Bureau (previously mentioned).

Fishing. You can fish in the lake, the freshwater bayous that feed it, or the Gulf of Mexico via Sabine Pass. Top game fish are speckled trout, red snapper, mackerel, billfish, and tarpon. A license is required except for party-boat excursions. For information on party boats, marinas, guides, and so forth, contact the visitors bureau, above. Fishing charters currently are available through Sabine Lake Guide Service; (409) 736-3023; www.sabinelakefishing.com.

Hunting. To see vast flocks of birds on the wing in sunrise light is unforgettable. Even seasoned hunters have been known to put down their guns in awe, though you rarely find one who will admit it. You can have that experience in the Port Arthur area; it's prime territory for duck and goose hunting, with four areas open to the public at various times during the November–January season. For overall information contact Sea Rim State Park, P.O. Box 1066, Sabine Pass, TX 77655; (409) 971-2559, or the J. D. Murphree Wildlife Management Area; (409) 736-2551. Other areas open for public hunting include the Texas Point and McFaddin Beach national wildlife refuges; (409) 971-2909.

La Rue des Soldats. This one-way drive tops Port Arthur's $89-million hurricane protection system, which forms a dike around the city. Open weekdays to vehicular traffic and accessed via the first drive to the left just past Gates Library on Lakeshore Drive.

Museum of the Gulf Coast. 700 Procter (on the ship channel in downtown Port Arthur). Before the construction of the Intracoastal Canal, there were beautiful sand beaches on Lake Sabine. Several sprouted luxury hotels that live on only in the photographs displayed with other area memorabilia in this interesting museum. The Port Arthur area also has spawned a number of noted musical artists, among them Janis Joplin, Harry James, Aubrey "Moon" Mullican, Johnny Preston, and Ivory Joe Hunter. Their legacies, complete with gold records and a replica of Janis Joplin's wildly painted convertible, are celebrated in the museum's outstanding Southeast Musical Heritage exhibit and Music Hall of Fame. *Also here:* extensive works depicting Gulf coast life over the centuries, the Robert Rauschenberg Art Gallery, the Snell Decorative Arts Collection, a maritime and petroleum hall, and a mammoth mural by Kerrville artist Travis Keese. Open daily. Fee; (409) 982-7000; www.museum.lamarpa.edu.

Oriental Village. 801 Ninth Avenue. More than 8,000 Vietnamese settled in the Port Arthur area in the early 1970s, 95 percent of whom were Roman Catholics and 5 percent of whom were Buddhists. Their culture and expressions of religion have changed the face of this town. Hoa-Binh (Area of Peace) shrine has a triple life-size statue of the Virgin Mary, surrounded by ornamental gardens. A block of Vietnamese shops is adjacent. The Buddhists bought an old Baptist church at 2701 Proctor Street and turned it into Buu Mon Buddhist Temple, complete with a lighted, four-tiered pagoda tower. Call for tours, (409) 982-9319.

There are dragon dances for Buddha's birthday and the Tet (New Year's) celebration every year, both public events.

Pleasure Island. In Sabine Lake, across the Sabine-Neches ship channel and south from metro Port Arthur. Follow signs to the Martin Luther King Bridge and Pleasure Island. This multimillion-dollar development is stirring things up, and there's more to come. For now there are miles of free levees for fishing and crabbing; a lighted fishing pier; a marina, restaurant, and golf course; condos; playgrounds; spots for picnicking and RV camping; an airfield for ultralights; boat ramps; and a ten-acre concert park that hosts musicals and festivals late spring through fall. Part of the lake around the island is reserved exclusively for sailboarders; (800) 235-7822 weekdays.

Pompeiian Villa. 1953 Lakeshore Drive. Believe it or not, this is a multimillion-dollar house. Built in 1900 by Isaac Ellwood, the "Barbed Wire King," it later was sold to the president of Diamond Match Co. He in turn traded it for $10,000 worth of Texaco stock worth millions on today's market—or so the story goes in Port Arthur. Whichever, this pink stucco villa is listed in the National Register of Historic Places and is now owned by the Port Arthur Historical Society. Open Monday–Friday. Fee; (409) 983-5977.

Rose Hill Manor. 101 Woodworth Boulevard. Built in 1906 as the family home of Rome Woodworth, a Port Arthur banker and mayor, this gracious home sits next to the Sabine-Neches Waterway. Docent-led tours can be arranged by calling in advance; (409) 985-7292.

Sabine Pass Battleground State Historical Park. Fifteen miles south of Port Arthur via TX–87 to Sabine Pass, then 1.5 miles southeast on Dowlen Road. Now a small settlement on the outflow channel from Sabine Lake, Sabine Pass (then known as Sabine City) was a major center for the shipment and trading of cotton as well as a supply center for Confederate forces during the Civil War. To protect this strategic entry into Texas from Union invasion, the Confederate forces began construction of Fort Griffin in 1863.

On August 29 of that year, 5,000 Union soldiers on twenty-two ships of various types sailed from New Orleans, accompanied by four heavily armed gunboats and one command vessel. Their goal was to capture Fort Griffin, invade Texas in the vicinity of Sabine City, advance to Beaumont, seize the railroad, and then take Houston and

Galveston from the north. An additional 10,000 troops would then be brought in from New Orleans to overcome all resistance.

But they didn't figure on Confederate Lt. Richard W. "Dick" Dowling and the forty-seven men he commanded at the not-yet-completed Fort Griffin. On September 8 the Union fleet arrived offshore of Sabine City. After the Union's initial shelling of the fort elicited no response, it was decided that the fort was deserted. When the gunboats got close to the fort, however, Dowling's forces opened fire. With extreme cunning and only six cannons, Dowling and his men destroyed two Union gunboats and took between 300 and 350 prisoners, with no Confederate casualties. The remainder of the Union fleet then panicked and fled back to New Orleans, the Federal invasion of Texas a total failure. A monument to Dowling's act of heroism now stands on what may have been the site of Fort Griffin.

This fifty-six-acre park also has four concrete ammunition bunkers (no guns) constructed during World War II. All this has given rise to a miniforest of historical markers.

Visitors will find exhibits about the Civil War battle, backdropped by huge oil rigs stacked offshore, awaiting deployment in the Gulf. A $1.9-million project in 2003 upgraded the park's boat ramp, as well as made the park more wheelchair accessible. Other activities include picnicking, camping, and fishing along the 0.25 mile of waterfront. Open daily, year-round; (409) 971–2559; www.tpwd.state.tx.us.

Sea Rim State Park. About 23 miles south of metropolitan Port Arthur on TX–87. Thanks to enlightened management, the sea rim marshlands between Port Arthur and Galveston are treated as the fragile natural resource they are. Important to the seafood industry as nursery grounds for shrimp and fish, they also provide a unique experience for visitors.

Sea Rim State Park is a perfect example; it is far more than the usual seaside camping and sunning spot. With more than 15,000 acres, this is the third-largest state park in Texas. Also the only marshland park, it is divided into two distinct areas. The beach unit has camping with and without hookups along 3 miles of sand; a main headquarters with rest rooms, hot showers, and concessions; an outstanding interpretive center; and the Gambusia Trail, a 3,640-foot boardwalk through the wetlands behind the dunes.

The second unit is a pristine marsh, easily explored on your own via a small powerboat or canoe. Be aware, however, that you must file a float plan with the rangers and that marsh maps are essential to safely navigate this wilderness. Inquire also about the airboat tours operated by park rangers at various times March through October (fee). You may surprise a flock of herons or egrets or see an alligator or two—unless they see you first. There are four camping platforms and observation blinds within the marsh; reservations required. Fee. P.O. Box 1066, Sabine Pass, TX 77655; (409) 971-2559; www.tpwd.state.tx.us.

Snooper's Paradise. 5509 East Parkway, Groves (at the northwest corner of Thirty-ninth Street and TX-73). For more than thirty-five years, these folks have been importing antiques from Europe, and their 40,000-plus-square-foot facility bulges with beautiful things, primarily from the 1860–1900 period. Delivery to Houston is all in a day's work. Open Monday–Saturday. □; (409) 962-8427; www.snoopersparadise.com.

Texas Marshland Tour. 3262 Bell Street. Fishing guide Jerry Norris capitalizes on his eighteen years' experience in the waters around Port Arthur to offer ninety-minute tours into the Big Hill Bayou portion of the J. D. Murphree Wildlife Refuge. This roadless wilderness, the largest freshwater bayou in the state, lies on Port Arthur's western city limits and is home to "alligators, alligators, and more alligators," according to Norris. He gets close to such wildlife and ten to fifteen species of migratory birds as well by utilizing the trolling motor on his 23-foot center console boat. Cost is $25 per person (for up to seven people) with a minimum charge of $75 per trip. Although advance reservations are preferred, feel free to call at the last minute; (409) 736-3023; www.marshland.com/marshland.html.

Veterans Memorial Park. On TX-187, in the shadow of the impressive Neches River bridges, this park pays tribute to veterans of all branches of the military. Visitors will find the names of more than 10,000 servicemen and women, spanning World War I to Operation Desert Storm. Kids and military buffs will marvel at all the hardware here, including an F4-D Phantom Jet, a Huey helicopter, and an M60A3 tank.

Vuylsteke Dutch Home. 1831 Lakeshore. This home was built in 1905 for the first Dutch consul to Port Arthur and contains its original furniture. Tours by appointment. Fee; (409) 984-6101.

White Haven. 2545 Lakeshore. Now owned by Lamar University–Port Arthur, this 1915 Greek Revival mansion is open for tours on

Monday, Wednesday, and Friday or by appointment. Fee; (409) 984-6101.

WHERE TO EAT

Esther's Seafood and Oyster Bar. 9902½ Gulfway Drive, Groves. If you're hungry for spicy Cajun seafood and steaks, search out this barge eatery at the foot of the Rainbow Bridge. Open for lunch and dinner daily. $$-$$$; ☐; (409) 962-6268.

Golden Gate Restaurant. 3444 Gulfway Drive. You'll find authentic Vietnamese food here, as well as a Chinese food buffet. Open daily for lunch and dinner. $-$$; ☐; (409) 982-3100.

Jivin' Java Coffee House. 4901 Twin City Highway. Although this building looks like a converted Dairy Queen, do not pass on by. Inside it's slickly designed and far more than a coffee spot. In fact, it's usually very busy with local folks enjoying peerless sandwiches, soups, and assorted pastries along with their cup of joe. Everything, even the cheesecake, is made on-site. If you're thinking of a picnic farther down the road, get the sandwiches and treats here. Open daily almost from dawn to late at night. $; ☐; (409) 962-1777.

WANDERING THE BACKROADS

The most logical and the swiftest access from Houston to the entire Golden Triangle area is via I-10 East. But if time is no problem and you prefer quiet country roads, detour south from the interstate just past the Trinity River Bridge and explore Wallisville and Anahuac (Day Trip 4, this sector).

Interested in rice farming? Plan a stop at the East Chambers Agricultural and Historical Museum in Winnie, open weekdays or by appointment; (409) 296-2231. Exhibits here include early farm equipment and an old crop-duster airplane. From I-10 take exit 829, turn south on TX-124, and turn east on LeBlanc; the museum will be 1 block down on the left. If you have children with you, take note of the very nice playground across the street. Winnie also hosts Old Time Trade Days on the first Friday–Sunday after the first Monday of the month. This event draws many of the dealers from First Monday at Canton and is of major interest to hunters of antiques and general junk (Day Trip 1, this sector).

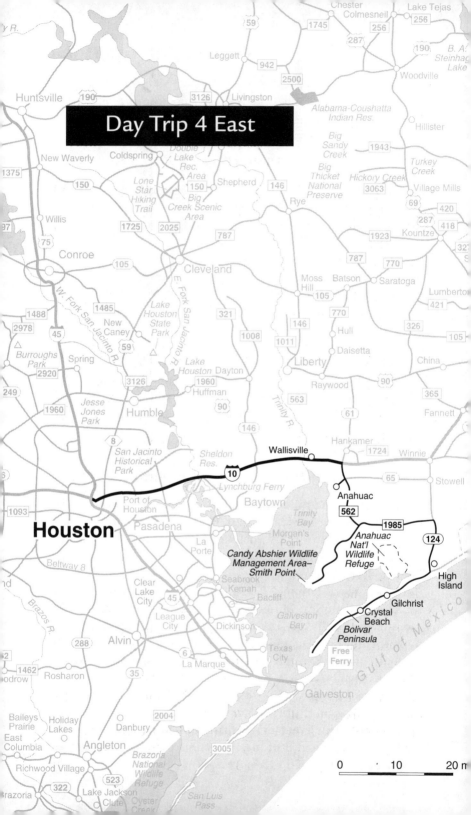

Day Trip 4 East

Chester
Colmesneil
Lake Tejas
256
59
1745
256
287
190
B. A.
Steinhag
Lake
Leggett
942
Woodville
2500
Huntsville
190
3126
Livingston
Alabama-Coushatta
Indian Res.
1375
150
Coldspring
Double
Lake
Rec.
Area
Big
Sandy
Creek
1943
Hillister
Turkey
Creek
New Waverly
Lone
Star
Hiking
Trail
150
Shepherd
146
Big
Thicket
National
Preserve
Hickory Creek
3063
Village Mills
69
420
287
418
97
Willis
1725
2025
Big
Creek Scenic
Area
787
Rye
1923
Kountze
32
75
Conroe
105
Cleveland
E. Fork San Jacinto R.
Moss
Hill
Batson
Saratoga
Lumberton
421
1488
2978
1485
Lake
Houston
State
Park
321
146
770
326
105
45
New
Caney
59
1008
1011
Hull
Liberty
China
1960
Jesse
Jones
Park
3126
1960
Lake
Houston
Dayton
90
Huffman
Raywood
90
365
Fannett
249
Humble
146
Trinity R.
563
61
8
San Jacinto
Historical
Park
Sheldon
Res.
Wallisville
Hankamer
1724
Winnie
10
Lynchburg Ferry
Baytown
65
Stowell
1093
Port of
Houston
Anahuac
562
Houston
Pasadena
La
Porte
Morgan's
Point
Trinity
Bay
1985
124
Anahuac
Nat'l
Wildlife
Refuge
Beltway 8
Candy Abshier Wildlife
Management Area–
Smith Point
High
Island
Clear
Lake
City
45
Seabrook
Kemah
Bacliff
Galveston
Bay
Gilchrist
Crystal
Beach
Brazos R.
League
City
Dickinson
Bolivar
Peninsula
Gulf of Mexico
288
Alvin
6
La Marque
Texas
City
Free
Ferry
52
1462
35
Rosharon
Galveston
odrow
Baileys
Prairie
East
Columbia
Holiday
Lakes
2004
Danbury
3005
Angleton
Brazoria
National
Wildlife
Refuge
0   10   20 m
Richwood Village
322
523
Lake Jackson
razoria
Clute
Oyster
Creek
San Luis
Pass

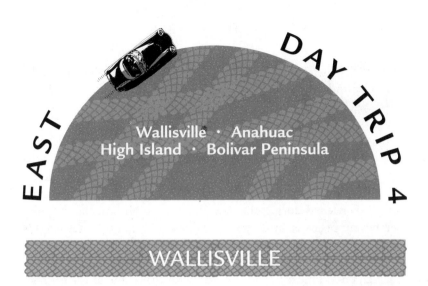

WALLISVILLE

One of the oldest towns in Chambers County, Wallisville was torn down in 1966 by the U.S. Army Corps of Engineers in preparation for a large flood-control dam that then remained stalled in controversy for many years. The project's scope subsequently was scaled back to being a barrier and navigation locks between the saline waters of the Gulf and the fresh water and marshes of the Trinity River. In the process a major new recreation area has been created (see "What to Do"). The original Wallisville townsite, however, remains green, rolling, and open. What once was a handsome, Victorian-era town is now just a fading memory.

WHAT TO DO

Cedar Hill Park. From I–10, take FM–563 north 2.8 miles and turn left on Lake Charlotte Road (watch for HATCHER'S CHRISTMAS TREE FARM sign); the park will be 1.1 miles down on the left. Although some will come here for the camping and pleasant picnic area by the lake, this park is of interest primarily as a birding and wilderness exploration site. A boardwalk and observation deck, lined with cypress trees, extends into Lake Charlotte; nonmotorized boats can be launched here, so come with a kayak or canoe. Bring a camera as well; this is a favored habitat for eagles and roseate spoonbills. For camping reservations call (281) 576–2243.

Lake Wallisville Ranger Station and Visitor Center. P.O. Box

293, Wallisville, TX 77957. From I-10 East take exit 807 and turn south on the first levee road. Operated by the Army Corps of Engineers (ACOE), this well-designed nature center has educational exhibits well worth a stop.

In addition to a visual history and maps of old Wallisville, visitors also are captivated by the large topographical map that explains the extensive and complicated Wallisville project. This also is where you file a float plan if you want to boat these waters. The locks operate hourly as needed during the day, plus their high walls are popular perches for pelicans. Birding trails follow several of the levees (apply at the visitor center for access).

The watery maze that makes up this recreational area tantalizes boaters, but all must file a float plan with the ACOE at the number below. The best put-in is via the Turnaround exit from I-10 on the west side of the Trinity River Bridge. Many water routes flow from there, one of which—the Cypress Swamp Canoe Trail—accesses Lake Charlotte when water levels permit. That I-10 exit also leads to a major birding trail that include two boardwalks over the marsh; an observation tower is planned. No motorized vehicles are allowed beyond the parking area. If the gate is closed, request a key at the visitor center. Open daily; (409) 389-2285.

Wallisville Heritage Museum. 20136 I-10 East (P.O. Box 16), Wallisville. Take the Wallisville exit (No. 807) and continue on the eastbound frontage road. Created in 1979 as a nonprofit foundation to restore the old town of Wallisville and preserve the adjacent El Orcoquisac Archaeological District, this small museum has three of Wallisville's old buildings on site. Only one—an 1869 school—can be toured; a lack of funds delays restoration of the others. Ancestor hunters also find an extensive genealogical library focused on America's eastern coast, the ancestral home of many Chambers County pioneers. Open Monday–Saturday; (409) 389-2252.

CONTINUING ON

From Wallisville take the Old Wallisville Road to its intersection with FM-563 and continue south to Anahuac. The road itself is a delight—no center stripe or traffic—and it's easy to imagine how things were when this was a horse-and-buggy route.

ANAHUAC

Founded as a Spanish fortress in 1821, Anahuac (pronounced *Ana-whack*) was the site of a fort and customs house constructed in 1831 by prisoners of the Mexican government. Built where the Trinity River empties into Galveston Bay, the fort was captured the following year by Texian forces under the command of William B. Travis, who subsequently met his doom at the Alamo. The site now is a large city park south of town (see below). Today Anahuac is both the Chambers County seat and the official alligator capital of Texas, a fact the town celebrates with Gatorfest every September.

WHAT TO SEE

Anahuac National Wildlife Refuge. On East Galveston Bay, 18 miles southeast of town via FM-562, FM-563, and FM-1985 (follow the signs). This 35,000-acre wildlife refuge hosts more than 270 species of birds (fifty-two of which nest here), twenty-four species of mammals, an extensive number of reptiles, and uncountable mosquitoes; wear industrial-strength repellent. When weather conditions permit, approximately 12 miles of graveled roads offer excellent opportunities to observe wildlife. A major stop on the Great Texas Coastal Birding Trail, this refuge offers birders an observation platform along Shoveler Pond and a footpath to The Willows, a major "fallout" area during the spring and fall tropical migrations; the rare palm warbler often is sighted here during spring migration. There also are two boat ramps if you want to explore on your own by shallow-draft boat. Hunting is allowed on three tracts in season; request information on times, restrictions, and required permits. Other activities include photography, fishing, and crabbing. Apart from rest rooms, there are no amenities, concessions, or picnic facilities; bring drinking water. All visitors must register at the Visitor Information Center. Refuge brochures and bird checklists are available here; a small bookstore sells natural history books related to the general area. For advance information and a birding list, contact P.O. Box 278, Anahuac, TX 77514; (409) 267-3337; www.southwest.fws.gov/refuges.

Anahuac National Wildlife Refuge also includes the East Bay

Bayou Tract on FM-1985, 7 miles east of the refuge's main entrance. Opened in 1998, this birding and fishing area has a 1.5-mile wooded trail along East Bay Bayou, a good spot for viewing migratory songbirds in the spring. Other activities include freshwater fishing from the bank or from three fishing piers. Nonmotorized boats also are allowed.

Candy Abshier Wildlife Management Area. At Smith Point on east Galveston Bay, 23 miles south of Anahuac via FM-562. Also a major "fallout" area for migrating birds in spring and fall, these 207 acres of oak-studded coastal prairie provide welcome roosts and cover for orioles, buntings, warblers, swallows, pelicans, storks, frigates, and raptors. Some twenty species of the latter have been sighted here during the fall migration (late August to early October; third week of September is prime). These Hawk Watches are sponsored by the Gulf Coast Bird Observatory; (979) 480-0999; www.gcbo.org. Apart from a 30-foot-tall viewing tower on the shore of East Bay, there are no other public facilities or water. Insect repellent strongly advised. Open daily. Guided tours can be arranged through the Texas Conservation Passport Program; (409) 736-2551.

Chambers County Library. 202 Cummings Street. What were the contents of the Chambers County Museum now are housed here. The library is open Monday–Friday, and until 1:00 P.M. on Saturday; (409) 267-8261. Outside you'll find two very old buildings on the library's lawn. The first, Chambersea, was built in 1845 and is one of the prettiest and most unusual homes remaining from that early statehood era. The other, a frontier doctor's office, was floated into Anahuac from its original home in Cedar Bayou. For access to either call the local historical commission, (409) 267-8225.

Fort Anahuac Park. Main Street at Trinity Bay. Diligent researchers here find traces of Fort Anahuac (circa 1831), built as a combination fort and customhouse by prisoners of the Mexican government. This also was the site of a skirmish between Texian and Mexican forces prior to the Texas Revolution. This is another major stop on the upper coast birding trail; visitors now find a lighted fishing pier on the Anahuac Barge Channel below the bluff; it's free and open around the clock. A paved, 1.9-mile-long levee road offers excellent wade fishing and wildlife observation, and the new Judge Oscar Nelson Boardwalk starts at the boat ramp and continues along the Trinity River.

Picnic and play places. Two parks make good leg-stretching stops in the Anahuac area. Double Bayou Park, on Eagle Ferry Road between FM–563 and FM–562, offers day-use areas, a covered pavilion, boat ramps, and other amenities. White's Park, on TX–61 south of I–10, has a rodeo area, bayou access for fishing and crabbing, a picnic area, and camping. Insect repellent is advised at both parks.

Upper Texas Coast Water-Borne Education Center. P.O. Box 518, Anahuac, TX 77514. This facility's goal is to provide on-the-water educational experiences to enhance the general public's understanding of coastal resources in general, the Trinity River delta in the specific. To that end they operate boat explorations within the Trinity River watershed (fee). Aimed primarily at groups, these trips last up to four hours. Activities aboard may include water testing, seining, specimen collecting, and so on. These are not pleasure trips in the general sense of the term; rather they are educational experiences. Nor do they use pleasure craft. Their fleet currently consists of one 21-foot outboard, one sailing and rowing boat, and two 45-foot-long boats configured with teaching facilities, tools, galley, air-conditioning, and overnight bunks. For additional information call (409) 267–3547.

WHERE TO EAT

DJ's. At the intersection of I–10 and US–61. This unfancy grocery store serves some of the best barbecue in the region, which you can eat at picnic tables under the trees. Open daily for lunch and dinner. $; ☐; (409) 374–2144.

Gator's Ice House. 306 Ross Sterling Road (FM–563). Stop here for hamburgers, pizza, and assorted forms of chicken-fried steak. On Sunday the cook stirs up a pot of something homemade such as chili or chicken with dumplings, a touch of home for folks on the road. Open Monday–Saturday for lunch and early dinner. $; ☐; (409) 267–3444.

Mitch's Kitchen. 400 Cummings Avenue (at Main). In addition to a daily steam-table meal, the menu here ranges from hamburgers and sandwiches to seafood, steaks, chicken, and quail. Open daily for breakfast and lunch, Wednesday–Friday for dinner. Closed midafternoon. $–$$; ☐; (409) 267–4000.

CONTINUING ON

To continue this day trip from Anahuac to High Island and the Bolivar peninsula, follow FM-562 south to FM-1985, then turn east (left) and go 15 miles to a south (right) turn on TX-124 to High Island. From that tiny community continue south on TX-124 to its intersection with TX-87 at the coast. *Warning:* The washed-out sections of TX-87 to the left of that last intersection are no longer passable, even with four-wheel drive.

After touring Bolivar you have two options for returning to Houston. The first is to ride the free car ferry that connects Bolivar's southwestern tip with Galveston and then take Broadway down-island to I-45 North. Or just park your car at the Bolivar ferry dock, walk aboard (no waiting) for a round-trip ferry ride, and then return home the way you came: TX-87 east up the Bolivar peninsula to TX-124 and High Island, then 20 miles north on TX-124 to I-10 west at Winnie. From there it's 63 freeway miles west to Houston.

HIGH ISLAND

Another major stop on the Great Texas Coastal Birding Trail, this tiny community, just 1 mile inland from the Gulf of Mexico, is particularly rewarding to birders from mid-March through mid-May. Following instinctive migration patterns, as many as 25,000 exhausted songbirds (wood warblers, tanagers, orioles, catbirds, buntings) make their first landfall here after flying 600 to 700 miles across the Gulf from winter homes in Mexico and Central America. Many carry colorful plumage in preparation for breeding and nesting farther north. Their favored landing trees are the one-hundred-year-old live oaks that shade numerous High Island sites. Four of those areas—Boy Scout Woods, Smith Oaks, Eubanks Woods, and the S. E. Gast Red Bay Sanctuary—are owned and operated by the Houston Area Audubon Society, (713) 932-1639; www.houstonaudubon.org. Bring binoculars, insect repellent, and your best manners; the birds must not be disturbed. Donations requested. For accommodations, contact the Birder's Haven Resort, 2081 Winnie, High Island, TX 77623; (409) 286-5362.

As you approach High Island on TX-124, stop at the High Island Roadside Park to locate the above sites and to check out the birds in that rest stop's sheltering oaks.

BOLIVAR PENINSULA

In contrast to Galveston's burgeoning commercial development, this 32-mile stretch of unrestricted sand flexes with the whims of Mother Nature, changing with every storm. As a laid-back, low-cost, somewhat funky getaway, however, Bolivar can't be beat.

Once on Bolivar you won't find much, which is its biggest attraction—just some fishing camps and stilt-legged residential developments, a seemingly endless beach, a few small communities, and an abandoned lighthouse built in 1872 and currently closed to the public. The latter was used some years ago as the set for the film *My Sweet Charlie.*

The beaches are open—you can drive, ride horses, or just walk for miles. There are waves to play in, sand to loll in, and enormous numbers of shorebirds to keep you entertained.

Two warnings: Apart from portable toilets, there are no public facilities on Bolivar's beaches, and the strand opposite the blinking light in Crystal Beach is locally known as "the Zoo," a mecca for unsupervised teenagers during Spring Break.

Love seashells? Time your visit to catch either an outgoing high tide or a minus tide. The beaches around High Island usually have the most abundant shells as well as an occasional fossil liberated from the prehistoric clay deposits that line much of the Gulf bottom. The flats at the southwestern tip of the peninsula also are good for shelling; wear insect repellent.

Bed-and-breakfast also is possible here, at Out by the Sea, (409) 684-1555 or (888) 522-5926; www.outbythesea.com.

Tip to oyster lovers: Locals consider oysters harvested from beds in Bolivar's East Bay to be among the best in the world. Local oysters are big deals on Bolivar menus; they're also sold by the pint and quart at several local markets.

For a vacation packet, birding list, and tourist information, contact the Bolivar Peninsula Chamber of Commerce, P.O. Box 1170, Crystal Beach, TX 77650; (409) 684-5940; www.bolivarchamber.org.

WHAT TO DO

Birding. Bolivar Flats, a 550-acre stretch of coastal beach near the southwestern tip of the peninsula, is considered one of the prime birding areas on the upper Texas Gulf coast. From TX-87 watch for Rettilon Road (reverse spelling of "no litter"), 3.7 miles east of the Bolivar ferry terminal. Turn south on Rettilon to a right turn at the beach and drive to the vehicular barricade. *Note:* Please stay on the beach and keep your animals on a leash. Entering the vegetated dunes and marshes is discouraged because of fragile nesting sites and poisonous snakes.

Fishing. Rollover Pass is the favored spot because strong currents bring large numbers of flounder, redfish, croakers, speckled trout, sand trout, and other game fish close to shore. This narrowest part of the peninsula got its name during Prohibition, when bootleggers would take delivery of barrels of hooch from ships on the Gulf side of the peninsula and then roll those barrels overland to local boats waiting in East Bay.

Fort Travis Seashore Park. South end of the peninsula, near the ferry. Noted as the spot where Jane Long, "the Mother of Texas," gave birth to the first Anglo child on Texas soil, it also has the remains of a fort built before the turn of the twentieth century. Now partially renovated, the fortifications provide stairs to a long beach and rocks for fishing; (409) 934-8100.

WHERE TO EAT

Alice's Restaurant & The Blue Moon Saloon. 2501 TX-87, Crystal Beach. Chef-owned, this "beachy" place offers a full menu, with emphasis on seafood. Open for lunch and dinner Monday–Saturday. $-$$$; ☐; (409) 684-3022.

Bob's Sports Bar and Famous Grill. 1755 TX-87, Crystal Beach. Locals favor this place for its hamburgers, shrimp, and barbecue. The 5-inch muffeletta is big enough for two. Open for lunch and dinner daily. $-$$; ☐; (409) 684-4929.

De Coux's Pub & Restaurant. 3150 TX-87, Crystal Beach. A good Sunday-drive destination in itself, this clean and classy eatery offers the chef's creations on a blackboard menu in addition to burgers, sandwiches, crabmeat nachos, crawfish in season, and so on. If the weather turns chilly, come enjoy their fireplace. Open for dinner daily year-round, lunch also on weekends. $-$$; ☐; (409) 684-0177.

Little Chihuahua. On ground level of Stingaree (see below), 1295 Stingaree Road, Crystal Beach. Looking for Mexican food minus the usual Tex–Mex twist? Try the seafood enchiladas and quesadillas here. Open only on summer weekends for dinner. $-$$; ☐; (409) 684-2731.

Mama Teresa's Flying Pizza & Italian Restaurant. 2770 TX-87, Crystal Beach. Nearly an icon for the area, this busy place serves highly praised, hand-tossed pizza and numerous other Italian entrees. The fettuccine shrimp alfredo is one of their top sellers. In winter this spot is open for dinner only on Thursday and Friday, lunch and dinner on the weekends. Dinner also is served Tuesday and Wednesday in the summer. $-$$; ☐; (409) 684-3507.

Outrigger Grill. 1035 TX-87, Crystal Beach. This family-oriented restaurant even has toys to keep the kiddies happy while you wait for a delicious oyster po'boy, giant burrito, Mexican plate, burger, steak, or whatever else takes your fancy on their long menu. Owner Skip Rohacek buys her fish fresh off local boats and guarantees that no one leaves her place hungry. Open daily for breakfast, lunch, and dinner. $-$$; ☐; (409) 684-6212.

Steve's Landing. 1290 Bay Vue Road, Crystal Beach. You can come by car or boat to this attractive place that overlooks the Intracoastal Canal, and then dine either indoors or on the screened-in patio. *Attention oyster-lovers:* On Thursday and Sunday during the winter, this lively spot offers all-you-can-eat oysters fixed seven different ways, in addition to the regular menu (seafood straight off their own boats, chicken, and steaks). From May 1 to October 1 they serve lunch and dinner Wednesday–Sunday, dinner only on Monday and Tuesday. From October through April they serve dinner only Wednesday–Friday, lunch and dinner on the weekends. $-$$$; ☐; (409) 684-1999.

Stingaree. 1295 Stingaree Road, Crystal Beach. Considered by many people to be Bolivar's premier eatery, this spot's specialties include barbecued crab, charbroiled snapper, honey jalapeño shrimp, and snapper throats (when available). Save room for the bread pudding with bourbon sauce. For drinks and appetizers, the second-floor deck, with its view of East Bay and the Intracoastal Canal, is the place to be on Bolivar. Open for lunch and dinner Wednesday–Sunday in winter; Tuesday–Sunday during Spring Break; daily during summer. $-$$$; ☐; (409) 684-2731.

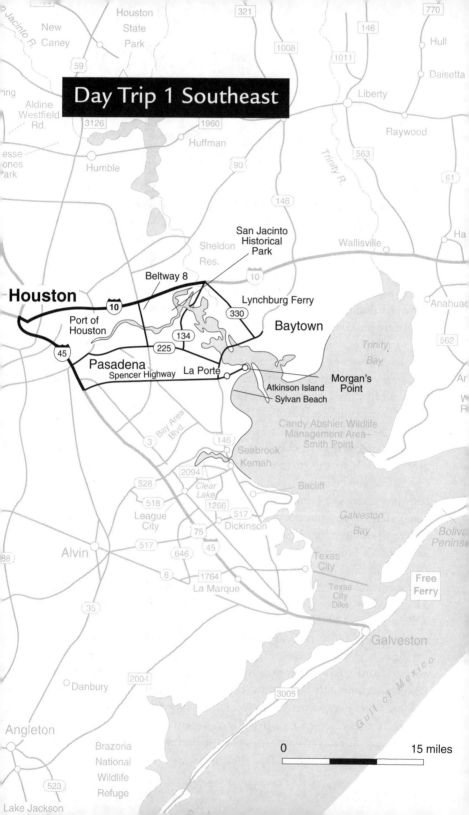

Pasadena · La Porte
Baytown · Morgan's Point

PASADENA

As you drive southeast from Houston on I–45 and look east to the vast industrial-chemical complex that is Pasadena today, it's hard to believe that this once was projected to be Houston's garden. Its bucolic future was altered permanently by two events: the completion of the Houston Ship Channel as a deepwater port in 1915 and the discovery of oil in nearby Baytown the following year.

Slightly off the usual Sunday drive itinerary, this upper bay region has several things to see and do. Start with a tour of the Port of Houston and the ship channel, and then head east on TX–225 to digest some history at San Jacinto Battleground State Historical Park in La Porte. From there ride the free Lynchburg Ferry to Baytown and return to the Morgan's Point/La Porte area via the Fred Hartman Bridge. En route you'll find crabbing, swimming, and bird-watching—all at a laid-back pace.

WHAT TO DO

The Beltway 8 Bridge. Accessible from either I–10 on the north or TX–225 on the south. No reservations needed here, just some toll change for a fantastic bird's-eye view of the port from atop the bridge.

  Our Family's Herbs and Such. 702 Llano. If you're interested in starting an herb garden, stop here. Lana and Bob Sims offer a garden full of herbs acclimated to our Gulf coast climate, as well as numerous "Taste of Texas" jellies, vinegars, salsa mixes, and so on. They also make herb-based toys and flea-repelling collars for domestic pets. Open Saturday March–October or by appointment; (713) 943–1937.

The Pasadena Historical Museum and the Strawberry House. 201 Vince Street (in Memorial Park). The museum's well-done displays include an authentic doctor's office, and an early kitchen, complete with water pump, is one of the features of the adjacent Strawberry House. That structure originally stood on a nearby Mexican land grant and is furnished to illustrate three periods: the early 1880s when it was new, the 1920s, and the 1940s. The museum is open Wednesday–Sunday; call for hours. Strawberry House is open those same days by request; (713) 477–7237.

Port of Houston. 7300 Clinton Drive, Houston (Clinton exit from Loop 610 East). The observation deck on the northwest side of the turning basin is open daily, but a boat tour is better. The free ninety-minute trip aboard the MV *Sam Houston* takes you close to huge ships from around the world, grain elevators, refineries, docks—the heart of the second largest port in America. This is an official inspection vessel, and reservations are required. Make them two to three months in advance, although you often can get reservations at the last minute due to cancellations. Closed on Monday, holidays, and for the month of September; (713) 670–2416; www.portofhouston.com.

LA PORTE

Founded by French settlers in 1889, this modest community now stretches north to include one of the state's most significant historic sites. See that portion of La Porte now, en route to the Lynchburg Ferry, and the Sylvan Beach area on the final leg of this trip.

WHAT TO DO

Jim Watson Texas History Museum. 826 San Jacinto. Now owned by the La Porte School District, this former home houses an outstanding review of Texas history from the 1820s through the Vietnam War. Each of six rooms covers a different era and is staffed with well-informed docents. You'll find antiques, as well as hands-on exhibits specifically designed for children. The admission fee includes refreshments. By appointment only; (281) 604–7000.

Little Cedar Bayou Park. 1322 South Broadway. From TX–146 in La Porte, turn east onto Fairmont Parkway, right on Eighth Street, and left on M Street. This pleasant city park has play and picnic areas, a mile-long nature trail that ends at Galveston Bay, and a WaterWorld–type wave pool (fee) that operates during summer; (281) 470–7275.

Lynchburg Ferry. From the cemetery and picnic area of the battleground park (see below), continue northeast on TX–134 to this free ferry, a relic from pre-freeway days. You are welcome to park your car and take the fifteen-minute round trip as a passenger, or you can drive aboard and then continue to Baytown. The ferry operates twenty-four hours a day, year-round; (281) 424–3521.

San Jacinto Battleground State Historical Park. 3800 Park Road. From Pasadena continue east on TX–225 to TX–134, and turn north to Park Road 1836. Here, in just eighteen minutes, Sam Houston and his ragged Texian Army defeated the Mexican Army in 1836. This event changed not only the future of Texas but that of the western half of continental America. The dramatic story is chiseled in granite and unfolds as you walk around the base of the 570-foot-tall San Jacinto Monument. There is no better capsule lesson in Texas history.

Inside, the interesting San Jacinto Museum of History has artifacts from the Spanish-Mexican period (1519–1835) and the Anglo-American settlement years (1835–81). A multi-image documentary presentation, *Texas Forever! The Battle of San Jacinto,* brings history to life in the museum's Jesse H. Jones Theatre for Texas Studies. The museum is free, but there are charges to see the film and to ride the elevator to the top of the monument. Open daily; (281) 479–2421.

The battlefield flanks the monument, and a free map available at the museum will guide you to markers and various positions of the Texas and Mexican armies. This oak-studded parkland also has numerous picnic sites along one arm of the bay and on the ship channel, so bring your lunch and crabbing gear.

The battleship *Texas* is nearby. Moored here since 1948, and now with a recently restored hull, it is billed as the only surviving heavily armed dreadnought-class battleship, a relic of both world wars. Open daily. Fee; (281) 479–2431; www.tpwd.state.tx.us.

Sylvan Beach. From TX–146 in La Porte turn east on Fairmont Parkway to where it ends at this park. This pleasant, thirty-two-acre county park has a playground, picnic areas, a bait and tackle shop, rest rooms, and a free boat launch but no swimming. There also is good crabbing here. The old train depot at the park's entrance now serves as a historical museum for La Porte and is open by appointment; (281) 326–6539.

WHERE TO EAT

Monument Inn Restaurant. 4406 Battleground Road. This long-standing favorite place still serves up whopping portions of seafood, chicken, and steak. House specialties include the "Monumental" salad and Key lime pie for dessert. A scrumptious cinnamon roll comes in your bread basket, just right for breakfast the next day. Open for lunch and dinner daily. $–$$$; ☐; (281) 479–1521.

Two Sisters Afternoon Tea Room. 101 East Main Street (inside Antiques and Gifts by Parker). Your nose will pick up on the fragrant, freshly baked sourdough bread and desserts as soon as you enter this combo establishment. Lunch offerings also include an interesting assortment of soups, salads, and sandwiches. Open Tuesday–Saturday from 11:00 A.M. to 3:00 P.M.; afternoon high tea served by advance appointment. $–$$; ☐; (281) 470–0247.

CONTINUING ON

From the San Jacinto Monument area and La Porte, the Lynchburg Ferry takes you across the ship channel to Baytown, where you continue on TX–134 to Decker Drive (TX–330). Turn southeast (left) and drive into Baytown. At the intersection with TX–146, a turn southwest (right) will take you back to La Porte via the Fred Hartman Bridge.

BAYTOWN

Both Lynchburg and Baytown were early Anglo settlements, the former an important trading post and the latter originally a sawmill and a store on Goose Creek near the junction of the San Jacinto River and Buffalo Bayou. What was then known as Bay Town boomed after the Civil War and again with the discovery of oil nearby in 1916. When Humble Oil and Refining Co. bought 2,200 acres for a refinery in 1919, present-day Baytown began to evolve. Antiques hounds may enjoy a stroll through the Goose Creek historic district (Texas Avenue and Defee Street between Pruett and Commerce).

WHAT TO DO

Baytown Historical Museum. 220 West Defee. This interesting look at the area's past is housed in a 1936 post office. Note the fresco on the lobby wall, painted by noted artist Barse Miller as part of a WPA project during the Great Depression. Other major exhibits include replicas of an Indian hut and midden; the poetry of the Sage of Cedar Bayou, John P. Sjolander; and Humble/Exxon memorabilia from the early days in the oil patch. The Texas Room has artifacts relevant to David Burnet, Sam Houston, and Lorenzo de Zavalla, all of whom lived in the area. Open Tuesday–Saturday; call for hours. Donation; (281) 427-8768; www.baytownmuseum.org.

Eddie V. Gray Wetlands Education and Recreation Center. 1724 Market Street. Opened in January 1998 and the activity hub for the Goose Creek Greenbelt, this 14,000-square-foot facility has much of interest to the traveling public. Aimed at teaching environmental education, the Wetlands Center includes a large display area and a Living Lab as well as numerous classrooms used by Lee College and the Goose Creek school district. For visitors the primary focus is the Living Lab, where indoor education blends with outdoor recreation, even in bad weather. In addition to taxidermist displays and touch tanks, it features the (indoor) Exxon Learning Trail, which simulates an outdoor nature trail experience. An aboveground pool replicates a cypress swamp, complete with fish, turtles, and two baby alligators. Call for current program and fees; (281) 420-7128.

Fred Hartman Bridge. Glorious double diamond-shaped towers mark this soaring structure over the waters between La Porte and Baytown. Total length of this portion of TX-146 equals eight football fields. Drive slowly and enjoy the views.

Goose Creek Stream Greenbelt. An ongoing project begun in 1990, this ambitious development currently is two-thirds complete, with a final phase scheduled to be finished soon. Visitors now find 1.5 miles of hike-and-bike trail along Goose Creek between Decker Drive and West Texas Avenue (bring your own wheels); a new pavilion, extensive playgrounds, fishing and boating piers, and other facilities at Goose Creek Park; similar redevelopment at Britton Park; and a 7.5-mile, concrete hike-and-bike trail from the Marina area (under TX-146 business) to Arizona Street. When completed this greenbelt will extend from downtown Baytown to Ninfa's Seafood Cantina (see "Where to Eat"), under the eastern end of the Fred Hartman Bridge.

Houston Raceway Park. 2525 FM-565 South. Take exit 798 from I-10 east of downtown, go south to TX-146, then right to FM-565. Billed as the world's fastest drag-racing track, this quarter-mile strip hosts the NHRA Slick 50 Nationals annually in late February/early March and the Jet Car Nationals in June. Want to test your wheels in pro territory? Come on a Wednesday night (March–December) and bring $12. Some type of racing or special event is on every Wednesday and weekend, year-round. Fee; (281) 383-2666; www.houston raceway.com.

WHERE TO EAT

Going's Barbeque Company. 1007 North Main. The name says it all at this locally popular spot. In addition to the usual meats/plates/ sandwiches, there's an all-you-can-eat evening buffet on Thursday. Open daily for lunch and dinner. $-$$; ☐; (281) 422-4600.

The Health Way. 407 West Baker. This health-food store has a nice deli and dining room in back, serving veggie burgers, salads, and sandwiches. Open for lunch Monday–Friday. $; ☐; (281) 427-9000.

Rooster's. 6 West Texas Avenue (at Main Street). This extremely popular locals' hangout specializes in steaks and burgers. Open for lunch and dinner Monday–Saturday. $-$$$; ☐; (281) 428-8222.

Veranda Cafe. 214 West Texas Avenue. Distinctively Italian in most of its menu—the Casa Martelli is a great choice if you love shrimp—you'll also find plenty of "Bubba" food (Texas standards such as steaks, chicken, and seafood) as well. For starters either the calamari or the seafood fondue will stretch your culinary horizon. Open for lunch and dinner Monday–Saturday. $–$$$; ☐; (281) 427-1705.

MORGAN'S POINT

Back in those good old days, Morgan's Point combined with La Porte to provide a beach and bay playground for Houstonians. Big-name bands brought crowds to the dance pavilion at Sylvan Beach, and folks drove around Morgan's Point just to see the handsome homes on the "Gold Coast."

A drive along Bayridge Road still takes you past some of those places, among them a grand replica of the White House, built by former Texas Governor Ross Sterling. It has been a landmark on the Houston Ship Channel for nearly three generations. At the end of Morgan's Point is an undeveloped beach area well known to birders. With binoculars you can watch roseate spoonbills and other species on Atkinson Island, a sanctuary in this upper portion of Galveston Bay.

WANDERING THE BACKROADS

From the San Jacinto Monument, you easily can skip tours of Baytown, La Porte, and Morgan's Point in favor of a jaunt to Clear Lake and Kemah (Trip 2, this sector). Just retrace your route to TX-225 and turn east (left) to its intersection with TX-146. Turn south (right) and go approximately 10 miles to Clear Lake and Kemah.

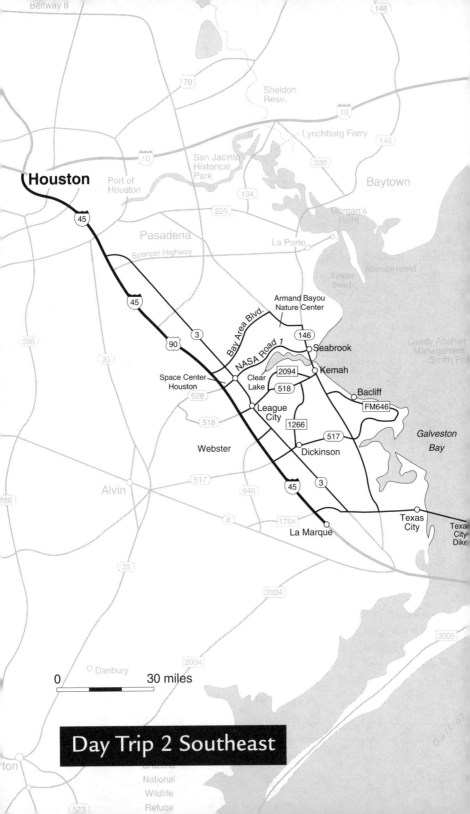

Beltway 8
146
70
Sheldon Resv.
10
Lynchburg Ferry
146
10
San Jacinto Historical Park
330
Houston
Port of Houston
Baytown
134
225
45
Morgan's Point
Pasadena
Spencer Highway
La Porte
Sylvan Beach
Atkinson Island
288
45
3
Candy Abshier Management Smith Po
90
Armand Bayou Nature Center
Bay Area Blvd.
146
Seabrook
35
NASA Road 1
2094
Kemah
Space Center Houston
Clear Lake
518
Bacliff
528
FM646
League City
518
1266
Galveston Bay
Webster
Dickinson
517
518
517
45
3
6
646
Alvin
88
1764
La Marque
Texas City
Texas City Dike
35
2004
3005
0   30 miles
Danbury
2004

Day Trip 2 Southeast

ton
Brazoria
National
Wildlife
Refuge
523

CLEAR LAKE

A drive south from Houston on I-45 brings you to NASA Road 1. Turn east to explore Clear Lake and the laid-back towns of Seabrook and Kemah.

The launching of *Sputnik* also launched America's space program and triggered the construction of the NASA/Lyndon B. Johnson Space Center. Visitors now access some portions of that facility via Space Center Houston, a neighboring $70-million educational/ entertainment project (see "What to Do" section) that's become one of the most popular visitor attractions in the state.

After investigating the exploration of space, you can challenge some new frontiers on your own. A few miles away is nature at its most primitive, a wilderness bayou seemingly untouched by civilization, and almost across the road you'll find the boating and water fun capital of Texas, Clear Lake. That 2,418-acre water playground sports more marinas, boat slips, and boats than any other Lone Star lake. Less adventurous folk enjoy the shops and docks in Seabrook and Kemah, a day's outing in themselves. Toss a cooler in the car to haul home some fresh fish. You'll also enjoy exploring the oak-shaded shops and tearooms in League City.

For information, contact the NASA–Clear Lake Convention and Visitors Bureau, 1601 NASA Road 1, Houston, TX 77058; (281) 338-0333 or (800) 844-5253; www.nasaclearlaketexas.com.

WHAT TO DO

Armand Bayou Nature Center. 8500 Bay Area Boulevard, Houston. One of the largest urban wilderness and wildlife refuges in America, this 2,500-acre haven is home to more than 370 species of wildlife. This refuge hits its birding peak during March and April as a major stopover for migrating flocks. A covered bird blind with interpretive materials allows an educated look.

A 500-foot-long teaching boardwalk leads from the parking lot to the nature center, and additional walking trails thread woods, prairie, and the bayou's edge. Also on the grounds are a restored prairie with two bisons and an observation platform, a new raptor house, and a three-acre exhibit farm focused on the 1890s–1900s. The latter includes a restored and furnished farmhouse (live demonstrations on weekends), a barn, outbuildings, and a vegetable garden. There's also a children's day camp program here in June and July.

The water portions of this wilderness park are best explored by canoe. You can either bring your own and put in at adjacent Bay Area Park, or you can participate (fee) in the canoe trips sponsored by the nature center (reservations required). Groups of ten to twelve also can reserve naturalist-led trips via pontoon boat (fee). Consider buying a family membership ($45) while you're at the nature center to help preserve this wilderness. Open Tuesday–Sunday. Fee; (281) 474–2551; www.abnc.org.

Boating and other water sports on Clear Lake and Galveston Bay. At this writing at least twenty sources provide charters, rentals, lessons, or excursions. The following are of particular interest to casual day visitors.

Several companies offer brief water trips on Clear Lake and/or Galveston Bay at various times and seasons. Here are two to consider: Kemah Baywatch Tours, (713) 962–6994; and Tropical Express, (281) 538–0773, www.tropicalexpress.com/.

Clear Lake Charter Boats and Clear Lake Powerboat Rentals, based at South Shore Harbor Hotel in League City and at the Nassau Bay Hilton, offer sailboat and powerboat rentals, bay and gulf fishing trips, and parasailing; (281) 334–4858.

Gateway Charters and Sailing School at the Kemah Boardwalk Marina (formerly Lafayette Landing Marina) in Kemah offers private sailing lessons, boat and breakfast, sunset and moonlight cruises (minimum eight people), and boat charters (with captain and crew, or without); (281) 334-4604.

Houston/Bay Area Rowing Centers, based at Watergate Marina in Kemah and at Clear Lake Shores Marina, teaches the fundamentals of rowing and sculling and rents equipment. Ask about the free introductory rowing excursions on Saturday morning and affordable club membership that gives members use of club craft; (281) 334-3101.

Parasail Clear Lake, based at the Nassau Bay Hilton Marina, offers parasailing as well as hourly and daily rentals of sailboats, Hobie-Cats, jet skis, wave runners, motorboats, and canoes; (281) 333-2816.

Windsurfing Sports, based at 3000 NASA Road 1 in Seabrook, offers sailboard, wakeboard, and kayak rentals by the hour or day; (281) 291-9199; www.windsurfingsports.com.

The following offer sailing lessons, boat charters, and/or fishing trips: At the Helm, based at Kemah Boardwalk Marina in Kemah, offers sailing and rowing lessons; (281) 334-4101; www.atthehelmgulf.com.

South Coast Sailing, also based in Kemah, is an ASA sailing school providing certification through several levels of instruction. They also offer fishing charters; (281) 334-4606; www.southcoast sailing.com.

School of Seamanship, based at the South Shore Harbor Marina in League City, offers ASA certification at all levels of boat training; (281) 997-0416.

Windward Seaventure Charters, based at Waterford Harbor in Kemah, offers sailing lessons as well as sailboat and powerboat rentals (with or without a captain); (281) 334-5295 or (800) 910-7245; www.windwardseaventure.com.

The following offer charters: Bay Area Sailing Association, (281) 334-1856; Majestic Ventures, (281) 333-3080; Sackett's Sailing Center, (281) 334-4179; Star Fleet, (281) 334-4692; and Ultra Sailing Charters, (281) 333-2063. Star Fleet offers a few public cruises at various times of the year; call for details.

Canoeing the bayous. There is canoe access at Bay Area Park and at the NASA Road 1 bridge at Clear Lake Park, 5001 NASA Road 1. Canoes can be rented by the hour or day at Cecil's Red Lantern Restaurant, 2908 Red Bluff Road (at the bridge on Taylor Lake), (281) 474-7660, and at Windsurfing Sports (see above). If you don't want to canoe at those specific sites, inquire whether the proprietors provide or rent car-top carriers or racks to transport canoes; you may need to bring your own.

You'll also find pleasant canoeing in Dickinson Bayou, which roughly parallels FM–517, both west and east from I–45. There is a good put-in and parking at Paul Hopkins Park in Dickinson, and then you have your choice of takeouts: a carry either at the FM–646 crossing (3.5 miles) or at Cemetery Road. This last section is the most beautiful and undisturbed. *Note:* Canoeing here is best on weekdays.

Galveston Bay Foundation. 1724-A North Highway 3, Webster. There's no need to go to Galveston to explore and enjoy bay waters. This volunteer nonprofit organization sponsors more than fifty activities and workshops annually, all focused on the natural ecology of Galveston Bay. Recent trips included canoe tours of Armand Bayou, Cedar Bayou, and Double Bayou; inspection by boat of the Houston Ship Channel; and a guided look at Anahuac National Wildlife Refuge. Emphasis always is on responsible ecotourism. Trips fill fast, and preference goes to members. Membership fees start at $15; (281) 332–3381; www.galvbay.org.

Space Center Houston. 1601 NASA Road 1, Houston. From I–45 South take the NASA Road 1 exit and go 3 miles east. Billed as "A Magical Place to Discover Space," this focal point for America's manned space flight program has interactive exhibits that are easy to understand and fun to operate. Care to try your hand at landing the shuttle? Intercepting an errant satellite in space? Performing space chores at zero gravity? You can do all three and more, courtesy of a large bank of computer stations in the "Feel of Space" section, on the left as you enter.

An ideal outing regardless of the season or weather, Space Center Houston has an IMAX theater, a full-size mock-up of portions of the space shuttle, a super display of moon rocks (you can touch one), and tram tours that scoot you around limited portions of Johnson Space Center, next door. Got children under twelve in tow? A $1.2-million Kids' Space Place offers numerous out-of-this-world activities designed specifically for that age group. Kids can now create a mock shuttle flight at Mission Kidtrol, experience what it feels like to walk on the moon, and so on. Plan to spend at least four to six hours here, more if you eat at the Zero G Diner, a cafeteria-style food court. *Nice to know:* If you just want to visit the gift shop, you have a forty-five-minute free period during which you can get your entrance fee back. There's also a day camp program for children in summer. *Also note:* The NASA–Lyndon B. Johnson Space Center, including Rocket Park, is no longer open to the public except through Space Center Houston. Open daily. Fee; (281) 244–2100 or (800) 972–0369; www.spacecenter.org.

WHERE TO EAT

The Cross-Eyed Seagull Restaurant & Bar. 1010 East NASA Road 1, Webster (at Egret Bay Boulevard). Happiness is chowing down on delicious shrimp while sitting on this cafe's over-bayou deck. The burgers, quesadillas, meat loaf, and pizzas are popular as well, and there's live entertainment nightly. Open for lunch and dinner daily. $-$$; ☐; (281) 333–3488.

Frenchie's. 1041 East NASA Road 1, at El Camino Real, Webster. This small, friendly place has been a local favorite since it was opened fifteen years ago by the Camera family, formerly of the Isle of Capri in Italy. You'll find scads of photographs on the walls, as well as a menu that ranges from family-style Italian to seafood and steaks. Although casual for lunch, it's a bit dressier for dinner. Open for lunch and dinner Monday–Saturday. $$-$$$; ☐; (281) 486–7144.

CONTINUING ON

From Clear Lake this day trip follows NASA Road 1 east to its intersection with TX–146 in Seabrook and then turns south. The area on the north side of the bridge is Seabrook. On the south side is Kemah.

SEABROOK AND KEMAH

Each of these small communities makes an ideal day trip destination in itself. The number of things to do in the general area keeps growing, however, so consider reserving overnight accommodations at the Boardwalk Inn on the Kemah Boardwalk, (281) 334–9980 or (877) 285–3624, www.kemah.com. Or check out and into one of the area's very interesting B&Bs: The Back Bay Inn, (281) 474–3869, www.backbaybnb.com; Beacon Hill Guest House, (281) 326-7643, www.visitbeaconhill.com; The Crew's Quarters, (281) 334-4141; or Pelican House, (281) 474-5295, www.pelicanhouse.com.

To overnight here in bayside luxury and still be within walking distance of nearly everything in Kemah, call the Captain's Quarters, (281) 334-4141; www.captsquarters.com. Owner Mary Patterson also puts on an elegant afternoon tea with live entertainment on the first Thursday of every month ($$; reservations required). Mary also operates four other B&Bs in the Kemah-Seabrook area.

Both Seabrook and Kemah are heaven for seafood lovers and boat watchers, but each has its own distinct personality. Their common boundary, the Clear Creek Channel under the Kemah–Seabrook (TX-146) bridge, is the only passage from Clear Lake into Galveston Bay, and views of the constant boat parade are great from the outside decks of Kemah Boardwalk's seven waterfront restaurants. If you want to buy shrimp and other Galveston Bay catches fresh and relatively cheap, check out the numerous fish markets that line the channel on the Seabrook side of the bridge. Seabrook's channel-front also sports several eateries.

Away from the water the quaint buildings of "Old" Seabrook now house assorted antiques stores, tearooms, and specialty shops. To find them follow NASA Road 1 east through the signal at TX-146 (it becomes Second Street) and turn right. If you like bazaars and flea markets, don't miss Seabrook's Back Bay Market (free admission) on the second weekend of every month, (281) 474-3869.

Always vulnerable to intermittent change by storms, Kemah's somewhat funky but charming fishing village character finally has been forever vanquished. Long loved by Houstonians as an unpretentious spot to sit, sup, and sip while enjoying the channel boat parade and the breezes off Galveston Bay, all of Kemah's channel-front now functions as a fourteen-acre entertainment theme park called the Kemah Boardwalk, courtesy of Landry's Seafood Restaurant, Inc., which bought out the entire strip in early 1997. Successful in the extreme, the Kemah Boardwalk now attracts more than three million visitors annually and provides an economic stability the region truly needed.

Visitors now find a slickly designed, upscale complex composed of seven themed restaurants (most of them names you know from other locations; see "Where to Eat"), retail shops, hotel, water park, and amusement zone, all connected by a wide and lighted boardwalk along the channel. The latter's a plus, something that the old Kemah lacked. You also can get around via a gas-powered choo-choo, the *C. P. Huntington,* which replicates an 1863 Central Pacific Railroad train. For information regarding ongoing events call (281) 334-9880 or (877) 285-3624; www.kemahboardwalk.com.

Kemah also has a delightful old-fashioned carousel, an enormous slide, and a 65-foot Ferris wheel on the edge of the bay. Also bring waterwear, the better to play in the "dancing fountains" in the hotel's courtyard. Pinwheel in shape, the fountains intermittently shoot water up to 12 feet through seventy-five jets, a handsome sight when lit by colored lights at night.

To reach all of Kemah's fresh splendor, turn east at the Sixth Street stoplight at the southern end of the TX–146 bridge; then go north on Bradford. You'll also find interesting shopping, several eateries, and the Kemah Boardwalk Marina (formerly Lafayette Landing Marina) on the streets immediately behind the channel area and bay front.

WHERE TO EAT

Of the seven restaurants on the Kemah side of the channel, four are major eateries travelers usually know well from other locations: Cadillac Bar, Joe's Crab Shack, Landry's, and Willie G's. Another popular chain, Pappadeaux, is across the channel on the Seabrook waterfront. If you're interested in other dining experiences, try one of the following.

In Kemah:
The Aquarium. No. 11, Kemah Waterfront, Kemah. Top-notch in every respect, this very fishy place delights as a sensory experience. Its two-story heart is a huge cylindrical aquarium filled with major salt-water fish; if you're there at feeding time, you'll see a scuba diver hand-delivering dinner to some of the aquarium's more reclusive denizens. The human food is equally spectacular; the multipage menu offers numerous entrees, and each will arrive at your table properly cooked and presented. You can economize a bit on the desserts; each easily serves two. Don't miss doing some time on the outside decks—that's what Kemah's really all about. Open for dinner daily, lunch and dinner on Friday–Sunday. $–$$$; ☐; (281) 334-9010.

The Flying Dutchman Restaurant and Oyster Bar. No. 9, Kemah Waterfront. Ask local residents where they take visitors for good and inventive seafood, and this place wins by a landslide. It's dressy duds upstairs, cutoffs and casual boating wear down. Unless the weather's at one of its uncomfortable extremes, try for a table on the deck, the better to watch the boat traffic. Open daily for lunch and dinner. $–$$$; ☐; (281) 334–7575.

The Kemah Crab House. No. 3, Kemah Waterfront. A more classy environment than Joe's Crab Shack, this spot offers entrees ranging from fresh fish to more than six different types of crab, along with Angus beef, pastas, and a well-stocked salad and shellfish bar. Food also is served on the deck overlooking the channel. Open daily for lunch and dinner. $–$$$; ☐; (281) 334–3360.

Sartin's Seafood of Kemah. 310 Texas Avenue. A small bit of Kemah as it used to be, this unflossy spot has a nice deck and some of the best barbecued crab ever served. The menu also stretches to fried-fish platters and lunch specials. If you're planning this stop, call in advance for a reservation. Open Wednesday–Sunday in winter; Tuesdays as well (usually) in summer. $–$$; ☐; (409) 892–6771.

T-Bone Tom's Meat Market and Steakhouse Restaurant. 707 TX-146. Why anyone would want a great steak, spicy sausage, ribs, chicken, or barbecue in the midst of fresh fish territory is beyond understanding, but if that's your pleasure, this is the place. Open Monday–Saturday for lunch and dinner. $–$$; ☐; (281) 334–2133; www.tbonetoms.com.

What's Cooking. 930 Highway 518. This cozy spot serves a broad Continental menu, but it's the Middle European dishes that really shine. Hungry for Hungarian? Authentic goulash soup is one of chef-owner Kristine Garbo's specialties. You also can't go wrong with the wiener schnitzel, rouladen, and sausage sampler, accompanied by potato pancakes and spicy red cabbage. You'll find fresh/never-been-frozen fish here and a great jazz brunch on Sundays, as well. No simple buffet on the latter; it's all table service with the food freshly prepared when you order. Open daily for lunch and dinner. $–$$$; ☐; (281) 334–3610.

In Seabrook:

Bay Thai Restaurant. 1101 Second Street. Tucked away in a pink cottage on a back bay residential street, this small, family-owned place has oriented its front door to the west, an omen for success suggested by a Thai fortune-teller. No need. The food at this eatery makes it on its own. Entrees on the a la carte menu range from traditional Thai dishes to specialties such as wild boar curry and emu with Thai seasonings. Owner-chef Gil Lobeck is Bangkok-born, and his love of fine food shows. Open for dinner Tuesday–Saturday. $$–$$$; ☐; (281) 474-4248.

The Crazy Cajun. 2825 NASA Road 1. No way can you stay in a bad mood in this relaxed and zany place. The waiters will charm you right out of the blues, a cup of gumbo will rev up your taste buds, and the Cajun Shrimp Combo will satisfy hunger pangs for hours. Open daily for lunch and dinner. $$–$$$; ☐; (281) 326-6055.

Frenchie's Villa Capri. 3713 NASA Road 1. Dress up here. This "Cucina d'Italia" is one of the prettiest places on Clear Lake, complete with an outdoor patio and Italian-style gardens stretching to the water's edge. Italian dishes get top billing, along with grilled seafood and steaks. Open for lunch and dinner Tuesday–Sunday. $$–$$$; ☐; (281) 326-2373.

Seabrook Classic Cafe. 2511-A NASA Road 1. This is a great place for weekend breakfasts, particularly if you have a fondness for those nifty little New Orleans doughnuts called beignets. Everything is fresh here and made from scratch. Open for lunch and dinner daily, breakfast on weekends. $–$$; ☐; (281) 326-1512.

Sundance Grill. 222 Jennings Island. Located in the Seabrook Shipyard immediately west of the TX–146 bridge, this waterfront eatery specializes in very creative seafood and salads. Try the Sausalito Salmon (topped with an avocado-citrus salsa), Shrimp Bimini (stuffed with a mix of crab, salmon, herbs, and choron sauce), or the double-frenched lamb chops (pricey but worth it). *Re desserts:* The crème brûlée is God's food, plus four of their pastry offerings are imported from Vienna. Don't come here if you're in a hurry; service (particularly on the outside deck) often has been slow here in the past. If that happens, and you have swimsuits, you're welcome to take a dip in their swimming pool. Open for lunch and dinner daily; reservations advised. $–$$; ☐; (281) 474-2248.

Tookie's. 1202 TX–146. When you are hankering for a hamburger, thick and sweet onion rings, and real iced tea (huge and made with freshly brewed hot tea), come here. Open daily for lunch and dinner. $; ☐; (281) 474-3444.

CONTINUING ON

From Kemah drive south on TX–146 to the signal at FM–2094 and turn west (right) to the FM–518 West intersection. That latter road becomes Main Street in this day trip's next stop: League City.

LEAGUE CITY

This community, at the conjunction of Clear Creek and Sugar Bayou—the site of a Karankawa Indian village in pre-Anglo settlement times—was known as Butler's Ranch and/or Clear Creek when it was first settled by ranchers around 1854.

Two decades later J. C. League acquired a large amount of local land and laid out his namesake townsite along the right-of-way for the Galveston, Houston & Henderson Railroad. League City melds its Victorian past with current tourism in several pleasant ways. Walking tour maps, available in several shops and cafes, lead you to more than two dozen historic sites, and both tearooms and antiques shops seem growth industries. For advance information contact the League City Historical Society, P.O. Box 1642, League City, TX 77574, or the League City Chamber of Commerce and Business Association, 621 Park Avenue, League City, TX 77573; (281) 338–7339; www.leaguecitychamber.com.

WHAT TO SEE

West Bay Common School Children's Museum Complex. 210 North Kansas Street (at Second Street). This award-winning, hands-on history experience captivates everyone regardless of age. A costumed "school marm" brings alive the rural education experience typical of Texas at the turn of the twentieth century; there's even a forty-five-star American flag. Sitting at old-fashioned desks in a real one-room school, youngsters use slates to learn the three R's from late-nineteenth-century textbooks, practice Spencerian penmanship in old-time pen and ink, and so on. The building itself was built in 1898 in west Chambers County and moved to the site of League City's original school in 1992. League City's 1927 icehouse and barber shop (1936) also have been moved here and restored as exhibits; an old barn serves as a regional museum. Open Monday–Thursday and on Friday mornings. Classes are conducted only for groups with advance reservations; (281) 554–2994 or 332–1644; www.oneroomschoolhouse.org.

WHERE TO EAT

Clifton by the Sea. P.O. Box 975, Kemah (at bay end of FM-646). Rising from the ashes of a disastrous 1997 fire, this spiffy eatery now has a diner atmosphere, great outdoor decks, and a patio that overlooks Galveston Bay. Nearly everything edible that swims in the Gulf dominates the menu, but they also offer steaks and one or two versions of chicken. Daily lunch specials ($) are good choices, as are the seafood po'boys. If your internal thermostat can handle it, try Clifton's Stuffed Jalapeños. Open for lunch and dinner daily. $–$$$; ☐; (281) 339–FISH.

Esteban's Cafe and Cantina. 402 West Main. One of the most appealing Mexican eateries in the greater Houston region, this family-owned spot makes its own sauces and tortillas from scratch daily. Don't miss either the spinach or crab enchiladas, just two of the house specialties. Open daily for lunch and dinner. $–$$; ☐; (281) 332–4195.

WANDERING THE BACKROADS

To return to Houston swing west on FM-518 to its intersection with I-45 North. If you want to extend this day trip, however, consider heading east on FM-518 to TX-146 and then turning south for a short drive to the Texas City Dike (signs). A 5-mile-long strip of road and breakwater jutting into Galveston Bay, the dike is popular with sailboarders and folks with small sailboats and catamarans because the winds are relatively dependable. Fishing and crabbing are wherever you find a spot. There also are boat-launching facilities and plenty of beach/auto access at the Texas City Dike Beach Park. Due to a major cleanup effort, the dike now is reasonably clean, with adequate parking available along the sides of the road. The numerous fish-camp shanties and ramshackle cafes that lined much of its distance for some years have been removed, and visitors now find open vistas of Galveston Bay, portable toilets, and even a few potted palms for atmosphere. There are no rentals or concessions, however, so bring everything you might need (water, shade, chair, sunscreen, food, bait, and tackle) with you. Also bring binoculars; the birding's often excellent.

As an alternate to the dike, sailboarders and wade fishers may prefer to turn left at the entrance to the dike onto Skyline Drive. Great kite-flying territory, it also offers a 6-mile view and water playground along the bay. Along the way you'll find an interesting hike-and-bike path, a lighthouse-styled pavilion with information panels, a rifle range (open Wednesday–Sunday), a small beach with rustic changing room and toilets, and the Thomas S. Mackey Nature Center. The latter is a thirty-five-acre wildlife habitat within the northern section of Bay Street Park, developed with the aid of local Boy Scouts and opened in 1998.

A third site in this same general area, the Texas City Prairie Preserve on Moses Lake, will be of interest to birders. Operated by the Nature Conservancy and usually open to the public on weekdays, the visitor center is primarily an educational facility for groups. Day-trippers with binoculars get good looks at shorebirds, but the surrounding land is a sensitive habitat for the endangered Attwater prairie chicken; please observe signs. *Note:* Neither dogs nor picnics are allowed here, and small children usually end up bitten by fire ants. For information, contact this preserve at 4702 TX-146 North, Texas City, TX 77590; (409) 941-9114.

Birders note: This Texas City area has a total of five sites on the upper Texas coast version of the Great Texas Coastal Birding Trail. Instructions for ordering that map are in the "Additional Resources" listing in the front of this book.

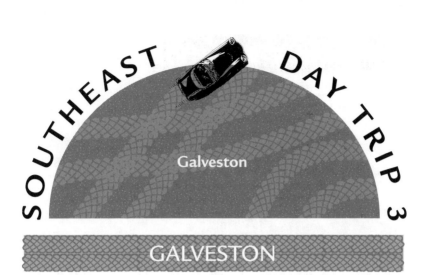

GALVESTON

Cabeza de Vaca found it first. Later a pirate named Jean Lafitte made this sliver of island his base of shady operations in 1817. Legend says his treasure still lies buried in the shifting sands, and hunting for it with metal detectors is a favorite Galveston pastime.

To Houstonians this small city, one hour's drive south via I-45, traditionally has been a relief valve, a place to escape from big-city life for a lazy day or weekend at the beach. But Galveston is far more than surf and sand.

Long before Houston was much more than a landing on Buffalo Bayou, Galveston was a major port and the threshold to Texas for thousands of immigrants. By the 1870s it was the wealthy and thriving "Queen City of the Southwest," and during the golden era of 1875–1900 some of the most remarkable architecture in America lined its streets.

A devastating hurricane in 1900 killed some 6,000 people and swept much of the city out to sea. Vulnerable to every passing storm, Galveston seemed doomed to follow the earlier Texas coast ports of Indianola and Lavaca into oblivion. To save the city and ensure its future security, two major engineering projects were undertaken, both remarkable for their times. The first was the building of a massive seawall, 17 feet tall and 10 miles long. The second was the raising of all the land behind that seawall from 4 to 17 feet.

These projects took seven years and were followed by another economic blow in 1915, when the successful completion of the

Day Trip 3 Southeast

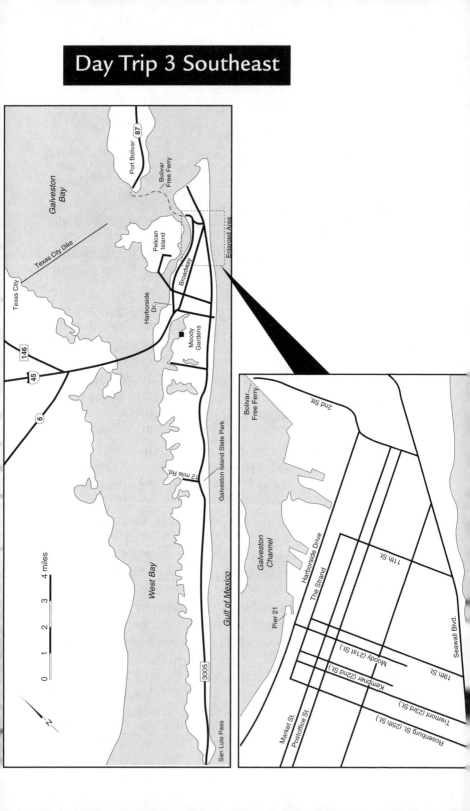

Houston Ship Channel began to draw off the cream of the port trade. Galveston never recovered its prehurricane commercial importance, and gradually it degenerated into one of the wildest gambling towns in the state. The Texas Rangers finally brought down the law in the 1950s, and after that Galveston slumbered along as a rather seedy seaside city for a time.

But all is changing and on the upswing once again. The renovation and restoration of many historic buildings and a growth in the hotel/convention sector has sparked fresh capital investment, and Galveston now is thriving. Don't miss a ride on the $10-million rail trolley system that connects, in 1890s–1920s style, the Strand Historic District with the seawall. Additionally, electric bus shuttles ($1.00 per ride) operate approximately every twenty-five minutes Thursday–Sunday on a route that includes several stops in The Strand Historic District, on the Seawall, and at the Moody Gardens Hotel/Entertainment complex. Information: www.islandtransit.net.

Bed-and-breakfast also is strong in Galveston; for booking information contact the Galveston Island Visitors Center noted below. *Fun to know:* You now can overnight aboard a 120-foot schooner conveniently anchored at the edge of The Strand Historic District. The Stacia Leigh Bed & Breakfast Aboard the *Chryseis* (circa 1906) has eleven staterooms with whirlpool baths.

Information on Galveston is available from the Heritage Visitors Center, operated by the Galveston Historical Foundation (GHF), 2328 Broadway, Galveston, TX 77550; (409) 762–3933. Other sources include the Moody Gardens Visitors Center, One Hope Boulevard, Galveston, TX 77554; (800) 582–4673; and the Galveston Island Visitors Center, 2428 Seawall Boulevard (at Twenty-fourth Street), Galveston, TX 77550; (409) 763–4311 or (888) 425–4753. The latter offers, by mail only, a free discount coupon booklet that gives reduced rates on some accommodations, attractions, and restaurants.

EXPLORING THE BEACHES

There are 32 miles of beachfront on the island and a variety of options. The decisions start after you cross the causeway from the mainland on I-45 and see the directional signs for East and West beaches. If you continue east (left lanes), I-45 becomes Broadway

Boulevard and runs in an easterly direction the length of the island. If you follow the signs to West Beach from I-45, you will cross the island on Sixty-first Street, which ends at Seawall Boulevard, the island's second east-west main drag. Turn right; West Beach starts where the seawall ends. The road becomes FM-3005 at this point and continues down-island to San Luis Pass. Do note that cars are not allowed on Galveston's beaches at any time of the year and that alcohol is banned both along the seawall and at Stewart Beach.

Good news: A $4.8-million replenishment program begun in 1995 is piping sand from an offshore reef to increase the width of Galveston's beaches by 50 feet.

Seafood tip: Want to buy fresh from the boats? Bring a cooler and check out the fish markets in the 1700–1900 blocks of Sixty-first Street.

There is one beach pocket-park on FM-3005, at 11 Mile Road. Operated by Galveston County, it has changing rooms, showers, food concessions, playgrounds, and picnic areas and is backed by protected natural dunes. Horseback riding, parasailing, sailboarding, and other commercial beach activities often are available nearby during warm-weather months. West Beach offers the best jogging and shelling, particularly near San Luis Pass.

In town you'll find numerous small beaches tucked between the rock jetties along Seawall Boulevard. Stop and watch the dolphins roll in the offshore swells and then walk out onto the jetties and chat with the fishermen. There are several places to rent roller skates, bicycles, and pedal surreys, and the wide sidewalk along the top of the seawall is a favorite promenade. The boulevard curves at the east end of the island and intersects Broadway at Stewart Beach. This city-run stretch of sand is popular with families because of its lifeguards, bathhouse, lockers, parking, and concessions.

A short drive farther east brings you to R. A. Apffel Park, a $2-million, 1980s development at the extreme end of East Beach. A favorite with fisherfolk and families as well as teenagers looking for like kind, it has excellent boating and fishing facilities and an 11,000-square-foot recreation center that includes a bathhouse and concessions. *Also here:* the Big Reef Nature Park with observation platforms for birding.

Galveston Island State Park. West of downtown Galveston on FM-3005 at the intersection with Thirteen Mile Road. Another beach facility with picnicking and camping, this 2,000-acre state park also offers bird-watching from observation platforms and nature trails along its north boundary; the latter faces the protected waters of West Galveston Bay. Some seven acres of freshwater ponds within the park often are stocked with trout during the winter months; (409) 737–1222 or (800) 792–1112. The park's Mary Moody Northen Amphitheatre features major musical productions during the summer; (409) 737–1744 or (800) 547–4697; www.tpwd.state.tx.us.

Palm Beach. West of town in Moody Gardens, 1 Hope Boulevard off Eighty-first Street. This three-acre freshwater swimming complex faces the bay. Facilities include whirlpools, lockers, a boardwalk, concessions, and lifeguards. This is the only beach in Texas with Caribbean-style white sand and palms. Fee; (409) 744–7256; www.moodygardens.com.

EXPLORING HISTORIC GALVESTON

Start at The Strand, once called the "Wall Street of the Southwest" and now the heart of one of the island's three historic districts. In itself The Strand is considered one of the largest and best collections of nineteenth-century iron-front commercial buildings remaining in America.

To reach The Strand area from the I–45 South causeway, take the Harborside Drive exit and turn east (left). To get to The Strand from Broadway, turn north on Twenty-fourth Street and continue 8 blocks. Most of the buildings along The Strand now house shops, galleries, businesses, and restaurants—more than ninety-five in all. Dickens-on-The Strand, a Victorian-themed Christmas festival on the first weekend in December, often draws crowds in excess of 70,000 and is covered by the national press.

The following major historic sites are either within the Strand Historic District or nearby:

The 1871 League Building. Strand at Tremont. One of the nicest restorations in the city and home to several interesting shops and The Brothers Petronella restaurant (see "Where to Eat").

The 1882 H. M. Trueheart–Adriance Building. 210 Kempner. This Nicholas Clayton–designed building is one of the most ornate and distinctive structures in the area. Its restoration in 1970 sparked The Strand's renaissance.

The *Elissa*/Texas Seaport Museum. Harborside Drive at Pier 21 (1 block north of The Strand). An 1877 square-rigged barque called *Elissa* rides at anchor here. One of the oldest vessels in Lloyd's Register of Shipping, she also represents Texas in assorted "tall ship" parades and is open daily for tours. Visitors roam (self-guided) through restored after-cabins, the hold, and the decks. In addition to a film detailing *Elissa*'s acquisition and restoration, the museum chronicles Galveston's rich maritime heritage through interactive exhibits and a wide-screen multimedia presentation on the age of sail. Open daily. Fee; (409) 763–1877; www.tsm-elissa.org.

Galveston Arts Center. 2127 Strand. If you like mixing art with history, drop in at this eclectic gallery, housed in the old First National Bank Building. Closed Monday from Labor Day to Memorial Day; (409) 763–2403.

Galveston Railroad Museum and Terminal. Strand at Twenty-fifth Street, Galveston. The top draw here is the original waiting room of Galveston's old train depot, where life-size sculptures of travelers are frozen in a moment of 1932; unusual "hear" phones allow visitors to eavesdrop on their conversations. Two exhibits in particular interest children: a 550-square-foot layout of a town in HO-scale, complete with rolling stock, entitled "A Day in the Life of an American Railroad"; and a small room off the main station lobby that houses The Childress Collection, nearly 2,000 models representing a variety of cars, trucks, and even ice-scraping Zambonis. Out back are numerous steam locomotives and assorted railroad cars, a picnic gazebo, and exhibits of steam-powered machines. A mini train offers rides for children on select weekends. Open daily. Fee; (409) 765–5700; www.tamug.edu/rrmuseum/.

The Marx and Kempner Building. 2100 block of The Strand. Can you spot the clever trompe l'oeil mural? The original window detailing of this building was removed decades ago, and what looks like several vintage facades actually is hand-painted artwork.

The Tremont House. 2300 Ship's Mechanic Row. This superbly restored 1879 building now houses one of the most elegant small hotels in Texas; (409) 763–0300, (713) 480–8201, or (800) 874–2300 (reservations only).

Driving is recommended to cover these more distant historic sites:

The Bishop's Palace. 1402 Broadway. The only East End Historic

District home open to the public, this massive place was built between 1886 and 1892 for the Walter Gresham family. Designed by noted Galveston architect Nicholas Clayton, it is considered one of the one hundred most outstanding residential structures in America. Even more interesting than its turreted, rococo exterior are the details and furnishings inside. Fee. Guided tours are given daily, year-round; (409) 762–2475.

The East End Historical District. This special area covers 40 blocks of Victoriana bounded by Broadway, Market, Nineteenth, and Eleventh Streets. It can be driven or walked, but the best way to see the most is by bicycle or on the historical foundation's Homes Tour in early May.

1839 Samuel May Williams Home. 3601 Bernardo de Galvez (Avenue P). One of the two oldest structures in Galveston, this charming restoration now looks as it did in 1839. Open weekends. Fee; (409) 765–1839; www.galvestonhistory.org.

1859 Ashton Villa. 2328 Broadway. This Italianate beauty was built in 1859 of bricks made on the island and survived both a disastrous island-wide fire in 1885 and the 1900 storm. It now is restored as the showplace of the Galveston Historical Foundation and home to the Heritage Visitors Center. An interesting urban archaeological dig exposes a small portion of the home's original raised basement, which was filled in when the level of the island was raised after the 1900 storm. Open daily. Fee; (409) 762–3933; www.galvestonhistory.org.

Galveston County Historical Museum. 2219 Market Street. The handsome City National Bank Building, circa 1919, houses more of Galveston's glorious past. Open daily, except major holidays; (409) 766–2340.

Galveston Island Trolley. Styled to resemble the trolleys operating in early-twentieth-century Galveston, this streetcar system has two routes. One downtown loop operates in The Strand area (free), and a fixed-rail, 4.7-mile-long route crosses the island between Twentieth Street and Strand and Twentieth Street and Seawall Boulevard. Fee; (409) 797–3900; www.islandtransit.net.

Garten Verein Dancing Pavilion. Avenue O and Twenty-seventh Street, in Kempner Park. Built in 1880 and freshly restored, this is a delightful, "very Galveston" spot to have a picnic or let children spend some energy; www.galvestonhistory.org.

The Hotel Galvez. 2024 Seawall Boulevard. Constructed in 1911 at a cost in excess of $1 million, this six-story Spanish Colonial Revival building was named after Bernardo de Galvez, the Spanish colonial governor who first charted the Texas Gulf Coast and for whom the island is named. The Galvez was the island's showplace and a celebrity playground during the 1920s and 1930s; its registers held the names of presidents and movie stars until it became U.S. Coast Guard housing during World War II. A multimillion-dollar renovation completed in 1998 has returned the hotel's public rooms to their original appearance, refurbished guest rooms to luxury status, and created seven over-the-moon suites. Day visitors are welcome to explore the lobby level; there's also an outstanding Sunday brunch; (409) 765-7721.

The Grand 1894 Opera House. 2020 Postoffice Street. The interior of this interesting building has been restored to its early-twentieth-century grandeur, and the stage once again hosts a variety of performing arts throughout the year. For box office information call (409) 765-1894 or (800) 821-1894; www.thegrand.com.

John Sydnor's 1847 Powhatan House. 3427 Avenue O. Home to the Galveston Garden Club, this handsome mansion with its oak-filled gardens is on the National Register. No high heels, please; they damage the beautiful pine floors. Public tours on Saturday afternoon. Fee; (409) 763-0077.

The Michel Menard Home. 1605 Thirty-third Street. Galveston's oldest home has recently been restored and contains an outstanding collection of nineteenth-century furniture. Open Friday–Sunday. Fee; (409) 762-3933; www.galvestonhistory.org.

The Moody Mansion & Museum. 2628 Broadway. This marvelous old home is the Smithsonian of Galveston. The city's grande dame, the late Mary Moody Northen never threw anything away—archivists even found Christmas presents in their original wrappings, with full notation as to year and giver—and her lifelong home has been restored to the way it looked at her debut in 1911. Open daily. Fee; (409) 762-7668; www.moodymansion.org.

Postoffice Street. Four blocks south of The Strand between Twentieth and Twenty-third Streets, this once-busy thoroughfare again bustles with life as the main artery of Galveston's evolving art and entertainment district. A stroll here finds shops, galleries, coffeehouses, antiques stores, and The Grand 1894 Opera House (see above).

The Silk Stocking Historical District. Biking or windshield tours of this 9-block area, loosely bounded by Rosenberg, J and N Avenues, and Tremont Street, are visual fun. Unfortunately, no historic homes here currently are open to the public.

TODAY'S GALVESTON

If you've had it with history or are burned out with beaches, there is still plenty to do.

Air tours of Galveston Island. For a bird's-eye view of this sliver of barrier sand, call P Factor Aviation. They offer one-hour tours ($150 for up to two persons, $50 per additional person) in a variety of aircraft; (281) 610–4925.

Bicycle rentals. Numerous shops along Seawall Boulevard rent almost anything that rolls.

Birding. An ideal location for either novice or expert, Galveston Island has more than a dozen prime birding sites on the Great Texas Coastal Birding Trail map for the upper coast. For a list of guided birding tours, call Galveston Island Visitors Center; (409) 763–4311 or (888) 425–4753; www.galveston.com.

Boat launching. Free facilities on Teichman Road, Sportsman Road, and at Washington Park on Sixty-first Street.

Carriage rides. Horse-drawn surreys leave daily from the vicinity of Twenty-first Street and The Strand on thirty- and sixty-minute tours of the various historic districts. Fee.

Fishing. In addition to the rock jetties along the seawall, there are commercial fishing piers at Twenty-fifth, Sixty-first, and Ninetieth Streets and at Seawolf Park on Pelican Island. Surf fishing is allowed along most of the open beaches; common catches are speckled trout, flounder, catfish, and redfish.

Party boats for fishing in either the bay or the Gulf leave early in the morning from Piers 18 and 19 and from the yacht basin. A Texas fishing license is required for everyone between the ages of seventeen and sixty-five unless you are fishing at least 10.5 miles offshore. Check to see if a license is required when you make your reservations. Common Gulf catches include red snapper, sailfish, pompano, warsaw, marlin, ling, king mackerel, bonito, and dolphin. Take precautions against seasickness before you go—the Gulf can get rough. For specific charter information contact Galveston Party Boats, Inc.,

(409) 763–5423; Williams Party Boats, (409) 762–8808; or the Galveston Charter Boat Association, (409) 762–2200.

Galveston duck tours. Twenty-first and Seawall. These amphibious transports scoot you around the city's tourist spots and then enter the water to cruise Offats Bayou, a ninety-minute excursion that shows off the island in an unusual way. Fee. Reservations advised during peak tourism months; (409) 621–4771.

Harbor tours. Galveston Harbor Tours, based at Pier 22 on Fisherman's Wharf, runs forty-five-minute narrated boat tours of Texas's oldest seaport. Dolphin sightings are frequent, so ask about the special Dolphin Watch tours on Saturday morning. Call the day before to check on weather and scheduling. Fee; (409) 765–1700.

Moored at Moody Gardens, *The Colonel* churns its way around Galveston's harbor and inner bay with old-fashioned, stern-wheeler style. There are three narrated cruises daily, weather permitting, as well as dinner-dance and jazz options. Fee; (409) 740–7797; www.moodygardens.com.

Horseback riding. Weather permitting, you can rent a steed at Gulf Stream Stables, Eight Mile Road; (409) 744–1004.

Kemp's Ridley Sea Turtle Head Start Project. 5000 Avenue U. Operated by the National Oceanic and Atmospheric Administration of the U.S. Department of Commerce and by the Galveston laboratories of the National Marine Fisheries Service, this research facility offers free tours three times a week. (409) 766–3670.

Lone Star Flight Museum and **Texas Aviation Hall of Fame.** 2002 Terminal Drive (next to Moody Gardens and Galveston International Airport). Aircraft from the 1930s to the 1960s—all restored and in flying condition—fill this immaculate facility. In all, this is considered the world's finest (and possibly largest) collection of mint-condition "war birds." Situated on what was a military airfield during World War II, this growing collection includes fighters, bombers, a rare F-7-F Tigercat, and one of only two P-47-G Thunderbolts remaining in the world. In 1999 this museum was expanded to include the $2.2-million Texas Aviation Hall of Fame, a series of exhibits and artifacts that document the careers and contributions of Texans to various military efforts. The gift shop carries World War II memorabilia, aircraft engines are on display, and the research library is a find for historians. Don't miss the remarkable essay on what World War II was all about, particularly if you have teens in tow.

Open daily. Fee; (409) 740-7722; www.lsfm.org.

Mardi Gras Museum. 2309 Ship's Mechanic Row. If you can't participate in the island's annual festival, a visit here is the next best thing. Fee. Open Wednesday–Sunday; (409) 765-5930.

Mary Moody Northen Amphitheatre. Galveston Island Outdoor Musicals, P.O. Box 5253, Galveston, TX 77554. This outdoor theater is in Galveston Island State Park, west on FM-3005 at the intersection with Thirteen Mile Road. Broadway favorites light up this stage Monday–Saturday from Memorial Day through Labor Day. Tickets are available at Houston ticket outlets, at the box office (409-737-3440), and at the gate. Insect repellent advised. Fee; (409) 737-1744 or (800) 547-4697.

Moody Gardens. 1 Hope Boulevard (near the Galveston International Airport). Don't come here in a hurry; this is a day-long experience that's well worth its somewhat hefty admission fee. In addition to a hotel/convention center, restaurant, ice-skating rink, and gardens, this $18-million, nonprofit project features three huge glass pyramids, each devoted to super family-learning experiences.

Start at The Rainforest Pyramid, one of the largest single structures under glass in the country. Beneath a 55-foot-high canopy of tropical vegetation, this conservatory's more than 170 animal and 1,700 plant species flourish amid waterfalls, cliffs, and caverns. Beautiful birds and butterflies are everywhere; some even perch briefly on visitors.

Nearby, The Discovery Pyramid features more than forty interactive, futuristic exhibits developed with the assistance of NASA's Johnson Space Center. Downstairs, America's first 3-D IMAX Theater presents images that seem to leap from the six-story-tall screen. *Also here:* the nation's first IMAX Ridefilm Theater with three separate screening rooms, each with an eighteen-seat motion base and a 180-degree wraparound screen. Folks over 45 inches high can fasten their seatbelts and "rocket" off into an asteroid adventure, a swim with dolphins, or an exploration of cyberspace. Whichever experience is selected, you'll feel as though you are "in" the film, not just watching it.

Moody Gardens' newest attraction, The Aquarium Pyramid, uses viewing tanks filled with more than two million gallons of water to showcase habitats common to the oceans of the North and South

Pacific, the tropical Pacific, and the Caribbean. Two viewing levels provide both shoreline and underwater looks, and the Antarctic Exhibit showcases three species of live, tuxedo-clad penguins. Diver-to-guest communications answer questions, while touch tanks make other aquatic exhibits extremely personal.

The Moody Garden complex also is home to *The Colonel* harbor cruises and the Palm Beach swimming area, both of which have separate listings. Fee; (409) 744-4673 or (800) 582-4673; www.moodygardens.com.

Ocean Star at the Offshore Energy Center. Pier 19. This $3.2-million combination museum and educational attraction puts you inside a full-size offshore drilling rig. Three decks of videos, equipment exhibits, and interactive displays bring alive the day-to-day world of offshore drilling and production. Open daily. Fee; (409) 766-7827; www.oceanstaroec.com.

Pier 21. This lodging/restaurant/marina/shopping complex adjacent to the Texas Seaport Museum also houses the Great Storm Theatre, a multimedia presentation on Galveston's devastating 1900 hurricane. Fee. For information contact Harbor House, (409) 763-3321.

Postoffice Street Arts and Entertainment District. Slowly assuming a distinct personality, this area is anchored by the historic Grand 1894 Opera House and includes art galleries, antiques shops, eateries, and taverns. Boundaries extend from Market to Winnie Streets and from Nineteenth to Twenty-fifth Street. A ghost town of sorts only a few years ago, Postoffice Street's more than twenty historical buildings are taking on new life. Shopping guides are available at many of the businesses.

Sailing, surfing, and waterskiing. These scenes are ever changing; for a list of operators, contact the Galveston Island Visitors Center, 2428 Seawall Boulevard, Galveston, TX 77550; (409) 763-4311 or (888) 425-4753.

Seawolf Park on Pelican Island. Accessible from either Broadway or Harborside Drive via a turn north on Fifty-first Street. Adults enjoy watching Galveston's busy harbor from this unusual vantage point, and children love scrambling over a series of naval exhibits that include an airplane, a destroyer escort, and a submarine. Fee. There is no swimming at Seawolf Park, but there are good facilities for fishing and picnics. Open daily. Parking fee.

Summer band concerts. If you're planning a June–August outing to the island, time your trip to take in the free summer band concerts on Tuesday evenings in Sealy Pavilion. The Galveston Beach Band performs patriotic marches, Broadway tunes, polkas, Dixieland, and Big Band music, while you stretch out on a blanket under the stars. Kids love the musical games and flag parade. For a schedule call (409) 762-3988, 744-2174, or (888) 425-4753.

Tennis and Golf. Information on specific locations is available from the Galveston Convention & Visitors Bureau. If you are a hotel guest, ask about membership privileges at private facilities on the island.

Treasure Isle Tour Train. The tram with the fringe on top takes you all over town on a ninety-minute narrated tour. Daily trips, year-round. Fee; (409) 765-9564.

WHERE TO EAT

Benno's on the Beach. 1200 Seawall. Don't let the converted Taco Bell building discourage you from trying this super-casual diner. The menu provides a primer in fine fried fare, but it's the Cajun dishes, including superior gumbo, jambalaya, and crawfish étouffée, that will make you yearn for your next visit. $-$$; ☐; (409) 762-4621.

Brothers Petronella. 2301 The Strand. Housed in the handsome and historic League Building (1871), this upscale restaurant specializes in seafood, chicken, and steaks. The extensive menu includes gourmet pizzas, panini, and pasta, but the management is emphatic that this should not be considered an Italian restaurant. Take them at their word and order the Snapper Petronella, a filet sautéed in butter and topped with large chunks of lump crabmeat. Open for lunch and dinner Monday–Saturday. $$-$$$; ☐; (409) 766-7266.

Clary's. 8509 Teichman Road (across from the *Galveston Daily News*). Don't judge this place by its low-key exterior. Locals think it serves some of the best seafood on the island, often with a Creole touch. An off-menu item, spiced shrimp, is a house specialty. Other memorable choices include Special Butter Lump Crab and the grilled oysters. Slightly dressy crowd here, so no beach clothes, please. Open Tuesday–Friday and on Sunday for lunch and dinner, Saturday for dinner only. $-$$$; ☐; (409) 740-0771; www.galveston.com/clarys.

Fish Tales. Twenty-fifth and Seawall. If you have only one casual meal to eat in Galveston, this lively spot's upstairs deck is a good choice. You'll be able to see out over the Gulf while filling up on seafood in all sizes and guises. The menu also has some nonfishy selections, along with a long list of appetizers, several of which are large enough to make a meal. Open for lunch and dinner daily. $-$$$; ☐; (409) 762-8545.

Fisherman's Wharf Seafood Grill. Pier 22. You'll find indoor and outdoor dining here, with great views of the port. The fresh seafood menu ranges from shrimp and oyster po'boys to full-course meals—the Shrimp-T entree is named for Houston Rockets coach Rudy Tomjonovich—and there's also a fresh seafood market with a tank where children can fish for perch. Formerly a shrimp unloading and cold storage facility until its reincarnation as a restaurant in mid-1995, this eatery's hardwood floors came from some of Galveston's old cotton warehouses, and the vintage photographs that line the walls are either family memorabilia or reproductions from the Rosenberg Library collection. Open daily for lunch and dinner. $-$$$; ☐; (409) 765-5708.

Gaido's. 3800 Seawall. Whether it's fried, broiled, or boiled, the fresh seafood here is excellent, partly because the dressings and sauces are made from scratch. The menu changes daily to reflect the best from the sea, but you can't go wrong with the grilled red snapper. Open daily for lunch and dinner. $$-$$$; ☐; (409) 762-9625; www.galveston.com/gaidos. *Tip:* If Gaido's is crowded, try Casey's casual family dining next door; they share a kitchen.

Landry's. Fifty-third and Seawall. Excellent steaks and seafood, often with Cajun touches, bring crowds to this eatery. Open daily for lunch and dinner. $$-$$$; ☐; (409) 744-1010.

Luigi's Ristorante Italiano. 2328 Strand. This outstanding restaurant brings a warming touch of Tuscany to its surroundings, the 1895 Hutchings-Sealy Bank Building. The wine bar is in the old bank vault, and the Piccola Tavola (chef's table; reservations required one week in advance) gives ten to twelve diners a close-up look at Chef Luigi Ferre creating culinary masterpieces in the kitchen. Open Monday–Saturday for lunch and dinner. $-$$$; ☐; (409) 763-6500; www.galveston.com/luigis.

The Merchant Prince. 2300 Ship's Mechanic Row (inside the Tremont House hotel). This quiet retreat really takes the edges off a hectic day, particularly when your psyche begins to respond to the piano music coming from the Tremont's lobby. Inventive food beautifully served is the rule here, but ultrafancy dress is not. Open for breakfast, lunch, and dinner daily. $–$$$; ☐; (409) 763-0300 or (713) 480-8201.

Mosquito Cafe. 628 Fourteenth Street. Basically a neighborhood cafe, this clean and trendy eatery is a good place to explore what's happening on the Galveston casual-food scene. Just how unusual are this cafe's choices? First-timers might try a Mosquito Benedict breakfast (a scone topped with portabello mushroom, shrimp, artichoke hearts, and asparagus, finished with a serrano hollandaise) or the Napa salad for lunch. The latter takes grilled breast of chicken, adds walnuts, Gorgonzola, apples, red grapefruit, and grapes, and then tosses all with greens and a raspberry vinaigrette. Worry not, if neither of those appeals; there's much, much more. Open for breakfast and lunch daily; dinner Thursday–Saturday. $–$$; ☐; (409) 763-1010.

Ocean Grill. 2227 Seawall. If you want to eat alfresco above the waves, this is the place. The gumbo is great, as are the mesquite-smoked fish entrees. Open daily for lunch and dinner (until 2:00 A.M. on weekends). $$–$$$; ☐; (409) 762-7100; www.galveston.com/oceangrill.

The Phoenix Bakery and Coffee House. 2228 Ship's Mechanic Row (1 block south of The Strand). Although the great sandwiches and salads will tempt, go straight for the New Orleans–style beignets and café au lait, and then head for one of the umbrella tables in the patio. It's not quite like New Orleans's French Quarter, but close. Open 7:00 A.M. to 5:00 P.M. Sunday–Thursday; until 7:00 P.M. Friday and Saturday. $–$$; ☐; (409) 763-4611.

Rainforest Cafe. 5300 Seawall. We're including this mighty chain restaurant for a number of reasons. One, because of its prime real estate, adjacent to the luxurious San Luis Resort on the Seawall. Two, because of its unusual exterior (its dramatic volcano spouts and spews every half hour from the otherwise flat island). And third (and perhaps most important), because the chain is owned by Galveston native (B.O.I.—born on the island, as they call it here) Tillman Fertitta, the entrepreneur also responsible for Kemah's Boardwalk and the entire Landry's Restaurants family. The food ranges from inspired to indigestible. Stick with the basics and enjoy the show. Open daily. $–$$; ☐; (409) 744-6000; www.rainforestcafe.com.

Rudy & Paco's. 2028 Postoffice Street (adjacent to The Grand 1894 Opera House). Another top entry in Galveston's fine dining competition, this extremely popular and interesting eatery specializes in Central and South American cuisine. Born and raised in Nicaragua, owner Francisco Paco Vargas has a management resume that reads like a list of Galveston's top restaurants, and his chef hails from Argentina. As a result, the empañadas and steaks with chimichurri sauce are outstanding, and you'll also want to try the *vuelva la vida* (back to life) appetizer, a combination of crab claws, shrimp, and calamari sautéed in a lightly spicy lemon-butter sauce. *Nice to know:* They serve both pre- and post-show dinners and also open on Sunday whenever there's something playing at the Grand Opera House. Open for lunch Monday–Friday, dinner Monday–Saturday. $–$$$; ☐; (409) 762-3696; www. galveston.com/rudypaco.

Saltwater Grill. 2017 Postoffice Street. Perhaps the most inventive restaurant on the island, this handsome dining spot is also one of the quietest—a nice contrast to the tourist eateries on the Seawall. A great favorite with Galveston's business community, it's also very well regarded by those who relish fresh fish, chicken, and beef properly prepared and efficiently served. Nothing has been frozen—there isn't even a freezer on the premises—and nothing is fried. Instead your selection will be pan-seared, grilled, or steamed to your specifications. Menus change weekly to capitalize on what's fresh in the markets, and the $6.95–$9.95 lunch specials are a good place to start selecting your meal. Consider the barbecued spiced oysters on a baguette or the lobster and shrimp tacos. If those don't interest you, it may be a good day for the Gulf blue-crab cakes or the veal chop with a wild-mushroom risotto. Whatever appeals, you'll definitely remember to come here again. Open for lunch and dinner weekdays; dinner only on Saturday and Sunday. $–$$$; ☐; (409) 762-3474; www.galveston.com/saltwatergrill.

Shearn's. 7 Hope Boulevard (on the top floor of the Moody Gardens Hotel). You'll want to dress up for this dining experience. The surroundings are lovely, the service exceptional, and the quality of the Continental food extremely high. Open only for dinner Tuesday–Saturday, and reservations are required. $$$; ☐; (409) 741-8484; www.moodygardens.com.

Shrimp & Stuff. 3901 Avenue O. Beach-weary folks love this simple place for its tasty shrimp and oyster po'boys, homemade gumbo, and ample fish dinners. Open daily for lunch and dinner. $-$$; ☐; (409) 763-2805; www.galveston.com/shrimpnstuff.

Sunflower Bakery. 527 Church Street. A greatly loved locals spot, this fragrant bakery takes you away from the tourist scene and back to the time when most folks bought their daily bread from the corner bakery. In this case, lucky Galvestonians still do—right here. Sandwiches and box lunches are the traveler's finds here—the day's offerings are painted on large pieces of fresh butcher paper and hung on the wall—and the desserts are nothing short of spectacular. Rest assured that all is fresh; each day's leftovers are given to the local children's center. Open weekdays 6:30 A.M. to 6:00 P.M.; Saturdays 7:30 A.M. to 4:00 P.M. $; (409) 763-5500; www.galveston.com/sun flowerbakery.

Yaga's Cafe. 2314 Strand. *Tropical* is the working adjective at this casual place, from decor to food to music. Try the spicy shrimp only if you have some very cool liquid to quench mouth fire. This is a good spot also for burgers and sandwiches, and it jumps with reggae at night. Call for hours. $-$$; ☐; (409) 762-6676; www.galveston. com/yaga.

WANDERING THE BACKROADS

Driving southwest on FM-3005 the length of the island brings you to great fishing at San Luis Pass. Go over the causeway, and it's another 38 miles to Surfside Beach and Freeport. For activities there see Trip 1, Southwest sector.

Heading east from Galveston along the coast is possible. Just take the free Bolivar ferry and continue on TX-87 (Trip 4, East sector). In Galveston the Bolivar ferry slip is at the end of Second Street (turn north from Broadway), but don't plan to take it on a prime-time weekend unless you love waiting in long lines.

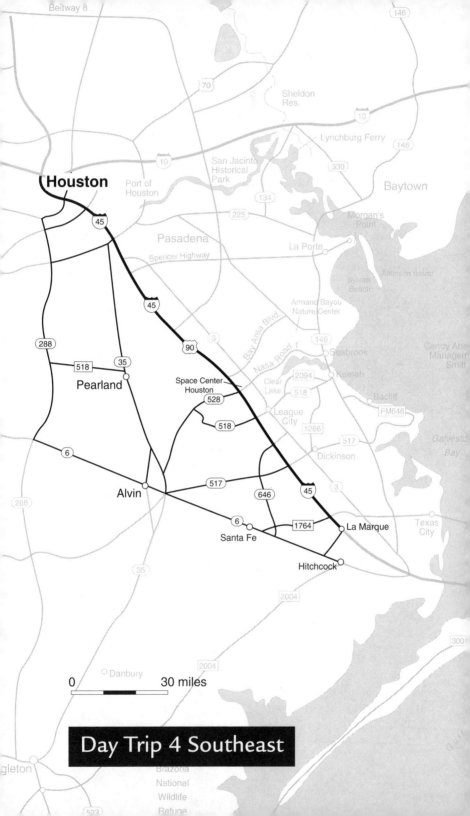

Day Trip 4 Southeast

ALVIN

Basically a farming community first settled in the 1840s, Alvin prospered with the coming of the railroad in the 1880s and remains a major agricultural center today. As a tourist destination its primary point of interest is the Nolan Ryan Exhibit Center at Alvin Community College, but you'll find several other things to do while you are in town.

Begin this day trip by taking TX–288 south from Houston to its intersection with TX-6 and then turning southeast (left) for 10 miles. En route, consider visiting the amazing Sri Meenakshi (Hindu) Temple on the outskirts of Pearland and buying some fresh fruits and veggies at Froberg Farms.

One of the nicest things about Alvin is the number of huge oaks that shade its older residential streets. A drive along either West Lang or Beauregard shows off a few century-old homes, as well. For more information contact the Alvin Convention and Visitors Bureau, 105 West Willis, Alvin, TX 77511; (281) 331–3944 or (800) 331–4063; www.alvintexas.org.

WHAT TO DO

Alvin Opry. Eighth Street at Sealy Street. Country and gospel music is the entertaining rule here on Friday and Saturday nights. Fee. Open year-round; (281) 331–8181.

Bayou Wildlife Park. 5050 FM–517. Take the Dickinson/FM–517 exit from I-45 and then drive west on FM–517 for 6 miles;

279

the entrance will be on the left. From antelopes to a zonky (a cross between a zebra and a donkey), more than 260 animals representing forty species roam this eighty-six-acre preserve. Many are either endangered or nearly extinct in their natural habitat. Visitors tour with a guide via an open-air tram, buckets of feed ($2.00) at the ready. This outstanding facility gives you a good look at major zoo-type animals roaming free in a natural environment. If you've never been nuzzled by a camel or scratched a giraffe's neck, this is the place. *Also here:* a children's barnyard (which includes pony rides in spring and summer), an alligator farm, a monkey island, and a feeding barn for young animals that need extra TLC. Although no human food is sold here, picnickers are most welcome. Open daily in summer, Tuesday–Sunday in winter. Fee; (281) 337–6376.

Froberg Farms. 11875 Country Road 190 (off TX–6, 3 miles northwest of downtown Alvin; watch for signs). This rural fruit-and-veggie stand features locally grown produce that draws buyers from miles away. Their store also sells gift baskets, jams, jellies, pumpkins, beans, nuts, and homemade pies. Usually closed in August and September. Open Monday–Saturday in winter; daily in summer; (281) 585–3531.

Nolan Ryan Exhibit Center. 2925 South Bypass 35. This relatively small but extremely interesting museum chronicles the life of Alvin's celebrity native son, baseball player Nolan Ryan. Open Monday–Saturday until 4:00 P.M. Fee; ☐; (281) 388–1134.

Shimek Gardens. On County Road 237 west of Alvin. This is a must-stop for daylily lovers, a beautiful garden lush with 850 different types of daylilies and literally hundreds of roses. The owners are hybridizers who have two new types of lilies to their credit, with others in development. Open by appointment only year-round, but prime time to come is mid-May through July; (281) 331–4395.

Sri Meenakshi Temple. 17130 McLean Road, Pearland. From TX–288 turn east on FM–518 toward Pearland and go 8 miles to a turn south on McLean Road. The temple is approximately 2 miles south. This honey-colored, highly ornate Hindu temple is a startling sight, tucked away amid assorted dwellings and small farms on a rural road southwest of downtown Pearland. The third traditional Hindu temple to be constructed in this country and the only one outside India that's devoted to a specific goddess (Shakti), this temple not only welcomes visitors but is a place of pilgrimage for

Hindus from throughout North America. Although you are requested to take off your shoes before entering any of the interior worship areas, you are welcome to walk around the courtyard grounds and take photos. A free, well-written booklet available in the temple's administrative office explains all, and guided tours (donation) can be arranged by calling (713) 467-3022. Should you visit sometime between Friday evening and Sunday afternoon you may find typical South Indian food being served at a very reasonable price, a real enhancement to this cultural experience. The temple is open Monday–Thursday from 9:00 A.M. to noon and 5:00 to 8:00 P.M., Friday until 9:00 P.M., and all day on weekends and holidays; (281) 489-0358.

WHERE TO EAT

The Homestead Inn Restaurant. 801 South Gordon (TX–35). Good country cooking here, either in the buffet or via the menu. Open daily for breakfast, lunch, and dinner. $–$$; ☐; (281) 331-4842.

Joe's Barbeque Company. 1400 East TX–6. Even the parking lot smells good at this plates-to-steaks place. You order at the counter—beef brisket, steaks, sausage, ham, chicken, or ribs—plus there's an all-you-can-eat steam table and salad bar. Open daily for lunch and dinner. $–$$; ☐; (281) 331-9626.

CONTINUING ON

TX–6 more or less follows the original railroad right-of-way between Galveston and Richmond, connecting Alvin with Santa Fe, the next stop on this day trip.

SANTA FE

Haak's Vineyards & Winery. 6310 Avenue T. From TX–6 South, turn right at Avenue T (the second signal) in Santa Fe and go 1.8 miles; the winery will be on your right. Established in 1980 by Raymond and Gladys Haak (and our only stop in this very small town), this boutique vineyard has four acres planted with two varietals:

Blanc du Bois (white) and Black Spanish/Lenoir (red). The results: an extremely fine port and a tasty white, both of which tend to be in short supply due to the limited production. Best bet, if you want to taste totally Texan wines, is to come here in late August when each year's wines debut. The Haaks also buy grapes from other Texas vineyards and import grapes from California's upper San Joaquin Valley. The chardonnay is fermented in domestic oak barrels, and the port ages for two years in oak. Wine production here also includes a chardonnay, sauvignon blanc, cabernet sauvignon, and zinfandel, all of which can be sampled in the tasting room at no cost. Tours include the vineyard, the crushing area, a state-of-the-art winery, and an 1,800-square-foot cellar where the wines rest until they come of age. Buy picnic fixings and enjoy a snack on the winery's covered pavilion. Want to help with the picking? Give them a call. Grape vine cuttings are available free in February, until they are gone. Open daily. ◻; (409) 925–1401; www.haakwinery.com.

HITCHCOCK AND LA MARQUE

Like Santa Fe, Hitchcock does not have a strong presence in and of itself. However, its lack of development is exactly why it's an ideal location for the following:

Gulf Breeze Downs. 7602 FM–2004, Hitchcock. Take exit 15 from I–45 and turn west to FM–2004 South for 1.2 miles. When you see huge cement pillars on your left (the remains of an abandoned blimp base), look to the right for the entrance to this training track for Sam Houston Race Park. Visitors are welcome to tour the barns and watch the daily workouts, and there are match races here on some Sundays in nice-weather months. Call in advance to check if that's important to your visit. Also, there's an exotic animal park in the making here. You can see zebras, elk, antelope, and other animals by driving to the fence at the end of the dirt driveway. Open daily, year-round, weather permitting. Free; (281) 337–8782.

CONTINUING ON

The next stop on this day trip is La Marque. To get there, or to I-45 North and home, return to TX-6 from Gulf Breeze Downs and continue southeast to a left turn on FM-519 to La Marque.

First stop here for shoppers is the Lone Star Factory Outlet complex on I-45 at Delany Road. However, the real reason for coming here is to go to the dog races, a day trip destination in itself.

Gulf Greyhound Park. P.O. Box 488, La Marque (30 miles south of Houston via exit 15 from I-45). This 110-acre, $50-million attraction is the world's largest greyhound racing facility—a Cadillac of racetracks—and when it opened in 1992, it offered the first legal parimutuel betting in the Houston area in more than fifty-five years. General admission is $1.00, parking is $1.00, and the minimum bet is $2.00. If you want to go first class, choose valet parking ($3.00) and lounge/clubhouse admission ($4.00). Expect numerous well-designed lounge areas, closed-circuit color TV, and plenty of instruction on the various methods of betting. Post times on this quarter-mile track are 7:30 P.M., Tuesday and Thursday–Sunday; 4:00 P.M. and 7:20 P.M. on "Winning" Wednesday; and 1:30 P.M. Friday–Sunday. Families are welcome; (409) 986-9500 or (800) 275-2946; www.gulfgreyhound.com.

CELEBRATIONS
AND FESTIVALS

Note: Many of the telephone numbers given are answered on weekdays only. For specific event dates consult the current issue of *Texas Highways* magazine. Also note that admission charges may apply.

JANUARY

Baytown's "Goose Creek Texas Chili When It's Chilly" Cook-off. (281) 422-8359; www.baytownchamber.com.

Festival Hill. Concerts followed by dinner and a classic film lure people to Round Top once a month from August through April—always enjoyable, but most welcome during the quiet days of winter. The dinner includes wine, and overnight accommodations are available in attractive studio residences as well as in historic Menke House. Reservations required. (979) 249-3129.

Go Texan Celebration. Clear Lake swings in late January. (281) 488-7676.

Janis Joplin Birthday Bash. Port Arthur celebrates a native daughter with concerts and special displays. (800) 235-7822 or (409) 722-3699.

Union & Confederate Skirmish. Events at Jesse H. Jones Park west of Humble take you back to the days of the Civil War with reenactments of drilling, recruiting, period music, and tending to "casualties." A question-and-answer session is part of the program. (281) 446-8588.

FEBRUARY

Clear Lake Annual Epicurean Evening. Area restauranteurs show off their best creations via booths at Baybrook Mall. (281) 338-0333.

Clear Lake Gem and Mineral Show. This show, on the fourth weekend of February, ranges from rocks and fossils to fantastic jewelry. Children welcome. (281) 481–1591.

Frontier Days in Old Town Spring. This mid-month family celebration includes a cowboy camp with reenactments, an Indian village, a buckskinners' gathering, a chili cook-off, a Civil War encampment, and demonstrations of common early-day life. "Goods and wares of the era" will be sold, along with food, drinks, and rides. (281) 353–9310 or (800) 653–8696.

Galveston Mardi Gras. This reincarnation of a long-gone tradition keeps the island swinging with parades and balls during the two weeks prior to Lent. (409) 763–4311 or (888) 425–4753.

Go Texan Parade in Conroe. Call for specifics of this early February event. (936) 756–6644.

Go Texan Weekend in Navasota. Plenty of good country fun, including boot-scootin', chili cook-offs, and horseshoes. (800) 252–6642.

Mardi Gras of Southeast Texas. Port Arthur swings on a long February weekend with a Doo-Dah Parade, the Majestic Krewe of Aurora Grand Parade, fireworks, art and auto shows, a carnival, more parades, concerts, and children's activities. (409) 721–8717 or (800) 235–7822.

Messina Hof. The Marriage of the Port at this Bryan winery celebrates a 200-year-old tradition. (979) 778–9463.

Texas Independence Day. Washington-on-the-Brazos relives its brief moment in the Lone Star limelight every year on the weekend closest to March 2. (979) 836–3695 or (888) 273–6426.

MARCH

Anahuac's Annual Wild Game Cook-off. Fort Anahuac Park fills with teams competing for the best chili, gumbo, fried foods, and barbecue of game, feather, fur, and alligator. A duck and goose calling contest and a field trial dog competition add to the day, along with a street dance and arts/crafts festival. (409) 267–4190.

Beaumont Festival of the Arts. Musicians and artists showcase their talents in late month. (409) 866–2398 or (800) 392–4401.

Bellville Garden Show. Surrounded by blossoming countryside, this small town shows off more flowers, shrubs, statuary, garden furnishings, and equipment early in the month. (979) 865–3407.

Bellville's Annual Great Exchange Antiques Show. This is a huge affair held mid-month at the Austin County Fairgrounds. Frills include a farmers' market and plant and flower sales. (979) 865-3407.

Calvert's 'Art of Texas Festival and Sale. A verbal play on the well-known "Heart of Texas" saying, this super celebration of the arts in late March puts you one-on-one with many of the major artists who are changing the makeup of this historic town. All-day demonstrations range from raku and potting to blacksmithing and soap making; entertainment and an open-air concert wrap up the day. (979) 364-3730 or (800) 670-8183; www.artoftexas.com.

Freeport's Joy Ride & Rod Run. This judged show mid-month features custom and classic cars (including pre-1949 street rods), a parade, entertainments, and door prizes. (281) 444-8680.

Heritage Day at Jesse Jones Park & Nature Center, near Humble. All the homely arts that ultimately tamed the Texas frontier are demonstrated, and the park's reconstructed homestead is open to the public. (281) 446-8588.

Kountze Spring Fling. This Big Thicket town swings with a carnival, craft booths, flea market, and music. (409) 246-3413 or 246-3414.

Liberty Jubilee. Lots of fun can be had at this family fun-fest in downtown Liberty in late March. Activities include three stages of live entertainment, a barbecue cook-off, car show, parade, street dance, and arts and crafts. (409) 336-3684

Montgomery County Fair & Rodeo. Everything from chicken flying to a barbecue cook-off keeps the fairgrounds jumping for ten days. (800) 283-6645 or (936) 760-3631.

Nederland Heritage Festival. Lots to do mid-month with a beauty pageant, parade, golf tournament, craft market, country music show, and fun run. On Boston Avenue, between Fourteenth and Seventeenth Streets. (409) 724-2269.

Renegade Round-Up. Humble hosts fun that includes a livestock show and rodeo. (281) 446-2128.

Round Top Herb Forum. Festival Hill hosts a one-day celebration of herbs that includes lectures, luncheon, and a plant sale. (979) 249-5283.

San Felipe's Annual Colonial Texas Heritage Festival. What was once one of the major colonial capitals of Texas celebrates its heritage in late March with Buffalo soldiers reenactments, arts and crafts booths, traders, exhibits, living history demonstrations, guided tours of historic San Felipe, and a buffalo barbecue. (979) 885-3222.

Springfest in Old Town Spring. A food and wine festival enlivens this old community near the end of the month. (281) 353-9310 or (800) 653-8696.

Spring Fling Flower and Garden Show. Brenham's downtown square welcomes the entire family to a festival on the fourth Saturday of the month. (979) 836-3695 or (888) 273-6426.

Walker County Fair & Rodeo. Huntsville hosts rodeo events, livestock exhibits, a barbecue cook-off, a carnival, contests, dances, and more in late March. (936) 295-8113 or (800) 289-0389.

Winedale Spring Festival and Texas Craft Exhibition. Expect pioneer demonstrations of old-time skills, an outstanding juried craft show with working artists, live musical entertainment, barbecued chicken picnic, and a barn dance. (979) 278-3530.

Woodville Western Weekend. The second largest trailride in Texas and an open rodeo kick off spring celebrations. (409) 283-2632.

APRIL

Big Bird Fly-in. This model-airplane jamboree enlivens Crockett. (936) 544-2359 or (888) 269-2359.

Blessing of the Fleet. Freeport hosts this festival annually. (979) 265-2508 or (800) 938-4853.

Bluebonnet Festival. Chappell Hill shows off its old things and wildflowers in a variety of art forms early in this best of Texas seasons. Expect cloggers, folk dancers, dulcimer music, hayrides, and pony and train rides for the children. (979) 836-3695 or (888) 273-6426.

Burton Cotton Gin Festival. This tiny town's wonderful old gin hums with activity again in mid-April while locals give tours and explain how it works. Lots of food and entertainment, as well as demonstrations of other old-time skills. (979) 836-3695, 289-3378, or (888) 273-6426.

Clear Lake Crawfish Festival. This shindig in Clear Lake Park raises funds for Fourth of July fireworks and celebrations. (281) 488-7676.

Dogwood Festival. Woodville celebrates the beauty of spring in the East Texas woods with this annual event in early April. Fun ranges from a parade and historical pageant to a beard contest, rodeo, and trail ride. There's also bluegrass and country music on an outdoor stage. Call for specifics. (409) 283-2632.

Eeyore's Birthday Party. Costumes are a tradition for this annual Winedale event, which also includes music, games, maypoles, a lollipop tree, and birthday cake for everyone. This is an ideal outing for families with small children. There's even Shakespeare in the evening in the old barn. (979) 278-3530.

Fayetteville's Antique Show and Midnight Madness. All shops and vendors stay open until midnight on the first Friday and Saturday nights following the first Thursday of the month. (888) 575-4553.

Folk Weekends at Washington-on-the-Brazos State Historical Park. There's something going on nearly every April weekend in Washington-on-the-Brazos State Park, from Buffalo Soldiers reenactments to a kids' day of frontier activities. (936) 878-2461.

The General Sam Houston Folk Festival. Sam and his cronies wander around the historic homes in Huntsville's Sam Houston Memorial Park, while citizen-soldiers show off camping techniques and equipment of the 1800s. Life-style skills of that period also are demonstrated; local ethnic groups are celebrated with food and music. (800) 289-0389 or (936) 294-1832.

Good Oil Days Festival. Humble's Main Street fills with food, crafts, and entertainment on an early April weekend. (281) 446-2128.

Kemah Boardwalk's South Sea Days. Polynesian dancers and drummers perform in the plaza. Call for date. (281) 488-8981, (800) 844-5253, or (877) 285-3624; www.kemahboardwalk.com.

Lumberton's Village Creek Festival. Festivities at this three-day affair in mid-month include a 5K run, carnival rides, craft and food booths, a pageant, and entertainment under a tent. (409) 755-0554.

Migration Celebration. Early in the month, Brazosport offers seminars, keynote speakers, a trade show, and field trips of major interest to serious birders. (800) 938-4853.

Montgomery Trek. Many of Montgomery's old homes open their doors to the public on the third Saturday in April. (936) 597-4155, 597-4899, or (800) 283-6645.

New Ulm's Arts Festival. Professional artists from all over Texas converge on this tiny hamlet every weekend in April. (979) 992-3337.

Round Top Antique Fair. Annually on the first weekend in April, Round Top's old Rifle Association Hall and two satellite sites brim wall-to-wall with antiques dealers showing their best. (281) 493-5501 or (877) 444-7339.

San Jacinto Festival. East and West Columbia and Varner-Hogg State Park celebrate the early days of the republic in mid-month with entertainment, a barbecue cook-off, a fajita dinner, an arts and crafts show, a pentathlon, a baseball-card show, a petting zoo, street dances, and tours of a replica of the first state capitol. (979) 345-3921.

Spirit of Flight Air Show and Walkabout. Galveston's Lone Star Flight Museum hosts World War II–era aircraft in reenactments of explosive dogfights. Many of the old "birds" are open for tours. (409) 740-7722.

Sylvan Beach Festival. La Porte relives its heyday with a parade, a chili cook-off, and entertainment. (281) 471-1123; www.laportechamber.org.

Wine and Roses Festival at Messina Hof. Grape-stomping, fun runs through the vineyards, the conclusion of the Texas Artist Competition, live music, equestrian shows, and a cook-off keep you busy in Bryan–College Station. (979) 778-9463.

MAY

Boat Show at Kemah Boardwalk. In addition to the usual passing parade of boats in the channel, you can see many others and auxiliary equipment displayed on land throughout the Boardwalk complex. (877) 285-3624; www.kemahboardwalk.com.

Clear Lake Greek Festival. Clear Lake Park hosts ethnic dancing, crafts, foods, children's activities, etc. (281) 326-1740.

Columbus Live Oak Festival. Columbus rolls back time the third weekend in May with an opera house performance, a historic homes tour, canoe races, music, storytellers, and antiques/crafts shows. (979) 732-8385.

Crockett's Annual Lion's Youth Rodeo. Call for list of events. (409) 544-2359.

Czech Fest. Rosenberg celebrates its ethnic heritage every spring at the Fort Bend County Fairgrounds. (281) 342-6171; www.fbcfa.org.

Fayetteville's Good Old Summertime Classic. On the first weekend in May, this small town sponsors bike races, a bike rodeo for children, and free lemonade and watermelon on the town square. Call for schedule and race-entry information. (979) 378-3001 or (888) 575-4553.

Homes Tour. Galveston's annual peek behind historic doors. One of the best in the state. (409) 765-7834 or (888) 425-4753.

Ice Cream Festival in Brenham. Enjoy a Blue Bell ice-cream eating contest, arts and crafts, and entertainment on the square in downtown on the first Saturday of May. (979) 836-3695 or (888) 273-6426.

International Gumbo Cook-Off. Orange and its Cajun folks relegate chili to the back burner in favor of every sort of gumbo brewed in the South. Other special events include Cajun and country music, a carnival, and arts and crafts. (409) 883-3536.

Keels and Wheels in Seabrook. The Lakewood Yacht Club is the place to go on the first weekend of May to view antique cars and classic wooden boats while enjoying music, entertainment, and food. (713) 521-0105.

League City Village Fair. This event offers food, a midway, and plenty of arts and crafts. (281) 332-3431.

Maifest. Brenham hosts the oldest spring festival in the state in the heart of wildflower season. (979) 836-3695 or (888) 273-6426.

Memorial Day Celebration at The George Ranch Historical Park. A traditional "Decoration Day" event at the family cemetery as well as dramatic vignettes at the Davis House bring real meaning to the holiday. (281) 343-0218 or 545-9212.

Neches River Festival. Beaumont celebrates water for a week with historical pageants, shows, a lighted boat flotilla, a skydiving show, and exhibitions all over town. (409) 835-2443 or (800) 392-4401.

Old Town Spring. The Texas Crawfish Festival brews up pots and pots of those tasty little critters, along with all the multistage live entertainment you can handle, on two weekends in May. (281) 353-9310 or (800) 653-8696.

Oleander City Festival. Any bloomin' excuse for a party in fun-loving Galveston. (409) 763-4311 or (888) 425-4753.

Pasadena Strawberry Festival. This mid-May event at the Pasadena Fairgrounds draws more than 30,000 people annually. Activities include a historical village with working artisans, a beauty pageant, circus, alligator show, magician, carnival rides and games, cook-offs (ribs, beans, fajitas, and briskets), a mud volleyball tournament, and the world's largest strawberry shortcake (covers more than 750 square feet and requires 3,000-plus pounds of fruit!). There's also a large children's activity area. (281) 991-9500; www.strawberryfest.org.

Pilgrimage/Maypole in Calvert. This old railroad town opens the doors of its vintage homes. If you love Victoriana and antiques, don't miss this on the first weekend in May. (979) 364-2582.

Red Steagall Cowboy Celebration at George Ranch Historical Park. You'll enjoy traditional cowboy/western music and poetry plus skills, crafts, and collectibles. (281) 343-0218 or 545-9212.

Taste of the Town. Sample the best dishes from Brazosport's restaurants, at the Brazos Mall. (979) 265-2505; www.brazosport.org.

Texas Crab Festival. Tiny Crystal Beach offers crab races, crab legs contests, and a crab cook-off to all comers on Mother's Day weekend. Activities also include live entertainment, a volleyball tournament, a sand-castle competition, tug-of-war, and a treasure hunt in the sands of Bolivar Peninsula. (409) 684-3345 or (800) 786-3863.

JUNE

Agricultural Society Barbecue. Cat Spring turns out for music, cake walks, crafts, and a dance on the first Sunday of the month. (979) 885-3984 or 992-3647.

Alabama-Coushatta Indian Powwow. The region's only Indian reservation (on US-190, between Livingston and Woodville) is your destination for this ethnic celebration the first weekend of the month. Expect a parade, along with authentic Indian foods, dances, and crafts. (936) 563-4391; www.alabama-coushatta.com.

Alvin's Annual Tour de Braz Century Bike Ride. You can spectate, volunteer, or compete in this U.S. Cycling Federation–sanctioned race, which also determines the Texas state champion. The competition is at Alvin Community College. Call for details. (281) 331-3944; www.alvinmanvelchamber.org.

Blues Festival in Navasota. Usually held on the fourth weekend in June, this celebration brings together top-flight Texas blues performers for two days of music. The program also includes a Friday night dance and special musical activities for children. (936) 825-3699 or (800) 252-6642.

Brazoria's "No Name" Festival. Want to know what's doing on the second weekend of the month? Give them a call. (979) 798-6100.

Bryan–College Station's Annual Bluegrass Festival. Music, food, and entertainments. (979) 361-3600 or (800) 777-8292.

Festival Hill Concerts. Outstanding classical music by some of the world's best young professionals highlights weekends June through mid-July. (979) 249-3129; www.festivalhill.org.

Firemen's Picnic. Frelsburg draws folks into town with music, an auction, and other shenanigans on the second weekend of the month. (979) 732-8385.

Galveston's Caribbean Carnival Festival. Kempner Park is the site mid-month of a Caribbean market, calypso and steel-band competitions, parades, limbo dancing, and so on. (409) 763-4311 or (888) 425-4753.

Grimes County Fair. Head for the fairgrounds in Navasota for this one. (936) 825-2508 or (800) 252-6642; www.navasotatex.com.

Gulf Coast Jam. Port Arthur rocks early in the month with headliner talent in Cajun, C&W, and rock music. (409) 722-3699 or (800) 235-7822.

Hay Day in Ledbetter. Draft horses and mules draw antique farm equipment on the roads and fields of this small community. Demonstrations of antique equipment, hay baling, and hauling as well as free buggy and wagon rides add to the old-fashioned fun. (979) 249-3066.

Juneteenth Celebrations. Emancipation is cheered with special events in Brenham, (979) 836-3695 or (888) 273-6426; George Ranch, (281) 343-0218; Huntsville, (800) 289-0389; Port Arthur, (409) 982-8040 or (800) 235-7822; and Bryan–College Station, (800) 777-8292.

Kolache-Klobase Festival. East Bernard celebrates its ethnic heritage in mid-June with a colorful costume parade, ethnic dancing, arts and crafts, and a cakewalk. (979) 335-4827 or 335-7907.

Montgomery Old West Festival. The second weekend of June brings a cattle drive and trailride to a nearby ranch. Entertainments include cowboy poetry and music performances, historic reenactments, crafts, foods, an Indian village, and children's activities. (936) 449-5604, 597-4155, or (800) 283-6645.

Sandcastle Building Contest. Galveston's contest, featuring more than fifty teams of professional architects and designers, usually is the weekend following Memorial Day. (409) 763-4311 or (888) 425-4753.

Sealy KC Summer Polka Fest. The Knights of Columbus Hall really rocks on the fourth weekend of June when major polka bands rev up their oompahs and hundreds of couples take to the dance floor. Home cooking and hamburgers provide fuel. Call for schedule. (979) 885-6786.

Summer Band Concerts in Galveston. Every Tuesday night, June through August, the Galveston Beach Band presents free evenings of music at the Sealy Gazebo. Bring a blanket to sit on. (409) 763-4311 or (888) 425-4753.

***Whispers in the Wind* in Woodville.** This historical musical plays the third and fourth weekends of the month at Heritage Village. (409) 283-2272, 283-2632, or (800) 323-0389.

JULY

Antiques Show. In Bryan, at the Brazos Center. (979) 776-8338 or (800) 777-8292.

Fireworks. The folks in Humble often can't hire a qualified pyrotechnician on the Fourth of July, so they shoot the works on the third. (281) 446–2128.

Fourth of July Celebrations. The following all have their own versions of an old-fashioned Independence Day: Baytown, (281) 420–6597 or (800) 782–3081; Beaumont, (409) 838–3435; Bryan–College Station, (979) 260–9898; Burton, (800) 225–3695; Chappell Hill, (979) 836–3695 or (888) 273–6426; Clear Lake, (281) 338–0333; Columbus, (979) 732–8385; Crockett, (936) 544–2359; Galveston, (888) 425–4753; George Ranch Historical Park, (281) 343–0218; Huntsville, (800) 289–0389; Kemah, (877) 285–3624; Lake Conroe, (936) 756–6644 or (877) 426–6763; Lake Jackson, (979) 297–4533; Nederland, (409) 722–0279; Palacios, (361) 972–2615 or (800) 611–4567; Round Top, (979) 249–4042; Seabrook, (281) 488–7676; and Sea Rim State Park, (409) 971–2559.

Freeport Jay-Cee's Fishing Fiesta. Fisherfolk from all over the state compete for prizes. (979) 233–4434.

Great Texas Mosquito Festival. Brazosport celebrates the area's bumper crop of buzzers on the last weekend of the month in Clute Municipal Park. Expect a Miss Mosquito Legs look-alike contest, a mosquito-calling contest, the Ms. Quito pageant, a "skeeter beater" baby crawling contest, C&W headliners, dancing, food, games, and both barbecue and fajita cook-offs. (979) 265–8392 or (800) 938–4853; www.mosquitofestival.com.

Hempstead Watermelon Festival. Here's your chance to test your seed-spitting skills for prizes. Other events include a parade, a street dance, and professional entertainment on the third Saturday of the month. (979) 826–8217.

Lake Conroe Boat Parade and Fireworks. Call for specifics. (936) 756–6644.

Lunar Rendezvous. The Clear Lake area celebrates all month with art shows, festivals, tournaments, and a decorated boat parade. (281) 338–0333 or (800) 844–5253.

Moody Gardens Watermelon Fest and Ice Cream Crank-Off. Call for specifics on this Galveston event. (409) 762–3933 or (800) 351–4236.

Pickers' Club & Harvest Weekend at Messina Hof Cellars. On Saturday mornings in Bryan from mid-July through early August, the pickers' training sessions begin at 8:00 A.M., after which you get to stomp the grapes. (979) 778–9463.

Shakespeare-by-the-Book Festival. Richmond's George Memorial Library amphitheater hosts a weekend of live theatrical performances, featuring the best of the Bard. (281) 341–2678.

AUGUST

Ballunar Liftoff Festival. Johnson Space Center in Nassau Bay opens its usually closed campus for this three-day event that includes more than one hundred hot air balloons in competition flights, team sky-diving, live entertainment, arts and crafts, concessions, and aviation exhibitions. Call for schedule. (281) 338-0333 or 483-0123.

Beaumont's Car Show. Billed as an "Automotive Extravaganza," this event in early August awards trophies in thirteen categories and includes food and vendor booths, games, entertainment, and a car "swap meet." (409) 880-3927.

Blessing of the Fleet. Kemah invokes heavenly blessings on the shrimp crop with a boat parade, a carnival, crafts, dances, and a cook-off. (877) 285-3624.

Fiddlers' Festival. Some old-time toe-tapping music in Crockett in mid-August. (936) 544-2359.

Firemen's Fiesta in Brenham. The Firemen's Training Center comes alive with dancing, water polo, pumper races, cook-offs, and both horseshoe- and washer-pitching competitions. (409) 836-1688, 836-3695, or (888) 273-6426.

Ice Cream Smorgasbord in Brenham. This is everyone's secret dream: all the Blue Bell ice cream you can eat, served inside the air-conditioned American Legion Hall in Brenham's Fireman's Park. (979) 836-3695 or (888) 273-6426.

Prazka Pout. Praha hosts its annual Czechoslovakian homecoming at St. Mary's Catholic Church in mid-August. (361) 865-3560 or (979) 743-4514.

Salebration in Calvert. This citywide sale on the second weekend of August brings out artists, antiques dealers, demonstrations, and Civil War reenactments. (800) 670-8183.

Schulenburg. This small town welcomes visitors to "A Texas Style Adventure" annually on the first weekend in August. (979) 743-4441 or 743-4514; www.schulenburgchamber.org.

Shakespeare at Winedale. The historic old barn at this open-air historical museum rings with the undying words of the Bard Thursday-Sunday evenings through mid-month, with weekend matinees. There's also a hunter's stew dinner before the Saturday evening show. (979) 278-3530.

Shrimporee and Fishfest in Palacios. There's a boat parade and blessing of the fleet, with anglers competing for cash fishing prizes. (361) 972-2615 (Fishfest); 972-2446 (Shrimporee); www.palacioschamber.org.

Woodville. Heritage Village presents tales and legends of Texas in "Ghosts of Texas' Past." (409) 283-2272 or (800) 323-0389.

SEPTEMBER

Bellville. Antique-car buffs host a swap meet for vintage cars and parts the first weekend of the month. (979) 865-3407.

Cat Spring Antique Show. This major event on an early September weekend draws primitive and country antiques dealers from all over the country to this community's historic agricultural society hall. (979) 865-5618.

County fairs. This is the month, so plan a trip to Brenham, (979) 836-4112; Columbus, (979) 732-9266; Hempstead, (979) 826-8217; or La Grange, (979) 968-5756 or 968-3911.

Davy Crockett Pioneer Festival in Crockett. This mid-month celebration has a pioneer village with costumed actors, arts and crafts, food, and entertainment. (936) 544-2359 or (888) 269-2359.

Dick Dowling Days. Sabine Pass turns out on the first weekend of September with special events to honor this Irish hero of the Confederacy. (800) 235-7822.

Fiesta Hispano Americana. This Wharton event celebrates Hispanic culture in Southeast Texas with food, music, and dancing. (979) 532-1862.

Heritage Days in Old Town Spring. Vintage cars line the streets, music fills the air, and reenactments bring back the 1800s throughout this small district on the last weekend of the month. (281) 353-9310 or (800) 653-8696.

Jazz Fest at Kemah Boardwalk. For information call (877) 285-3624; www.kemahboardwalk.com.

Kite Fest on Galveston Island. What could be more fun than taking advantage of the beach's constant breeze? This annual event has sport kite demonstrations; two-man, four-man, and mega-flyers; exotic kites from around the world, and so on. You can learn to fly a kite here as well and even take a ride in a bike-powered buggy. (888) 425-4753.

Mexican Heritage in Port Arthur. Call for specifics. (800) 235-7822 or (409) 982-8300.

Shrimpfest. Port Arthur's Pleasure Island comes alive mid-month with a gumbo cooking contest, a shrimp peeling/cooking contest, shrimp food booths, music, arts and crafts, and a carnival. (409) 963-1107.

Texas Gatorfest in Anahuac. The "Alligator Capital of Texas" celebrates the opening of gator season. Come prepared for the Alligator Roundup, carnival rides, live entertainment on dual stages, a 5K run, airboat rides, a street dance, petting zoo, arts and crafts, and an exhibit of live gators. Food includes alligator delicacies. (409) 267-4190.

Texas Pecan Festival in Groves. This two-week celebration mid-month includes sporting events, carnival, concessions, cooking with pecans, arts and crafts, and more. (409) 962-3631 or (800) 876-3631.

Texas Rice Festival. The small town of Winnie (west of Beaumont on I-10) celebrates its prime crop with a carnival, parades, art and antique auto shows, rice-cooking contests, street and square dances, barbecue cook-off, horse show, a fiddling contest, and professional entertainment. (409) 296-2231 or 296-4404; www.winnietexas.com.

Texian Days in Anderson. This historic little town celebrates its history with home tours, a Texas Army encampment, a flea market, a beauty contest, and live entertainment. (936) 825-3386.

Wendish Fest in Serbin. This annual event celebrates the roots of this tiny community north of La Grange. Events include costumed folk dancing, Wendish crafts (egg decorating, noodle making, sausage stuffing, quilting, and butter making), and a typical Wendish meal at the Serbin picnic grounds. (979) 366-2441.

OCTOBER

Antiques Show. Bellville traditionally has one of the most extensive shows in the state on the fourth weekend in October in the city park pavilion. Also on the grounds are a farmers' market, folk art, a quilting bee, rug weaving, and country cooking. (409) 865-3407.

Bay Day. Sponsored by the Galveston Bay Foundation in mid-month, this official celebration of Galveston Bay features a wetlands tour, an air show, fireboat and Coast Guard helicopter rescue demonstrations, a kids' fishing derby, and plenty of fireworks, all at Sylvan Beach in La Porte. (281) 332-3381.

Bluegrass and Gospel Music Festival. In late October bands from all over the United States converge on the Coushatte Recreation Ranch (between Bellville and Sealy) to perform at this event. Expect several stages of live music, and do come ready to perform yourself. Call for directions and performance schedule. (281) 376-2959.

Bryan–College Station. The Continental Antique Show brings more than ninety dealers to Brazos Center, usually in mid-October. (979) 260-9898 or (800) 777-8292.

CAF Wings over Houston. Ellington Field hosts Confederate Air Force air-power demonstrations with authentic World War II planes and a flight show. Expect aerobatics, jet dragster speed demos, flight simulators, and a large military aircraft exhibit. (281) 531-9461 or 488-7676.

CavOilcade Celebration. Port Arthur celebrates its economic base with a street parade, an old-timers' breakfast, golf and tennis tournaments, Hungry Artists' show, antique automobiles, and a thieves' market. (409) 985-1247 or (800) 235-7822.

Conroe Cajun Catfish Festival. This three-day celebration mid-month is filled with music, food, arts and crafts, children's activities, a parade, and dancing in the streets. (936) 756-6644 or 539-6009; www.conroe.org.

County and Regional Fairs. Try the Fort Bend County Fair at Rosenberg (ends on the first Saturday in October), (281) 342-6171; the Harris County Fair near Bear Creek, (281) 550-8432; the South Texas State Fair in Beaumont, (409) 832-9991 or (800) 392-4401; or the Tyler County Fair in Woodville, (409) 283-2632 or 283-2272. Other possibilities include the Brazoria County Fair, (979) 849-6416; and the Austin County Fair with its PCRA-sanctioned rodeo in Bellville, (979) 865-3407 or 865-5995.

Fair-on-the-Square in Huntsville. Downtown's historic heart hosts entertainment, arts and crafts, and so on, on the first Saturday in October. (936) 295-8113 or (800) 289-0389.

Fayetteville's Antique Show and Midnight Madness. All shops and vendors stay open until midnight on the first Friday and Saturday nights following the first Thursday of the month. (888) 575-4553.

Harvest Festival and East Texas Folklife Festival. Woodville's Heritage Village literally comes to life with artists, craftspersons, musicians, and demonstrations. (409) 283-2272 or (800) 323-0389.

Historic Richmond Business Association Pecan Festival. Test your pecan-shelling talents at this event. Other activities include dancing, fire department demonstrations, a pecan bake-off, and a fun run. (281) 341-1575.

Houston International In-the-Water Boat Show. Four days in late September to see the latest and greatest in power- and sailboats, luxury yachts, fishing boats, and so on, at Watergate Marina in Clear Lake

Shores. (281) 338-0333 or 334-1511; www.watergatemarina.com.

Lickskillet Celebration. Fayetteville relives its heritage with crafts, reunions, and a parade on the third Sunday of the month. (888) 575-4553.

Pasadena Stock Show and Rodeo. This weeklong event at the rodeo grounds includes a barbecue cook-off. (281) 487-0240.

Polk County Pioneer Days. Livingston hosts street dances, trail-rides, timber exhibits, food and BBQ cook-offs, crafts, and more in Petticoat Park on the US-59 bypass. (936) 327-4929.

Renaissance Festival. Sixteenth-century England is re-created every weekend this month and through mid-November in the woods between Magnolia and Plantersville. Amid parades, jousting, races, and games of skill, you'll chat with Robin Hood, assorted wenches, minstrels, comics, jugglers, knights and their elegant ladies, and other anachronistic characters. Dress to the theme and join in the fun. (281) 356-2178, (979) 894-2516, or (800) 458-3435.

Rice Festival in Bay City. Parades, concerts, carnival, and other events fill a week. Call for specifics. (979) 245-8333.

Round Top Antiques Fair. Always held on the first full weekend in both April and October, this event draws dealers and buyers from all over the country. Main venues are Round Top's venerable Rifle Hall and Carmine's Dance Hall. A third site on SH-237 is devoted primarily to folk art. (281) 493-5501 or (877) 444-7339.

Scarecrow Festival. Chappell Hill's biggest event of the year includes arts and crafts booths, continuous entertainment, historical church and home tours, hayrides, a quilt raffle, and a scarecrow contest. (979) 836-3695 or (800) 225-3695.

Seabrook Music Festival. A carnival, arts and crafts, live music, a silent auction, assorted cook-offs, and an antique car show. (281) 244-2144 or 474-3838.

Texian Market Days. Reliving the early days of ranching, this late-October weekend event has pioneer-life demonstrations, arts and crafts booths, entertainment, and tours of two old homes at the George Ranch Historical Park near Richmond. *Also here:* a reenactment of an 1860s Confederate military camp and the 1820s settlement of Stephen F. Austin's first colony, including a working farm. (281) 545-9212 or 343-0218.

Trinity Valley Exposition and Rodeo. Liberty gears up the third week of October with a variety of family activities, including a baby parade held annually since 1909. *Also here:* concerts, a barbecue cook-off, PCRA-sanctioned rodeo, and a mule show. (409) 336-7455 or 336-8168.

NOVEMBER

Christmas previews. You will find "welcome to the holidays" celebrations at various times and in a variety of styles at the following: Bellville, (979) 865-3407; Conroe, (877) 426-6763; Crockett, (936) 544-2359; Galveston, (888) 425-4753; Groves, (409) 962-3631; Lake Jackson, (979) 297-4533; Rosenberg, (281) 342-6969; Tomball, (281) 351-7222; Wharton, (979) 532-1862; and Woodville, (409) 283-2632.

Civil War Weekends at Liendo Plantation. Encampments and reenacters look right at home in this beautiful historic matrix. Held Friday, Saturday, and Sunday prior to Thanksgiving. (979) 826-3126; www.liendo.org.

Fall Festival and Texas Heritage Days at Armand Bayou. All the old-time skills are demonstrated, including cane pressing and hay baling. Add a pie-eating contest, animal demos, and horseshoes for family fun. (281) 474-2551.

Fall Festival of Roses. Independence's Antique Rose Emporium hosts seminars, exhibits, demonstrations, shopping, and food the first weekend of the month. (979) 836-5548.

Fly Day at Lone Star Flight Museum in Galveston. The state's largest collection of old warbirds, including B-25 bombers, takes to the skies. Displays, exhibits, and speakers explain all. (409) 740-7722 or (888) 425-4753; www.lsfm.org.

Home for the Holidays. Old Town Spring celebrates the holiday season each weekend until Christmas with special events, evening programs, and beautiful decorations and lights. (281) 353-9310 or (800) 653-8696.

Messina Hof Wine Cellars. Wine Premier brings visitors to this Bryan–College Station attraction. Expect an international theme, food and wine tastings, elegant dinners and a jazz brunch, culinary seminars and demonstrations by noted chefs, hayrides, and an art exhibit. Reservations and tickets required for most events. (979) 778-9463.

Pioneer Days at Jesse Jones Park & Nature Center, near Humble. All the homely arts that ultimately tamed the Texas frontier in the 1830s and 1840s are demonstrated, and the park's reconstructed homestead is open to the public. (281) 446-8588; www.cp4.hctx.net/jones.

Poinsettia Celebration. Ellison's Greenhouses on the outskirts of Brenham brim with 80,000 blooming plants for this special benefit weekend, just before Thanksgiving. Booths feature plant care, holiday designs, food, and entertainment. (979) 836-0084; www.ellisonsgreen houses.com.

Round Top Arts Festival. This juried art show on the first weekend of the month includes paintings, sculpture, carvings, and ceramics. (979) 249-3308.

Twilight Firelight at Fanthorp Inn State Historical Park. Celebrate with a journey back to the 1850s when Anderson's historic inn opens its doors for this event on the Saturday of Thanksgiving weekend. Visitors first board a replica stagecoach for a ride down Anderson's Main Street. Arriving at the inn, they are entertained by costumed actors with stories, poetry, music, wassail, and good cheer. (936) 873-2633; www.tpwd.state.tx.us.

DECEMBER

Bellville's Small Town Christmas & Holiday Home Tour. This also includes walking carolers and a show at the square on the first Friday of the month. (979) 865-3407.

Brookshire Christmas Festival. Santa, caroling, dancing, and a carnival welcome the season on the first full weekend in December. (281) 375-8100; www.westI10chamber.org.

Campfire Christmas. The George Ranch in Richmond lights up with campfires, a holiday feast, wagon rides, and so on. (281) 545-9212 or 343-0218.

A Candlelight Christmas. Varner-Hogg State Park in West Columbia celebrates the season with interpretive tours of this Victorian and seasonally decorated plantation home. (979) 345-4656.

Candlelight Christmas Tour, An 1845 Celebration. Two of Beaumont's historic jewels, the McFaddin-Ward House and the John Jay French Museum, glow with celebration on the first Sunday of the month. You may get to help costumed French characters decorate an oldtime tree. (409) 898-3267 or (800) 392-4401; www.beaumontcvb.com.

Christmas at the Depot. Burton sponsors a holiday celebration at its restored historic train station. (979) 289-2863 or (800) 225-3695; www.brenhamtexas.org.

Christmas Bird Count in Brazosport. Birders from all over the country gather here between Christmas and New Year's for this annual event. As many as 226 species have been sighted some years; 326 overall. Binoculars are essential. (979) 265-2508; www.tourist-info.org.

Christmas Fantasy of Lights in Sealy. The entire town turns out for a Christmas market and lighted parade on the first Saturday of the month. (979) 885-3222; www.sealy-tx.com.

Christmas in Calvert. Antiques sales and five or more old homes that are open for tours brighten the first weekend in December. (979) 364-2559, 364-2710, or (800) 670-8183.

Christmas in Humble. Historic Main Street comes alive with carolers, choirs, and Santa. (281) 319-6619 or 446-2128; www.humbleareachamber.org.

Christmas in Old Montgomery. Tour lovely old homes dressed for the season, as well as a cookie walk, arts and crafts show, and community dinner. (936) 597-4155, 597-4899, or (800) 283-6645; www.conroe.org.

Christmas in Round Top. Wagon rides, singing, shopping, and decorations liven up the town square early in the month. (979) 249-4042.

Christmas on Lake Sabine. Port Arthur glows all month with more than 700,000 lights depicting biblical scenes. Eleven different ethnic groups display holiday trees and traditions, on December's first weekend. Call for details and home-tour schedule. (409) 984-6101 or (800) 235-7822; www.portarthurtexas.com.

Christmas on the Boardwalk. Kemah's waterfront glows with a tree-lighting spectacular. (877) 285-3624; www.kemahboardwalk.com.

Christmas on the Colorado. Columbus puts on a three-day celebration in its historic downtown district early in the month. Expect guided walking tours, open houses in vintage homes, a market, *Messiah* in the old opera house, and cowboys serenading. (877) 444-7339; www.columbustexas.org.

Christmas Open House at Winedale. All the old German Christmas traditions seem right at home for this one-day event. (979) 278-3530.

Christmas Traditions in Orange. This town's beautiful W. H. Stark House wears its seasonal decorations. Call for information. (409) 883-0871.

Christmas trees. There are more than five dozen commercial Christmas tree farms within the area covered by this book. For a list by county, contact the Texas Department of Agriculture, Box 12847, Austin, TX 78711; (800) 835-5832 or (713) 666-8491.

Clear Lake Area Christmas Boat Parade. Clear Lake, Seabrook, League City, and Kemah join floating forces on December's second weekend to celebrate the season in their own unique way. Clear Lake Park and the Kemah-Seabrook channel are the best public viewing sites. (281) 338-0333; www.nasaclearlaketexas.com.

Clute's Christmas in the Park. Decorated trees, foods, and crafts of the season, for four days early in the month. (979) 265-8392.

Country Christmas in Chappell Hill. On the second Saturday Santa arrives via fire engine, choirs sing and ring hand bells, and children with teddy bears dressed for the occasion parade down Main Street. It's also open house at several historic homes. (979) 836-3695 or (888) 273-6426; www.brenhamtexas.com.

Country Christmas in Fayetteville. Santa arrives on the square the first Saturday of the month, along with entertainers, crafters, wassail, home tours, and gingerbread. Free wagon rides pass by decorated homes. (888) 575-4553.

Country Christmas on the Square. Coldspring celebrates the holiday with East Texas spirit on the second Saturday of December. Expect varied entertainments, a country market, a lighted Christmas parade, choirs, a fun run, and scads of food. (936) 653-2184; www.coldspringtexas.org.

Dickens-on-the-Strand. Galveston's famous Strand becomes a 4-block stage for Victorian Christmases past. Dress up in your best period duds and join the fun. There will be a mix of characters from Dickens: town criers, British bobbies, carolers, bell-ringing choirs, horse-drawn coaches, and more. (409) 765-7834 or (888) 425-4753.

Downtown Christmas Stroll in Brenham. Special shopping and holiday events, including a 4-H Christmas tree auction, fill historic downtown Brenham on the first Friday and Saturday. (979) 836-3695 or (888) 273-6426; www.brenhamtexas.com.

Griffin House Christmas Candlelight Tour in Tomball. The traditional songs and wassail of Christmas on the second weekend of the month. (281) 255-2148 or 351-7222; www.tomballchamber.org.

Holiday on the Brazos. Bryan–College Station welcomes December with a parade on the first Sunday, followed by light displays, church plays, and special arts and crafts events throughout the month. (800) 777-8292; www.bryan-collegestation.org.

Kreische House Christmas Tours. Groups of ten or more visiting Monument Hill in La Grange experience the holiday in an early German atmosphere. (979) 968-5658.

Light Up the First Capitol. West Columbia celebrates on December's first weekend with a night parade, caroling, story time with Mrs. Claus, Santa Claus visits, and holiday home tour. (979) 345-3921.

Messina Hof. This wine cellar and vineyard in Bryan welcomes the holidays with a Mulled Wine Weekend early in the month. (979) 778-9463; www.messinahof.com.

A Nineteenth Century Christmas. Washington-on-the-Brazos State Historical Park demonstrates how the citizens of the Texas Republic celebrated the holiday more than 150 years ago. Children get to make ornaments and rag dolls, and candlelight living-history tours light up Independence Hall and the Anson Jones Home. (936) 878-2214; www.tpwd.state.tx.us.

Spirit of Christmas in Galveston. Several of Galveston's grandest homes are at their best during this annual event. (409) 765-7834 or (888) 425-4753.

Trail of Lights in Huntsville. This town's historic central square glows with holiday lights throughout the month. (800) 289-0389.

Woodville's Christmas Extravaganza. A twilight tour of Heritage Village, along with a craft fair and bluegrass fiddling, highlight this event on the first Saturday of the month. (409) 283-2272 or (800) 323-0389; www.heritage-village.org.

ABOUT THE AUTHOR

CAROL BARRINGTON

Odds are good that in any given month a Carol Barrington photograph or story graces the travel pages of America's magazines and newspapers. Although she specializes in Texana—she considers the entire Houston-Galveston region her "backyard"—her general story/photo beat has covered the world. During her twenty-five-year, prize-winning career as a travel journalist, her work has appeared in more than fifty publications. Her professional memberships include the Society of Media Photographers, American Society of Journalists and Authors, and the Society of American Travel Writers, of which she is a past president.

ABOUT THE EDITOR

SYD KEARNEY

Reporting from far-flung places such as Turkey and Botswana, Syd Kearney has spent the past decade sharing travel stories with the readers of the *Houston Chronicle*. But there is no place she'd rather talk about than her native East Texas. Kearney's travel stories and photographs have appeared in newspapers across the country. A longtime member of the Society of American Travel Writers, Kearney also is a founder and past president of the Houston chapter of the Association for Women Journalists.